A SOLDIER'S
GENERAL

A SOLDIER'S GENERAL
AN AUTOBIOGRAPHY

GENERAL J.J. SINGH

Dear Kundan & Susubhin,

With best wishes & grateful thanks for the lovely function organised by you.

General, 11 Nov 12

HarperCollins *Publishers* India
a joint venture with
THE INDIA TODAY GROUP
New Delhi

First published in India in 2012 by
HarperCollins *Publishers* India
a joint venture with
The India Today Group

Copyright © General J.J. Singh 2012

ISBN: 978-93-5029-133-7

2 4 6 8 10 9 7 5 3 1

General J.J. Singh asserts the moral right to be identified
as the author of this book.

The views and opinions expressed in this book are the author's own and the facts are as
reported by him and the publishers are in no way liable for the same.

All rights reserved. No part of this publication may be reproduced,
stored in a retrieval system, or transmitted, in any form or by any means,
electronic, mechanical, photocopying, recording or otherwise,
without the prior permission of the publishers.

HarperCollins *Publishers*
A-53, Sector 57, NOIDA, Uttar Pradesh – 201301, India
77-85 Fulham Palace Road, London W6 8JB, United Kingdom
Hazelton Lanes, 55 Avenue Road, Suite 2900, Toronto, Ontario M5R 3L2
and 1995 Markham Road, Scarborough, Ontario M1B 5M8, Canada
25 Ryde Road, Pymble, Sydney, NSW 2073, Australia
31 View Road, Glenfield, Auckland 10, New Zealand
10 East 53rd Street, New York NY 10022, USA

Typeset in Minion Pro 11.5/15
Jojy Philip, New Delhi 110 015

Printed and bound at
Thomson Press (India) Ltd.

For
the great Indian Army and my family

Contents

	Preface	ix
	Acknowledgements	xiii
	Part I: Ancestry and Early Life	**1**
1.	A Family Military Tradition	3
2.	Bonds of Blood with the 'Mahrattas'	7
3.	The Spirit of a Warrior	10
4.	Impact of Second World War and Partition	18
5.	Growing Up in Army Cantonments	22
	Part II: Cadet to a Colonel	**31**
6.	The Cradle	33
7.	Regimental Soldiering	40
8.	Sharpening the Cutting Edge	56
9.	The Crucible – Command of the Battalion	73
10.	Military Attaché in Algeria	91
	Part III: Flag Rank: From One Star to C-in-C	**95**
11	Brigade Commander – Containing the Fire	97
12	Operation Mousetrap	115
13	Death Sentence to Brigadier 'Shaitan Singh'	121
14	Gateway to the Top	134
15	Masterminding Operations	144
16	Stand-off in Siachen	147

17	Kargil – The Pakistani Misadventure	155
18	Command of Strike Corps and Exercise Poorna Vijay	174
19	Colonel of the Regiment	184
20	Attack on Parliament and Operation Parakram	188
21	Army Commander – The Penultimate Rung	191

Part IV: The Pinnacle — **195**

22	'Jangi Laat' – Becoming the Army Chief	197
23	The Security Perspective	204
24	Internal Security and Countering Terrorism	208
25	Chief of Defence Staff – The Way Forward	228
26	The Nuclear Dimension	233
27	Snow Tsunami and Earthquake in Kashmir	236
28	Defence Diplomacy and Neighbourhood	240
29	Preparing for the Future	261
30	Leadership and Command Experience	267
31	The Man behind the Machine	282
32	Sports and Adventure Activities	296
33	Adieu	301
34	Musharraf and I	306

Part V: Governor of Arunachal Pradesh — **309**

35	The Second Innings	311
36	A Proactive Approach	317
37	Development of North East and 'Look East' Policy	323
38	Upliftment of Rural Areas and Tourism	326
39	Captives of Geography	334
40	A New Dawn	337

Part VI: Reflections — **341**

| 41 | A View from the Verandah | 343 |

| Appendices | 357 |
| *Index* | 373 |

Preface

There comes a time in life when there is an inner voice urging you to write about your experiences, and chart the course of your life, with all its ups and downs. One day in November 2007, when my second innings in life was just beginning, Patwant Singh said he would like to help me write my memoirs. I thanked him but said I needed some more time. Alas, unluckily for me, that was not meant to be, for Patwant passed away soon thereafter.

At that point in time, some publishing houses had also expressed an interest in publishing my story – even if it meant waiting for a few years. Further, my family, some fellow officers and friends, including media persons, kept asking me 'when' or 'if' I was coming out with my book.

Therefore, I decided to pen down my thoughts before my memory started to fade and the whole exercise became futile! What this book contains are my *personal views*. The constitutional position held by me has to some extent prevented me from writing about certain sensitive issues or writing more freely about some others. Frankly, I did face a moral dilemma while undertaking this project. Should I describe my achievements objectively, even if they might appear as self-praise, or take the mellow approach. My decision was to write about events as they happened and while doing so, be as factually correct as possible.

Perhaps I had more than my fair share of 'field' or operational-area assignments. As a result, the conflict in my mind between duty and family was often palpable. However, not once did I ask anyone to exert an influence on the course of my career. Going through this journey on my own terms, taking the good and bad bounces, as happens in every round of golf one plays, nothing has been able to distract me from giving a full 100 per cent while doing an assigned task. Known for being 'cool' under stress, I don't lose my composure easily, and it is not easy to take away the smile from my face no matter how great the challenge or daunting the circumstance. A famous and highly decorated cavalry regiment of ours, The Skinners Horse, has the motto 'Himmat-i-Mardan, Madad-i-Khuda' (God helps the courageous), which is close to my heart. My own regiment, The Maratha Light Infantry, has the credo, 'Duty, Honour and Courage,' which is equally dear to me.

Hard work, sincerity, dedication and destiny bestowed upon me the pride and honour of becoming the first chief of army staff from the elite Maratha Light Infantry Regiment, and the first Sikh to reach this rank. My tenure at the top of the pyramid was of two years and eight months, from 31 January 2005 to 30 September 2007. Regarded by commentators as a soldier, a professional and a thinking general, I brought into limelight that we were not just tough soldiers but that there was a 'humane face' of the army too, that it was a people's army. Zero tolerance was displayed by me with regard to false reporting and human rights violations and the unsound emphasis on 'killings' and the 'numbers' game. In 2007, the army came out with the doctrine of low intensity conflict, in which many of my precepts and ideas have been articulated, the most important one being the concept of an 'iron fist and a velvet glove'.

It is a matter of great pride for me to have been appointed as the governor of Arunachal Pradesh, a strategically important state of our country. The variety of experience that life had in store for me, and the dreamlike army career that took me to the top of the ladder despite some close brushes with death and near-disasters, makes this the story of a survivor and a winner – 'a lambi race ka ghora,' as some friends have described me! Was it destiny or was there an element of luck? Frankly speaking, it has been difficult to fathom everything that has unfolded in life so far.

This then is my autobiography, although strictly speaking, the style is a little unorthodox and different. There is some experimental sketching of my innermost thoughts and a recreation of scenarios, a description of personal experiences and perceptions, and an account of the vicissitudes of life spanning six-and-a-half decades. I have endeavoured to be as objective, down-to-earth and truthful as possible, but have no pretensions to literary excellence. It is an account of a simple and straightforward soldier born without a silver spoon in his mouth, who reached the top without any godfather.

My gratitude to my immediate family – my parents, my wife, Rohini, and children, Vivek and Sonia – who had to face the challenges of life so often without me, and suffer the pangs of separation. My wife perhaps understood my compulsions, but I am not too sure if my children could always comprehend them. Perhaps now, when they read this, the culmination of a personal and intensely passionate endeavour of mine for the last few years, they will understand me better.

Acknowledgements

This book has been the outcome of five years of research, interactions and delving into the inner recesses of my mind. It wouldn't have materialized but for the encouragement, guidance and support of my friends, colleagues and family, who readily and graciously gave their time and inputs to make the text more accurate and suggested valuable improvements.

I would like to thank Khushwant Singh for his invaluable advice and for being a constant source of inspiration. Every time I happened to meet him during the last three years, he would ask, 'General Saheb, what is the progress on your autobiography?' I am indebted to the media adviser, Prime Minister's Office; the Photo Division, ministry of defence; the Army HQ; the Press Information Bureau, Government of India; the Department of Information and Public Relations and Tourism, Arunachal Pradesh; my regiment, the Maratha Light Infantry, and specially, the units and formations which I commanded and the officers who served with me, for their assistance in this work. Further, my team has earned my greatest admiration and gratitude for its unstinted help and valuable inputs. It comprised Venkat Gouder, Bunny Chetinder Singh, Pammi Pannu, Vivek Chadha, Aloke Dutt, Prashant Lokhande, Ankur Garg, Ravi Gonte, Manik Bhardwaj, Kuldeep Dabral, Rajesh Punia, Satbir Bedi and Atum Potom. The blessings of my father, Lieutenant Colonel J.S. Marwah, my mother-in-law, Prabhjot Kaur, and the boundless encouragement, patience and support of my wife, Rohini, during this period, when my computer and I were mostly inseparable, are gratefully acknowledged. I was also fortunate to have a dedicated and industrious secretarial staff comprising S.B. Rana, Pradeep Kumar and Mahesh Kumar.

I am grateful to the authors, publishers and other copyright holders whose inputs and material I have used in the book. I also would like to place on record the encouragement of well-wishers like Marshal of the Air Force Arjan Singh, Shekhar Gupta, Lieutenant General V. R. Raghavan, Sushil Gupta, Anil Malhotra, Sant Singh Chatwal, Hardev Akoi, Laxmi Narayan, acclaimed photographers Henry Dallal (his work appears on the cover) and Captain Suresh Sharma, Major General Manjit Dugal, Ranjit Singh, Colonel Basudev Maitra, Ajit Singh Sawhney, Harpreet Chadha, Surinder Kandhari, Ini Bawa, G.S. Kochar, and many of my services and golfing friends. I would also like to thank Jyoti M. Rai, Indrim Boo, Bandeep Singh and Pramod Kamble for their contribution to the project.

Finally, my greatest appreciation goes to Amit Agarwal and his team at HarperCollins. Their conceptual ideas helped me in evolving and formatting the manuscript correctly while keeping the focus in place. They meticulously edited and processed my work and thereby made an admirable contribution. *Merci beaucoup a tous!*

Part I
ANCESTRY AND EARLY LIFE

Atma Singh   Jaswant Singh   Joginder Jaswant Singh

Three generations in the service of the army.

*And how can man die better
Than facing fearful odds,
For the ashes of his fathers,
And the temples of his Gods.*

                      T.B. Macaulay, 1842

1

A Family Military Tradition

Three generations of my family – from 1914 to 2007 – have served in the great Indian Army, making it almost a century of family military tradition in the service of the nation. And rising from the 'ranks' to a four-star general in this period has been a unique achievement for us.

Our family roots take us back to the Aryans, or so was the conviction of my great-grandparents. I would like to believe this even if it is a myth! There appears to be a difference of opinion about the advent of the Aryans (between 2000 BC and 1500 BC) in the Indus Valley, the plains of Punjab and beyond up to the Indo-Gangetic region. Marwaha (Merwaha), our clan, is believed to have come to the Punjab from Merv or Marusthal, and claims to have its origins in Central Asia. They are said to have entered southwest Punjab through the Bolan Pass, and their earliest traceable settlement was at Goindwal, near Amritsar (Sketch 1.1). They belonged to the Khatri Sarin group and were descendants of Bhai Balu of Goindwal, who was appointed by the third guru of the Sikhs, Guru Amar Das, and whose shrine is at Dadan, near Ludhiana.[1]

My grandfather, Sepoy Atma Singh, was a burly Sikh. A fair-complexioned man, his rosy cheeks used to turn ruddier under the summer sun. He was a simple, down-to-earth sipahi, a private in the army. An accomplished drummer, he was in the Pipes and Drums platoon of 1/67 Punjab Regiment (presently 1st Battalion, the Parachute

---

[1] *A Glossary of the Tribes and Castes of the Punjab and North-West Frontier Province*, compiled by H.A. Rose, based on the census report for Punjab 1883 and 1892, pp. 524 and 697, and *Phulkian States Gazetteer*, 1904.

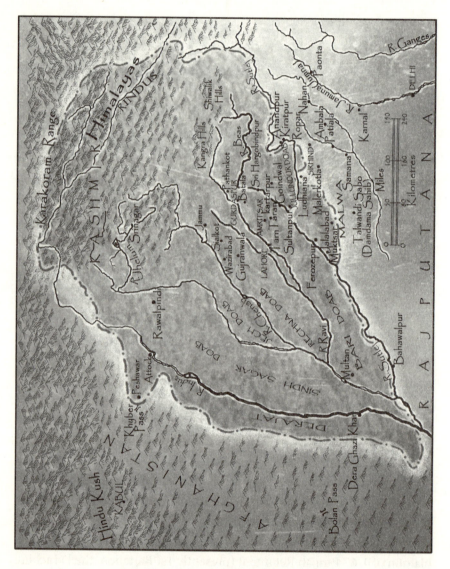

Sketch 1.1: Punjab and the Sikh Empire.

Regiment). In the good old days, the 'pipers' were the traditional vanguard of the infantry battalions and led them into the battlefield. My grandpa's pay was a meagre seventeen rupees or even less! We grew up hearing Colonel Bogey's march, or other martial music of the army, which he used to play with his knuckles on the dining table at dinner every day. He made us kids recite the 'mool mantra', the first stanza of our holy scripture, before food was served. After dinner, he would regale us with stories of the Great War. We would hear him with rapt attention.

Once, he recounted a story about his return to Daultala, our ancestral village near Rawalpindi, when he was discharged from the army after the war in 1918. As he had been wounded and his right hand had been incapacitated, he could not maintain his beard and long unshorn hair. Consequently, he had to shave them off. On reaching home, he knocked on the door but my grandmother, Ram Rakhi, refused to let him in, asking, 'Who is this firanghee', the native word for a European. She could not recognize him. Besides, he had acquired an even fairer complexion while recuperating in a hospital in the south of France. Theirs was a child marriage, as was customary then in the Punjab and in many other regions of India. It was only when he recounted to her some intimate details that she realized that he was, in fact, *her* Atma Singh, and she let him in. Then she asked him, 'What have you done to yourself?' He simply raised the right sleeve of his shirt and uncovered his dangling arm. That said it all! Some in the family had told her that those who crossed the seven oceans didn't ever come back. Of course, thousands didn't – they died in Kut-el-Amara or in Flanders. So she was delirious with joy and relief at my grandfather's homecoming and couldn't contain her tears.

When I was commissioned from the Indian Military Academy, Dehradun in 1964, my grandfather asked me, 'Kaka, kedi "paltan" mili hai tainu?' (Son, which regiment did you get?) When I told him it was the Maratha Light Infantry, he was very pleased, saying, 'Mahratte[2] bade bahadur te tagre honde han; taan hi unhan noon "lite infantry" da khitaab us jang vich milya si' (the Marathas are a very brave and

---

[2] The British called the soldiers from the region 'Mahrattas' and not Marathas as we do today.

hardy race; that is why during the war they were given the title of 'Light Infantry'). The bravery of the Marathas in battle was renowned from the days of Shivaji, and Maratha soldiers have been traditionally called ganpats. During the First World War, a letter from a German soldier describing the valour of the Indian soldiers and printed in the *Frankfurter Zeitung* said this:

> Today for the first time we had to fight against the Indians and the devil knows that those brown rascals are not to be underrated. At first we spoke with contempt of the Indians. Today we learned to look on them in a different light – the devil knows what the English had put into those fellows...with a fearful shouting thousands of those brown forms rushed on us.... With butt ends, bayonets, swords and daggers we fought each other.[3]

Grandpa was proud to see me, a wiry young officer of nineteen, wearing my new olive-green uniform with one pip, a green lanyard around my neck, and a red-and-green hackle, one of the few regiments with such unique embellishments, on my turban. Moreover, he was pleased that I had joined the infantry and that too the Maratha Light Infantry. One fine day in 1965, when he was in an emotional and reflective mood, he patted me on my cheek, and said, 'Kaka, rab rakha, sepoy da beta karnail, te karnail da beta jarnail banega.' (God be with you, the son of a soldier will be a colonel, and the colonel's son shall be a general!) I just smiled innocently. At that juncture, my father was a major and I was a young second lieutenant, fresh from the mint. Destiny has its own way, and these words proved to be 'prophetic'; although, at that time, they were taken merely as the blessings and good wishes of a respected elder.

The grand old man passed away peacefully in his sleep a few years later, when he was in his late seventies. 'Son, when one's path is "righteous" and the cause is "just", one is bound to succeed,' was grandpa's refrain, and his words still ring true.

---

[3] Philip Mason, *A Matter of Honour*, EBD Educational Pvt Ltd, Dehradun, p. 413.

2
Bonds of Blood with the 'Mahrattas'

During the First World War, in the campaign in Mesopotamia, my grandfather's battalion, the 1/67 Punjabis, had fought alongside five 'Mahratta' battalions.[1] These included the 5th Royal 'Mahrattas' as part of 6th Poona Division led by Major General Charles Townshend. Life has a way of coming full circle. This was the same battalion that I had the great privilege to command from 1985 to 1987 in Hyderabad, seventy years later.

In the siege of Kut-el-Amara (in present-day Iraq), the 6th Division of the British Indian Army was surrounded and cut off by the Turkish forces as shown in Sketch 2.1. During this battle, which lasted from November 1915 to April 1916, the defenders had to go on half-rations, then on a quarter, and finally, they had to eat their own mules or starve to death. The 'Mahratta' soldiers refused to eat horse flesh. It was then that Chhatrapati Shahu Maharaj, their king and descendant of Chhatrapati Shivaji Maharaj, appealed to the soldiers in a cable that 'survival is more important and essential than superstitions and taboos'. Finally, famished, exhausted and depleted, the division had to capitulate. All the gallant officers and men ended up as prisoners of

---

[1] These were: the 103rd, 1 Maratha LI (Jangi Paltan), the 105th, 2 Maratha LI (Kali Panchwin), the 110th, 2 Para (converted from 3 Maratha LI), the 114th, presently the Maratha LI Regimental Centre (converted from 10 Maratha LI in 1922), and the 117th, 5 Maratha LI (Royal).

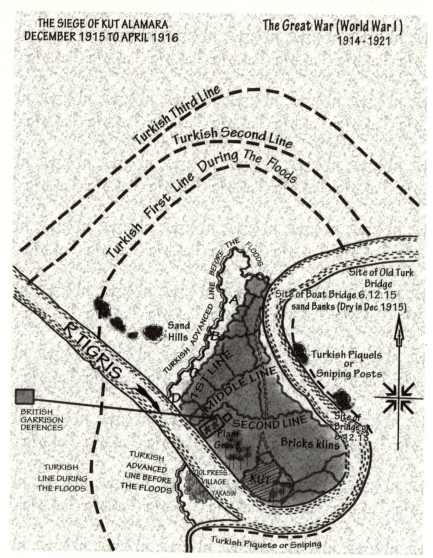

Sketch 2.1 (From *A Royal Tribute* by Major General E. D'Souza, ARB Interactive, Mumbai 2005.)

war (POWs) of the Turks. These POWs were made to march across the Iraqi desert to Syria. Further, they had to undergo hard labour and were employed by the Turkish army to construct the railway to connect this region with Syria and Turkey. Some were even subjected to torture while in captivity. Most of them perished due to sickness, malnutrition or torture.

In a way, my grandfather was fortuitous to have been wounded in an earlier phase of the siege, and was evacuated by the Red Cross and taken out of the theatre along with the other casualties. He took a machine-gun burst on his right elbow, and the joint, along with the radius and the ulna, got shattered. As a young soldier all of twenty years, he was sad to be *hors de combat*, even though there was no way he could have remained in the theatre of operations. He lost the use of his right arm; but fortunately, it was saved from amputation by timely medical attention. Seriously wounded soldiers were sent to hospitals in the UK or the south of France. Grandpa spent many months recuperating in a hospital in France on the Mediterranean coast. Once, his eyes gleaming, he told us, 'Asi te memaa samundar kande nangiya nahandia wekhian san!' (We saw European ladies bathing in the nude on the beaches). This was how and when the 'French connection' of our family commenced.

For the 'Mahrattas', the Mesopotamian campaign was an epoch-making phase of their impressive and ancient martial tradition of bearing arms. As a mark of honour for the regiment's impressive display of gallantry, steadfastness, and ability to withstand the harsh battlefield conditions and severe deprivations in the First World War, it was given the title of 'Light Infantry'. All the paltans (battalions) suffered heavy casualties; some had to be re-raised during the war itself, albeit with reinforcements from sister battalions and with fresh recruitment. It was during this campaign that the 117th Battalion, now the Fifth Battalion, was given the honorific title of 'Royal' for conspicuous gallantry and the most outstanding standards of conduct, discipline and dedicated service.

India – Punjab and Maharashtra, in particular – lost thousands of young men in foreign lands, for the British Empire, for a free world, for the glory of their 'paltan'. They lived and died for 'naam', 'nishaan', 'namak', 'dastur' and 'izzat' (their name, colours, loyalty, tradition and honour). These were simple, disciplined, sincere and hard-working men from rural backgrounds but when required, they could be ferocious fighters and second to none in gallantry. It wouldn't be wrong to say that they remain so even today.

3

The Spirit of a Warrior

Certain aspects of one's psyche, culture and behaviour are innate reflections of one's upbringing and influences. 'Punjabiyat' and 'Sikhi' have been my heritage, bestowed on me by the collective consciousness of Sikhism. Having been brought up in the typically heterogeneous, secular and typified environs of army, I may not have been aware of it in a conscious manner in my early years. However, though I held dear the olive-green values as the greater cultural connect of my life, the tenets of my faith have been a guiding beacon during the journey.

In my childhood, every day at dusk, we used to surround our mother as she recited the Rehras Sahib, a prayer from our scriptures. We understood little, but by repeatedly listening to it, portions of this prayer got embedded in our minds. My Nanaji (maternal grandfather), a pious man, was in service as an office superintendant during the Raj period in Rawalpindi. One fine day he just resigned from his job, saying that he would from that moment onwards be in the service of Wahe Guru. At the time of Partition, he, along with his family, migrated to Patiala. In childhood we often spent our holidays with them. His letters to me, written in English, were very inspiring. When I was growing up, I recall that Nanaji, whom we used to respectfully address as Khalsaji, always encouraged me to speak in the gurdwara on occasions like Gurpurab, on religious subjects such as 'the life of Guru Nanak'. He made a great contribution to my spiritual evolution. These childhood convictions in the Gur Baani or the holy scriptures, and Rehatnama, the code of life for the Sikhs, played a great role in my understanding of the value of being a 'warrior for the cause'.

Imbibing certain intrinsic values, the most fundamental amongst which was to be a good human being, was a part of growing up. My spiritual study is anything but profound but there are certain endearing universal values of Sikhism that guide me during difficult times.

Sikhism was founded and evolved by Guru Nanak in the fifteenth century. It evolved as a distinct faith with its own cultural and physical identity and ideology through the teachings and legacy of ten gurus till the end of the seventeenth century. The term Sikh is derived from shishya, a Sanskrit word meaning a disciple or follower. A majority of Guru Nanak's disciples were from the peasantry of Punjab, the fertile 'land of five rivers' lying between the rivers Indus and the Sutlej. His followers were from both the dominant religions of the times, Hinduism and Islam, mainly because of the simplicity of his message, and its appeal to humanity. Guru Nanak was always accompanied by two of his ardent and highly devoted followers, one of whom was a Muslim named Mardana, a proficient rebaab[1] player, while the other was Bala, a Hindu.

Deeply etched in my mind is Guru Nanak's philosophy based on the three basic precepts of 'naam japo', 'kirat karo' and 'vand chako'. The first enables man to link all dimensions of life to the omnipresent God, and helps him purify his mind and heart and face the vicissitudes of life with courage and fortitude. The second exhorts the Sikhs to balance the spiritual and physical aspects of existence, and live a full life with a sense of creativity and dynamism, while remembering God. The third envisions a social order in which one shares the God-given bounties with others in a spirit of love and service.

When the guru's end was near, as a story recounted in Khushwant Singh's comprehensive and authoritative *History of the Sikhs* puts it: 'Said the Mussalmans: "we will bury him"; the Hindus: "we will cremate him; Nanak said: "You place flowers on either side, Hindus on my right, Muslims on my left. Those whose flowers remain fresh tomorrow

---

[1] Rebaab is a traditional stringed musical instrument. Mardana, the closest disciple of Guru Nanak, was always seen with it.

Guru Nanak Dev and his two disciples (From *Japjee: The Sikh Morning Prayer*.²)

shall have their way." He asked them to pray. When the prayer was over, Baba pulled the sheet over him and went to eternal sleep. Next morning when they raised the sheet they found nothing. The flowers of both communities were fresh'.³ Guru Nanak is still reverently looked upon and remembered as, 'Baba Nanak Shah Faqir – Hindu ka Guru, Musalman ka Peer' (learned Nanak, the King of Fakirs – Guru of the Hindus and Sage of the Muslims).

Guru Arjan Dev, the fifth guru, compiled the scriptures called 'the Adi Granth, containing more than 7000 hymns rendered lyrically',⁴ the precursor to Granth Sahib in its final form. His spiritual period of twenty-five years also saw the emergence of Amritsar as the seat of Sikh religion. Amritsar, which means 'amrit sarovar' (lake of nectar), was chosen by his father, Guru Ram Das, to build the Harmandir Sahib (House of God). Jehangir, son of Mughal emperor Akbar, was intolerant of the secular preachings of Sikhism, unlike his father, and

---

² *Japjee: The Sikh Morning Prayer*, Himalayan Books, p. 34.
³ Khushwant Singh, *A History of the Sikhs*, Vol. I, Oxford University Press, p. 35.
⁴ Patwant Singh, *The Sikhs*, Rupa & Co, p. 36.

he arrested Guru Arjan Dev and had him tortured to death in 1606. This resulted in a tumultuous period of transformation and evolution of Sikhs in the next 150 years. They were compelled by circumstances to take up arms and become a 'race of warriors' to defend their nation, faith, community, fertile lands and their freedom. Guru Arjan Dev's son, Hargobind, became the guiding force for developing Sikhs into a formidable martial community to protect the Sikh faith and beliefs. By the time of his death in 1644, Guru Hargobind had rallied the community and also formalized the institution of the gurdwara – 'the abode of the guru', the Sikh house of piety and prayer, with the Granth Sahib consecrated in it.

Under the Muslim rulers, especially during the reign of the Mughal emperor Aurangzeb, the Hindus and the Sikhs were the targets of many indignities as they were seen as 'kafirs' – non-believers. Forcible conversions were the order of the day. Guru Gobind Singh, the tenth guru, took a stand to protect the Kashmiri Pundits and others. He stands as a stoic symbol of unwavering faith and supreme sacrifice for a just cause. He is deferentially referred to as 'Sarbansh Daani', one who sacrificed his whole family – his father as well as four sons attained martyrdom. Two of his minor sons were 'bricked' alive in Sirhind when they refused conversion. It was Guru Gobind Singh who formalized the transformation of Sikhs into the Khalsa (the pure) or Singhs (lions). The guru ordained his followers to always possess the five 'K's: 'kesh', uncut hair and beard; 'kirpan', the sword; 'kara', the iron bangle; 'kanga', the comb; and the 'kachha', the shorts. In addition, the turban became an integral part of the Khalsa attire. Guru Gobind Singh composed 'deh shiva bar mohe', a classic 'baani' (spiritual words) in the form of a 'shabad' (devotional poetry), so as to inspire and motivate his Khalsa followers and the Sikhs to live by his principles, fight against injustice, be victorious in every endeavour, and when the time came, to lay down their lives fighting courageously. This remarkable transformation of peasants into warriors had a profound impact on the history of the Punjab.

Eventually, it was Guru Gobind Singh's vision and wisdom that just before his death in October 1708, he consecrated the 'Granth Sahib', as the eternal guru of the Sikh faith, the guiding force for personal and ethical conduct. The Guru Granth Sahib is the compilation of the 'baani'.

Thus, Sikhism became a religion with a sacred Book. Qualities like courage, bravery, determination, initiative, sacrifice, and selfless service for the community became ingrained amongst the Sikhs. As recounted by Patwant Singh, '"a will was created in the ordinary masses to resist tyranny, and to live and die for a national cause", as two Sikh historians have it'.[5] Sikhism emerged not as a synthesis of established religions but as an alternative to them, characterized by its cultural and conceptual distinctiveness, which allowed equality between men and women and a classless society, a precept which has still not been addressed by cross-sections of Indian society.

The formidable Khalsa Empire was established by Maharaja Ranjit Singh between 1801 and 1839 in the Punjab (see Sketch 1.1). The Khalsas were quite a match even for the well-trained British Indian Army, as evidenced by the closely contested battles during the Anglo-Sikh wars, and the high attrition taken by both sides. The Sarkar Khalsaji, as the government of Ranjit Singh was called, held sway over the entire stretch of territory from the Hindu Kush and the trans-Indus areas, including Kashmir, and going right down to the Sutlej river. He established Lahore as his capital, which was the heart of the civilization of the Punjab.

Once in place, the Sikh Empire effectively blocked the route of the invaders who poured in through the Khyber and Bolan passes, and brought peace to the Punjab for a few decades. Hari Singh Nalwa, a famous general of Maharaja Ranjit Singh, carried the banner of the Khalsa Army far and wide, and had the awesome image of a ruthless warrior. However, after each Anglo-Sikh war, the Sikh Empire was clipped, till it completely fell apart because of the ineptitude of the rulers, palace intrigues and a disunited army. Not losing any opportunity to cut the Sikhs down to size and employing Machiavellian strategies, the British became masters of the whole of the Punjab by 1849. Even though they had succeeded in their strategy, the innate potential of the Sikhs as warriors was not lost sight of by the British. As a masterstroke, they got them on their side.

Well before a number of French and other officers were inducted into the Sikh army to train and organize this force on the lines of

---

[5] Ibid., p. 72.

The Spirit of a Warrior 15

contemporary European armies, Captain A.H. Bingley wrote in 1818 that Ranjit Singh's 'battalions were a formidable body of troops, well disciplined and steady. Their endurance was remarkable and it was not unusual for whole regiments to make 30-mile marches often for days at a time'.[6] The courage and resilience of Sikh soldiers was underlined when twenty-one of them, from a single unit (the 36th Sikhs) and in a single day, fought to the last and were posthumously given the highest military decoration – Member of the British Empire (MBE) – that Britain could bestow on soldiers of the Indian Army. This action took place on 12 September 1897 at Saragarhi in North West Frontier Province, and is acknowledged as a feat of gallantry and sacrifice unsurpassed in the annals of military history.

The 'warrior' in my psyche has a lot to do with the Sikh history, tradition and culture. In one of my fantasies, I see myself as a 'Sikh warrior' of yore, on a mission to wreak havoc against the savage and cruel invaders who came frequently from the northwest frontiers of Hindustan, and whose primary objectives were conquest, pillage, abduction, rape and plunder. Our band of warriors has pledged to fight for the defence of the dharma and our lands, and save our countrymen from slavery and tyranny of the conquering forces. With revenge on our faces, we would swoop down on the camps or caravans of the returning alien forces, and play 'merry hell' with them. Much like the nineteenth century Sikh cavalryman described brilliantly by Major General Sir George Younghusband in Philip Mason's book, *A Matter of Honour*, 'Some of our men lost their turbans... A Sikh, with hair long as a woman's streaming in the wind, bending low and hard forward, yelling like a fiend and bringing his curved sword down on all and sundry, with a soft whistling drawing cut, is like a demon of dark dreams. There was no mercy for those fleeing enemies than they would have shown themselves.'[7]

We would rescue many hostages and prisoners and recover as much of the ill-gotten booty as possible. In particular, we would endeavour

---

[6] Ibid., p. 133.

[7] Philip Mason, *A Matter of Honour*, EBD Educational Private Limited, Dehradun, p. 367.

to rescue the women and children who would have otherwise been sold as slaves somewhere in the bazaars of Peshawar, Kabul, Kandahar or Central Asia. This was an essential part of my wandering surreal thoughts. But the 'reverie' wouldn't end at that. When we asked the liberated women or children as to where they came from, and whether or not they would like to be escorted back to their families, they said that they would rather stay with our folks as there was no question of their being accepted back, not even by their parents. The traditional norms of Hindu and Muslim society of that period were very harsh. As per the strictly enforced rules, such unfortunate women and girls who had been violated, were no longer pure, and therefore, were unwelcome. So, we had another challenge ahead, that of rehabilitating these victims of destiny. Eventually, most of these destitute women and children made a new life for themselves in the vibrant, hard-working, secular and egalitarian communities of the Punjab, where they were given shelter and protection.

Historians who have written about the Punjab during this period have described these types of guerilla tactics used by Sikh bands against invaders carrying ill-gotten booty and slaves. This role – of some kind

Sikh Warriors (Painting by Smyth, courtesy Imperial Hotel, New Delhi).

of a knight in shining armour – has been enshrined in my psyche, and therefore has become a part of me.

I have derived my inspiration and pride as a soldier from the exemplary leadership and saga of sacrifice of our gurus, warriors and military leaders such as Guru Gobind Singh, Chhatrapati Shivaji Maharaj, Maharaja Ranjit Singh, Rana Sangha and generals like Hari Singh Nalwa, Lachit Borphukan, Tipu Sultan and Zorawar Singh.

I imbibed certain values as part of growing up. I don't profess to have a profound knowledge of Sikhism, but I sincerely endeavour to be a good Sikh in my own way. My god has never failed me and has answered my prayers. At the same time, I have always cheerfully accepted whatever has happened in my life as my destiny. But most importantly, faith and religion for me are issues that are very personal. All through my career these did not have any place in my professional life, and have been an intensely private matter for our family. The spiritual strength derived from my faith has given me the confidence to stand on my feet and face the ups and downs of life.

4

Impact of Second World War and Partition

My father, Lieutenant Colonel Jaswant Singh Marwah, is a sprightly ninety-one-year-old Second World War veteran. In April 1943, after graduating from the Indian Military Academy, Dehradun, he was commissioned into the Royal Indian Army Service Corps (RIASC). He thus became the first 'afsar', or commissioned officer, in his family. Though he was commissioned in the RIASC, my father's heart was set on serving in the Indian Electrical and Mechanical Engineers (IEME) from the very beginning, as he had majored in subjects like higher mathematics, physics and chemistry for his graduation from the University of Punjab. He was thus happy to get transferred to the IEME in 1948. 'Frankly speaking, I wasn't either enjoying or feeling comfortable doing the assigned duties in the RIASC,' Dad would tell us. It was from the same academy, twenty-one years later, that I would also graduate and get my commission.

In 1944, my father was posted to the Reserve Supply Depot at Karachi Port, after completing the basic young officer's course at Kakul and a few weeks' attachment at the RIASC Centre at Ambala. The Karachi depot stocked rations for the army deployed in the Punjab and the North West Frontier Province, particularly items like tinned fish and milk imported from the UK. He married Jaspal Kaur in December 1944 in Rawalpindi, and took her to Karachi. They were in Karachi for a brief period during the war. My father recounts that he would take my mother out to the sea quite often by motor boat, and they would also go for long walks on the beach. It was exciting for them to be near the sea – it was like a honeymoon posting. However, sadly for them, it lasted only a few months.

In February 1945, he was posted as the commanding officer of a rail-based petroleum sub-depot at Samasata, about 20 miles from Bahawalpur, a princely state in the Punjab. Being the only officer, he also doubled as the station commander of the small military set-up there, with a few junior commissioned officers and soldiers under his command. It was almost like a one-man-and-a dog team. As my mother was expecting me, her first child, great love and care was lavished on her by my father. A box of 'bedana' (seedless) grapes from Chaman, near Quetta, that my dad arranged for her at that time was something that she remembered all her life. It was in this small, dusty and remote military cantonment that I was born on 17 September 1945. My mother had a forceps delivery, and both she and I survived, in an era in which there were many deaths during childbirth.

While the Allies were winning the war in 1945, colonial India's domestic political scene was witnessing turbulent times. The British had realized that India could no longer remain their crown jewel: the sun was setting over the empire, and the future of the subcontinent had to be decided soon. There was a growing feeling amongst the people of India that independence was round the corner. At the same time, rumours that India was being partitioned were spreading like wildfire. In this wartime scenario, the Indian Army, particularly the Indian officers, junior commissioned officers and other ranks, faced great uncertainty. Once the war ended, this feeling got accentuated even more. The sad prospect of serving in different armies once Hindustan was split into two nations was not easy to digest. It was ironical as armymen, irrespective of whether they were Hindus, Muslims, Sikhs or Christians, never thought of themselves as anything but Hindustanis. But at this juncture of history, the officers and men had become a confused and perplexed lot. Time was running out and the soldiers had to decide quickly whether they wanted to serve in the Indian or Pakistani army!

Many people in the Punjab had a flicker of hope till the very end that they might not be uprooted from their land, home and hearth.

Such sentiments were understandable. However, a great catastrophe befell the Indian subcontinent on 3 June 1947, when the Mountbatten Plan was announced for the partition of India. The date fixed for the division of British India was 15 August, and the proclamation of the Radcliffe Award, which would define the exact alignment of the border between India and Pakistan, was scheduled for the next day, 16 August. This was wrong, in my opinion, as people who owned properties didn't want to abandon them till they were sure of the boundary. Some of the landlords even converted to Islam and stayed behind to keep their lands! Till the time the Radcliffe line was clearly established, there were millions of affected people who couldn't take any decision about their future. When they finally did make up their minds, it proved to be too late and calamitous for many of them, for in the bargain they lost their lives too.

My grandparents and other family members, who were mainly Punjabi Khatris, both Sikhs and Hindus, were uprooted and devastated. My grandfather, a disabled veteran of the First World War and his family, and that of Anupama (I call her Rohini), my future wife, had little choice but to migrate to the Indian part of the subcontinent.

They were not only a witness to many horrendous incidents, but also suffered untold pain and misery themselves. An example in our family was the assumed violent death of Rohini's elderly grandmother; her body was never found. This period thus had an indelible and traumatic effect on this generation's psyche and life as also that of their children. Khushwant Singh's unforgettable book, *Train to Pakistan*, gives a moving account of this tragic period. The whole thing was a human tragedy of unimaginable dimensions, and possibly avoidable, according to some contemporary historians.

As a result of this Partition, the armed forces and their assets were also divided between the two nations. Regimental histories were torn asunder. Vertical splits and division of manpower and equipment took place in various regiments of cavalry and artillery, and in infantry battalions of mixed-class composition. The farewells were carried out in a spirit of bonhomie between the parting soldiers, who were comrades-in-arms till that day. Barring a few exceptions, the Muslims on one hand and the Hindus and Sikhs on the other, went their different ways. Little did they realize then that within a few months both the armies would get embroiled in a war over Kashmir. My grandfather, whose battalion, the 1/67 Punjabis, was similarly divided, was quite heartbroken about this and once remarked, 'The "paltan" that was built by our blood, sweat and toil over a century or two, disintegrated overnight with the stroke of the pen of the Mulki Laat, the Viceroy!'

It was a time of great stress for my parents. Between March 1946 and February 1948, my father, who was just a captain, was shunted around to eight different military stations in various units! So was the case with a large number of commissioned officers and men too. Things would never be the same again for officers and men of the British Indian Army. The effect was traumatic as well as tragic in many cases, particularly for those soldiers and their families who happened to suddenly find themselves living in the wrong country.

5

Growing Up in Army Cantonments

Life in the military cantonments in the 1950s was very different. I grew up in small towns or army cantonments like Patiala, Meerut, Babina (near Jhansi), Secunderabad and Jammu. Some of these places had no schools except for a few primary schools run by the government. The medium of education was Hindi or the regional languages. The army helped in the setting up of English-medium schools in many remote areas. Some of these were run by missionaries, and land and other facilities were made available to them. I recall the dedication and sincere commitment of the Portuguese and Goan fathers who taught us in St Francis Xavier School in Babina in the early 1950s.

In two places, the schools I went to happened to be convents meant to provide education to girls. These were St Anne's Convent in Bolarum, Secunderabad, and St Mary's Presentation Convent in Jammu. Wards of military personnel, including boys, as special and exceptional cases, were readily given admissions in these schools. Quite unlike the case today, we sometimes even got 'double promotions' based on our performance. I was quite good at studies and also had a decent handwriting. The question of any extra tuition or coaching never arose.

In some of these quaint little places, life was adventurous, easy-paced and rustic. There were very few amenities or avenues for entertainment, other than what was available in the cantonments. There were no malls, multiplex cinemas, TV, music systems or mobile telephones.

Even ordinary phones were the status symbols of important people – I had seen none till I entered my teens! Those were the days of the gramophone, and even that was rare. Therefore, we grew up spending a lot of time outdoors in the countryside, exploring nature, hunting for 'ber' (wild berries), playing games like cops and thieves, marbles, 'gilli danda', kite-flying, spinning tops and later, badminton or cricket. Once we kids were invited to the flag staff house at Secunderabad, to fly kites with Major General Niranjan Prasad. We had great fun and enjoyed the hospitality of the large-hearted general!

We learnt to swim by being thrown into a deep 'hauzi' or water tank, with a rope tied around the waist. Once in the water, we had to splash around and keep afloat. We eventually learnt to swim, but the hard way. I had a sharp eye, a strong left arm that enabled me to chuck stones very effectively, and I was very accurate with my catapult too.

As boys, we gave a tough time to our parents as we would always be up to some mischief. When I was about ten or eleven years of age, I liked a girl and wrote 'ILY' followed by her name with a white chalk on the road that she would usually take to school. It was puppy love, I suppose. But I was found out, and the sound thrashing I got for this prank made me forget all such funny ideas thereafter! On another occasion, because of my long hair, I was asked to do the role of a lady in the school play. I raised quite a ruckus as I didn't want to be seen wearing female attire. The nuns then made me act as a 'princeling' with my hair curled up.

I am a left hander, also called a 'khabchu', like my late grandfather. However, in his case, he was compelled by circumstances to become a 'lefty'; as described earlier, he had been shot through his right elbow during the First World War. As a child, it was tough for me to stand constant nagging from family and friends for using the inauspicious or 'wrong' hand. Often, I would retort and say 'dadaji wang mainu vee doli lagi hai' (like grandpa, I too have a gunshot), pointing at my right hand. Hearing the stories of the Great War from the grand old soldier was the best pastime for us kids in that era.

The officers club used to be the hub of all social activities in the cantonments. There were sports facilities like tennis, badminton, squash and billiards, as well as a swimming pool. We made good use of these facilities. Besides, we loved the Sunday tombola and brunch, whose menu was simple and wholesome and alternated between biryani, dosa or chana bhatura and a dessert. We also looked forward to the weekly movies shown outdoors on the noisy projector system. Whenever the film reel finished, there would be a short break while the operator replaced it. We grew up watching movies like *To Hell and Back*, *Gone with the Wind*, *From Here to Eternity* and *Ben Hur*. Most of them highlighted courage, comradeship, patriotism and other qualities of warriors, and were an important factor in motivating us to choose the army as a career. There were other social functions like the New Year's Eve or the May Queen Ball. However, in those days, children were not permitted to attend them.

The annual sports meet of the station was a great hit with the kids. The march past, relay races and the sprints were most exciting and we would lustily cheer our dad's team. The tug of war was always the last event, extremely prestigious, and thus hotly contested. The grand finale was the band display, capped by the beating of the retreat and high tea. Our sights by then would be set on goodies like chocolate pastries, samosas and gulab jamuns. To access the best delicacies we had to sneak into the enclosures meant for senior officers and do a quick job. All said and done, it was a healthy and simple life that we led.

Transfers of my father were fun occasions, too. Those were the days of steam engines, and the trains moved at a snail's pace. I remember the long journey of two or three days from Jhansi to Secunderabad. Ours being a large family, dad was entitled to a whole first-class compartment. During the Raj period, such compartments were reserved for the whites. The carriage had three cushioned berths and three bunks above them. There were nice lights and small but noisy fans on the ceiling. We would make it our temporary home. In summer, the compartment got very hot, and to keep it cool the railways provided us huge tubs with slabs of ice. These ice slabs were replaced only at big junction stations. It was not a very effective solution but there was no alternative. Because of the heat, we travelled wearing nothing except our shorts. Food could be ordered in advance, and it generally was served later than planned, because it was rare for the trains to adhere to scheduled timings. On one particular day, we were provided dinner after midnight! However, mother had packed enough homemade food and snacks to keep the insatiable hunger of her four brats under control. We used to make tea in a unique manner. Mom had carried a big thermos, tea leaves, milk powder and sugar. When the train halted at a station, she would ask one of us, the older siblings, to walk up to the engine and fill up the thermos with hot water released from the boiler. The engine drivers would never say no to us. Tea brewed from this water, courtesy the railways, tasted quite nice!

The train journeys were always eventful. However, either all or one of us Marwah brats would land up in some mess or the other during the days immediately preceding the posting of our father. On one occasion, at a farewell lunch, we tried to bring down a huge beehive hanging from a tree in the host's garden. We did succeed, but paid a heavy price for this silly act. We were attacked by so many bees that all of us had swollen faces like sumo wrestlers, and had to be under medication for quite a few days. The next time around, it was I who was bitten by the foul-tempered and moody Alsatian dog of our neighbour. He seemed to have taken a dislike for me and was perhaps angry about having been given a cold water bath by the servant. It tore into my leg just a day before we were to leave on our train journey. During the voyage, a doctor from the railways would come as per schedule and give me the anti-rabies shot. In my opinion, the Indian Railways has always been a most disciplined, efficient and professional organization, developed by the British on the lines of the army. Consequently, like the army, the railways has also played a major role in integrating our country and in nation-building.

At the end of 1956, my father was posted to Jammu. We joined St Mary's Presentation Convent, a well-established English-medium school. After two uneventful years, in 1958, when I was in my final year of middle school, I was forced to change my school. This was because the Mother Superior was visiting from Ireland, and the school authorities didn't want her to see that boys had been admitted in the convent. Although we realized there was no other option but to leave, it was difficult to overcome the feeling of being ditched so brazenly by the nuns. I had to join Model Academy, which was situated in the heart of the town, and finished my matriculation from there in 1960. Though it was a Hindi-medium school till the middle section, the standard of education was very good, and the teachers were very sincere and committed. I still remember the principal, Harbans Lal Gupta, and his wife, Shanta, as both of them took the classes for the tenth standard. I secured 8th position in J&K University in the matriculation examination.

During this period, Major General S.H.F.J. (Sam) Manekshaw was the commanding general (GOC) of 26 Infantry Division in Jammu. Flamboyant and dashing, he was one of the primary motivating factors in my decision to join the army. A story doing the rounds at that time was that one evening, while Sam Manekshaw was taking a stroll on the road leading to the officers' transit camp, he came across a young officer returning from leave, and struggling with his luggage. On finding him in a spot, the general, then in his 'civvies' (civilian clothes), promptly helped the officer carry his bags to the transit camp. The guards on duty smartly saluted their GOC. A bit perplexed, the young officer guardedly enquired of him, 'thank you, sir...but might I know who you are?'

Sam replied, 'Oh, I help soldiers like I just did, and in my spare time I command the division!'

In 1959, even though dad was posted to Udhampur, we continued to stay on in Jammu. In those days, there used to be no accommodation other than a 'basha' (an innovation of the Indian Army, this was a temporary structure made of mud and stone with a thatched roof) or a tent at Udhampur, and almost everyone lived in 'bashas' or under canvas. It was quite an experience to have a huge tent known as 'English Pattern Indian Police' (EPIP) for a house, whenever we went there for a holiday from Jammu. At night we were often woken up by huge bandicoots scurrying all over, foraging for something to nibble at, including our toes or nose.

Kashmir has been a part of my life since I was a child of twelve. My father was posted as the commanding officer of the Recovery Company at Jammu and Udhampur military stations for four years, from 1957–60. Our house was located in Satwari square, a suburb of Jammu, where the officers of the J&K state forces used to stay. Some houses were given to the army and we were lucky enough to get one of them. There were about forty houses in a hollow square configuration in that locality, flanked by the Ranbir canal. Named after Maharaja Ranbir Singh, the ruler of J&K from 1857–85, the canal carries ice-cold water from the Chenab river and originates from the barrage at Akhnur. In those days, this canal was used by us to refrigerate fruit, soft drinks and even beer bottles, and people sat on its bank and dipped their feet and literally cooled their heels. It was a challenge to swim in its freezing waters, but our spirit of adventure and taking 'pangas' (uncalled for hazardous or risky ventures) made us not only dive into the canal, but also swim through the aquaducts under the bridges. In those freezing waters we couldn't stay submerged for more than a minute or two. But it was great fun. The canal was also a popular place for a walk or a drive, as one got to see the beautiful Dogri damsels bathing in it! Since the road ran parallel to the canal and in close proximity to it, we learnt that many army trucks ended up driving into the canal or had accidents, because of this distraction.

Once, while celebrating the lohri festival that signifies the end of the winter season in north India, we augmented our collection of firewood by stealing all the wooden name boards from the gates of houses in our colony, so that we could enjoy the bonfire for a longer time. Our mischief was discovered within a day or two. We received a proper dressing down by our parents, but finally, it was laughed off as no house had been spared.

I have vivid memories of two visits to the Kashmir valley as a teenager, during 1957–60. The first one was by three of us siblings, all by ourselves. A huge recovery vehicle was being repositioned from Jammu to Srinagar, and we hitched a ride. It turned out to be an amazing journey, and maybe a record of sorts! The driver's cabin was spacious, and the three of us made ourselves fairly comfortable on the rear bench. We stopped for the night at various locations en route such as Batote, Ramban and Quazigund; places where there were recovery posts established by Dad's unit. Batote can be quite cold on a rainy day, which was the case when we halted for the night.

This was one of the first occasions when we had a tot of rum mixed in our milk, a 'night cap' to keep our body temperature above the freezing point. We had four army blankets over us, which were of such a rough texture that it hurt our skin. We used our handkerchiefs to cover our faces and soon went off to sleep. It must have been the tranquilliser effect of the army rum! Later on, during my military career, our civilian friends would often request us to serve them canteen rum. The most common pretext was that the army rum had more 'dum' (punch) than what was available in the market. It was a gift that was universally accepted and appreciated.

Our journey up to Srinagar, though interesting, was quite uneventful. J&K was a peaceful state in those carefree days. One could pick up fruits like peaches, plums or apples from the trees and eat them with relish and saunter about with gay abandon. The Kashmiris looked content and we felt welcomed.

The second trip was *en famille*. During this summer holiday, we travelled in a military convoy from Jammu and stayed in transit camps for the night halts. We reached Srinagar on the third day. My father had hired a house in downtown Srinagar, which we made into a temporary home – it was furnished to minimalistic standards and old newspapers served as curtains. This modest abode became our 'firm base', so to say. Such an arrangement would be quite unthinkable in the present times!

We used to go for long walks and covered all the tourist spots in Srinagar, including the Dal Lake, the Char Chinar island, and the wonderous Mughal Gardens – Shalimar, Nishat and Chashma-Shahi – and the Shankaracharya Temple. The town was one-third the size of what it is today. The mode of travel of the common people was the bus or 'tonga'. The visits to Kokernag and Verinag, the source of the Jhelum, were unforgettable. We saw hundreds of trout in the crystal-clear spring water, including the rarely found rainbow trout. Unimaginably and ironically, thirty years later, I was combating terrorists in the same area as a brigade commander.

Barely in our teens, what interested us then were our studies and games. In the absence of a vibrant media in those days, we were neither aware of the political undercurrents nor very concerned with them. These aspects have been discussed in more detail in Part III of this book.

Our parents did not send us to any boarding school, perhaps because they couldn't afford it. My father was the only commissioned officer in the entire family, and had the responsibility of bringing up not only his children but many others too. Besides, my parents believed that children could be given greater personal care, and also taught family traditions and spiritual values better, at home.

My parents have had the greatest influence on me as a child, my late mother in particular. Rani Jaspal Kaur was a wonderful person and an excellent homemaker. She brought up a large family very efficiently and lovingly. I was her first-born, and perhaps because of that, she had a special attachment to me. A pious lady, she sacrificed everything for her family. Though frail in health towards the end, she lived to see her son become the army chief, and died peacefully in her sleep in February 2005, a fortnight after that event. She was cremated in a befitting and dignified ceremony at the Brar Square in Delhi Cantonment. This was the same place where my grandfather's last rites were conducted with appropriate military honours.

My father is ninety-one, and by the grace of God, in good health. He is caring and devoted to his very large family of six children, thirteen grandchildren and fifteen great-grandchildren! At one point in time before his retirement, he was a proud father having three sons serving in the defence forces. My elder brother, Squadron Leader S.J.S. 'Satti' Marwah, was an ace fighter pilot and acclaimed flying instructor in the Indian Air Force; I was serving in the Maratha Light Infantry; and the third, Captain B.J. Singh, was an exceptionally gifted and talented doctor in the Army Medical Corps. Satti served as an instructor in Iraq's Air Force Academy at Tikrit for two years, as a member of our air force training team. My father retired as a lieutenant colonel in 1973, after meritoriously serving the EME and the army for over thirty years. For our family, it was a matter of pride and an honour with four of us serving the nation at the same time: more so during the Indo-Pak war of 1971. Here I would like to make a mention of my younger siblings – Inderjeet Singh, who distinguished himself as an entrepreneur; D.J. Singh, an enterprising international banker; and Veena, the youngest and only sister, a bright scholar, educationist and administrator who lives in Norway. This makes up my immediate family.

Part II
CADET TO A COLONEL

Commissioned into 9 Maratha Light Infantry – 2 August 1964, Belgaum.

6

The Cradle

My four-and-a-half-decade-long journey in the army started in January 1961. I was all of fifteen years and three months old at that time, and like most others of my age, didn't know where this journey would end. Along with my half-brother, I left home for the National Defence Academy (NDA), Khadakwasla, near Poona, to join the 25th Course. Mother prayed for us and did the 'ardas' before we left. I don't know of any other case where two brothers joined the NDA in the same batch. Though my brother, S.J.S. Marwah (Satti to me), was elder to me by almost two years, we got through the NDA examination and the interview by the selection board together. I was fifteenth in the overall merit list from amongst a couple of thousand who sat for the entrance examination. In those days, the results used to be published in the national dailies. Sadly, it's not the case any longer. Satti opted for the air force, while I chose the army, though I liked the navy too.

The NDA is a world-class training institution; importantly, it is one of the few tri-service academies of the world. It was the vision of Jawaharlal Nehru that resulted in the creation of such an outstanding academy. Today it is the cradle of our military leadership.

We travelled by train for a day-and-a-half from Ferozepur, where my father happened to be posted at that time, and reached Poona on the appointed day. There we were received by a team from the NDA. After an hour's bus ride we reached the academy. I remember that moment so vividly even today.

The first view of the NDA from the main gate at the top of the hill was simply stunning. A straight and wide avenue led us to the heart of the academy. Having reached the cadets' living area, we got down from the buses, identified our baggage and put name tags on them. We were told that our boxes would be sent to our rooms (called 'cabins' – a naval term), but a warm reception awaited us on the way. That was our first experience of ragging. We were expecting it, because everyone who knew about the NDA had warned us about it, but what we experienced was unbelievable. At times, it was cruel, sadistic and almost inhuman! We measured the distance to the cadets' mess not by walking but by 'front-rolling', a term denoting a human ball rolling on the tarmac. We soon learnt how to fold our torso in a round configuration, perhaps a shade better than when we were in our mother's womb. It did not take us time to realize that while riding our cycles we exposed ourselves to being saddled with a 'golden necklace'. That meant continuing our journey carrying the cycle around our necks in case we failed to pay compliments to our seniors, were out of line or simply because we crossed the path of a mean son-of-a-bitch. The worst part of it was that the senior cadet who awarded the punishment generally vanished, without giving any orders about the termination of the punishment. For all it mattered, a sincere and disciplined first-termer could be on his haunches leaping like a frog, front-rolling or running around an 'imaginary tree' the whole night.

It wasn't difficult to spot a first-termer as we were in civilian clothes till our uniforms and 'mufti' outfits were tailored and issued to us. Besides, our body language gave us away even when we had received our uniforms, later in the term. There appeared to be a stamp somewhere on our person which nailed us. The whole issue of ragging seemed bizarre and silly. In our squadron, we had a daily dose of ragging after dinner; the physical aches and pain made it difficult for us to laugh it off, and it was pointless crying. There was no one to comfort us. It was like the 'death lane' in the equestrian training area, where the rider and the horse were put in a barricaded enclosure with a series of jumps which the horse was trained to clear with or without the rider in the saddle. The latter eventuality was a frequent occurrence. So we learnt to get on with life by ourselves – graduating into manhood.

Since the NDA was designed to train cadets of all the three services, using the terminologies of the army, navy and air force was *de rigueur* in the academy. We found terms of the three services being used in a random mix. At first, it sounded a bit odd to learn that in the drill square there was a 'quarter deck'. Our instructors were amongst the finest officers from the three services. It was common to have a squadron commander from the navy or a battalion commander from the air force. The army cadets were called 'pongos' and the hospital a 'sick bay'! With my army background, I found the whole thing quite funny and confusing at times.

One Sunday morning I was in the barber shop, standing in the queue with a serious look on my face. A senior cadet present there found it very amusing – a Sikh cadet waiting for a haircut.

'Bloody fool (the normal way a fresher was addressed), what are you doing here. Don't you know this is a barber shop?' he barked at me.

'Yes, sir,' said I.

'Then get lost before I make a monkey out of you,' he hissed like a king cobra.

'But I can't do that, sir. I am standing in for Vinod Sir,' was my timid response.

'Disappear immediately, will you? I will sort out your Vinod Sir as well!'

I ran from that area as fast as I could and sought the refuge of my cabin. After that day, I wasn't ever asked by Cadet Vinod (name changed) to do anything stupid.

The daily routine at the academy was very tough. From 6 a.m., when the reveille was sounded, till 10 p.m., when it was lights out, we were kept so busy that we didn't know whether we were coming or going. The day would generally start with PT, drill or equitation. Then, after breakfast, we had classes till lunch. Thereafter, we would have games, followed by a quick shower, and then getting into mess kit for dinner nights or civvies on certain days, and doing self-study before going to the mess for dinner. By the time we returned from the mess, we would be dog-tired and go off to sleep as soon as 'lights out' was announced. The academic curriculum was designed to give us an educational background upto graduation level, though in those days we never got any formal degrees.

The overall aim of training was character building, esprit de corps, mental and physical robustness, leadership and a sense of keen observation. Besides this one learnt inter-services aspects of the armed forces, developed interest in extracurricular activities, and inculcated the spirit of the 'honour code' as well as ethical and moral values. We were obliged to study a foreign language as an additional subject. The popular languages were French, German or Italian. However, I was allotted Arabic. By the end of our course, I had achieved a fairly good standard in this language and even passed the advanced diploma Part I exam. There were some clever guys who never passed their basic Hindi test and therefore, did not have to study a foreign language. They were losers in the long run, as I believe knowing another language is an asset in life.

When I joined the NDA, I was nominated to the Alpha squadron, but on rejoining after the first-term break, I was astonished to learn that my squadron had been changed to Juliet. This was a new squadron and cadets had to be transferred from all other squadrons to make it full strength. Being a new squadron, we had to forge ourselves into a team and soon we began to make a mark by excelling in various inter-squadron competitions. By the end of my stay in the NDA, we were amongst the best squadrons of the academy. As of now, there have been many two- and three-star generals, air marshals and admirals from the Juliet squadron, though I have been the only cadet to become a chief.

For relaxation, we used to look forward to the weekly movie. On occasions there was a dose of ragging and punishment at the end of the cinema show, if any of us misbehaved, whistled or jeered during it. We also used to have end-of-the-term social evenings, which were a cause of much amusement. We were permitted to go on an outing to Poona on Sundays or holidays and this was referred to as 'liberty'. Many of us got into serious problems getting back to the academy on time. Stopping of liberty was a very effective punishment. Studies were taken very seriously and we had to report back earlier for a retest in case we failed in two or more subjects. Only once during my stay of three years in the NDA did I have to take the re-examination. As a tradition in the final term, the passing-out cadets became the juniormost for a day or two. It was fun to see them being ragged by everyone. Generally, those who were very harsh or strict with their juniors were singled out for special treatment. When I was graduating, very few of the juniors came looking for me, and I got away lightly.

The Sino-Indian war took place during October-November 1962. This war over disputed borders came as a rude shock. I was in the fourth term at that time. All of us volunteered to go and fight for the defence of the motherland. I vividly recall that our deputy commandant, Brigadier Hoshiar Singh, a gallant soldier and an experienced war leader, was nominated to command a brigade under 4 Infantry Division in NEFA (now Arunachal Pradesh) and moved posthaste to the northeast. That brigade was tasked to occupy a defensive position at the formidable Se La pass.

We had great faith and confidence that his brigade would stall the Chinese advance and stem the tide. Unfortunately, the 4th Division withdrew from Se La without giving much of a fight. During this phase of the war, Brigadier Hoshiar Singh died in action against the Chinese. We as cadets felt very sad to lose such a fine officer, and it would be hard to forget those days. As a result of this debacle, quite a few heads rolled in the army, and the overall responsibility had to be accepted by the then defence minister, V.K. Krishna Menon, and the army chief, General P.N. Thapar. In a way, this setback to the image of India affected the stature of our first prime minister, Jawaharlal Nehru. He felt stabbed in the back by the Chinese. He never recovered from this catastrophic event and died due to a heart attack in 1964.

After their traumatic defeat in 1962, there was a large-scale expansion of the armed forces. To make up for the shortfall of officers, emergency commissions were given to a few thousand young men from 1963–65. They were given training at the academies for only six months instead of two years. At the same time, our one-year training period at the Indian Military Academy (IMA), Dehradun, was compressed to seven months, and we got commissioned as second lieutenants in August 1964. It was a hectic period for hundreds of us milling around in Premnagar and Clement Town areas of IMA, Dehradun. There was a lot of ad hocism and curtailing of the training schedules being resorted to. Further, due to the increased numbers, there was an unavoidable dilution of standards of the living conditions of the cadets, particularly in the Clement Town area where I was undergoing training. We were made to live in barracks made during the Second World War to house Italian prisoners of war! My memories of that seven-month period are quite lacklustre. Except for the passing-out parade and our commissioning, I do not recall any other event. During those days, we always appeared to be in a big rush, doing one thing after another.

However, I do remember vividly the bashing up I got in the semi-finals of the boxing championship. Being from the NDA, it was assumed that I was a boxer. Every cadet had to participate in the novices boxing competition in the NDA. But that did not mean we became good pugilists. Without so much as asking my concurrence, I was fielded in the bantamweight category of the IMA Inter Company Championship. I somehow managed to do well in the preliminary bouts. Being a 'southpaw' had its advantages. In the semis I had to face an adversary who happened to be a university champion and was from the emergency commission cadets' stream. In the first two rounds, I fared reasonably well. I gave him a few punches and one odd left hook, even though he had landed many solid knocks on my face, which, by then, was badly bruised. In the third round, he showed his true colours and went for me. I didn't give up. Flinging my arms about wildly and missing the target most of the time, I took a lot of beating. Barely able to stand in my corner, all that I remember was that the referee announced 'well fought red, green is the winner'. The multicoloured stars that we saw in comics as kids were all that I could see wherever I turned my eyes, and my head was pounding. Then I passed out and had to be admitted in the military hospital, where I was kept under observation for two days. Fortunately, there was no 'brain damage', or so I assume, but I had to go around with a black eye for many days. My company commander happened to watch this fight. I suppose he must have raised my ranking in the order of merit a couple of notches higher, for displaying grit and determination and taking the bashing in a manly way. That was the last time that I boxed.

My father came to attend my passing-out parade and the pipping ceremony on 2 August 1964. He put on a single star on each of my shoulders and embraced me. He had tears in his eyes as he recalled his own commissioning at this very same IMA parade ground in 1943. This was the dawn of a third-generation soldier of the Indian Army. To celebrate, my father offered me my first glass of beer, and we clinked our glasses as we said cheers. Then my father said that henceforth, we shall be 'brother officers' first, and father and son later. It was one of the happiest days of my life. How I wished that my mother was also there to bless me and share this moment of joy. But she couldn't come as she was supervising the construction of our house in Defence Colony in Delhi.

7

Regimental Soldiering

After a brief holiday, I left home in August 1964 to report to the Maratha Light Infantry Regiment Centre (MLIRC) at Belgaum. As the train steamed into the Belgaum railway station, I got into my summer uniform and packed my valise and the black steel trunk. Those contained my only worldly possessions at that point of time. I was received by the duty officer and directed to proceed to the MLIRC officers' mess. Outside the station, there was no transport waiting for me. So the coolie carrying my luggage suggested that I take a tonga instead. The mess was on a small hill and the poor scrawny little horse found the going quite tough! The driver had to dismount and put his shoulder to the wheel and push. I paid him one rupee, a princely sum those days, and he left giving me a salaam. Finally, on reaching the mess, the havaldar (sergeant) offered me a welcome cup of tea. When I asked him to show me my room, he smiled wryly and said, 'No rooms are available and Sir, you will have to make do with a tent!'

One of the mess waiters took my baggage and put it in the tent. It had already begun to drizzle. This drizzle continued for the next three days. I knew of the monsoons but had never experienced anything like this. The low clouds passing around the hills made my abode damp and cold. I sat on my trunk and looked around. The tent was no bigger than a hundred square feet and its interiors were bare; besides a cot and an easy chair, there was a folding table and a camp stool. The only light in the tent was from a single 40-watt bulb hanging by a cable on the centre pole. The uneven floor was covered by light brown coir matting. The attached bathroom was even more luxurious! It was a dingy little tent lit by a 'hurricane lantern' (a kerosene oil lamp). The space inside it was barely enough for a commode and a towel stand. For the bath there were two buckets placed in a corner, which was raised from the soil with the aid of a few bricks joined together. It was dry sanitation at its simplest. The commode, humourously also called the 'throne' or 'thunder box', would be cleaned every morning by a sweeper, and the bath water would drain out into a temporary underground septic tank nearby. The only consolation was that I was not alone; there were a few more unfortunate souls like me living in that tented colony.

I was attached by the Army Headquarters (HQ) to the Regimental Centre till the commencement of the raising of the 9th Battalion, the Maratha Light Infantry (LI), on 1 October 1964. There were many more young officers posted to the centre at that time. A majority of them were emergency commissioned officers. I was the only NDA graduate amongst all of them, and I held a regular commission. In every combat unit, besides the commanding officer, there were two or three field rank officers, a captain and the rest were subalterns. The joke was that if one threw a stone in the air, it would most probably land on the head of a young officer!

Even though our habitat was frugal, more like the rear area of war zone rather than a peacetime cantonment in the south, we enjoyed all the free time we got. We followed a set timings and work schedule at the centre – PT with the recruits at 6:00 a.m., followed by breakfast, supervision of the training of budding soldiers, lunch, and then games with the troops followed by dinner in the officers' mess. Thrice a week we would have a dinner night – a formal affair for which we had to wear the summer mess kit or the blue patrols in the winter. The menu would generally be a three-course Western meal. The helpings were so small that often we would go to our tents and sleep on a hungry stomach! On all other days, we would cycle down to the club or the town and have a good time. I had bought myself a new cycle, which was the only transport most of us could afford, and that too on monthly instalments. One's salary as second lieutenant was around four hundred rupees and barely sufficed to keep one's head above water. Yet we managed to behave like 'sahibs' of the Raj period, wearing white sharkskin jackets and black bow-ties with Wellington shoes and spurs for informal mess functions. We used to go to the gymkhana at the cantonment, and made a few Anglo-Indian and Goan friends. We would organize dance parties once in a while, mostly on Saturdays. Everyone pooled in for the food. We were most sought after as we took care of the drinks, and rum was the favourite, particularly the XXX Hercules rum from the army canteen! At one of these 'dos' I met an attractive Bengali girl. We became friends. We enjoyed dancing together, particularly the foxtrot, the quickstep or the cha-cha-cha. I had become proficient in ballroom dancing at the NDA. She wanted to learn from me and I agreed to teach her. However, this was when I learnt that she was married, and she became off-limits as far as I was concerned. Shortly thereafter we moved to Naga Hills.

As young officers, after clearing our monthly mess bills and other dues, we were left with very little out of our meagre salary; and by the twentieth day we would be almost bankrupt! What would we have done without our regimental banias? They readily helped to bail out the 'rank and file' financially whenever we were broke. Of course, they would take their pound of flesh and never forgot to charge us a hefty interest. But loans were not a problem, and unlike banks the bania never took a holiday or stuck to fixed working hours. It was 24×7 the year round for this tribe.

This petty trader, contractor and private banker all rolled into one has existed as an institution in the Indian Army since ages. We must give credit to the British for this unique invention. We have known of two or even three generations that have served with certain battalions and regiments. The battalion in which I was commissioned forty-seven years ago, has seen three generations of the first unit bania, Har Narayan Aggrawal, who began his trade along with the raising of our battalion. Now his son and grandson run the show. A century or two ago, this breed was among the important camp followers moving behind the conquering armies. Their loyalty, dedication and commitment and the readiness to bear privations along with the soldiers whom they served was indeed commendable, and this tradition continues till date. Of course, the fact that there have been some real sharks also amongst them cannot be denied!

The 9 Maratha LI was raised on 1 October 1964 at Belgaum. The battalion was created from scratch. The first day of our existence was historic for all of us who were present. I had to merely step across from the Regimental Centre at Belgaum to the new unit, and happened to be among the first few officers to join the battalion. First of all, there was a prayer ceremony attended by us, the pioneers. This was followed by a 'Sainik Sammelan' (a formal interaction with all ranks) by Major K.L. Awasthi, the second-in-command. The gathering on that occasion comprised a few officers, including myself, some JCOs and about 300 soldiers. It was an unforgettable experience for all of us. Major K.L. Awasthi officiated as the commanding officer (CO) till Lieutenant Colonel M.B. Wadke arrived and took charge of the battalion.

We received orders to move to Nagaland in mid-1965. The battalion moved by a special military train from Belgaum to Dimapur. Though the journey was a great experience, it took us forever to reach our destination. Being a peacetime move, our train was given the lowest priority, even lower than goods trains. The rolling stock or the bogies that formed the train were the worst available and in a poor state of maintainance too. The batteries which ran the lights and fans in the compartments required to be charged very frequently. We would spend hours sweating it out in the oppressive heat and unbearable humidity. Nights were comparatively cooler but often without any lights.

For a youngster like me, it was the strangest train journey. The train was the mobile home for 800 troops for over ten days. The officers had a first-class compartment, the junior commissioned officers were given a second-class one, and the rest of the train comprised third-class bogies. Ordinary covered wagons meant for goods were converted into kitchens. The conditions inside these metal boxes were hot as hell, perhaps a shade worse than the boiler room in a steam ship. We really marvelled at the capacity of the cooks to be able to make food in such horrible conditions. We had meal halts and also technical halts for the engines to be changed or refuelled. Sometimes, we had unscheduled halts to allow higher priority trains to pass. At major stations we would get fresh rations and huge blocks of ice for cooling our compartments. Air conditioners were unknown in those days.

We had installed a 20-line field telephone exchange and telephones for key officers and the engine and the guard at the end of the train. Wherever we got an opportunity, we would go for a jog on the platform or the railway siding. The officer commanding of the train had entrusted me with the most thankless and enervating task of keeping a detailed record of all halts on this long journey. Therefore, I had to be on my toes 24x7 throughout the journey to maintain this log. I couldn't sleep peacefully either during the day or night. I had a few additional hands to help me in this task. Eventually, after many days, we reached Guwahati after crossing the mighty Brahmaputra over a very long bridge. This dual-purpose bridge had two decks, the lower one for the railway and the upper deck for the highway. The bridge was an engineering marvel and was reportedly constructed by Indian engineers. Though work on it started in 1958, the foundation stone was laid by Jawaharlal Nehru in January 1960 and it was commissioned in June 1963. Prior to that, the trains terminated at Amingaon on the north bank of the river. From there, the passengers and baggage were transferred into huge steam ferries and taken to the south bank, where there was a railway terminal at a place called Pandu, near Guwahati.

Facing the Naga Underground

From Guwahati to Dimapur in Nagaland, the railroad passed through thick tropical forests. We had heard of trains being stopped by the insurgents by felling trees across the track and by firing at the coaches. Therefore, we were ordered to be in combat gear with weapons at the ready, prepared for any eventuality! At times, when the train stopped dead in the middle of a forest, we were told that there was a herd of wild elephants on the track; hence we could only restart our journey once they moved back into the jungle. Finally, we reached our destination – Dimapur – and the battalion detrained on a railway siding. We were piped in by pipes and drums of a sister battalion, and warmly welcomed by a reception committee from 81 Mountain Brigade. It was a huge effort to unload everything, specially the arms and ammunition and other controlled stores. After a thorough check, an 'OK report' was rendered by all the company commanders to the CO. Over the next few days, we were inducted by road into our area of responsibility in Phek, ahead of Kohima.

As the monsoon had already set in, the roads were in a big mess. There was only one major artery connecting Dimapur to Kohima and Imphal. Besides this highway, there were hardly any other black-topped roads in those days! Beyond Kohima it was a dirt track fit for vehicular traffic only in fair weather. In the event it had turned into a quagmire of slush. The wheels of the trucks had made ruts that were two feet deep at places. We had a few cases where the vehicles skidded off the road and fell down the hill. Fortunately, we had no casualties and were able to recover the vehicles as they were saved from going too far down the slope because of the dense forests. The battalion took over a week to settle down and the companies moved forward to their posts over the next ten days or so.

Since there was a ceasefire between Naga rebels and the government in force during that period, we had no armed encounters with the hostiles. There was an uneasy peace prevailing at that time, and seven rounds of talks had taken place between the Government of India and the underground 'Naga Federal Government'. Besides that, there was a peace mission established that was playing the role of a mediator. It had a peace centre and an observer team in Kohima. Dr Aram, a Sarvodaya worker, was one of its prominent members. Taking advantage of the ceasefire, we used to carry out a lot of patrolling to familiarize ourselves with the area of our operational responsibility. I was the intelligence officer (IO) and therefore my work station was at Phek. Whenever the CO moved out for operations or reconnaissance missions it was my task to accompany him, and look into the coordination aspects. Besides, the IO generally functioned as an understudy to the adjutant of the battalion, and as per the normal practice, took over that appointment in due course.

It was on one of these reconnaissance missions that I accompanied Lieutenant Colonel Wadke to the Indo-Burmese border area, about ten kilometres ahead of one of our company posts at Khanjangkuki. The trek to the top of the mountain was one of the most fascinating climbs of my life. We walked along a foot track from Khanjangkuki to the border along the Patkai mountain range. This area was known as the Somra Tract and had a very dense rainforest cover. I had never seen forests like that before. There were tall trees with a canopy branching out on the top and with very little undergrowth. One could not see the soil as the ground was covered by a soft and moist carpet of dead leaves and decaying branches of fallen trees which had lichen and fungi all over. All of a sudden my eyes fell on a ground orchid in full bloom.

This was the first time I had ever seen orchids in the wild. It was a stunningly beautiful sight. We bivouacked for the night in this area and returned the next day to Jessami, the road head. From there we drove back to the Battalion HQ at Phek. The CO did not share with me the reason for this reconnaissance trip. The track we followed had witnessed the Japanese cross the Chindwin river and advance to Kohima during the Second World War. After their defeat in the Battle of Kohima, the British Indian Army under General (later Field Marshal) W.J. (Bill) Slim chased the Japanese back over the Patkai range into Burma.

While we were camping in the forest, we received a wireless message that a vacancy for the intelligence course had been allotted to the unit, and the name of the officer detailed to undergo the course had to be communicated to the Brigade HQ without delay. I was able to prevail upon the CO and get a decision in my favour. As I was functioning as the IO of the battalion, I felt it would be appropriate if I was nominated for it. This decision of Lieutenant Colonel Wadke had far-reaching consequences in my life. Yet it might also have caused some heartburn among others who wanted to do the same course. I attended the course and topped it despite being the juniormost, and later on was posted as an instructor at the Intelligence School at Poona in 1970.

As young officers we were unaware of the political developments in Nagaland, and confined ourselves to the limited realm of doing our assigned duties in the battalion. We had to carry out a number of long-range patrols in order to get to know the area, just in case the 'ceasefire' with the Naga underground got abrogated. As good regimental officers we shared the hardships with the men and did our best to be their role models. Sometime during 1966 the battalion got orders to be deployed closer to the border with Burma, with company and platoon posts being established all over in the Tuensang district. We became experts in creating infrastructure and rudimentary habitat with bamboo and grass. Most of these new posts were maintained by air. We became adept at using the cotton parachutes to line the interiors of our thatched shacks, so as to protect us from the rain and cold breeze. We learnt that a large group of Naga rebels, including many young recruits, had crossed over to Burma under self-styled General Thinoselie and other leaders of the Naga underground. They were reportedly headed for Yunan province of China to receive training and arms. It was very interesting to know that this group had crossed over from the area where we were now deployed and that they were given traditional feasts with mithuns (semi-domesticated animal of the ox family) being slaughtered, and local drinks like madhu, a variety of rice beer, flowing liberally.

The year 1967–68 was momentous for all of us serving in 8 Mountain Division in Nagaland. Intelligence reports had confirmed that in December 1967, another large gang of Naga underground rebels, led by self-styled generals Mowu Angami and Zuheto Sema and stalwarts like Isaac Swu and T. Muivah, had gone across from the Tuensang area of Nagaland to China, for training and procuring arms. This was a blatant violation of the ceasefire policy. Over 300 young men had been recruited from the Angami, Sema, Ao and Tangkhul tribes for this mission. 'Thinoselie, who had gone to China in November 1966, began his return journey in mid-January 1968. He brought with him more than 400 Chinese weapons, including a few mortars, machine guns, rocket launchers and wireless sets, mines and ammunition. Naga tribes living on the Burmese side of the border helped Thinoselie enter Nagaland.'[1]

The government and the Army HQ were livid with Eastern Command and 8 Mountain Division, in particular, for not being able to intercept and prevent this huge group of rebels from exfiltrating across the border into Burma, and thence to China. Neither were they able to catch Thinoselie's gang on its return. 'By April 1968 it had become clear that Mowu Angami and his gang were planning to return to Nagaland

---

[1] Colonel R.D. Palsokar, *Forever in Operations, A History of 8 Mountain Division*, Vol. I, pp. 63–73.

in the near future.'[2] Hence, 9 Maratha LI was moved from Phek to Kiphire near Tuensang. We reinforced the thin deployment of 8 Assam Rifles along the border, and were placed under the command of 162 Mountain Brigade commanded by Brigadier A.S. Vaidya, MVC. Some other battalions were also moved to plug the gaps in this border area.

The general officer commanding-in-chief (GOC-in-C) of the command was Lieutenant General Sam Manekshaw, and Major General N.C. Rawlley was our divisional commander. A warning was sent out down to the battalion level that the heads of the COs and the company commanders would roll in case the Chinese-trained gang managed to slip into Nagaland undetected this time. With the guillotine facing us there was tremendous tension in the air. Lieutenant General Manekshaw was looking at becoming the army chief and similarly, Major General Rawlley knew his future depended on the level of success that would be achieved by his division in neutralizing the infiltrating gang. Lieutenant Colonel K.L. Awasthy, our CO, also had a nagging suspicion that he might face the axe if we did not perform as expected or if the commanding general had his way, since he didn't appear to like his face! But we had a great team of youngsters like Baban Shinde, M.N.S. Thampi and D.B. Shekatkar, and we strove to ensure that the battalion or our CO was never let down. We built up strong bonds with the tribes of the border areas, like the Yimchungers, Noktes and Wanchoos. That rapport was one of the primary reasons for our success subsequently.

This was achieved by our exemplary conduct and people-friendly activities. While the insurgents were away from Nagaland for about a year, the security environment of the remote Indo-Burmese region in Tuensang district changed drastically. There was much greater presence of the army along the border and more effective surveillance. Besides, we had won over the hearts and minds of the people. A mistake made by the leaders of the insurgents was that they had included very few men from the border tribes, whom they considered inferior to their own tribes from the heartland. That attitude hurt the pride of these border tribes. As a result they willingly cooperated with us and provided very

---

[2] Ibid., p. 66.

valuable information and logistical help where required. News kept trickling in of the return of the gang led by Mowu Angami, Issac Swu and T. Muivah. But the question on everyone's mind was when, and from where, will they re-enter Nagaland? We were palpably nervous and anxious.

On 2 or 3 March 1969, I was asked by the CO to take out a patrol and go right upto the border on the top of the Patkai range, carry out surveillance, and try and get some specific information on the gang. I left for my mission by the afternoon with a mixed group of soldiers from my battalion and 8 Assam Rifles. Very early the next morning, we reached the highest point of the mountain. There the track meandered on a plateau covered with a thick forest. It was a kind of a 'no-man's-land'. As we crept forward, the track began to descend sharply. I wasn't sure of our position, and besides, in those days, we had no GPS to help us out either. Going down the steep slope in the jungle as silently as we could, we suddenly heard noises. We froze at once. I went up to the leading scout and, from the cover of a large tree trunk, saw an incredible sight. There were about fifteen to twenty armed men. It was difficult to make out whether they were Burmese Army soldiers or members of the insurgent gang! I had about ten soldiers and most of them were from Assam Rifles. There was no possibility of ascertaining the identity of these aliens. Further, if they noticed us they wouldn't let us get away unscathed. In such a situation the one who spotted the adversary first, had all the advantage. In this case not only were they unaware of us but we were also on higher ground and thus dominating the area. I had to make up my mind quickly. Ultimately, it was us or them! I took a calculated risk and decided that if the group moved up the hill towards us, we would open fire, and if not, we would wait and watch. There appeared to be no other option in that fog-covered and densely forested environment of the Patkai range.

Fortunately, they fell in and after checking their weapons and equipment in an orderly manner, started moving back. This was an indication that they were from the Burmese Army, and I heaved a sigh of relief. Had they moved towards us, it could have resulted in an unsavoury incident, a firefight with international ramifications, and probably the end of my military career! That incident would also have spelt doom for our CO as the buck would have stopped at his level, and consequently, a serious setback for our unit.

Even to this day I get the shivers when I recall the events of that dawn. I had a local guide whom I then despatched, with some rum and cigarettes, as my emissary to get some news of the gang. In fact, he actually followed the Burmese patrol till they reached their post. Waving a white handkerchief he approached them and handed over the gifts. He was then told by the Burmese that a large Naga gang had been chased across to our side the previous night. He thanked the Burmese post commander and returned posthaste to the place on the border where I was waiting for the news. Having got the vital information, we literally ran back to the Battalion HQ, believing we had 'breaking news'. On reaching Anutangre, I briefed Lieutenant Colonel Awasthi on the map, and gave the news obtained from the Burmese Army. He appeared preoccupied and was not greatly enthused with the inputs I had brought. In fact, our troops had been informed by the villagers of the presence of jungle 'manus', a local terminology for the insurgents, and were already in contact with them at a few places. He told me to coordinate the ongoing operations and function as the adjutant.

There had been a few encounters in the past twelve hours. As a result of that the gang broke up into smaller groups and tried to get away through the dense foliage. As we were more familiar with the area, our battalion was given the task of combing the dense jungles. Therefore most of our officers and men were tasked to search the jungles as subunits or special mission patrols. Additional units were moved into this sector and deployed on the ridgelines. They became the anvil and we acted as the hammer. This was to ensure that we captured the whole gang. We did our best to ensure that none of them was able to escape from the dragnet. Since the insurgents were not giving a fight, while fleeing they ran into the ambushes along the ridgelines, and the troops deployed there captured them and took the credit. But the real slogging was being done by us.

In one encounter, we had killed some of them but we lost one soldier. The first insurgent we caught was quickly brought to the Battalion HQ. As the officiating adjutant, I was the one who did the preliminary interrogation. The insurgent, a Sema lad who looked barely in his teens,

My parents after their wedding, in wartime Karachi, 1944.

A content child, 1945.

High school graduate, May 1960.

Second term at the NDA, July 1961.

The graduating class with the principal of Model Academy, Jammu, 1960 (I am in the top row, sixth from right).

Sixth term at the NDA, November 1963. Kneeling: Virender Kochhar, Satish Kapur and I; Standing: P. Vig, R.B. Menon, G.R. Sud, C.M. Mehta, Captain Surjit Kumar, M.M. Toteja, R.K. Singh and Subhash Kumar.

AT BANERJEE, SP BHATIA, MAJ DP THAPAR, MAJ KL AWASTHI, LT COL MB WADKE, MAJ NV SUBBARAO, 2/LTS MNS THAMPI   TD PATIL   KG MAHAJAN   AS KHARE   JJ SINGH   RC TULI

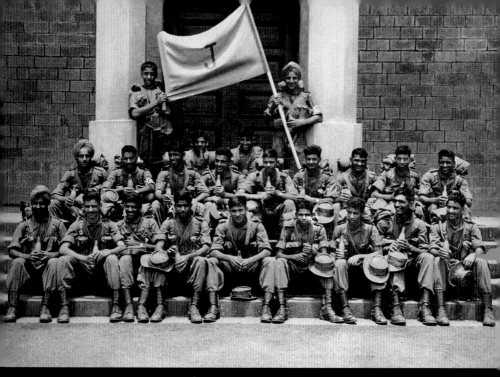

Enjoying a refreshing drink after a gruelling camp, NDA, 1962. First row: Hari Pal Singh, V. Kochhar, Subhash Kumar, K.B. Menon, Y. Malhotra, R.B. Menon, M.M. Toteja, C.M. Mehta, S. Kapur; Second row: I, P.R. Potnis, K.K. Sainani, S.K. Malik, P. Vig, G.R. Sud, Laxman Singh, T.R. Mullick, A. V. Bhat; Third row: S. Satpute, R.K Singh, N. Menon and G.S. Kahlon (holding the flag).

Raising of
9 Maratha LI,
1 October 1964.

NDES, Y S SHINDE, PETER DALGADO
AN AGASHE   SR KALE

Adjutant of the battalion, Hyderabad, 1969.

Receiving the Colours for 9 Maratha LI from President Zakir Hussain a Maratha LI Centre, Belgaum, 1968

Learning to be mountaineers, HMI Darjeeling, 1966.

Tenzing Norgay and I at base camp, 1966 (Mountaineering Course at HMI Darjeeling).

Delhi Cantonment, 1966. Sitting: I, Veena, dad, mom, Satti; Standing: Bhupi, Inderjeet and Deepak.

Looking at the future, Anupama (Rohini), 1971.

Lt Col J.S. Dhillon, the CO 7 Maratha LI, flanked by (left to right) Capt S.L.A. Khan, Maj N.K. Balakrishnan, the RMO, Capt M.S. Shekhawat and I, Tangdhar, Kashmir, 1978.

Tying the knot with Rohini, 9 May 1971.

Elder brother Flying Officer S.J.S. Marwah and his 'Gnat' fighter, 1965-66.

Rohini's parents, Poona, 1948.

Younger brother Lt Col B.J. Singh, a medical specialist in Army Medical Corps, 1993.

Receiving the Vishisht Seva Medal for distinguished service as CO 9 Maratha LI from Gen A.S. Vaidya, MVC**, chief of army staff, Army Day 1984.

With my company commanders: Pritam Bhandral, M.N.S. Thampi and J.R.F D'Souza, and warriors of Tirap, Arunachal Pradesh, November 1981.

Rohini and I with Prime Minister Indira Gandhi at Army House, New Delhi, January 1984.

As company commander on the Line of Control, Tangdhar, Kashmir, 1978.

Winners of 'skill at arms' championship, Bison Division, Hyderabad, 1986.

Seeking the blessings of Chhatrapati Shivaji Maharaj on taking over the command of 9 Maratha LI, Tezu, Arunachal Pradesh, February 1981.

One of the first surrenders by a militant, Baramulla, 1991.

As brigade commander, controlling operations in Kashmir, September 1991.

A display of arms and ammunition captured during Operation Mousetrap, November-December 1991.

'For he's a jolly good fellow, so say all of us,' Chandi Mandir, January 2005.

Traditional farewell from Western Command – ceremonial buggy of four-in-hand, January 2005.

Rohini and I with the kids – with scary yet regal escorts, Tezu, Arunachal Pradesh, 1981.

Rohini and Sonia with a Tuareg tribesman in Sahara desert, Algeria, 1988.

Presenting the Colonel of the Regiment Trophy to Col M. D'Souza during the bicentenary celebrations of 5 Maratha LI (Royal).

Sonia, Rohini and I, Atlas mountains, Algeria, 1989.

Receiving the Ati Vishisht Seva Medal from President K.R. Narayanan, 2001.

Decorated with the Param Vishisht Seva Medal by President A.P.J. Abdul Kalam, 2004.

was carrying a sack that weighed no less than 30 kilograms, and had been walking for days on end. When I saw the arms and munitions he was carrying, I was shocked. It could have been a metal pack. Surprisingly, there was a small red-coloured pocketbook dedicated to Mao Tse-tung in the pack. There were no rations, only some brown gooey stuff which I was told was opium. No wonder he was famished and fatigued. So the first thing I ordered was a mug of tea and some food for this poor boy, which he devoured as fast as he could. He recounted his story of how he left his village in December 1967 and walked all the way to Myitkyina in Burma, with the rest of the gang. From there they went by road to a place near Kunming in Yunan province of China. There was a training camp where they were given training for a few months. When they first reached there, as recalled by this insurgent, they were asked to pray to their God for providing them with food. So they remained hungry. Only when they praised Mao Tse-tung was food served to them.

Talking of his journey back, he said that they were moved in buses upto Myitkyina and then started trekking through the forests of northern Burma towards Nagaland. En route they had a number of clashes with the Burmese Army and even suffered some casualties. They pressurized the Burmese villagers to give them food and shelter, without giving them adequate compensation. Sometimes they went without food and survived on opium. When he was caught by our troops during the first week of March 1969, he was so fatigued that he could not resist or fight, as they had been marching continuously for seventy-eight days. That was the first time we saw an AK-47 rifle, over four decades ago! As soon as we informed the Division HQ about the capture of an insurgent from the gang led by Mowu Angami and Issac Swu, Brigadier S.S. Malhotra, the deputy GOC, himself flew down to our Battalion HQ at Anutangre by helicopter to take him back for gaining as much information as possible, in order to plan further operations. Time was at a premium so he did not stay for more than half-an-hour or so. The brigadier congratulated the battalion for the good job done before he left.

A fine account of this operation has been written in the history of 8 Mountain Division, '.... the gang was first located on the international border by the Marathas. It was on 4 March 1969 that a commando platoon patrol of the 9 Maratha LI led by Maj. Y.S. Shinde spotted a large gang near Tinmaung on the border, due east of Zunheboto. Mowu, who could not cross in the Chakhesang country, had moved north, but was not keen to make his way in the Sema-dominated territory. It was later reported that one of his (Mowu's) men pointed a pistol at him and insisted that he cross at Tinmaung. His men were tired of carrying heavy loads up the hills and down deep gorges in the past couple of months and were keen to get some rest in their own land. They had no footwear, and their clothes were in tatters.'[3]

Finally, Mowu Angami, the C-in-C of the Naga army, and the rest of his gang were cornered at a camp near Koiboto. Many camps of the underground had already been destroyed by us as the ceasefire had been abrogated by the Nagas by getting arms from China. Mowu's complete gang was effectively cordoned off by troops of 8 Mountain Division, and nearly a fortnight later they were forced to capitulate. Once they were warned of the serious consequences if they refused, they had no choice but to surrender, which they did. There were 169 insurgents in all, and they also handed over about 100 Chinese-made AK-47 rifles, machine guns, carbines, rocket launchers, stick grenades, pistols and a lot of ammunition that they had brought from China. Mowu Angami was taken into custody. The defence minister, Sardar Swaran Singh, informed Parliament on 1 April 1969 that the security forces had captured Mowu Angami and his gang with their weapons. The prime minister congratulated Major General Navin Rawlley and the troops under him for this signal success. This operation was a great achievement for 8 Mountain Division.

However, Isaac Swu and T. Muivah broke up their group into small parties and managed to escape. Still, many of them surrendered later on. Overall, the performance of 9 Maratha LI during the extended four-year tenure was indeed praiseworthy, and even though we were a young battalion, we made a mark. Major Y.S. Shinde and Naik Balwant Sawant were decorated with Sena medals, and a few more gallant soldiers of the battalion got the chief of army staff's commendations. We did not have a single case of human rights violation or molestation in an area where the women of the Nocte and Wanchoo tribes, as per their traditions,

---

[3] ibid., p. 68.

Surrender by Naga rebels, March 1969:
Top: Inspecting the first AK-47 captured by us. Above left: The first Naga rebel captured by us. Each of the rebels was carrying arms and ammunition loads weighing 30–40 kgs. Above right: Chinese weapons captured from a small group of General Mowu Angami's gang (AK-47, pistol, rocket launcher, sniper rifle, stick grenade, ammunition and mortar bomb).

did not cover their bosoms. We were very proud of our conduct as leaders, and for this we must give credit to our commanding officers who brought us up with a strict code of conduct, and impressed upon us that we were 'officers and gentlemen' above all. Lieutenant General Manekshaw, or 'Sam Bahadur', as he was fondly called by the rank and file of the Indian Army, was the epitome of 'the officer and a gentleman' tradition. He had inspired all of us so much as our army commander that we were ready to do anything to implement his strategy and directions relating to counter insurgency. We had outstanding successes such as the neutralization of almost the entire gang of Naga hostiles led by Mowu Angami. I realized that he was not only a great military leader, but also had many other qualities, such as being lion-hearted, particularly in adversity. He also had an uncanny sense of humour, and seldom lost his cool.

During this tenure in Nagaland, I did the basic and advanced courses in mountaineering at the Himalayan Mountaineering Institute (HMI) at Darjeeling under the legendary Tenzing Norgay, Nawang Gombu and Lieutenant Colonel Narinder Kumar. I got an 'A' grade on both and was even recommended for a Himalayan expedition. Subsequently, I went to the HMI as an instructor for an adventure course for school children, including a few boys from Australia. I loved the mountains and discovered that I had a natural flair for climbing. Moreover, I could stand high altitudes better than most.

In 1968, our regiment, the Maratha LI, celebrated its bicentenary and was presented the colours by President Zakir Hussain. Each battalion had to select an officer to receive the colours from the president at a presentation ceremony. I consider myself extremely fortunate to have been nominated to receive the colours for 9 Maratha LI by our commanding officer, Lieutenant Colonel Awasthi. At a glittering ceremonial parade in our Regimental Centre at Belgaum, the colours were first consecrated by religious teachers and priests, and then they were presented to each battalion in turn by the president as the commander-in-chief of the armed forces. Our older battalions, whose origin dated back from 1768 to 1800, laid to rest their old colours presented by the British monarchs during this parade. In his address, the president said, 'Your regiment has, during the last 200 years of existence, added many brilliant chapters to the glorious annals of the Indian Army.'

My parents, along with my elder brother, Flying Officer Satti Marwah, and sister Veena had come to witness this historical event. Later, when I took over the command of the same battalion in 1981, it was a rare personal achievement. Not every officer who received the colours that day was destined to command the same battalion.

8

Sharpening the Cutting Edge

After a long but successful stay in Nagaland, our battalion moved to Hyderabad for a well-deserved peace tenure. The unit lines were near the Golconda Fort. I had been appointed as the adjutant, which is a key assignment in a unit. Training and sports are the core activities during peace-time soldiering and these kept us busy.

As it happened, I couldn't stay long with the battalion at Hyderabad and was posted to the Intelligence School, Poona in 1970. I stayed there as an instructor for three years. This assignment played an extraordinarily important role in shaping my military career, and in honing my professional skills and enhancing my knowledge base. In those days we did the General Intelligence Course for a duration of three months. It was called the mini-staff course. The most important thing we learnt was how to do an intelligence appreciation, that is, analyse the various options available to the enemy or adversary and deduce his most likely course of action. Our own plans should only be evolved thereafter. Later, as an instructor, this approach to problem-solving became second nature to me.

The biggest weakness in many of us in the defence forces is that we seldom give adequate consideration to the enemy's plans; we tend to make excellent plans in which the enemy's actions are made to 'fit' into our scheme of things. Therefore, such plans are likely to go awry when the enemy adopts a course of action that we have not anticipated. In any case, we need to remember that the best of plans hardly survive the first engagement. There must be inbuilt flexibility to modify, change or adopt Plan B to exploit any unexpected opportunity. At the Intelligence School, we also learnt to articulate ourselves with precision and logic, both orally and in writing.

It was also a great posting for me personally, as I met a very charming and talented young lady, Anupama, who was doing her graduation from Wadia College, Poona. We met at the New Year's dance, fell in love, and got married in May 1971. The circumstances under which we met were quite interesting, and made news when I became army chief. One media account went like this:

> *The scene was straight out of a movie. Across a crowded room, a young officer saw a beautiful girl escorted by her parents at a New Year's party at an army club. Most faces looked familiar as only members frequented the club. Only the girl stood out. The curiosity built and the brash captain entered a bet with his friend (Captain Ramesh Bhatia) that he would have a dance with her. The girl refused; and to drive home the message that she was not interested, she went and sat next to her mother to deter the young man. This is what they call an obstacle in military training. Being deft in negotiating obstacle courses, he walked up to the mother and asked her politely if he could have a dance with her pretty daughter. Faced with this impudence what could the poor mother do. And Captain Joginder Jaswant Singh had his first dance with petite Anupama, who became his wife in just a few months.*[1]

Anupama (whom I call Rohini), is also from an army family. Her father, Colonel Narenderpal Singh, was commanding the ordnance depot at Dehu Road, near Poona, at that time. Both her parents are also literary figures. Her mother, Prabhjot Kaur, is a famous poet who has been honoured with a Padma Shri. Her parents are also recipients of the Sahitya Akademi award for Punjabi literature, a rare achievement for a couple. Colonel Narenderpal Singh was commissioned in the Sikh Light Infantry during the Second World War, and served in the Middle East. Later, during the 1950s, he was transferred to the ordnance corps. Rohini soon realized that she had married a professional whose first love was the army. She once asked me what role she had as an army

---

[1] Ghazala Wahab, *Force*, March 2005.

wife. My reply was, 'the soldiers will give their life for the nation on my orders so you must take care of their families first, and then look after our children and our home'.

As per army customs, we are required to take permission from the CO for getting married. This was perhaps done to ensure that officers did not tie the knot with the wrong girls. I followed the rules and sought approval (the letter is reproduced below).

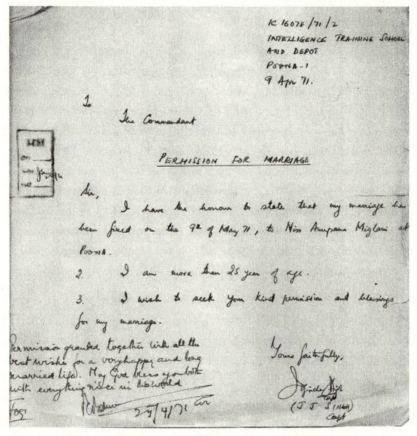

My letter to my CO asking for permission to get married.

We settled down in a small house within the precincts of the Intelligence School, and made it our home for two wonderful years in Poona. We had no worldly possessions to do up the house, except the bare essentials. We used 'matkas' (earthen pots) to store drinking water and an ice box to cool the fruit and vegetables. Basic necessities like a refrigerator or air conditioner weren't affordable. Yet Rohini made our home comfortable, and gave it an artistic touch with a minimalistic look. Till she put up her paintings and sketches, I never knew that she was a good artist. She had held her painting exhibition at Bal Gandharva Rang Mandir in Poona a few months before our wedding. Later she told me that she had studied art at Academie Julian in Paris, when her father was posted there as the military attaché in our embassy from 1966 to 1969. As a teenager, she had travelled all over Europe during their three-year stay in Paris. Earlier, as a child, she had lived in Kabul, when her father did a stint as the defence attaché in our mission in Afghanistan. With all her foreign travels and exposure to the advanced countries, I sometimes wondered how she would take to living with an infantry man. To our credit, we made it work, though it was tough.

We are both fond of the outdoors and sports. When we were about to be married, she asked me very innocently, 'I hope you don't play bridge or golf.'

'I do,' was my frank response. When she asked me to give up these games, we made a deal. I would not play bridge provided she joined me in golf. We have kept our word. We are avid golfers and surprisingly, enjoy playing together. I find golf a great stress-buster.

It was during this period that I received a communication from the Army HQ asking me to report for the pre-Everest expedition trials at the Himalayan Mountaineering Institute, Darjeeling. Having done well in the basic and advanced courses, I felt I could make it to the Everest expedition if I volunteered. But in that case, my life thereafter might have been that of a mountaineer. When I asked Rohini for her advice, her response was that I should carefully analyse the pros and cons and then decide. Further, she conveyed that she would respect my decision. As it happened, I decided to continue soldiering. Importantly, I also continued to enjoy the mountains while serving at the northern borders along the great Himalayas.

In 1971 Pakistan was going through a political crisis. In the elections to the national assembly, the Awami League, led by Sheikh Mujib-ur-

Rehman, had won a majority by making a clean sweep in East Pakistan, winning 160 seats, whereas Zulfikar Ali Bhutto's Pakistan People's Party won about half that number. Taking a rational view, there appeared no option other than to make Sheikh Mujib the prime minister of Pakistan. As this did not happen, the internal situation in East Pakistan worsened. Eventually, the Bengali people of East Pakistan revolted and on 23 March 1971, independence was declared and Bangladeshi flags were unfurled all over. On the evening of 25 March, Sheikh Mujib declared the creation of the People's Republic of Bangladesh. In a broadcast, he stated, 'From today Bangladesh is independent. I call upon the people of Bangladesh to resist the army of occupation to the last….'

In an act of vengeance, the same night, the Pakistan Army unleashed Operation Search Light, a ruthless and repressive campaign to subdue the alienated population. Sheikh Mujib was arrested and whisked away to jail in West Pakistan. Hundreds were killed or arrested and many other atrocities like rape and pillage took place. Streams of Bengali refugees, both Muslims and Hindus, started pouring in from strife-torn East Pakistan, which was witnessing a civil war between the 'Mukti Bahini' freedom fighters and the Pakistan Army.

As a great diplomatic move, India signed a treaty of friendship with the Soviet Union on 9 August 1971. 'Andrei Gromyko, the Soviet foreign minister, visited New Delhi and signed this treaty. It was one of the best-kept secrets in Indo-Soviet relations.'[2] The most vital and crucially important aspects of the treaty were contained in Articles VIII to XI, 'which provided for an all-encompassing commitment of defence cooperation and mutual defence assistance in case of either party being subjected to threats to their territorial integrity and security,' wrote J.N. Dixit. This treaty reshaped the politics and geography of our region.

The intensity of the skirmishes between the 'Mukti Bahini' and the Pakistan Army along the Indo-East Pakistan border increased in the later part of 1971, leading to a conflict situation. Open hostilities in the eastern theatre commenced on 29–30 November, and the Indo-Pak war broke out on the evening of 3 December 1971, when the

---

[2] J.N. Dixit, *Across Borders: Fifty Years of India's Foreign Policy*, Picus Books, 1998, p. 106.

Pakistan Air Force carried out a pre-emptive attack on our airfields, military and civilian targets. The retaliation by the Indian armed forces was swift and massive. All our service training institutions were temporarily shut down, except the training facilities for recruits and officer cadets. I was posted to Western Command and told to report at Jalandhar Cantonment, where the operational headquarters of Western Command had been established. I worked in the intelligence branch, which, as usual, was one of the most hard-pressed. Everyone wanted to have the latest information. It was a thankless yet challenging task to meet the demands of the Corps and Division HQs. In a short-duration war, real-time, hard and actionable intelligence is difficult to come by. But we tried our best.

Eventually, in the eastern theatre, the Pakistan armed forces were inflicted a crushing defeat. In a brilliant campaign, the Indian Army, Navy and Air Force, ably supported by the Mukti Bahini, the paramilitary forces, the BSF in particular, and people on both sides of the border, liberated Bangladesh. On 16 December 1971, the Pakistani forces formally and unconditionally surrendered and a new nation emerged. Bangladesh became a reality. For this brilliant land campaign, the credit rightly went to the armed forces leadership, in particular the army chief, General Sam Manekshaw; the GOC-in-C Eastern Command, Lieutenant General J.S. Aurora, his corps and division commanders and all other subordinate commanders and staff officers. I do not subscribe to the exaggerated claims for a larger-than-life role played by some other senior staff officers. We must not forget that in the defeat of 1962, the heads that rolled were of the army chief, the corps commander and other leaders, and not of their chiefs of staff or other advisers. The ultimate responsibility and accountability of achieving the mission rests on the shoulders of the commander concerned. On the western front, on 17 December 1971, a ceasefire was unilaterally declared by India and accepted by Pakistan. India had won a decisive victory, and we took 93,000 prisoners of war. It was one of our best-fought wars. The nation celebrates 16 December every year as Vijay Diwas.

After the war was over, I returned to Poona and resumed my duties. Soon I was ordered to proceed to Dhana, a small military station in central India, where we had set up a camp for Pakistani POWs. I was assigned to interrogate the important POWs. There were almost a thousand prisoners in that camp. It was very interesting to hear their account of the war. There were some who did not reveal anything more than their name, rank and unit, and kept shut. There were many others who, when engaged in a conversation, revealed everything they knew. There was a third category of POWs who were angry with their leadership and their generals who had put them in this mess and brought humiliation to Pakistan. They were the most forthcoming. I remember one of them telling me that we Indians didn't even know 'how to kill' someone properly! I did not realize the import of his statement at that time. (Three decades later, when a few of our soldiers' badly mutilated bodies were returned after the Kargil War, these words flashed back in my memory.)

All 93,000 Pakistani POWs were treated fairly by us as laid down in the Geneva conventions. No third-degree methods were employed, as there were strict orders to that effect. There were many families in the station, particularly the ladies, who wanted to see the Pakistanis. I remember one middle-aged major who was the second-in-command of 31 Baluch, an infantry battalion that was defending Jamalpur. In his diary he had recorded a graphic description of the battle of Jamalpur, of how brilliantly the Indian Army engaged them frontally, while they cut off the rear by placing an effective road block. Thereafter, the Baluchis were attacked from the exposed flanks and the rear where their defences were weak and uncoordinated. I asked him, 'How is it that you lost so badly?' He replied that it was because the 'awaam' (the public) was against them and that this was also due to good leadership displayed by the Indians. This gallant action was undertaken by 1 Maratha LI (Jangi Paltan), led by Lieutenant Colonel K.S. Brar, who was decorated with a Vir Chakra for this operation. The battalion got a large number of gallantry awards for this action and most importantly, the 'battle honour' of Jamalpur. I gave a brief of this historical account to Lieutenant Colonel K.S. Brar, VrC, while doing the staff college course in 1976, as he was my instructor at Wellington.

After two months or so at Dhana, I returned to Poona and it was once again back to the normal grind. Like me, most of my colleagues had served for eight to ten years, and we all aspired to do the Staff College Course. The entrance examination was in February 1973, and as is the norm, all of us were hopeful of doing the pre-staff course and taking leave to study for the exam. However, the commandant of the Intelligence School, Colonel Balakrishnan, was faced with a dilemma. How could he run the institution with five of his instructors being away? Therefore, he gave a ruling that none of us would be given leave or a chance to do the pre-staff course. Now it was up to us to decide whether to sit for the exam or not. Practically all of us accepted the terms of reference and took the exam from the 'line of march', so to say. I appeared for the Part 'D' promotion exam in November 1972, and two months later sat for the Staff College entrance exam along with the others. In between both these exams, our son, Vivek, was born on Christmas day, a little after midnight. When the results came out in May or June 1973, out of five of us, three had qualified in the examination, including me (the other two were Captains S.S. Mehta and Satpal Sandhu). I proved to be the dark horse, the only one to get a competitive vacancy (amongst the top twenty in the order of merit). This tenure was professionally and socially very stimulating and active. We were a young and energetic team of instructors in the process of enhancing our professional knowledge, and had a good circle of friends.

On completion of my tenure, I was posted back to 9 Maratha LI. The battalion was stationed in Malari, a high-altitude area on the Indo-Tibet border, beyond Joshimath. My stay in the 'paltan' was shortlived as I was required to join the Staff College at Wellington in January 1974. My daughter, Urvashi (also called Sonia), was born in Delhi just before we moved to Wellington.

The Defence Services Staff Course was an enriching experience as for the first time, I had an exposure to a tri-service and an all arms and services environment. Besides, one got to meet and interact with some of the brightest brains of our armed forces as also those from friendly foreign countries. We were taught how to analyse a problem in a logical and pragmatic manner and to express it succinctly in writing or orally. The art of problem-solving in a focused way and in a compressed time frame was something that has remained with me ever since. Being one of the juniormost and among the first few in my batch on the course, I was fairly disadvantaged as I had no 'previous course knowledge', famously known as PCK. Many senior guys on the course were well-armed in this regard. They played golf or partied after submitting their solutions in good time, whereas I would be tearing my hair and struggling to finish my work till the last minute, with the directing staff breathing down my neck. There was a lot of sporting activity as well as a hectic social life at Wellington. It was one of the best periods of my life. We actually practised the maxim 'work hard and play hard'. We made some lifelong friends and this association has stood me in good stead all my life.

The year in the Staff College passed very quickly. Before we knew it we were packing our bags. Rohini and the kids moved to Delhi and I to New Mal, a godforsaken little non-family station in the Dooars of North Bengal, as the brigade major (BM) of 123 Mountain Brigade. Our formation had the task to defend our border in the eastern theatre. When the postings were out, a lot of my friends pulled my leg saying, 'JJ, it's good you are going as BM to "Stiffy" Vadehra. He will sort you out, nice and proper.' Brigadier P.S. Vadehra had a reputation of being a hard taskmaster, a thorough professional and a fitness freak. He was a soldier who had a vice-like handshake.

When I reported to him, he sized me up and his first remark was, 'Where did you get these fancy shoes from?'

I was taken aback, but not unnerved, and replied, 'These are authorized pattern brogue shoes, Sir.'

'But don't you know that we are a mountain brigade?'

'Yes sir, I do,' I said, looking at the big boots that he was wearing. I got the message. Thereafter, not only did I procure the boots but also the ordnance pattern socks that our soldiers wore!

We had an important brigade-level exercise in a high-altitude area in Sikkim. During the exercise we were rehearsing our operational role. At a critical juncture, the brigade commander's wireless operator collapsed and there was no one to carry the radio set. It was raining and freezing cold. I remained cool and just picked up the set and strapped it on my shoulders. I told the COs I was manning the radio set, and that it would help if they responded when I called. The command and control was more effective this way. The exercise went off well, and Brigadier Vadehra was more than happy. Thereafter, I couldn't do any wrong. After a few months, we were permitted to bring our families to the station. So I asked Rohini and the children to join me. We lived in a bamboo-walled structure with a roof made of CGI (corrugated galvanized iron) sheets. Wherever we have lived in the last four decades since our marriage, Rohini has made the house into a home. One night the whole thing was shaking and we felt as if there was an earthquake, only to be told that there was a herd of elephants around and that we should switch on our lights and not venture outside. We were also told that our Brigade HQ was located in the middle of an elephant trail, so they had the right of way.

Once we narrowly escaped being trampled by a rogue elephant. This incident took place when we were travelling in a jeep to Siliguri. Seeing many vehicles crowded at a point, the driver slowed down. I presumed that there had been an accident and told the driver to press on. As he did so, the jeep came to a halt after about a hundred yards. As the driver got down and lifted the bonnet, we noticed a wild elephant advancing towards us from the forest. We just froze, me on the front left seat and Rohini, the kids and a maid at the back. The elephant had come so close that we could smell his body odour. Suddenly the driver began to chant 'Jai Ganesh, Jai Ganesh' quite loudly. When I thought that we had just about had it, the rogue elephant turned around and retreated into the thicket. I looked back and saw people watching the drama. Somehow the jeep started and we quickly drove off, thanking our stars.

Our relationship with Brigadier (later Lieutenant General) Vadehra and Taran Vadehra, his very warm and affectionate wife, remains very close even today. He made me into a tougher soldier. After a year or so, there was a change of commanders, and Brigadier N.K. Talwar took over. His was a different leadership style – softer and yet fairly effective. I noticed that several people tried to cosy upto Brigadier Talwar and said a lot of things to please him. I didn't change my colours and my loyalty to the previous brigade commander, while being equally loyal to the successor. Brigadier Talwar, an exceptional professional, was mature enough to see through it all. He was very happy with my work and I continued to contribute towards the operational effectiveness of the formation, with his guidance. We also have a wonderful relationship with Nikki and Kusum Talwar, and we have kept in touch ever since. I learnt a lot from both of my brigade commanders.

On completion of my stipulated tenure of two years as a brigade major at New Mal, I was posted back in February 1977 to my battalion 9 Maratha LI, which was located at Jalandhar Cantonment. It was nice to be back home – back to regimental soldiering. I was appointed as 'A' Company Commander. In no other command assignment is an officer closer to his men than in this post. Our focus was on training, administration and sports. The aim of every company commander was to win the inter-company championship trophy. Every tournament we played was like a battle. Even the ladies and children joined in to cheer up the teams. Vivek and Sonia, my son and daughter, would always take on the mantle of the 'screaming brigade', and be the cheerleaders. The battlefield was the Katoch Stadium. Nearly twenty-eight years later, on the same sports field, I would address a 'Sainik Sammelan' of 11,000 officers and men of 11 Corps, led by Lieutenant General P.K. Singh, an outstanding leader. Such a large gathering was some sort of a record. I was the army commander of Western Command and the chief of army staff-designate at that time. It was a very moving event for me.

We did well in many of these sports and professional competitions. I was able to train and motivate my company to a high pitch. Our focus was to be the best company of the battalion and we worked very hard to achieve our objective. Consequently, 'A' Company won the championship trophy for the year 1977. My sole aim was to earn the respect of my men and be remembered as one of the best company commanders. 'B' Company under Major M.N.S. Thampi was the one that gave us the toughest competition. Six years later, he succeeded me as the commanding officer of the battalion. One interesting aside during this tenure was that I nearly got assigned on the five-month-long battalion support weapons course. There was a vacancy on the course allotted to our brigade, and there was no junior officer available to go for it. Since surrendering of a course vacancy was not acceptable to the higher HQ, my name was forwarded. It was really a joke for someone who had done the Staff College and been a brigade major for two years, to be sent for this course meant for captains and lieutenants. All because I was below thirty-two years of age! Somehow, wisdom prevailed at the Division HQ and I was taken out of this assignment, although for me it would have been like a paid holiday.

Unexpectedly, the next summer I got a posting to a remote field area in Jammu and Kashmir, in the Tangdhar sector. It was graded as a 'high-altitude and uncongenial climate' area. I did not think it fair to be sent to an operational area once again, but I was told that 7 Maratha LI needed officers of my seniority to command companies deployed along the line of control (LoC), as the posted strength of officers in the unit had become very low. Some had been declared medically unfit and had to be moved out of the battalion. Therefore, during mid-1978, after the usual farewell dinner, I moved to join 7 Maratha LI. My wife and kids stayed behind at Jalandhar. This was my first posting to the LoC in J&K.

The overnight train journey to Jammu was uncomfortable because of the hot and muggy weather. From there it was a gruelling three days' journey by road to Tangdhar, a distance of about 250 kilometres. The movement beyond Jammu was in a controlled convoy system, with scheduled halts at the transit camps en route. After a night halt in a beautiful transit camp by the side of the turbulent Chenab river at Ramban, I reached Srinagar the following day.

The rundown transit camp at Srinagar could be made out even at a distance of half a kilometre, by the bluish grey smoke emanating from the coal-fired 'bukharies' being lit in the evenings, particularly during the winter. The fine soot of these heating devices had, over the years, coated everything in sight black. The faces and hands of the bearers and other workers in the camp had been darkened by the smoke. It reminded me of the poor chimney sweeps I had read about, while in school. Pollution and degradation of the environment at its best, I mused.

The next day, after a tedious and tiring journey on an even more potholed road, the convoy halted at the logistics base for the troops serving on the LoC. During the winter the journey beyond had to be on foot or by helicopter due to the enormous amount of snow on the

Shamsabari range. Because of the danger of avalanches, the next stage of the journey, to the Nastachun Pass and beyond into the valley of Tangdhar, had to be undertaken at night. The steep snowy slopes were comparatively stable during that period.

After a refreshing mug of tea at the pass, we proceeded ahead and reached the Battalion HQ in the evening. I was welcomed by the commanding officer, Lieutenant Colonel J.S. Dhillon. The next day, I was formally interviewed by him and 'dined in'. From the Battalion HQ to my company piquet it was a strenuous uphill trek of about two hours. My post was at an altitude of about 8000 feet. I was received there by the subedar sahib and shown around. The barbed-wire fence and the skull-and-bones warning boards inside the minefield indicated the LoC. The proximity of the adversary could not be taken lightly.

After the formal briefing, I entered my bunker and had a hot bath. The water was stored in an improvised bucket made from an empty oil tin with a wire handle. It relaxed me as much as a tub bath or a shower in a five-star hotel! The bunker was heated by a bukhari. The warmth exuded by the burning wood was very comforting. I knocked down two quick shots of rum and some appetisers comprising fried liver, pakoras and namkeen. For me, in that wilderness, it was the equivalent of champagne and caviar!

The company commander's bunker was a huge dugout of about 200 square feet with a small bathroom adjacent to it; it had a ceiling made of wooden logs with about twelve inches of sand bags and earth placed above to give it protection from shelling. It had walls made out of planks of the deodar (pine) trees, which were plentiful in that area. It had an agreeable fragrance of old wood, quite like some high-end perfumes. I wondered if it could withstand a direct hit of an artillery shell. But then I wouldn't be in it, as during a hot war I would be directing the battle from the command post – a fortified fighting bunker.

The next morning was bright and clear. Coming out of my bunker, I was stunned by the landscape. What a glorious welcome. As the sun rose over the Shamsabari range, the ultraviolet rays reflected off the snow-covered higher reaches, and directly hit the retina. I shouted for my snow goggles, and wore them over the balaclava. I loved the feel of the goggles and the soothing effect they had on the eyes.

At places the LoC went along the Kishanganga river, with villages on both sides of the river divided by an artificial line. Entire families had been split into two. Elsewhere, the boundary followed the ridgeline or went midway between the top and the valley, cutting across the mountainside. This created complications of its own. The countryside was peaceful and tranquil and the people were mostly poor farmers. They looked for jobs with the army so that they could have a steady income. Though the area was incredibly beautiful, because of its remoteness, there were hardly any visitors or tourists. It was famous for its walnuts, whose outer cover could be crushed by hand. They are commonly called as the kagazi, a paper-thin variety.

The task of my company was to defend the assigned area along the LoC. For that we had to maintain an elaborate observation system to keep a watch all along the border. The daily routine on the post involved, besides the surveillance of the border, morning and evening 'stand-to', patrolling and the laying of ambushes to prevent intrusions, and the improvement and maintenance of our defence works. Occasionally, I would order stand-to or alert at odd times to test the readiness of my troops to get into battle positions quickly. Every morning, I would go around the company-defended locality and meet with the soldiers, and then attend to the administrative issues and some office work. Later, after lunch, I would play basketball or volleyball with the men. I got to know each of them well in a short time. Life was lonely as I was often the only officer on the piquet. There were no means of communication except the field cable and antiquated telephones for communicating within the battalion and with the units on our flanks. Letters were awaited eagerly and Rohini and I would write to each other regularly. But letters usually took longer than a week or even up to a fortnight to reach. Sometimes two or more letters would arrive at the same time, and it was fun to decide which one to open first.

Time passed and soon it was winter. In view of the heavy snowfall, troops on both sides of the LoC would keep a low profile. But I ensured that we never lowered our guard. In those days we had first-generation black-and-white televisions with the screens no bigger than today's laptops. We unfortunately couldn't receive the transmission of Doordarshan. Instead, we saw the Pakistani TV programmes. Their news bulletins were mere propaganda – India-bashing. But their plays were good and some English serials like *Star Trek* were absorbing. However, we did send a larger number of soldiers on leave during the winter. As the journey in transit from the rail head at Jammu to Tangdhar usually took over a week in the winter, the men were encouraged to avail of four months' leave at a time, for the current year and the following year as well, and thereby save time in movement.

I vividly recall my first experience of heavy snowfall at my piquet. I had gone to visit one of my forward posts, situated deep in the gorge but on our side of the Kishenganga river. It was a classic case of eyeball-to-eyeball confrontation separated by a 100-odd metres with the river in between. Each side could watch the activities of the other. A visit by the company commander was an important event and the Pakistanis were keenly watching the happenings. I always insisted on having a 'Sainik Sammelan', an address to the soldiers, followed by a regimental song and battle cry, and a community lunch during such trips. This raised the morale and level of motivation of all ranks and helped me to create esprit de corps among my team. This became my leadership style. It was a gruelling one-and-a-half hour climb back to my company HQ and there was already some snow in places on the track. Besides, it started snowing as we reached the half-way point. The final ascent to the top was very steep as usual. I was quite fatigued by the time I finally reached my bunker. A hot bath and a large peg of rum along with the usual snacks relaxed me.

The next morning I was greeted by a thick carpet of three-to-four-feet of virgin snow all around. It was a complete 'whiteout', something I hadn't witnessed before. The purity of the white colour of the snow is beyond comparison. The deodar branches were drooping with the weight of lumps of soft snow, many having collapsed and fallen to the ground, unable to bear the weight. With a thud, a huge white ball would suddenly fall off these trees and strike the earth, as I walked around the post. It was the most fascinating and beautiful sight I had ever seen.

In the summer of 1979, Rohini and the children came on a month's vacation in Tangdhar. Lieutenant Colonel Dhillon told me that I could spend time with my wife and kids, but would have to be back in my piquet at night. So, it was a lot of trekking for me those days. Coming down to the Battalion HQ, I used to literally jog and reach in 45 minutes or so. Going back was tough. Rohini felt bad for me, but it was better than being far away in Jalandhar. At least we could meet and snatch some moments together. Besides, it was much cooler in Tangdhar as compared to the hot summer in the plains of Punjab. When their holidays were about to finish, I took leave for a week and we travelled to Jalandhar. On the way we spent two days at Gulmarg with 2 Maratha LI being commanded by Lieutenant Colonel Har Ranjit Kalkat. We were welcomed very warmly and our stay with the Kali Panchwin (the Black Fifth, as this battalion is traditionally known) was memorable. In those days, Kashmir was peaceful and the people were friendly.

The tenure of the battalion got over by mid-1979 and we got orders to move to Poona. I was happy because we were going to a good peace station where we could be together once again. It had good schools where our children could study. I was approved to become a lieutenant colonel in 1980 and by then had become the second-in-command of the battalion. Normally, I should have been made the commanding officer of 7 Maratha LI itself, but the colonel of the regiment, Major General Bachittar Singh, was requested by all ranks of 9 Maratha LI that I must be reverted back to be their CO. It was conveyed to him that there were some problems in the unit, and it would be in the best interests of the battalion if I took over the command from Lieutenant Colonel A.F. Fernandes. So once again I had to move to an operational area, this time to Tezu, a remote place in Arunachal Pradesh.

Life had been tough for Rohini and the children, who were growing up in the absence of their father. From 1973 to '81, within a span of eight years, I had had eight postings alternating between peace and field.[3] One must admit that it was some 'yo-yoing'! There was great turbulence and insecurity in our family life which seriously affected the education of my children, Vivek and Urvashi. Things had got so

---

[3] Field is a short form of describing an operational or field-area deployment along the border or in counterinsurgency areas like J&K, where the families are generally not permitted.

bad that if ever they saw Rohini and me packing our bags for the weekend or a holiday, they would ask, 'Papa, are we transferred again?' This has been the true facet of life in the infantry. We are proud of the fact that we took all this in our stride. I never represented against any of these postings.

9

The Crucible
Command of the Battalion

Sometime in February 1981, I reached Tezu to take over as the CO of 9 Maratha LI. The brigade commander, Brigadier Harwant Singh, warmly received me and asked my predecessor, Lieutenant Colonel Tony Fernandes, to take me to our operational area and brief me. Before we went on our reconnaissance, the brigade commander was kind enough to promote me and graciously put the epaulettes of a lieutenant colonel on my shoulders. Then off we went to Hayuliang. This involved a road journey of over 200 kilometres over a bumpy and treacherous mountainous road snaking up along the Lohit valley. Lieutenant Colonel Fernandes was driving rather fast and at times a bit rash, as he wanted to come back the same day. I advised him to take it easy, but to no avail. Unfortunately, we met with an accident due to brake failure and consequent loss of control. The jonga (an army SUV) crashed into the hillside and took a side roll and overturned with all four wheels looking up at the skies. Something like the stunts one sees in the movies, only much better, because it wasn't rehearsed! One more roll would have meant the end for all of us, as beyond the edge of the road was a sheer drop of about 1000 feet into the turquoise-blue Lohit river.

It was a miraculous escape. All of us, with the exception of Lieutenant Colonel Fernandes, got away with a few cuts, bruises and blunt injuries. Sadly, Tony's right hand was crushed between the superstructure and the steering. He needed to be evacuated to the hospital at Guwahati urgently.

Enroute from Tezu to Hayuliang – a miraculous escape for us, February 1981.

No briefing or 'handing over' could be done under the circumstances. What a way to start my innings as the battalion commander, an assignment that has meant the most to me in my life as a soldier.

I became the sixth CO of the battalion, the first to have been commissioned in 9 Maratha LI. I had a single-minded resolve to be one of the best commanding officers of the battalion. I held my first 'Sainik Sammelan' and addressed the troops, and spelt out the key result areas that we had to focus on. The first and foremost task was to improve our operational and administrative efficiency. My emphasis has always been on good man-management and I assured them that they would get a fair deal as far as promotions, leave and postings were concerned. I had literally grown up with the 'paltan'. Some of my junior commissioned and non-commissioned officers had been enlisted as soldiers in 1964, when our battalion was raised. So we knew each other like family.

Before I took over the 'paltan', I was cautioned by the colonel of the regiment that the subedar major (SM), the highest ranking soldier, was the cause of bad blood between the previous CO and the second-in-command and could be replaced if I wished. I came to know that he

The Crucible – Command of the Battalion

was unwanted in the unit also because he was an inductee brought in from another battalion by my predecessor. It was a serious matter and therefore I took my time to decide. I wanted to get on with the task of commanding the battalion rather than being bogged down by an unsavoury event right at the beginning. I had a frank talk with the SM and told him that the battalion could do without him. I didn't have to remind him that I was commissioned in this very 'paltan'. The only job I asked him to do was to come up with one good idea for the welfare of the troops every week. He was forbidden to sneak around and do 'chugli' or carry tales about others to me. That's what happens in many units. His acceptability began improving by the day and in due course the issue died down.

After a few months, the battalion was selected for a special mission. In preparing for that task, we were put through a mock exercise in which we were required to locate an insurgent camp in a thick forest and then attack and destroy it. A number of patrols were launched by me to find the target but we remained clueless till the very end. It was like finding a needle in a haystack. Eventually our perseverance paid off. Major P.S. Bhandral's patrol chanced to locate the suspected camp. The challenge now was to somehow link up with the patrol. I had ordered Major Bhandral to remain in the close vicinity of the target and, if possible, send someone along the ridgeline, where we would marry up. I trusted my map reading, and having plotted the insurgent camp, we set off towards the camp.

On the way we bumped into Havildar Vinayak Thosar, who was sent to guide us to Major Bhandral. It got dark and soon a heavy downpour commenced. We moved very slowly and cautiously, trying to ensure that the long column moving through the dense jungle did not break contact. Sure enough, somewhere a goof-up took place and just before dawn, when we reached the insurgent camp, only half the battalion showed up. The umpire, who was another battalion commander, was breathing down my neck and wanted to know my decision. I decided to go in for a raid on the camp with the force that was available with me. When we assaulted the camp, the insurgents (a company of 7 Guards) were taken unawares. The company commander of the insurgents was literally caught with his pants down! We took him into custody in his

A pep talk to motivate the officers, JCOs and men before an operation.

white kurta pyjama and when he requested me to allow him to change into uniform I refused. This was the best proof of the degree of surprise we had achieved. Our performance came in for a lot of praise during the summing up, and the exercise was terminated.

Thereafter, we were asked to keep ourselves prepared for the real task. To ensure a high standard of fitness we used to run 8–10 kilometres everyday. I was barely thirty-five years old and in good shape and took pride in running with the soldiers.

Sometime in November 1981 we were given orders to destroy a major camp of the insurgents on the Indo-Myanmar border. In order to spring a surprise, we made a non-stop move from Tezu for a distance of about 200 kilometres, and launched our operation. We were able to apprehend a few insurgents, while a majority of them escaped into Myanmar without putting up a fight. We destroyed the camp and returned to our base. The brigade commander, Brigadier V.R. Raghavan, a clear-headed, mature, soft-spoken professional and a man of few words, conveyed in a letter to me that 'the execution of the operation by the battalion was like clockwork'. A 'clasp' to the general service medal was instituted for all ranks who participated in

The Crucible – Command of the Battalion

this operation. Besides this, Major P.S. Bhandral of our battalion was given a gallantry award, the Sena Medal. Havildar Vinayak Thosar (now an officer) and a few other ranks received the commendations of the chief of army staff, and I was decorated with the Vishisht Seva Medal (distinguished services medal). The battalion returned to Tezu and resumed its usual activities – operational recces and discussions, professional and sports events and routine administration. The other battalion, 9 Dogra, which was given a similar mission as us, did equally well but had one or two casualties. We were fortunate to have had no mishap.

In February 1982, the mother of all sand model discussions took place at the Division HQ located in Dinjan. This was on the concept of mobile defence in the mountains. The brainchild of the GOC, Major General Misbah Mayadas, the subject evoked a lot of interest amongst all officers, particularly the brass. Most of them, including Lieutenant General A.S. Vaidya, MVC and bar, the GOC-in-C of Eastern Command and downwards, were present during the deliberations. There were three or four syndicates formed. Each of them was led by a brigade commander with three members, who were handpicked battalion or regiment commanders. Unfortunately, the discussions ran into heavy weather on day one itself! Our syndicate was led by my brigade commander, Brigadier Ved Prakash Airy, MVC, also a highly decorated war veteran. He was a frank and outspoken officer, and I was one of his battalion commanders.

The preliminaries were over, and the new concept was being described to us when Brigadier Airy got up and remarked that he did not agree with it. 'This idea will not work,' he continued. 'I have serious reservations about the practicability of the concept, and further deliberations are going to be a waste of time,' he added, looking at the army and corps commanders. Thereafter, an argument started between him and the GOC, Major General Mayadas. There was consternation on our faces as the drama unfolded itself in the elaborately prepared sand model room that had an excellent three-dimensional depiction of the entire area. Realizing that the ugly episode was causing embarrassment to all, particularly the younger lot of officers, the army commander ordered a halt to the proceedings.

The GOC announced a tea break. We dispersed while the brass went into a huddle. After a suspenseful hour or so, we were assembled in the sand model room and told that the discussion had been terminated. We were stunned. Such an abrupt end to an important training event was unprecedented – nor did it happen again in my career! The august gathering was then informed that an exercise with troops would be conducted on the ground soon, to decide on the feasibility and viability of the concept. Further, my brigade commander was tasked to run that exercise under the directions of the GOC of the division. Brigadier Airy had an enthusiastic, intelligent and professionally sound brigade major, Deepak Summanwar – a happy-go-lucky and warm-hearted young man. He was a friend of mine, and would go out of his way to see that my battalion got a fair deal. At the same time, I sought no favours.

We returned to our units and awaited further instructions. I was sad to leave because Rohini and the kids were staying in army accommodation in Dinjan, and I had been looking forward to spending a few days with them. Alas, it was not to be!

A month or two later I received a call from the general staff officer (operations) of our division, Lieutenant Colonel G.S. Uban, as in those days there were no colonel general staff.

'The GOC,' he said, 'has decided that your battalion will carry out the task of mobile defence of a given area in the forthcoming exercise, and hence, he would like to discuss the matter with you.'

'Why my battalion, sir,' was my query.

'The GOC thinks highly of you and your battalion, and he feels that you would be the best person to execute the mission involving this new concept,' replied Lieutenant Colonel Uban.

I promptly spoke to my brigade commander, Brigadier Ved Airy, who told me to disregard any orders that came directly from the Division HQ. I had an uncanny feeling that my battalion and I were likely to get embroiled in this personality clash between my immediate boss, and his boss. And that too, just because we were doing well professionally, and were counted amongst the best battalions!

Armies all over the world are hierarchical organizations. Violation of the chain of command is taken as interference and undermining of the authority of the subordinate commanders. I presumed that my brigade commander did not appreciate direct orders being given to me by the Division HQ, bypassing the Brigade HQ, and rightly so, too.

Therefore, Brigadier Airy picked up the phone and called up the GOC, Major General Mayadas. The conversation went something like this:

'Sir, I am given to understand by Colonel J.J. Singh that you wish to see him regarding the imminent exercise with troops,' queried the brigadier.

'Yes, I wanted to brief him about his task during the exercise. I would like 9 Maratha LI to execute the mobile defence concept,' the GOC replied.

'Sir, I may be wrong, but I was under the impression that it was my responsibility to conduct this exercise?' said Brigadier Airy.

'But of course, Ved. It's your exercise,' admitted the general grudgingly.

'In that case, please let me decide the specific missions for my battalions, and which one would act as Blue or Redland. Further, I would request that no direct orders are conveyed by your staff to my units, sir,' Brigadier Airy emphasized.

'Okay, Brigadier Airy, do as you like,' said the general in a gruff tone. Ved Airy put the J7[1] field telephone on its cradle with a triumphant look.

Thereafter, Brigadier Airy held a conference of all his commanding officers and directed all of us to prepare for the exercise. After that he called me separately to his office and spoke to me in confidence. The sum and substance of our discussion was that my battalion would do the task of Redland, the attackers. The other battalion, 3 Garhwal Rifles, would act as Blueland, and defend its territory employing the tactics of mobile defence. Before I left his office, Brigadier Airy asked me, 'JJ, tell me frankly, what do you think of the proposed concept?'

---

[1] The J7 telephone had replaced the Second World War field telephone set. It had a crank handle to send a ring and the handset had a 'pressel' switch that had to be pressed while talking. The handset fitted snugly in a small metal box for easy carriage.

'Considering our present organization, weapons and equipment state, particularly the radio communications, I do not think that the new concept would work in such a harsh and rugged mountainous terrain, sir,' was my unambiguous reply.

A smile lit up his rustic face as he took a puff from his cigarette, and shrugged the ash off in true Haryanvi style, with a twitch of his left hand.

'In that case,' he said, 'I would like to see your battalion tearing this silly idea to shreds. Do you get it, JJ?'

'We will do our best, you can be sure of that, sir,' was my confident reply, as I looked into his eyes. He then took a final gulp of his tea with a typically rustic slurp, and lit another cigarette.

All the participants had been mulling over the mobile defence issue ever since the infamous sand model discussion. I had also discussed the matter with my officers to get their views, and the consensus was against the new concept.

The Division HQ had taken upon itself the task of close monitoring and supervision of the conduct of the exercise. The level of 'closeness' was unprecedented. For example, an umpire of the rank of brigadier was nominated to report on the activities and conduct of the commanding officer of an infantry battalion of the rank of lieutenant colonel! The general norm is to have an umpire of the same rank as that of the officer being exercised. And the two COs and their battalions were the guinea pigs under the scanner. However, the stakes being so high, such things were to be expected. The professional reputation of all the key players could be made or unmade in the exercise. As the event got closer, the tension became palpable.

Around the end of May 1982, 9 Maratha LI, 3 Garhwal Rifles with their attached troops, and other arms and services participating in the exercise gathered at their respective rendezvous, and readied themselves for the exercise. It had taken the units from a week to ten days to reach their exercise locations as they had to march on foot beyond the point where the road ended in those days. 9 Maratha LI had to do the longest trek, as we had to establish our firm base the farthest, and then commence the offensive into Blueland. It required a colossal effort to move everything required for the exercise on foot. There was a large requirement of porters to carry the head loads. We also organized a system of 'fighting porters' from the available manpower; they comprised soldiers meant for logistical, clerical and other non-combat roles during peace time. However, during combat in such terrain, every man mattered and had to be mustered.

Even though it was summer, the monsoon was not far away. In those days, there were no satellites to give us weather data. The controlling HQ of the exercise was established by the division near the roadhead to enable the control HQ to decide the outcome of the battles that would be fought, in real time. A fairly elaborate camp was set up there to accommodate the high-profile visitors and observers from all over the Eastern Command. Never before was an exercise of a brigade with two battalions, in such a remote area, witnessed by such a galaxy of brass. In addition to our GOC, Major General Mayadas, there were the corps commander, Lieutenant General Ranjit Singh Dyal, MVC, and the GOC-in-C, Lieutenant General A.S. Vaidya, MVC and bar, and a host of other two-star and one-star ranking officers to give them company.

Before the manoeuvres commenced, the commanders of Redland and Blueland were directed to present their plans. My battalion was representing a brigade of the Redland forces, and I was tasked to launch an offensive to advance and capture territory up to a given point. Contesting my offensive was an infantry battalion group of the Blueland.

My plan was to advance on two axes. A battalion group represented by a company would be astride the main foot track, and the rest of the force was to advance along the crest of the mountain range. The aim was to divert the attention of the Blueland by initially contacting the defenders along the main axis, carry out probing attacks there, while outflanking the enemy positions by a hook from the right. For this action, we planned to advance cross-country along the ridgeline. There was a wide river flowing all along the main track. As it was not fordable, it posed a major obstacle to any operations from the northern flank. Notwithstanding this challenge, I planned to move a small special mission force on the far bank as well. This was tasked to get behind the enemy positions. I did not know the Blueland plans, but I had carried out a detailed appreciation and analysed their likely options for defence of their assigned area, before finalizing my own plan.

As soon as I had finished my briefing, Brigadier V.P. Malhotra, the commander of the artillery brigade, whom I had never met before, came up to me, shook my hand, and introduced himself. He went on to say that he was the chief umpire for Redland, and his brief was to stay with me. I told him that he was most welcome to do so. But, as he was not acclimatized to the higher altitudes at which my HQ and the major offensive force would be operating, my advice to him was to keep to the main track, and accompany the force operating along it. However, to my surprise, he would have none of it, and insisted on going wherever I went.

We commenced the exercise and the Redland forces launched the offensive as planned. Though the sky was overcast and it became pitch dark, we did not find any problem in advancing into the Blueland territory. At about 11 p.m., when we had penetrated up to about ten to twelve kilometres, we came across the first signs of resistance from the Blueland forces. This was at a big nullah that joined the main river, making a deep gorge. This was held by Blueland, which engaged advancing elements on the main axis with heavy machine guns, small arms and intense mortar fire. I ordered Major A.N. Agashe, the commander of the force moving along the main track, to plan for the capture of that position or keep the enemy engaged till our main force was able to cross the obstacle upstream and then attack them from the rear.

In the meanwhile, the weather suddenly deteriorated, and it started raining heavily. Visibility dropped to a few metres. We were operating at an altitude of over 10,000 feet, and within a few minutes we were drenched to the bone. In Arunachal Pradesh, the annual rainfall in places is perhaps even more than in Cherrapunji, which used to be considered as the rainiest place on earth. But, on this day, it appeared to be worse, something like a cloudburst. The nullah became a raging torrent and impossible to cross, something highly unusual and unexpected during May. I asked Major M.N.S. Thampi, the leading sub-unit commander, to do whatever was required to be done, but he said that even huge pine trees that they had attempted to place across the stream were being washed away like straws with the force and velocity of the water. We decided to wait for the rain to stop but the intensity of the rain increased further.

By now my brigade commander was quite restless. Even though I had kept him informed of the events as they were unfolding, he could not fully comprehend the situation we were facing, though he was a hardcore infantryman himself. He began to push me harder and harder. The pressure building up in our brigade HQ was becoming palpable. However, I did not pass on this pressure to my subordinates, and tried to remain cool. I was sure my company commanders were doing their best.

Around 3 a.m., it was still dark and raining when Brigadier Airy came on the air again. I told him the situation had only become worse.

'JJ, dammit, have you chickened out? I thought you were made of sterner stuff,' said the agitated brigadier.

'No, sir. But there is no way anyone can get across this nullah. Yet my boys haven't given up and are still trying,' was my response.

'That does not impress me, JJ. The fact is that your forces have been stuck up at the same place for half the night, and it seems to me that not enough is being done,' shouted Brigadier Airy.

'That's not right, sir. Anyway, how many casualties are we ready to take?' I asked brusquely.

In actual war or combat one takes many calculated risks. It's the done thing. If we lose lives while doing so, that is understandable. However, in this situation during peacetime, I was convinced that playing around with the lives of our officers and men would be nothing short of being foolhardy, and thus not justified. Even the local Mishmi guides from that area refused to be coaxed or bribed into making an attempt to cross the waters. The chief umpire, Brigadier Malhotra, was really having a tough time. On an impulse, Brigadier Malhotra took the handset from me and said, 'Ved, the battalion commander is damn right, the nullah is in spate and it is next to impossible to cross it in this state.'

There was an ominous silence and then there was no answer for quite some time. I think that was enough of a hint for a pragmatic and war-decorated soldier like Brigadier Airy. It was not only a pitch-dark night but the whole area was covered by a thick blanket of fog as well.

Till the break of dawn we were moving about like blind men, even when we used pen torches. At one point, as I was trying to go forward to the nullah, I nearly fell off the cliff. Till now I haven't been able to figure out what made me stop from taking that final step into what appeared like a black hole. Many others in my battalion would have had similar close calls with destiny that night.

After a few hours during which my troops were still trying to get across, it was conveyed to us by the Control HQ that the exercise had been frozen for the next 24 hours. However, as there was no sign of the rain abating, and the fact that all of us, including the umpires, were wet and freezing, it made no sense to keep us dangling in our high-altitude refuges for another day.

As the CO, safeguarding the lives of my men was my fundamental and sacred responsibility. Therefore, I called the Control HQ and told them it would be prudent to call off the exercise, allow the combatants to rest and refit, and then restart the match after two or three days. The chief umpire, who was at the end of his tether, also agreed with me.

Eventually, the exercise was called off for two or three days and we were asked to fall back to the start point. This time, the exercise went off smoothly with some successes and failures on both sides. Many lessons were learnt, and the good as well as the not-so-good actions were highlighted by the umpires and the Control HQ during the summing up. We were fortunate to have had no casualties during the entire exercise. A professional army must be prepared to accept some casualties during such exercises, as they ought to be conducted in conditions as close as possible to an actual war. However, I believe that losing lives due to callous and unjustifiable decisions in peacetime and even during war, is not justified.

Finally, on completion of this exercise, neither the commanding general nor the brigade commander could prove their points. The 'mobile defence' idea died a natural death within a year, once the principal players departed from the scene. No heads rolled and none was axed; the GOC and brigade commander both became lieutenant generals in due course, and of the two hard-pressed poor lieutenant colonels commanding the Redland and Blueland forces, one went on to command the Indian Army whereas the other retired as a colonel!

After a few months, I had to go on duty to Walong, my fourth visit to that remote corner of India. In those days, a round trip from the roadhead of Hayuliang to Walong and back was around 250 kilometres, and it was a gruelling trek of eight days. The portly but energetic brigade major, Deepak Summanwar, dissuaded me from going on foot and suggested that I accompany him in the Caribou aircraft doing a ration sortie to Walong. We took off from Tezu in that cargo plane at about 8 a.m. with fresh rations and provisions, including about twenty live goats and sheep (called 'meat on hoof' in army lingo) for the garrison.

Within an hour we were approaching the tricky and small air strip. As I recall, the aircraft followed the narrow valley, made a 'U' turn and then another small turn, and finally came in to land. Just before touching down the pilots realized they had overshot the runway, so the captain wisely decided to abort the landing and pulled up the joy stick. The aircraft, an old war horse, struggled to gain height and we barely missed crashing into the spur at the end of the runway. A few seconds' delay and we would have definitely flown straight into the hill. We were fortunate to have escaped death and were so shaken up we didn't realize that we had slid backwards in the cargo compartment and had a lot of sheep excreta all over us. The pilot tried the same approach a second time and managed to land safely. We were ashen-faced and heaved a sigh of relief. 'Never again,' I said to Deepak, and decided to do the return journey on foot after completing my mission. Today there is a motorable road all the way to Walong and even beyond towards the border.

Another episode that I would like to share happened when we went to our operational locations during October 1982. After the stipulated number of days we sent the report to the Brigade HQ that our defences were not yet ready. As it happened, the other units had given a completion report. The brigade commander wanted to know why we were taking so much time. In those days we did not have computers and the software to make slick powerpoint presentations, yet I requested the brigadier to come to my battalion tactical HQ where I could brief him properly. The seasoned soldier that he was, Brigadier Airy came up to my HQ and I presented to him the facts, logic and rationale of our build-up and preparations. He was convinced. Now the question arose as to how the others were claiming to be ready. When he asked for the details, he found out that some of the units had given an incorrect readiness report. He did not spare the defaulters.

Around the end of January 1983, I received a personal letter from a friend, Lieutenant Colonel Ashok Chaki, who was posted in the Army HQ. It read, 'congratulations on two counts, firstly, for the well merited award of Vishisht Seva Medal and secondly, for being selected for the Higher Command Course, which would be commencing in June 1983.' Although I felt extremely elated, I really did not know how to deal with this bit of news. As official correspondence took many days, sometimes even weeks, to reach Tezu, breaking news like this became a dilemma for me. I preferred discretion and after a few days told Rohini about it. Since she was staying in separate family accommodation in Dinjan, I did not want her to talk about it to anyone. But she told the kids. Sure enough the next day it was the news in the station that we might be posted to Mhow. After a month or so the nomination reached me through the official channel.

After completing this eventful and successful tenure of three years in Arunachal Pradesh in April 1983, the battalion moved to Binaguri (near Siliguri), to a peace station on rotation. Although initially we were disappointed to have been given a station far away from Maharashtra, there were some advantages of this too, such as adequate accommodation for the families and a central school for the children's education. The battalion settled down quickly and over a hundred families arrived to join their menfolk. It was then conveyed to us that there was an exercise in the offing for the division in the high-altitude areas of north Sikkim during May-June. All of us who were selected for the Higher Command Course were asked to report to the College of Combat (now renamed Army War College), Mhow in the first week of July after taking annual leave. My brigade commander asked me to forego leave and stay on for the exercise, and even went to the extent of saying that the higher command course would be like a year's holiday! I was perhaps the only officer who arrived at Mhow without taking a spell of leave.

The Crucible – Command of the Battalion

The year-long higher command course was introduced after the Indo–Pak war of 1971. Its aim is to train selected colonels and equivalent ranks in the operational art of war and in the planning and conduct of operations at the corps and field army level, with special emphasis on jointmanship. It is the only course where there is no grading or report written on the officers. This has been decided consciously so that the officers can speak freely while discussing operational plans or security issues at the highest level. Once again, I was the first in my batch to do this prestigious course, with most of the others being two or three years my senior. We discussed issues related to national security and war-gamed various scenarios. The emphasis was on out-of-the-box thinking.

On completion of the course, I was expecting my first posting to the Army HQ based on my qualifications and experience, and having put in twenty years of service. Instead, I got posted to Jammu in HQ 26 Infantry Division. Mine was an 'early bird' problem. I was not due to become a colonel for another year and therefore, I was posted as assistant quarter master general in the rank I was holding. This tenure in J&K was for a year. My charter of duties mainly involved the planning and execution of logistics support to the units and formations in the division. Logisticians are the unsung heroes in most armies. Good logistics planning can be a great force multiplier and morale booster. Whereas an operational staff officer faces a challenge only when there is war or during an exercise in peacetime, the logistics staff officer faces a challenge everyday – war or no war! We remained quite busy as Jammu has always been a very important administrative base for J&K, right from the days of the Indo–Pak war of 1947–48. There is never a dull moment as Jammu is a road, rail and air hub for the army deployed in Kashmir. We had to coordinate the movements, and provide logistics support to men, animals (mules), transport and material. The tonnages were mind-boggling.

Life in the Jammu cantonment was peaceful. Since my high school years (1957–60), a lot had changed in Jammu. It was not a one-street town any longer. It was a nice feeling when we met old friends there. Consequent to the sad and unfortunate assassination of Prime

Minister Indira Gandhi on 31 October 1984 by her guards, anti-Sikh riots broke out in many parts of the country, particularly in north India. We had a sizeable Sikh population in Jammu. Major General J.S. (Jimmy) Rawat, who happened to be our commanding general at Jammu, discussed the matter with his staff and ordered precautionary flag marches by the army in vehicles. I think the GOC's mature and wise decision had probably saved many innocent lives, as there were hardly any incidents of rioting reported in Jammu area and communal harmony was maintained. In fact, it is a matter of great pride for the Kashmiris that even during the partition of India in 1947, there were no communal riots.

During the Jammu tenure, the results of our promotion board were announced, and I stood approved for the rank of colonel. Normally, I should have been promoted in the same branch as my immediate superior, the colonel administration, was due for a posting. However, that was not to be and once again regimental interest prevailed. The Army HQ asked each infantry regiment to absorb two vacancies of colonel's rank in the appointment of commanding officers. My colonel of the regiment decided that I should take over 5 Maratha LI, which happened to be in Hyderabad. Consequently, I was posted as the CO of the 'Fifth Royal', a 185-year-old battalion, which was raised on 21 December 1800. As mentioned earlier, 1/67 Punjab (in which my grandfather was serving) and 5 Maratha LI had fought together in 1914–15 at Kut-el-Amara during the First World War. For me to command the same battalion was therefore a matter of great pride. I would be with my 'ganpats' once again. Regimental soldiering is the bedrock of leadership in the army and this experience further cemented my belief that command of troops cannot be substituted by any other form of leadership training.

During my command of almost two years, the battalion did well in training, sports and administration. For the first time in its history, the entire battalion was airlifted to an airfield secured by a para assault. This was when we participated in Exercise 'Trishakti', a joint army, navy and air force exercise conducted in Goa. Before this exercise, I was asked

The Crucible – Command of the Battalion

to make a presentation to the officers of the division on the subject of an air assault division. I was allowed to go to the Army HQ to search for reference material for this presentation. When I was given this task, the brigade commander's first question was, 'JJ, when can I see the rehearsal?' My response was, 'Sir, if you have confidence in me, then you don't need to see any rehearsals.'

As I was the only colonel commanding a battalion in the entire division, my performance was being watched. There was no option but to produce results. Besides doing quite well in professional competitions, we worked hard to create excellent teams in shooting and cross country. We achieved a top-ten finish in the inter-battalion cross-country competition. Subsequently, my best long-distance runner, Naik Parshuram Chaugule, won four golds and was declared the best athlete of the division. Within two years Chaugule represented India in an international cross-country competition in Australia.

During this period, we nearly had a flare-up with Pakistan. It was an escalation of tensions due to Exercise 'Brass Tacks' being conducted in Rajasthan. All of a sudden, we received orders to move by air from Hyderabad to Delhi. Over two nights in February 1987, we were airlifted to Delhi. Our formation was earmarked as an Army HQ reserve in case of an emergency. During the stay in Delhi for about six months, my name came up for an interview for an assignment abroad as a defence attaché. Interestingly, it was soon after Holi, when a basketball match is traditionally held in the Fifth Royal between the officers and junior commissioned officers. Unfortunately, I had a fall on the cemented court and fractured my right forearm. It was a compound fracture and there were cracks on both the radius and the ulna. I remained with a plaster cast for about ten weeks. A specially stitched uniform was provided to me for the interview, and it was the first time I saluted with my left hand. I was selected to be our first defence attaché in Algeria. My sportfulness must have enhanced my interview scores! Twenty-three years of regimental soldiering came to an end with a warm and befitting farewell from the Fifth Royal in July 1987. Hereafter, in a broader perspective, I would be serving the Indian Army and not a particular regiment. I joined the army to be a soldier and on commissioning, my aim was to become the commanding officer of my 'paltan'. I had already commanded my own 9 Maratha LI and the Fifth Royal, and that too for a period of almost four-and-a-half years. 'What more could one ask for. Anything else that comes my way now shall be a bonus,' I said to myself.

10
Military Attaché in Algeria

My preparations for the new assignment comprised briefings at the Army HQ, visits to various defence and industrial installations, and language training. The Army HQ insisted that I relearn Arabic, whereas we were told that in Algeria, French was more commonly spoken. We left for Algiers in December 1987. For me and our children, Vivek and Sonia, it was the first time we had left the shores of India. Rohini had lived in Afghanistan and France, where her father had been posted as a defence attaché, and had even travelled all over Europe and UK. Besides, she spoke French fluently and taught me as well. So she was our French teacher, guide and interpreter during the initial period of our stay in Algeria. Later, I joined the Alliance Francaise and took the French language course. Within a few months, I began to speak and write reasonably well; well enough to read *Le Monde*.

Our ambassador, Vijay Nambiar, was an outstanding diplomat. He and his wife, Malini, were very warm towards us and helped me to start the defence wing in our mission in Algiers. My task was to represent the armed forces of our country and build bridges of friendship between the two militaries. It is the second largest country in Africa and one of the most beautiful. It extends from the Mediterranean Sea to the middle of the Sahara desert. I got an opportunity to visit the length and breadth of this country and also some of its defence formations and establishments. Since they had mostly Soviet-origin equipment like T 72 tanks, Mig 21 aircraft and naval ships and submarines, they were keen to collaborate with us, particularly in the repairs, maintenance and overhaul of such equipment. Unfortunately, we could not help them much because of the shortage of spare parts. I was able to work out an official visit of our air chief but it had to be cancelled at the last minute due to tension with Pakistan along our western border in the early part of 1990. I had convinced the Algerians to ask for an Indian Air Force training team to train them in handling IL 76 aircraft, which they were planning to acquire. Their navy wanted to acquire submarine batteries from India so they were asked to get in touch with the ministry of defence. Their armed forces did subscribe for some courses of instruction, but then language was a hurdle as very few amongst them spoke or understood English.

During this tenure I was fortunate to have had the opportunity to attend three defence expositions: the Defendory in Greece, the Paris airshow and the Euro-Satory, also in Paris. It was almost unbelievable to see a Mig 29 flying barely 200 feet above us and crash in front of our eyes. The pilot was doing a cobra manoeuvre and when he pulled up there was a system failure. Luckily there were no casualties. The pilot ejected and was lucky to survive. I believe the Russians sold a lot of their ejection systems. The other thing I could not get over was a modern helicopter making a full circle. During this manoeuvre, at one stage the fuselage was on top of the rotor blades and the chopper was flying upside down!

This diplomatic assignment gave us an excellent opportunity to travel across the Maghreb, Europe and the UK. We invested in a complete set of camping equipment – tents, sleeping bags, mattresses, etc. Our most memorable outing in Algeria was a week-long camping tour in the wilderness of the great Sahara desert. We drove all over Europe, and enjoyed a vacation every summer, camping wherever we found a nice camping site. Interestingly, we slept out in the open one night in Switzerland, nicely snuggled in our sleeping bags besides our Peugeot 405, in a parking space on the side of the road! The thought that such an action was against the rules never occurred to me. Besides, we were dog-tired after travelling for the whole day, and all camping grounds had closed for the day. We woke up early in the morning and drove on.

We were able to visit many countries in this gypsy mode, as it was a very inexpensive way to travel. We travelled to Morocco, Spain, France, the UK, Belgium, the Netherlands, erstwhile Czechoslovakia, erstwhile East and West Germany, Austria, Switzerland and Italy. A day or two after the Berlin Wall fell, we happened to drive into Berlin. There was chaos and confusion all over. The police, customs or border control personnel were nowhere to be seen. Like everyone else, we also tried to chip away a piece of the famous wall. We succeeded in doing that and preserved that piece for many years, till one of our orderlies threw it away thinking it was junk!

I recall a discussion between my son Vivek and me in a camp in Spain. He said he wanted to join the army and continue the family tradition. I said it was a fine idea, but he needed to bear in mind that as he rose higher, he would lose out on the age factor by a year or two, because of changing so many schools and having moved to Algeria. He could lay the blame squarely on me for that. Besides, I said, 'there aren't going to be wars in the future, only low-intensity conflicts. It might be a century where economic wars are going to be fought. So, why don't you consider being an economic warrior for the country?' That is what he is doing today.

We happened to be in Algeria when Pakistani President Zia-ul-Haq's plane crashed mysteriously on 17 August 1988. On that day there was a children's party and my son and daughter were at the house of a friend whose father was an ambassador. All of a sudden, there was commotion there. My son found out the cause and informed me. In turn, I apprised our ambassador of Zia-ul-Haq's death. This was about two hours before the BBC broke the story. Our ambassador was very impressed with my networking. Only this time I didn't reveal my source! Vivek got a nice treat from me for his alertness and presence of mind.

Another memorable event at the end of our stay in Algiers was an exhibition of paintings by Rohini. The theme was the people of Algeria. The ambassador, C.P. Ravindranathan, was not only kind enough to inaugurate the exhibition, but also included it as one of the activities of the mission for the year. The Algerians were warm to us – they loved India because of our moral and diplomatic support to them during their freedom struggle; they also loved our food, music and films. The Algerians would do anything to acquire an audio or videocassette of a Bollywood film. Besides that, quite often, the people would ask me,

'Are you from India?' When I nodded, they would effusively continue, 'Le pays de Gandhi! Quel grand homme et quel magnifique pays!' (The country of Gandhi! What a great man and what a magnificent country!) This is indeed a true reflection of India's soft power.

At the end of my stay of three years in Algeria, I received orders to take over 79 Mountain Brigade on promotion to the rank of brigadier. This brigade was in the Kashmir valley. Our son had already joined the university in Le Havre, a port town near the coast of Normandy, to do a masters programme in commerce. And our daughter had returned to India a little earlier, to join the Army Public School in Delhi. We flew back to India after a few days' stay at London and Paris, where our military attaché, Brigadier (later lieutenant general) Raj Kadyan, and his wife, Anita, hosted us warmly.

Towards the end of our stay in Algeria, we saw changes taking place in its society. People were getting under the influence of fundamentalists and new mosques were being built with funds reportedly coming from Saudi Arabia and other sources. One day our daughter's Algerian friend told her that she couldn't move out of her house anymore without wearing a hijab (head scarf) and that she would have to be escorted by her brother. Soon after we left in December 1990, Algeria went through a vicious cycle of religious extremism and terrorism. The situation became so bad that for some time we had to close down our mission in Algiers. All the hard work done by us to build bridges and enhance cooperation in the political, diplomatic and military fields was undone.

Part III

FLAG RANK: FROM ONE STAR TO C-in-C

As brigade commander of north Jhelum sector, Kashmir, 1991.

11

Brigade Commander
Containing the Fire

'The mantra for success in counterterrorism/insurgency operations is an "iron fist" for the terrorists and a "velvet glove" for the people.'

On New Year's day in 1991, I took the flight from Delhi to Srinagar for my new assignment. As the plane flew over the beautiful snow-clad Pir Panjal range, I remembered the first time I had crossed the Banihal Pass in 1958 as an excited wide-eyed teenager. A lot of water had flown down the Jhelum in the past three decades. I had just been promoted as a brigadier and was on my way to take over the command of 79 Mountain Brigade. This was my third posting in J&K and the most important of them all, as Kashmir was aflame.

The picketing on the roadsides and heavy security during army movements made it look like a war zone. It was the peak of insurgency in Jammu and Kashmir. I could sense the tension in the air. It was going to be a make or break assignment for me and the intensity of operations was going to be immense. We were caught up in a classic case of irregular warfare – a proxy war and insurgency where the lead role was being played by non-state actors and their masters were across the LoC.

Pakistan was the mastermind of this stratagem, also referred to as 'Operation Topac'. Innocent Kashmiris who were losing their lives were like sacrificial goats, a price that did not hurt Pakistan directly. The jehadis from Pakistan or other countries who were ready to die for the 'cause' were cannon fodder produced by jehadi factories in

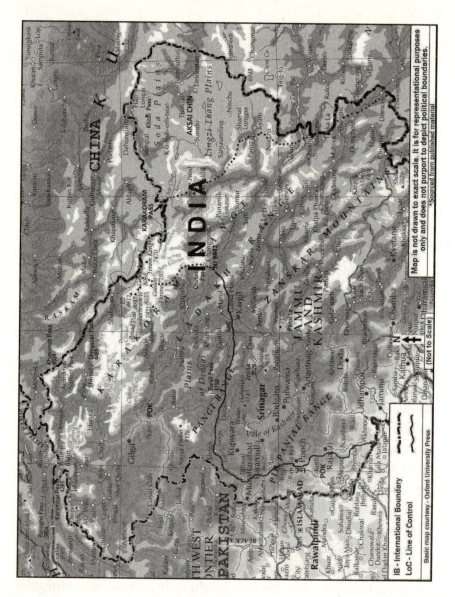

Map 11.1: Jammu and Kashmir.

Pakistan or PoK. They were brainwashed and sent across the LoC with the assurance of going directly to 'jannat' (heaven), if they embraced 'shahadat' (martyrdom). It was going to be a vicious and deadly war imposed upon the Indian state by an insidious, treacherous and ruthless adversary. The stakes being so high, it was clear to me that we could not afford to lose this war – it had to be won at all costs.

HQ 79 Mountain Brigade, the Himalayan brigade, was located at Khreuh, about 25 kilometres from Srinagar. I took over from Brigadier K.C. Dhingra at a time when the people were restive, and the feeling that 'azaadi' (freedom) was round the corner was gaining currency. Massive demonstrations by people chanting 'azaadi' slogans were the order of the day. This Machiavellian plan of Pakistan to wrest control of Kashmir was kept as a closely guarded secret. It was an unconventional war with an avowed aim of bleeding India by a thousand cuts. During the Indo-Pak war of 1965, Pakistan infiltrated a trained guerrilla force, including officers and soldiers from the regular army, for carrying out acts of sabotage, violence and subversion in Kashmir as part of Operation Gibraltar. This operation was an unmitigated disaster due to the effective response of the Indian Army, and also because Pakistan's action received no support from the Kashmiri people.

Therefore, this time, as part of Operation Topac, Pakistan planned to train and indoctrinate Kashmiri youth and subvert the system from within. In the next phase, the aim was to destabilize the state administration with low-level insurgency and keep the Indian Army engaged by small-scale attacks in vulnerable areas. In the third phase, Pakistan hoped to carry out large-scale infiltration and armed action to grab Kashmir.

In actual fact, by 1990, a large number of young men had been given training and indoctrinated with jehadi ideology, and a fair amount of subversion of the state administration had already been achieved. In particular, this included some politicians, elements of the police, public health engineering, telecom, and forest departments. Infiltration across the LoC was being reported from many areas. And an extremely violent phase of Kashmir's history was beginning to unfold. Phases 2 and 3 had not taken off until then. Nonetheless, the jehadis carried out ethnic cleansing by forcing about three lakh Kashmiri pundits to flee the valley. Farooq Abdullah's government fell and the state remained under president's rule from January 1990 to October 1996. Thereafter, Farooq Abdullah was again elected and was chosen to lead the National Conference government till October 2002.

Our brigade came directly under the Corps HQ. Lieutenant General M.A. Zaki, who was our corps commander, told me to carry out operational reconnaissance of all my tasks without worrying about the snow conditions. So I had to go on foot from the main road to the top of various hills, through knee-deep snow at places. This exercise was better than any treadmill and I got to know my area of responsibility, besides getting fit quickly. It was a dramatic change of scene from the peaceful environment of Algeria, and it didn't take me long to forget all about Algiers.

On being given any assignment, it has been my principle to convey my professional key result areas (KRAs) and concepts to my subordinate commanders and staff officers, as soon as I have got the picture myself. Therefore, I held a conference within a fortnight of my assuming command of the brigade. During this interaction, first, the operational and administrative issues were covered by my staff, then the commanding officers briefed me about the state of their units, and finally, I gave out my directions and policy. My first KRA was that we should have a high state of operational readiness. The next were training and administration issues. We were aware that many Kashmiri and foreign terrorists had infiltrated into J&K in the previous one or two years. They had also carried out some violent acts in the recent past. There were indications that the situation was likely to worsen. Therefore, I impressed on my battalion commanders that the stakes were very high, and that the challenge was to be met by the highest standards of leadership by all of us. As such, we needed to reorient ourselves and our commands to undertake counterterrorist operations. We must accord the highest importance to human rights while carrying out any task, I added, at the same time laying great emphasis on honest reporting.

Within a few days, we were tasked by the Corps HQ to rescue some people taken hostage by a small group of terrorists at Kokernag. One of my battalions, located nearby at Khanabal, on the outskirts of Anantnag, was asked to plan and execute the task. The CO decided to send two companies under the second-in-command to undertake this operation. The plan was to move close to the objective in two prongs, and thereafter advance on foot and cordon off the area where the terrorists were holed up. Apparently, one of the company columns got ambushed on the way. They lost a few soldiers and some others were wounded. The company fought through the ambush, and halted a little distance away. This happened at about 8 p.m. This company never reached the objective at all. During the night, the CO moved up and helped in controlling the situation. Along with the casualties, he pulled back this company to Khanabal, without taking a clearance from the Brigade HQ or even informing us. We were misinformed that the two companies had linked up near the objective area. As a result, throughout the night, we kept conveying incorrect reports to the higher HQ. The next day, when we reached Kokernag, most of the terrorists had slipped through the cordon. One or two of them who were still there threw a few grenades and a splinter hit the corps commander near the eye. Fortunately, it was not very serious, but nonetheless it was a close miss. In the melee, the remaining terrorists also made good their escape. It was a botched-up operation which embarrassed all of us.

As the brigade commander, I accepted full responsibility for the failure of the operation and apologized to the corps and division commanders, namely Lieutenant General Zaki and Major General V.P. Malik (he later became the chief of army staff), respectively. I assured them that we would take corrective measures and ensure that such mistakes did not recur.

At the same time, I took a very serious view of the lapses that had occurred. Tactical mistakes could be understood and corrected, but I could not accept the deliberate act of lying or misinformation by the CO. I requested both the corps and division commanders to consider replacing either me or the CO, as there had been a grave breach of faith between the two of us. Resultantly, I could no longer trust the CO. Having explained the whole scenario to them, I demanded a decision on the spot. Generals Zaki and Malik went into a huddle and after a while took me aside and said that the CO would be relieved from command. I thanked them for the decision and then sought their approval to my proposal that the battalion be disengaged from active operations and trained under my supervision for a month at Khreu. This was also agreed to. But this was not the end. It was clear to me that my performance hereafter would have to justify the strong stand that I had taken or I ought to be prepared to face the guillotine! Like the CO who was sacked, for me also the writing was on the wall: 'perform or perish'.

As a result of this bungled operation, my brigade and I had gone down below the zero line in operational performance. I had barely done one month in command. However, we took up the challenge, and our results in the months to follow spoke for our actions. In the next one-and-a-half years, the same battalion, the 2/11 Gorkha Rifles (GR) led by Colonel N.K. Pradhan, became one of the most decorated units in the entire corps. The battalion received the 'Unit Citation' from the army chief in recognition of its performance during 1991–92. The other units did equally well and contributed handsomely to make our brigade's achievements the envy of the rest of the command.

Intelligence was received by the Corps HQ that terrorists were planning to unfurl the flag of independent Kashmir on 26 January 1991 at Pahalgam, which had been declared as 'liberated territory'. Moreover, the situation in Anantnag had deteriorated so much that the deputy commissioner and the superintendant of police were functioning from their residences south of the Jhelum river – it had become unsafe for them to operate from their offices in the town. My brigade was ordered to move to Anantnag forthwith. I deployed one battalion, the 12 Rajputana Rifles, in Pahalgam and Aish Muqam areas and the other two, 17 J&K Rifles and 2/11 GR, in Anantnag. I was given one more battalion, the 1/11 GR, and we cordoned off the entire town of Anantnag, which had a population of over 50,000 people, and other important areas. Entry and exit was controlled by establishment of checkpoints on all roads leading to the town. Something like this had never been attempted before. This step took the terrorists by surprise and they were definitely caught on the wrong foot. Nothing untoward happened on Republic Day and even thereafter. The situation became almost normal.

As part of the plan to sanitize Anantnag and its environs, we launched Operation 'Just Resolve' on 14 March 1991. The town had been divided into segments for the purpose of search, which began at about 7 a.m. We had no hard intelligence inputs on the hideouts or locations of the terrorists, so we didn't expect anything much to come out of this operation. But we were in for a surprise. As soon as the searches commenced, I moved my tactical HQ to the hill in the centre of Anantnag town. From there we had a 360-degree view of the town. Within an hour, an exchange of fire took place between one of our search parties and terrorists hiding in the attic of a house. I learnt that in the shootout our soldiers had killed one terrorist and caught one alive. Both were armed with AK-47s.

I asked the company commander concerned to bring that terrorist to my location immediately so that we could find out all that he knew, and take follow-up actions. Based on my experience and whatever I had learnt in the Intelligence School, I am convinced that information can be extracted only in the initial stages, when the subject is under shock, unstable and afraid. In this case, he broke down very easily and told us of a huge cache of weapons and ammunition in a shop in the nearby market. I ordered the company commander to proceed with the terrorist and unearth the cache. However, the terrorist lost his nerve on reaching the area, claiming he couldn't identify the exact place. We combed the area by searching each shop systematically and eventually our perseverance paid. We hit a veritable gold mine – a large cache of arms and ammunition in the heart of the town, the first such seizure in Anantnag. These included a sizeable number of rifles, machine guns, rocket launchers, large quantities of ammunition, grenades, rockets and other items.

A realistic but sad dimension of this conflict came to my notice when I was listening into the radio communications on the 17 J&K Rifles net. The conversation on the radio network centred around a baby found abandoned in our area of operations. The unwanted child, probably fathered by a militant, was handed over to an orphanage. Unfortunately, a number of such cases have been reported during this so-called jehad.

The corps commander and the GOC of the division, Generals Zaki and Malik, drove down to congratulate me and my units. Their visit was a great morale booster for us.

As my baggage had arrived in Delhi from Algiers, I took some leave in May '91, to help my wife and daughter settle down in army accommodation at Pratap Chowk in Delhi Cantonment. When I returned from leave I was astonished to learn that my Brigade HQ had been ordered to move out of Anantnag, to be redeployed in a counterinfiltration posture. We had been given the operational responsibility of guarding the LoC of a newly created sector in Baramulla area and also to counter any infiltration or exfiltration from this sector. It was a strange decision to take away some of my original battalions and instead, to place under my operational command one infantry battalion and a BSF battalion. But what took the cake was that the annual confidential reports of the COs and other officers of these units were not to be initiated by me, but by their brigade commander sitting 40 kilometres away at Uri! To my mind, this was a perfect recipe for disaster as far as the functional efficiency of a formation was concerned. To make a commander responsible for an operational task on the LoC without having the power to seek accountability from his subordinates was certainly unreasonable, if not irrational. Unless one is given the authority to report on the operational performance of his subordinates, it becomes a herculean task to get the best out of them. I often wonder how I saved my goose from being cooked. Undeterred, I took up the challenge and managed to produce results, though it was extremely demanding on me, physically and mentally. At times, it felt as if I was playing with my life. Why, I cannot say! Had a streak of fatalism crept in?

'JJ, the next time you go for any cordon-and-search operation, I would like to come along. I have heard a lot about your address to the people and the "khopdi" (skull and bones) drill, and its impact on their minds,' said Major General Kevin D'Souza, the GOC of 19 Infantry Division. My response was a cryptic, 'Okay, Sir,' but I wondered how he came to know of it.

Very soon, I got an opportunity to satisfy the GOC's curiosity. Based on some intelligence inputs, we launched a cordon-and-search operation in a village named Fatehgarh on the way to Uri. Furthermore, we organized and played an impromptu cricket match with the young men of Fatehgarh. Much to the delight of the village youth, after a friendly ten-over game, we presented the cricket gear to them and shared a cup of tea with them. Such a thing was quite a rarity in those days, and the GOC's staff almost went into a state of consternation when the idea was first mooted. But the general went back suitably impressed.

So what exactly was our modus operandi in 79 Mountain Brigade when we conducted a cordon-and-search operation, including the famous 'khopdi' drill?

The first step was always to get the maximum information on the terrorists' activities and their presence in a given area, and more importantly, to get actionable intelligence in real time. Sometimes this intelligence would come from our own sources and at other times, from the higher HQs. Frequently, the commanding general would call me to his office or residence, and we would discuss and work out the broad operational plan based on the information provided by the sources. Before meeting the general, I would issue the warning order for the mission to the unit concerned.

This would set in motion the preparations for the operation by the troops. With an aim of deception, the vehicles were lined up facing the wrong direction. Very often I would order the movement to be on foot all the way to the target – a rapid march at night covering up to 20 kilometres or so. Surprise is indeed critical for success and in my opinion, it is one of the most important principles of war. In fact, I advised all junior leaders to ask themselves whether the plan they had evolved had an element of surprise or not. In case the answer was 'no', that plan would have to be trashed and a new one devised.

Generally, the plan involved convergence on the objective from two or three directions. The outer cordon would be established well before first light and the noose tightened at twilight. This kind of encircling action confused the terrorists, and made it difficult for them to escape even if they got wind of our movements during the night. In case anyone attempted to break through the cordon before daybreak, the person would be challenged and asked to stop. If the person tried to run away, we would first try and apprehend the individual, and when compelled, open fire. At night, the villagers generally stayed indoors and rarely ventured to go out. Besides, we had warned the people that in case of an emergency, they should make use of a lantern or torch while moving around. On the other hand, the terrorists moved about in a furtive manner at night and avoided making any noise. In fact, on many occasions, they ordered the Kashmiri villagers to do away with their dogs, so that their movements were not announced by the sound of barking.

After daybreak, we would enter the village and ask all men to assemble in a central place like a school or the Idgah. Women, children and the elderly were told to stay at home. We would then commence the search of the village in a systematic manner, based on the intelligence provided by the sources. Our endeavour was to prevent the trapped terrorists from moving from one hideout to the other. We had to isolate each locality or 'mohalla' before commencing search operations. It was ensured that a local police constable and a village elder accompanied every search party.

A clearance was obtained in writing after a house was searched so as to safeguard our soldiers from false accusations later. Many terrorists were detected and caught from hideouts and cavities cleverly made under the floor, behind the walls, or in the attics. Some were caught hiding in the cattle sheds. At times there were shootouts between our troops and the hiding terrorists. Some of these hideouts were very ingeniously configured and camouflaged, and thus remained undetected. Once a terrorist was captured from a house, the owner begged forgiveness. His plea would be that the terrorists threatened him with dire consequences if he refused to cooperate. That was indeed so in most cases – they had to acquiesce to save their lives.

While the search operation was on, it was my practice to address the men folk who had been assembled at a central place. Moreover, during this period, they were also screened individually and made to pass by a 'cat', a spotter who was a former terrorist. Anyone identified and pointed out by the cat was segregated and questioned separately.

I considered targeting and influencing the minds of the people more important than catching or killing a few terrorists. Winning their hearts and minds with the velvet-glove approach and a humane touch was an important facet of counter-insurgency operations in my command. My talk and interaction with the people, conducted in Urdu, would go something like this:

Brigade Commander – Containing the Fire

Kashmir Valley, 1991–92

Dear brothers and fellow Kashmiris. I feel sorry to put you through the inconvenience caused by the crackdown (the name given by the locals to a cordon-and-search operation). But were it not on account of the reported presence of terrorists in this area, we wouldn't be here.

We are the army of the people, and are here for your security. You are our countrymen, and I firmly believe that over 95 per cent of you are innocent. My troops will treat you with respect and your dignity will be upheld. There shall be no misbehaviour with women, harassment of the children and the elderly people, or wilful damage and destruction of your property.

Terrorism has turned your beautiful state into a veritable hell. God had given you a paradise. What will your children inherit from your generation? Maybe a generation or two would never see peace and prosperity. Progress will remain a chimera. Without your cooperation, terrorism cannot be rooted out. Look at Mizoram and Punjab. It was only when the people stopped supporting the terrorists, peace could prevail. Those people are now enjoying the 'peace dividend.' Do the terrorists realize or care as to how much damage they are causing to their own community?

I hear your refrain very often, 'Jenaab, ham to aapki aur jehadi bandook ke beech me mare ja rahe hai' (Sir, we are caught in between two guns, one of the army and the other of the jehadi). I can say with confidence that we are fully responsible and accountable, 'jimmewar' and 'jawabdar', as far as our actions are concerned, but the same cannot be said for the jehadis. If you don't display courage, nothing will change. Put up a united stand – they dare not even touch you as long as you are all together.

What is it that they are promising you, 'Azaadi'? It is not so, as they have an 'agenda' of their own. What 'azaadi' are they talking about? With just a flag, a small landlocked area like the valley cannot be 'azaad' in a meaningful way. It would be a state always at the mercy of others. And if the neighbours choose to block the roads and cut off the valley, you would be on your knees. Kashmir does not produce everything the people need. Your needs will, therefore, have to be met by imports from outside of Kashmir. We must draw the lessons from what is happening in the rest of the world. Europe is witnessing the emergence of the European Union, wherein all countries of that region have got together for a brighter future for their citizens. Boundaries are hardly visible, enemies have become friends, and the economic power of that block of countries is growing.

They (the jehadis) are using you; your children are the sacrificial goats! I am very moved when I see youthful lives snuffed out so needlessly. The lifeless bodies of young, handsome and innocent lads whose faces reminded me of my son and made me feel sorry for these poor Kashmiri boys. They were armed to the teeth and carrying the AK-47 – the death warrant, as I would call it. Does any country allow people carrying weapons to infiltrate across their borders? Did you give birth to them to die in this manner? Where are the children of the 'tanzeem' (jehadi organizations) leaders? Getting degrees and higher education in Bombay, Bangalore or abroad! How many of them have died for this 'cause'? Who are the people making palatial houses all over Kashmir, and where is the money coming from? Please ask these questions to the 'khalifas' or the leaders of the 'tanzeems' when we finish our operation and go away. (Recently, much noise was created when Asiya Andrabi, the head of a belligerent Kashmiri women's organization named 'Dukhtaran-e-Millat', wanted her son to go to Malaysia for higher studies – I had advised the Kashmiris to beware of such leaders twenty years ago!)

Meanwhile, one of my officers would hand over to me my AK-47, which I never failed to carry. At the same time, much to everyone's astonishment, a soldier would fix a small target with the picture of a 'skull and crossed bones' on the nearest tree. I would then load the rifle in a swift motion, and ask someone sitting in the audience as to which part of the target I should aim at. The bullet would be out with a loud bang before I received the response to my question. I seldom missed the centre of the target. I would fire a few more shots at the target. This had a spellbinding effect on the audience. At times, the womenfolk would come running towards the congregation thinking of the worst.

I then made the point that as a brigade commander, it was not my job to shoot, but to make plans and evolve the strategy. Yet if I could still hit the bullseye, my men could shoot through a coin. Therefore, what chance did novices like their son or brother have against the well-trained soldiers of the Indian Army? It would be an unequal fight.

After this, I would have a handwritten letter read out by one of the young men sitting in the gathering. This letter, from the person of a dead terrorist, was from someone undergoing training in a camp located in 'Ilaqa Gair', the no-man's-land between Pakistan and Afghanistan, to his family back home. Unfortunately, a bullet had stopped its courier from reaching his destination. Not only had the projectile pierced through the chest of the terrorist, it also went through this letter found in his breast pocket. It read something like this:

... Mai yahaan par theek hoon. Allah ke raham se aap sabh theek honge. Yahaan ke haalaat bahut kharab hai. Yeh log hamko sabz baag dikhaate rahe. Asli baat kuch aur hai. Hamse barha bewaqoof koi nahin ho sakta. Ham inki baton men aa gaye. Aur kisi ko yahaan mat aane dena.... (I am okay here. With the grace of Allah, I hope you all are fine. The conditions here are terrible. These people have been showing us gardens which appear greener than they actually are. The reality is something else. There is no one who is a bigger fool than us. We got taken in by their words. Don't let anyone else come here....)

Continuing my interaction, I would go on:

Dear Kashmiri brothers, get a hold of your destiny. The outsiders have come with their own designs. They have no love lost for you and your future generations, who are being made to pay the price for this violence and strife. There is much talk in the valley of 'azaadi' or freedom. Jammu and Kashmir is much more than the valley. Therefore, it would be wrong to assume that the people from the valley represent all Kashmiris. We have to bear in mind that there are diverse views on this issue. We cannot ignore the people of other areas and regions of J&K such as Jammu, Udhampur, Doda, Kishtwar, Poonch, Kargil and Ladakh. This state also comprises swathes of territory in Gilgit, Skardu, Hunza, and other parts of Pakistan-occupied Kashmir such as Muzzafarabad and Mirpur (Map 11.1 and Panorama 11.1). What about them?

The valley, with a small area about 55 kilometres wide and 108 kilometres long, would be unviable as an independent entity. India is an emerging power and a subcontinent with huge natural resources and a large population. Perhaps a way could be found by a dialogue on the

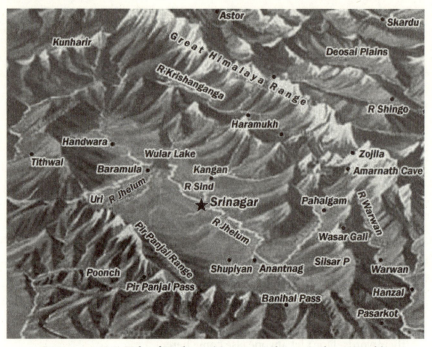

Panorama 11.1: Vale of Kashmir (Courtesy: Shanta Serbjeet Singh).

basis of more autonomy. Kashmir has always been a part of Hindustan, encircled by the Hindu Kush and Karakoram ranges to its north and northwest, and the Pir Panjal and Shamsabari ranges in the south and west. It has been one of the cradles of the Indian civilization since early days, and evolved as a homogenous 'melange' of Brahmanism, Buddhism, Islam, Sikhism and Sufism.

The ruins of the magnificent ancient temples at Martand, Harwan and Awantipur, which your ancestors built centuries ago and which have been described in the scriptures, reveal the greatness of your culture. Those huge blocks of granite didn't fall from the skies. So how can you forget your history, beliefs and way of life, particularly the spirit of Kashmiriyat derived from the philosophy propounded by famous saints like Sheikh Noor-ud-Din or Nund Rishi? He was also known as 'Allamdar-e-Kashmir', and is regarded by all of you as the patron saint of Kashmir. History tells us that your forefathers embraced Islam around the twelfth century. Therefore, you cannot disown your ancestors whose blood flows in your veins and your heritage.

Despite the imperfections we are a vibrant democracy. You have been participating in the election process for over four decades. Why don't the leaders of the jehadis stand for elections and serve the people if they are able to get the mandate? The fact is peace and progress don't suit them or fit into their scheme of things. The outsiders are imposing on you a way of life that goes against the grain of your culture. As written by one of your ilk in the letter that was just read out, they are misleading everyone. Whatever customs and practices they are forcing on you and your womenfolk in Kashmir, why aren't they being insisted upon in Karachi, Lahore or Islamabad?

Muslims who chose to migrate to Pakistan at the time of Partition stand permanently branded – they are referred to as 'mohajirs' [refugees] even today. Did they make a mistake? In comparison, my grandparents and their entire clan of Khatri Punjabis left their lands and property in Rawalpindi, Lahore, or Gujaranwala areas, and migrated to India. My father was a lieutenant colonel, and I have risen to the rank of a brigadier. Likewise, all others have resurrected themselves admirably. We are proud Indians, and no one refers to us as refugees.

Take the case of the Bihari Muslims who sided with the Pakistan Army and even laid down their lives during the Indo-Pak war of 1971, when Bangladesh was created. They were given assurances that they would be resettled in Pakistan. They are having a miserable existence in camps in Bangladesh even today, as Pakistan has been unable to give them a place to resettle in. Weren't they loyal and good Muslims?

You must, therefore, neither entertain any wrong notions nor be under false illusions. Pakistan will continue to do its best to keep the fire simmering in Kashmir. Don't get taken for a ride any longer, my wise Kashmiri brothers. It is time for you to say enough is enough!

This is the manner in which I used to interact with the villagers, and convey my ideas as the brigade commander to the mostly ignorant populace – the suffering poor of the valley. In the meanwhile, my units and sub units would complete their assigned operational tasks and thereafter, we would return to our base.

The 15 Corps commander, Lieutenant General Zaki's assessment in 1991 that there was large-scale infiltration taking place in the north

Jhelum sector, the corridor between the Shamsabari and the Jhelum river – was proved right by the phenomenal successes my units began to achieve. The previous brigade commander had claimed that not even a bird could get through his sector undetected and that no infiltration was taking place. The results produced by us definitely surprised him the most.

We intercepted and neutralized a number of infiltrating groups within a period of about eight months in 1991. Terrorist organizations like the Hizbul Mujahideen, Lashkar-e-Toiba and Jaish-e-Mohammad, and their mentors across the LoC found the new counter-infiltration set-up in the Baramulla sector fairly difficult to penetrate. They identified me as the thorn in their flesh, as other than a change of command of the sector, nothing much had changed in the force level or deployments. Therefore, they decided to do away with me, and began making plans to achieve this mission. My formation was referred to as the 'Shaitan' (Devil) Brigade, and I was nicknamed as 'Shaitan' Singh. I was happy with both these appellations. It signified that we had been able to put the fear of God in the 'tanzeems'.

We launched a number of seek-and-destroy missions. The majority of the population acted as fence-sitters during such operations, keenly watching the contest between the jehadis and the army. As was expected, they usually gravitated to the winning side, and we appeared to them as clear winners due to our professional approach and the results of engagements. The terrorists were no match for us and the outcome showed it. We hardly lost any of our men, whereas we killed or apprehended many terrorists. Gradually, we won the people over to our side, specially in the rural 'kandi' (foothills) belt.

We always kept our principle 'iron-fist-and-velvet-glove' uppermost in our minds. This phrase was used by me during this tenure as a brigade commander. The iron fist was for the terrorist while the velvet glove was for the people, a vast majority of whom were innocent. We ensured that collateral damage was confined to the barest minimum. I had zero tolerance for any human rights violations, and made my views clear to all of my subordinates. The projection of the humane face of the army has always been my aim. By killing a terrorist or two the insurgency won't come to an end, but by killing or maiming innocents we were going to create many more terrorists. Very often I used to advise my COs to let go of an odd terrorist, in case the action to get him was going to lead to loss of innocent lives or cause unreasonable collateral damage.

A particular CO once told me that I was flogging his troops. He had mustered the guts to say so either because he knew that his confidential report would not be written by me or else, he was convinced that his troops were really overstretched. When this incident happened, 7 Sikh, the battalion in question, was deployed near the LoC. The next morning, I walked up to the Battalion HQ. It was a tough march uphill all the way and it took me about two hours or so. Besides, it was my third trip there in as many months. When I questioned the CO as to what prompted him to make such a remark, he tried to make excuses to justify that his battalion was fully stretched.

'How many times has the previous commander been here in the last one year?' I asked.

'Once, Sir,' was the colonel's reply.

'Look here, my friend, this is my third visit to your unit and therefore, if I am not sparing myself then you and your battalion jolly well get used to it. We are all here to do our assigned missions to the best of our abilities. Do you get me?'

'Yes Sir,' he said. Things fell into place without any problems thereafter.

Earlier, another incident happened with the same unit. I got a call from their previous brigade commander, who asked me to let the CO visit his administrative base at Uri at least once a week. I did not agree as I felt that the operational situation demanded the presence of the CO. Infiltration was increasing and the challenge had to be met. I was okay with the CO going to Uri once in a while but not every week. But the brigadier carried on and on, and tried to convince me of how important it was for the colonel to visit his rear HQ. Finally, I proposed to the brigadier that since he was insistent, the CO could remain at Uri permanently. I would be quite content if all operational responsibilities were entrusted by him to the second-in-command. That was the last I ever heard on this issue.

Soon this battalion carried out a successful operation and effectively intercepted and eliminated a large group of heavily-armed infiltrators.

That was the beginning of their success story. The battalion ended up with a large number of decorations because of their hard work, and the CO was proudly wearing a Sena Medal for his gallant leadership less than a year later. His citation had been initiated by me. He apologized for his earlier remarks, and in an accolade-filled demi-official letter to me, expressed his grateful thanks. Surely, 7 Sikh, the Choinar Battalion and its CO would always remember this eventful tenure.

The new corps commander, Lieutenant General Surinder Nath, visited me during the latter half of 1991. Since I had only ad-hoc arrangements for my office, I decided to brief him on the ground. He landed by helicopter and I gave him a rundown of the operations we were conducting. He appreciated the work being done by us. I told him I could do even better if he gave me additional troops and financial support to reward the sources and agents who were giving us information on the terrorists. He assured me of a positive response, and wished us good luck before returning to the Corps HQ.

12

Operation Mousetrap

During the latter part of 1991, we conceived a series of counterinfiltration operations called 'Mousetrap'. In these operations we adopted a dynamic matrix of positions in tiers that we changed frequently. As a result, we achieved quite spectacular results. Our success story was covered prominently in *Frontline* magazine of 31 January 1992.

In Operation Mousetrap we had one of our finest counterinfiltration actions. It began very unexpectedly. On the morning of 27 November '91, when I was having breakfast, I heard the sounds of a shooting engagement from across the Jhelum river. I asked my brigade major, R.P.S. (Rajpal) Mann, to find out what was happening. He enquired from the battalion on the LoC if there was an encounter going on with terrorists somewhere. They said no. The exchange of fire continued nonetheless and from the sound of gunshots, it did not appear to be happening too far away. I therefore decided to move with my protection party and quick reaction team (QRT) towards the action site. 'Let's go,' I ordered Captain V.K. Singh, the brigade education officer, as our convoy sped off. VK was officiating as the general staff officer (intelligence) of the brigade. We crossed the bridge over the Jhelum and had barely gone a kilometre or so when we saw twenty-five to thirty soldiers running down the road towards us. When we asked them about the firing, they displayed total ignorance. I almost lost my shirt at their lack of interest, but it was amusing to learn that in the middle of this battle, these soldiers were going through a point-to-point map-reading test! I asked if they were carrying any ammunition along with their rifles. On getting a positive nod, I asked them to hop on to the protection vehicles and we proceeded ahead. We reached near the site of the encounter within an hour, dismounted from the vehicles and proceeded cautiously till we closed in. Up to this moment we had no idea whatsoever as to who was fighting and with whom. Soon Captain S.S. Anjaria of 2/11 GR crept up to me and started to brief me about the situation. Before he could begin, I told him that I had with me about fifty soldiers who could be employed to beef up his force. So it was decided that the motley group of men doing the map-reading test could be used in squads of eight men to form an outer ring to isolate the area and prevent the terrorists from escaping, whereas the QRT and my protection party would engage the terrorists hiding in the folds of the sloping ground. This timely arrival of additional troops gave the hard-pressed men of 2/11 GR a shot in the arm.

Thereafter Anjaria proceeded to brief me, and I was truly impressed with the actions of this brave officer and his outnumbered gallant Gurkhas. Despite the odds, they had hemmed in about twenty-odd heavily armed terrorists coming down the hill from the direction of the LoC. By this engagement, they had prevented the infiltrators from entering a nearby village. Once there, the terrorists could have easily escaped by merging with the locals and concealing their weapons and equipment (see Sketch 12.1).

In this skirmish, the young captain and his men had knocked down eight to ten terrorists, and sporadic yet intense exchange of fire was continuing. We had no casualty from our side thus far, and we could count at least ten dead terrorists lying around in the broken ground ahead of us. It was around 11 a.m. and I was confident that in a couple of hours we would be able to take care of all of them. At that moment, I felt a sudden piercing pain. The realization that I had been shot struck me when I felt some warm fluid flowing down my left leg. It was blood oozing out from both wounds.

I slumped to the ground, and was assisted by VK and taken to a somewhat secure place nearby, away from direct fire of the terrorists. Someone got hold of a field dressing and tied a bandage over the wound as the pain kept increasing. I told Anjaria and V.K. Singh that I did not want to be evacuated till someone responsible could take control of the operation. It was about 11.30 a.m. by then.

The brigade second-in-command, Colonel U.R. Chaudhri, arrived with the medical officer in about an hour. The tactical situation was explained to him and he took charge. Meanwhile, the doctor dressed my wound afresh and gave a shot of morphine, a very effective painkiller and the saviour of wounded soldiers ever since the First World War. As taught in medical schools, he put down details such as the dose administered along with the time at which the tranquillizer was injected, on the huge white sterilized bandage itself, and wrote out a brief medical report. As happens with a 'high velocity and spinning hardnosed' bullet of a 7.62-calibre 'Dragunov' sniper rifle, which I suspect was the type of weapon used to target me, it went through my groin making a hole the size of a small coin, but the exit wound in the buttock was about two square inches of shattered blood vessels, nerves and flesh, with blood all over! Intermittent firing continued to take place as I was evacuated on a stretcher to the road where a jonga (MUV) ambulance was waiting. From there, it took us about two hours to reach the nearest helipad, and I was flown to Srinagar in the waiting chopper.

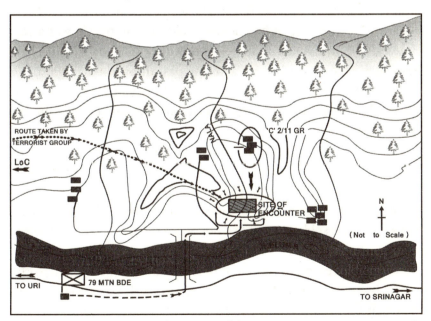

Sketch 12.1: Encounter with terrorists during Operation Mousetrap, 1991.

We landed at Badami Bagh, the cantonment of Srinagar, at around 4 p.m. Once again I was put into the ambulance, and taken straight to the military hospital. I was feeling very weak and exhausted and in shock, because of substantial loss of blood and the pain. The effect of the morphine was still there, though my leg felt dead as a log of wood! Soon we arrived at 92 Base Hospital and I was wheeled on the stretcher directly to the operation theatre. The surgical specialist, Lieutenant Colonel Brij Mohan Nagpal, opened the field dressing and asked the paramedic to get an X-Ray done. Fortunately, there was no bone injury, thereby making the surgery less complicated. General anaesthesia was then administered to me. Once tranquillized, I lost consciousness. Later, the nursing officer told me that the doctors took two-and-a-half hours to complete the surgery. They did it with great precision and professionalism, as is their wont, and I can swear on that now. After the operation, I was taken to the intensive care unit.

I got back to my senses at about 7 p.m., when the effect of the anaesthesia wore off. I enquired about the encounter and was told that it was still continuing, that there had been no further casualties on our side, while about twenty terrorists had been shot dead. My younger brother, Lieutenant Colonel B.J. Singh, who was a medical specialist in the army, on learning of the incident, told me, 'Brother, it was a very close call for you. A few millimetres on either side and it could have been fatal – the femoral artery and vein pass through that region. It is divine intervention that has saved you!' 27 November 1991 was a long day and I can never forget Lieutenant Colonel Nagpal, the surgeon who saved my life.

A lot of visitors, including Corps Commander Lieutenant General Surinder Nath and Lieutenant General M.A. Zaki (Retd), the security adviser to the government of J&K, came to the hospital to wish me a speedy recovery. Captain S.S. Anjaria was decorated with a Sena Medal, and a few of his soldiers were also honoured for their gallant actions in this operation.

At some level, questions were raised as to why I had gone so far ahead. It was as if I had done something wrong! It was my considered view that I must always try and be upfront, share the same risks that my soldiers were facing, and damn well get to know what's going on. Irregular warfighting is often so messy and complicated that decisions of far-reaching consequences have to be taken there and then, in real time. For example, if women congregate and attempt to storm and effect the release of a detained terrorist leader, and further, if terrorists wearing burqas and masquerading as women are amongst them, and they open fire at our troops, what would you do? One faux pas is enough to ignite a storm. Those of us who have handled such situations and survived are the unsung heroes of this dirty war in J&K and the northeast and elsewhere in the world, be it Afghanistan, Iraq or Bosnia. As a leader I would like to be in the picture and importantly, in the front, rather than in my office. I am convinced that all commanders up to the rank of brigadier should consider themselves as field commanders and act accordingly. Beyond that rank, the general officers should decide for themselves as to when and where their presence would be necessary in the combat zone, so that they can motivate the troops, guide the formation and unit commanders, and get a feel of the ground.

The nurse told me that my wife, Rohini, was on the way and would be joining me soon. It was the best possible news I could have received and it made me feel brighter. On arrival, she gave me a lovely bouquet of roses, and her presence cheered me up no end. For a few hours it was just the two of us. Rohini was full of questions, and we kept talking.

Many years later I asked Anjaria, who had become a colonel by then, to give me an account of how he saw the events on that memorable day. This is an extract of what he had to say: 'Since the column of 2/11 GR was grossly under strength due to the numerous stops and ambushes already out, the QRT which arrived was most welcome. During the process of engaging the ANEs [anti-national elements] the Cdr, Brig JJ Singh, VSM was identified and spotted by the ANEs. A short burst of AK fire hit the Cdr in the groin. Despite being injured and bleeding profusely Brig JJ Singh, VSM continued to coordinate the operations and even spoke to the GOC 19 Mtn Div on the Radio Set.'

It is not in my nature to talk about this gunshot wound. But over the years, many people have wanted to know about my injury. Besides, it is rare for an officer of flag rank to get wounded in action against terrorists, and not every soldier is fortunate to be bloodied in battle. Therefore, this experience finds a place in this narrative.

The Lashkar-e-Toiba and other terrorist groups against whom we were pitted celebrated my 'killing'. It appears that they had already claimed the prize money for my scalp from their 'tanzeem'.

I rejoined my brigade instead of taking sick leave after being discharged from the hospital. The terrorists found it unbelievable, and thought it was not me but my ghost. Their masters across the border were livid. They ordered the divisional commander of the terrorists to return the claim money and warned him against giving false reports in future. At the same time, they were told to make another plan to finish me off as soon as possible. This information was passed on to us by one of our sources.

During the next three to four months, we notched up many more successes in our operations against the terrorists. More than seventy young men who had gone across the border for training and come back with an AK-47, deserted the ranks of their 'tanzeems'. They had realized the futility of their mission, and surrendered to my battalions. To avoid the penalty of Rs 20,000 that would have to be paid to the 'tanzeem' towards the cost of the gun, they asked our troops to enact a kind of drama and capture them from pre-arranged spots. As an incentive, we helped to secure jobs for them in the Uri civil power project being executed by a Swedish company in 1991–92. Some of them were appointed as security guards! Today, we have a surrender policy under which these misguided young men are rehabilitated so that they can join the national mainstream.

In November 1991, we were delighted to receive this telegram from the chief of the army staff:

REFERENCE OPERATIONS OF 79 MTN BDE IN OP MOUSETRAP II ON 22 AND 23 NOV 91 (.) REQUEST CONVEY APPRECIATION AND CONGRATULATIONS OF CHIEF OF THE ARMY STAFF TO CONCERNED TROOPS IN OP MOUSETRAP II.

13

Death Sentence to Brigadier 'Shaitan Singh'

The terrorist organizations started carefully monitoring my movements. They noticed that I used to visit the Division HQ frequently, to brief the GOC, Major General Inder Varma. Accordingly, they worked out a meticulous plan to get rid of me in an urban ambush in the heart of Baramulla town at Tashkent Chowk. It was something like the ambush of the Sri Lankan cricket team in Lahore some years ago. I often wonder how we escaped death that day.

As I recall the events on that clear summer day in 1992, based on my memory of the interrogation of captured terrorists, information from local sources, and a vivid description given by an officer who happened to be on leave and present in Baramulla that day, I have reconstructed the deadly ambush.

Terrorists' Hideout – Baramulla, July 1992

'This b-----d of a brigadier, "Shaitan Singh," is becoming a pain. We have to get rid of him,' said the leader in a deep voice.

'Tomorrow, I understand he is likely to drive through Baramulla. Though the son of a bitch never follows a predictable routine, my "source" is very sure of his information this time. We shall give this infidel such a reception that he and his protection team wouldn't know what hit them. None of these motherf-----s of the "Shaitan" Brigade should get away alive.' He then unfolded his plan to his handpicked comrades in a cool and deliberate manner, leaving no room for error.

'Have you understood? Koi shak *(any doubts),*' he asked. The others just nodded.

'Okay then get on with it, and Insha Allah, we shall be crowned with success. I must caution you – never underestimate these kafirs and their commander. I know this "harami" well. He is a cat with nine lives. But, we will not let him get away this time. See to it that he is despatched to his God,' said the leader with a chuckle.

'Hello Zulu 1, "Phantom" leaving for "Taj Mahal" now….ETA [expected time of arrival] 0950 hours…over,' was the cryptic transmission by Captain Suresh Kumar, the general staff officer (intelligence) of the brigade, informing the Division HQ about my move.

'Yankee for Zulu 1 – roger out.'

Soon our convoy of four vehicles was snaking its way along the mountainous road. 'Move it,' I commanded the driver. The Nissan Patrol's two-litre engine revved up as the driver pressed on the accelerator.

'Don't you know that someone who moves slowly would be a f…..g dead duck, in this combat zone.'

'Yes sir,' was the prompt reply.

In normal practice, the convoy was led by a 1-tonner that carried the leading protection detachment of six soldiers. A machine gun was fitted on a bracket in the front with a swivel mounting, so that it could be fired in any direction. The commander of this detachment sat in the front cab, hawk-eyed and ever alert. A similar detachment was mounted in the other 1-tonner at the tail of the convoy. Sandwiched between them was my Nissan jonga and the Rover jeep (communication vehicle). I am convinced that in war, to do the expected or being predictable means disaster. Therefore, I did my best to achieve an element of surprise. 'The terrorist could appear from anywhere, and what is worse – at any time,' I would often remind my officers. 'Remember, that's the reason I am ready for action day or night and I and this loaded AK-47 are inseparable,' pointing towards my gun.

The convoy halted after taking a sharp turn five kilometres short of Baramulla. 'All seems quiet today, Sir,' said Captain Suresh, with a twinkle in his eye. Belonging to the artillery, he, apart from Captain V.K. Singh of the Education Corps, had seen more bullets being fired at him than many infantry officers. These youngsters were always brimming with enthusiasm and itching to prove their worth. While having tea, we watched the Jhelum river as it hit the rapids.

'Fly the pennant and uncover the star plate,' I ordered. This was something I never did normally. Why I took this decision on this day, I cannot explain.

'Today, I will lead the convoy through the town upto the Division HQ', I said to myself as I drove off with a zip, with the other three vehicles following behind.

'Sir, did you notice the looks of the young man at the tea stall where we had stopped for tea,' remarked Suresh, looking earnestly at me.

'Yes, indeed. I felt he appeared nervous and fidgety, I wonder why!'

'I think he was a terrorist,' said Suresh.

Soon our convoy entered the town. The highway passed right through the middle – as in a typical Kashmiri town. There were rows of houses and shops on both sides. It seemed a normal winter morning. Children were on the way to school, and the shopkeepers and wayside fruit and vegetable vendors were laying out their wares. Horse-driven carts, the primary mode of conveyance in a town like this, were moving to and fro. Just like any other day.

We had barely gone beyond Tashkent Chowk, the main crossroads in the centre of Baramulla, when all hell broke loose! Hot and lethal metal spewed by machine guns and rifles rained down on my convoy from houses and rooftops, and loud explosions of grenades and rockets enveloped the area in a cloud of dust. There was bedlam and one could notice people running helter-skelter for cover. Some just dived to the ground to get out of the line of fire, and shielded their heads. Fortunately, there were no fatalities, but some were wounded or had a close shave and were under shock.

A surge of adrenaline pumped into my bloodstream automatically, as bullets and shrapnel whizzed past. It felt that the next burst would hit us. The shock effect lasted a few seconds.

Regaining my composure, I yelled into my radio, 'Hullo all stations Zulu, keep moving, I repeat, keep moving – and don't stop till we are out of this hellhole! Shoot your way through, and keep the b-----ds' heads down'.

Stopping there would have been a grave mistake. The elaborately laid ambush was spread over 150 metres. As ordered, the troops carried on firing and fighting through the flak, mounted on their vehicles, as rehearsed by them many times. Once we were out of the killing area, I stopped and asked the men to quickly dismount from the vehicles and return fire from whatever cover they could find.

'Phew, that was indeed a close shave for all of us,' I remarked.

The ambush plan was immaculate; thought out in minute detail. The terrorist in the tea shop on the highway gave the early warning. The stops were deployed on both ends of the ambush point, and the firing party covered the killing zone effectively. The getaway routes were well reconnoitred and mock rehearsals carried out in advance. The ambush was to be sprung on the command of the leader. This was what was going to decide the success or failure of the mission. The timing had to be perfect.

Scene of Ambush – Tashkent Chowk, Baramulla, July 1992

'Get them! Don't let them escape,' shouted the leader of the terrorists. He realized that he had delayed the signal to open fire by a few seconds. It was only because he wanted to be sure of getting his kill, and not act prematurely. However, he never anticipated the commander to be up ahead and leading the cavalcade.

'The commander is in the leading vehicle. He is in the jonga! Take him on with the machinegun, fire the RPG, bring down fire of all weapons, kill him, kill the b------d,' shouted the leader. The machine-gunner tried his best to execute the orders of his leader, but he couldn't aim at the jonga as by then, it was obscured by the 1-tonner. Frustrated, he emptied the whole magazine in a long burst through the truck, not sure if he had got his target. His colleague got excited and pressed the trigger of the rocket launcher but missed the jonga. He saw the rocket explode with a loud bang in the school playground which lay in the flight path beyond the intended target!

Realizing the futility of continuing with the action and the fact that his prey had gotten away this time too, the terrorist leader ordered his companions to abandon their positions and make good their escape as quickly as possible.

'Break contact. Cover each other while you do so and get away. I will meet you at the Maulvi's house in Shera village as soon as you all reach there. Ensure no one is left behind,' yelled the leader before slinking away with his bodyguards to the 'getaway car' parked in a lane nearby.

'Yeh saala Shaitan Singh is waqt bhi haath se nikal gaya hai. Allah hi usko bacha raha hai' (this b------d has gotten away this time too. Allah seems to be saving him), said the leader to his mentors on the walkie talkie. The firing continued in spurts for a while, as the terrorists thinned out and disappeared into the alleys of the old town.

The diagrammatic plan of the elaborately conceived urban ambush to eliminate me was recovered by chance from the person of an apprehended terrorist named Nissar some days later (see Sketches 13.1 and 13.2).

The detailed planning that the terrorist group had carried out is evident from the sketch. The reverse side of the hand-drawn plan had the names of the terrorists, their locations and tasks. In all there were about twenty terrorists who took part in this ambush.

Quickly, Suresh regained control of the group, and it was then that he realized that the last vehicle of the convoy was nowhere to be seen. It had got detached from the rest in a deliberate blocking action by a truck that appeared from the opposite direction. However, the leader of the rear protection party, a thorough professional, did not play into the terrorists' hands. He wisely deployed the men at the far end of the ambush site, and did not blunder into the killing zone. Had they tried to join up with the rest of us, none of them would have survived the murderous onslaught.

It was a deliberate strategy of the terrorists to execute this action in the marketplace so that the blame for the civilian casualties and other collateral damage could be attributed to the army. They could always count on the support of their overground workers and the local media.

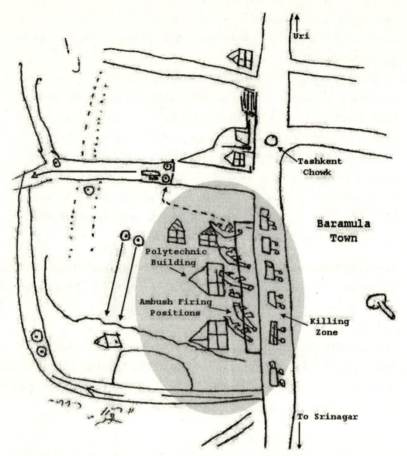

Sketch 13.1: The terrorists' ambush plan at Tashkent Chowk, Baramulla.

In the race for sensational 'breaking news', some reporters were ready to look the other way.

We were old hands at this game and did not oblige the terrorists. Our response to this provocation was measured and cool. We fired accurately and purposefully and for effect. During the fierce encounter in the bustling market, it was amazing that only a few civilians had got injured in the crossfire.

Having deployed the available troops, we took stock of the situation. I was happy to see that there were no fatal casualties amongst my men. The Rover, which stood out because of its antenna, bore the brunt of the deadly ambush, and its driver got hit by a burst of a machine gun. Yet this brave soldier kept on moving.

Sketch 13.2: Names of terrorists who were part of the ambush.

Suresh ordered the men to fan out from both sides, and in a pincer movement they carefully advanced towards the site of the ambush. The terrorists had hastily abandoned their positions and vanished.

The ambushers had deployed themselves behind a wall so that they could take us on at point-blank range, from both sides of the road. There were impressions of their boots on the tables placed behind the wall of the polyclinic, from where the murderous fire was unleashed. A large number of fired cartridges of the AK-47 and the universal machine gun were scattered all over. There were blood stains on one of the tables. The trail of the blood stains ended in the alley from where, possibly, the injured terrorist was picked up by a vehicle. Finding nothing more, the search was called off. I led the convoy to the Division HQ at the other extreme of the town.

'Thank God, you are safe. What is your plan of action now?' asked the brigadier who was the officiating GOC. 'Sir, I would recommend a cordon-and-search of Shera village at the earliest. I am sure these b-----ds have gone there, and would soon disperse,' I said, based on confidence that comes only from experience.

'Go right ahead, you have my okay,' said the officiating GOC. The cordon-and-search operations were carried out and over the next few days, we caught a few of these terrorists. I addressed the people as usual, and mockingly asked them to convey to the terrorists that they must go back and do some more training. They wasted so much of ammunition in the ambush!

Twelve years later, I was amazed when the story of this ambush was recounted by an officer whom I had never met before. During my farewell visit to 2 Corps at Ambala in December 2004 as the chief designate, a retired lieutenant colonel came up to me and said he was present in Baramulla on a holiday in 1992. He was staying with a relative whose house happened to be on the main highway, very close to the place where the terrorists ambushed me. He had heard rumours floating around about the plan the previous evening, but was scared stiff to move out or to do anything about it, like sending word to the 19 Infantry Division HQ, about half a kilometre from there. I asked him why he had kept silent for so long. 'It was due to remorse and a feeling of guilt, but I prayed for you,' he replied. He wrote a letter describing the incident which is given in Appendix 1.

While conducting another operation, one of my sub-unit commanders had an interesting experience. As Ravi (name changed) and his boys were passing by a small hamlet they noticed that someone peeped out and then closed the window. There appeared something suspicious and unusual about it. Quickly, that area was encircled and Ravi knocked on the door. After a few minutes, a terrified old woman opened it and asked, 'Who are you? What do you want?'

Ravi identified himself and demanded to know if there was anyone else in the house.

'Only my daughter-in-law,' she stuttered unconvincingly, pointing to a corner of the dimly lit room, where a young woman sat huddled up.

Even in the poor light, Ravi could see her petrified look; she had fresh henna patterns on her hands.

'You have my word that no harm will come to you, but I have to search this place,' said Ravi with authority.

Quickly his men positioned themselves around the house, and the nominated search party commenced their job. Within five minutes they located a small hideout under the floor, accessible through a trap door, which was covered by a worn-out rug. When challenged, out came a nervous young man with his hands raised above his head.

'Why were you hiding there?' demanded the major.

'Sahib, mujhe maut ka khauf hai (I was scared for my life)', he cowered in fear.

'What is your name?' asked Ravi.

'Abdul Majid, sir', he replied, shaking.

Ravi took out his notebook to check his list, which confirmed his suspicions. When confronted with information about his terrorist background, Abdul Majid broke down and fell at the major's feet, seeking forgiveness.

The old woman, in a state of shock, began sobbing. Regaining her composure after a few moments, she came up to the major and touched his chin as a gesture of respect and deference. 'Sahib, don't take him away. He is my only son and his "nikah" was done only a few days ago. Take pity on this young bride,' she implored. The girl looked stunned and slowly slid to the ground.

'Mother, tell him to be honest and to cooperate. I assure you of his life and safety', said Ravi to the woman.

'He will, he will; and may God bless you,' she responded.

Abdul Majid went up to the first floor of the house escorted by a soldier and took out his AK-47 alongwith four fully loaded magazines. These had been cleverly concealed in the attic. Giving them to the major, he said, 'Sahib, this is all I have. Though I had gone across the border for being trained for jehad, khuda kasam, I have never taken part in any action against the security forces. I have never used this gun! I am innocent – I swear by Allah.'

'Do you know the way to Shera village through the forest,' asked Ravi.

'Yes, sir', replied Abdul Majid.

'Okay, then come with us, and quickly guide us to that place.'

He couldn't be late and delay the mission of the entire battalion. He had to make up for the lost time. Grabbing Abdul Majid by the arm, he led him out of the house.

'Don't take him away, he is innocent. Have you forgotten your promise, Major Sahib?' begged the old woman.

'Ammi, I am a man of my word, and take pride in this uniform that I am wearing. Your son will not be harmed. We in the army are responsible and humane. I am sure he shall be forgiven for taking up arms against the state, provided he promises to mend his ways. Also, for the sake of this bride of a few days, he is not going to be sent behind bars! He will be back by the evening', assured Ravi. Before leaving the house, Ravi asked the accompanying policeman to take an all-clear certificate from the two women so that there would be no scope for false allegations later on. When I was informed of this incident, I ordered that the gun should be confiscated and the young man be let off with a stern warning. This action brought us a lot of praise and the goodwill of the people.

In another action during the month of February, I was accompanied by the GOC, Major General Inder Varma. We walked in the snow the whole night and cordoned off two villages with one battalion each. One of these was Khaitangan. The next morning nothing happened till about 9 a.m. So the GOC decided to go back to his HQ. He must have barely reached when one of my battalions hit a gold mine. They discovered two terrorists holed up in a hideout in one of the villages and on being interrogated they told us that there were about ten of them hiding in different places. So the search was intensified. I was addressing the menfolk who had been asked to congregate in the school compound, when a police inspector whispered to me that a serious development had occurred in an adjacent area, and that it needed my attention urgently.

On reaching the spot indicated by the inspector, I saw a bizarre scene. In an open ground there was the second-in-command of 8 Bihar flanked by two terrorists with AK-47s slung on their shoulders and a grenade each in their hands. While we had cordoned off the entire area, Lieutenant Colonel Harjit Singh was taken hostage right in the middle of the village by two fanatics who were ready to commit mayhem and were prepared to die. They conveyed that they would like to negotiate with none other than the brigade commander. They were tall, smart and a bit cocky in their attitude. But I must admit that I was impressed by the cool approach of Harjit Singh. If anyone had panicked, the outcome could have been catastrophic. Standing out of grenade-throwing range, about 50 metres away behind a hedge, I conveyed to them through Captain Shakeel Ahmad, a brave officer of the battalion, that their entire gang had been caught but in case they let go of the officer, they would not be harmed. They asked for some water and a bottle of water was placed near them. Both of them surveyed the deployment of troops all around them and must have realized that there was no way they could escape.

In the meanwhile Lieutenant Colonel Harjit Singh somehow broke away from their clutches and joined us.

The terrorists spoke to each other and all of a sudden lobbed the grenades in my direction and opened fire with their Kalashnikovs. We dived and hit the ground. The grenade splinters flew all around us and bullets whizzed past overhead. Fortunately, the brunt of the attack was taken by the embankment in front of us. Our faces and bodies were splattered with the melting snow and mud which flew in all directions when the grenades burst. I had a feeling that I had been hit by splinters but luckily it was only muck formed by the melting snow and mud. Both the terrorists were killed in the shootout that followed their suicidal attack. Once again I appeared to be the target, and was lucky to survive. There were no other casualties. Captain Shakeel Ahmad and a few others from 8 Bihar were decorated with gallantry awards for this operation. Till this day I have not been able to fathom the reason for the terrorists' refusal of my offer of a safe passage.

I cannot help writing about a notorious terrorist guide, Fatta Sheikh, from Maiyan village, close to the LoC in the Lachhipura sector. In an operation conducted in Baramulla area, we apprehended a suspect hiding in a cattleshed. Inside that dark shed there were scores of sheep huddled together. It would have been impossible to spot someone lying on the floor, but for the ingenious method devised by a JCO of 2/11 GR. He got hold of a long bamboo pole and started combing the shed by sliding it along the floor. At one place it hit some obstruction and he realized that there was someone hiding there. He warned in a loud voice that he would shoot if the person didn't come out. Lo and behold! a man stood up with his hands raised. He was taken to the CO, who asked him a few questions. Fatta Sheikh's alibi was that he was a gujjar (a nomadic tribe of herdsmen) and that it was his occupation to take the cattle of various owners for grazing in the higher reaches of the mountains every summer. He told his captors that he had come to return the cattle and take his wages from the villagers. He was innocent and he hid himself in the cattleshed out of fear, because of the army crackdown.

The CO was not aware of his background and was about to let him go. I was informed about it, but the circumstances under which he was caught rang a bell. When I was told that his name was Fatta Sheikh, I enquired if he was from Maiyan village. 'Positive,' said the CO. Then I told the colonel that we had been looking for this man for almost a year. He was a notorious crook and a mercenary who had guided more than thirty terrorist groups across the LoC. He was a storehouse of information regarding infiltrators and their Pakistani mentors. Only when he was threatened with dire consequences did he admit his involvement. He also dug out a few weapons wrapped in a polythene sheet that he had buried in a forested area near his village. He was handed over to the police and convicted for his criminal activities. His neutralization was a big blow to the activities of the terrorists in the Lachhipura sector. Fourteen years later, during a visit to Uri as the army chief, I met Fatta Sheikh. 'Abhi bhi badmaashi karte ho?' (Are you continuing your misdeeds), I asked. 'Nahin Jenab' (No sir), was his reply. I gave him a shabash, a pat on the back, alongwith a gift.

In my tenure of two years as the brigade commander of 79 Mountain Brigade, we conducted between 150–200 operations, both big and small, and got good results. We helped the locals make a jeepable road upto Lachhipura from the Uri highway. During this period we lost only five soldiers, whereas we killed over 130 terrorists and apprehended 870. Around seventy-five terrorists surrendered with their AK-47s. Overall, we had recovered 565 weapons and a large number of rockets, grenades and many thousand rounds of ammunition. We did our best to ensure that no innocent was harmed. It was an act of faith for us. Our iron fist was only for the foreign mercenary terrorists and hardcore militants who spread 'dahshat', or terror, amongst the populace. My brigade received seventy-one decorations during this tenure, including one Kirti Chakra, one Shaurya Chakra, eight Sena Medals and over sixty commendations of the chief of army staff and the army commander. Our brigade and the 68 Mountain Brigade were undoubtedly the top achievers of Northern Command during 1991–92, when insurgency in J&K was at its peak. Four battalions that served under me in the brigade, namely, 17 J&K Rifles, 2/11 GR (SHINGO), 15 Punjab (Patiala) and 7 Rajputana Rifles, were awarded unit citations by the chief of army staff for their outstanding contribution to peace in the valley during this period. In addition, 15 Punjab had the unique distinction of also being awarded the unit appreciation of the GOC-in-C Northern Command – the only unit to get both.

Based on my performance as a brigade commander, and my overall track record, I was selected to attend the highly regarded National Defence College course at the end of this assignment, and awarded the commendation of the chief of army staff.

14

Gateway to the Top

The National Defence College (NDC) Course is the most prestigious for armed forces officers of one-star rank, as well as officers at the level of joint secretary in the government. Therefore, only the best brigadiers and their equivalents are selected by the armed forces for this year-long course. This is the first formalized teaching imparted to us in our military careers, where the focus during all discussions and deliberations is at the national level. The aim is to enable the future policy-makers to get an overall understanding of the impact of international, regional and national issues relating to national security, and a focused exposure to political, military, economic and scientific dimensions that are vital for evolving national strategies. Besides this, the course is an excellent opportunity to interact with officers from the armed forces of friendly foreign countries. The highlights of the course are talks given by a vast array of experts, intellectuals and specialists in diverse fields; tours within India and to foreign countries; and presentations on India by study groups of students.

I was fortunate to visit the USA and Poland during the foreign tour in mid-1993. Post Cold War, we were the first students from the NDC course who were allowed to visit the USA. Our programme included interactions with the department of defence officials in the Pentagon, a visit to an airbase in Virginia, where we saw the F-7 stealth fighter from very close, and we were also taken on board the nuclear-powered aircraft carrier, USS John F. Kennedy, at the naval base in Norfolk. It was amazing to learn that the nuclear power plant on the carrier could light up a small town. During the interaction at the Pentagon, I raised the issue of double standards shown by the US in being a champion of democracy on one hand and supporting dictatorships on the other. The frank reply was revealing indeed – 'our national interests will always predominate while deciding foreign policy, double standards notwithstanding.' This was realpolitik! We were then taken to California, where we were briefed at the headquarters of the US Army National Guard. We returned via Tokyo, so it virtually turned out to be a trip where we went round the globe. A great experience, indeed.

On graduating from the NDC in December 1993, I was posted as the deputy director general of operational logistics (DDGOL) in the Army HQ. This was my first assignment in Delhi since my commissioning in 1964! For no fault of mine, I had been denied the experience of serving in the 'mad house', as the Army HQ is jocularly referred to, and widening my horizons. Despite my high profile and sound professional track record, I never got a Delhi posting for the first thirty years of my service in the army. This was because there is a category of officers in every army of the world, and I would prefer to call them 'parasites'. We have them, too. These selfish specimens of humanity neither care for others, nor for the good of the army. They repeatedly wangle their way and get plum postings at Delhi or other sought-after stations like Pune, Chandigarh or Kolkata, while the straightforward guys have to grind their arses in unattractive places like Binnaguri, Tibri, Talbehat or Danapur, or in remote field areas, and bear more than their share of the hardships. This situation is mainly attributable to such officers.

The exposure at the Army HQ at the level of a brigadier was an eyeopener. Since I had never served in a staff appointment above a Divisional HQ before, there was a lot of bureaucratese that I was clueless about. My boss, Major General Samay Ram, was a highly decorated and experienced soldier, a veteran of the low-intensity conflict that we had engaged in against the LTTE in Sri Lanka in the late 1980s. We had never served together before. In fact, we met for the first time when I reported on duty at the Army HQ in January 1994. Both of us were forthright and practical but with different backgrounds and operational experiences, and hence, quite often we did not see eye to eye. I have always found it difficult to impress superiors at first sight. Initially, despite my best efforts, things did not go as well as I would have wanted. I had a tough time making the general agree with my views and recommendations in quite a few cases. Not to be deterred, I endeavoured to learn my job as fast as possible.

Returning from a tour one fine day, he called for me and said, 'JJ, I didn't know that you were such a good combat leader, and that you had commanded your brigade so well in Kashmir. Your men are very proud of you even today.' I wondered as to who had spoken to him about me. Subsequently, I learnt that during a recent tour he had got talking to a junior commissioned officer (JCO) from a Rajputana Rifles battalion who had been detailed as his liaison officer in Jodhpur. That battalion had served under me in Kashmir during 1991–92. The JCO must have recounted some operational experience where I had figured prominently. All I can say is that the rest of my tenure with General Samay Ram passed smoothly. A good spoken reputation does matter for us soldiers, particularly if the praise comes from someone who has served under one's command during operations.

During this tenure there were some important assignments or events that took place. I was called by the master general of ordnance (MGO), Lieutenant General R.I.S. Kahlon, in early 1995 and told to carry out a study that would review the requirements and scale of transport in units of the Indian Army, prior to the introduction of the new family of vehicles. Over the next five years the new generation 2.5-ton 'Azad Super' and 5/7.5-ton 'Stallion' vehicles would replace the existing 1-ton and 3-ton vehicles that were based on the obsolete technology of the 1960s. The MGO gave me only three months to complete this study whose implications would have an impact for decades – an almost unachievable task.

The only way I could do so was to cut out the red tape and long-winded bureaucratic procedures, and go down to the grassroots level of units and sub units directly. This innovative approach involved the creation of a study group comprising officers of the rank of colonels of all arms and services of the army. The next step was to form sub-teams to look into specific areas. After initial discussions with my team, I gave the concept, logic and rationale on which they would base their study. Then we sent questionnaires to different types of units serving in various theatres and diverse terrain and climate zones and asked them to provide details of the utilization of their existing fleets as authorized to them.

I was told that the ministry desired to see a corresponding reduction in the authorization based on the increased carrying capacity of the new generation of vehicles. My response was that if it was purely a mathematical formula, then there was no requirement of this study. A team of clerks with computers could do it! We had to study the operational and functional requirements of vehicles for each type of unit before the authorization could be recommended. If we had not adopted this unconventional procedure and merely followed the chain-of-command route, a study of this magnitude could well have taken a year or more. As soon as we got the response from the units, the sub-teams started finalizing the new scales based on the logic mentioned earlier. We finished our study on time.

The recommendations of the study group were accepted by the ministry of defence without any changes, and the revised authorizations notified to all concerned. Accordingly, new war and peace equipment tables were issued to all units of the Indian Army. We did achieve an overall reduction in the numbers of vehicles in the inventory of the army and a commensurate saving to the state. We also quantified the financial saving by the introduction of these new fuel-efficient vehicles. The ministry of defence and the Army HQ were very appreciative of our study.

When these vehicles were entering service, I decided that the highest priority should be given to J&K. As the first consignment was being sent to a transport company in J&K, I asked to see a Stallion vehicle from that lot. It was brought to Sena Bhawan in the Army HQ and though I was the DDGOL, a brigadier, I did not hesitate to drive it around to get a feel. After all, this was going to be the workhorse of the Indian Army for the next four decades. I noticed that instead of a bucket seat for the driver, the vehicle had an ordinary bench type of seat. How had the quality assurance guys okayed it? Based on my report, those responsible for the lapse were taken to task, and the vehicles introduced into service after due rectification.

We were asked by the UN to deploy an infantry brigade in Somalia in August 1993, when the US forces suffered heavy casualties and were deinducted. Initially we were able to stabilize the situation, but the conflict between two rebel factions began to worsen by the day. Our forces were fired upon a number of times and we suffered a few casualties. The UN asked us to do contingency planning for the worst-case scenario of extrication of our forces by a fighting withdrawal. I realized that we could not do so unless the operational and logistics staff from the Army HQ and the air force had an opportunity to familiarize themselves with the area and the operational situation. Hence, I proposed to Lieutenant General V. Oberoi, director general of military operations (DGMO), that we fly to Somalia, study the ground situation and then finalize the plan. The air force readily agreed and our team, led by the DGMO, flew via Muscat (a refuelling halt) to Mogadishu, the war-torn capital of Somalia. In fact, Air Marshal Jimmy Bhatia flew the plane himself. We were briefed at the UN Mission located there. From there we flew to Baidoa, the location of our Brigade HQ. We were briefed by the brigade commander and discussed various options, including evacuation by sea from Kismaayo or, in the worst case, moving through Kenya and embarking from Mombasa. An attempt had been made to simulate a war-zone effect while we were being briefed. But the small-arms and machine-gun firing pattern had no semblance to an actual encounter or a skirmish.

The put-on act failed to impress me. I was accommodated for the night in an EME workshop, because I am an EME brat. Everyone lived in tents there. We had a pleasant evening in the brigade officers' mess. During this period, Indian naval ships also came up till Kismaayo. Thereafter, we flew back via Nairobi, where we had discussions at the highest level with the Kenyan armed forces and civilian officials. They were most supportive, and assured us of all possible help as and when the situation demanded. This kind of planning process involving the three services of a country was quite unprecedented in contemporary UN history, and it helped in enhancing our image in the region and the world. It most certainly had an effect on the belligerents in Somalia and they did not mess around much with our force thereafter.

My promotion board was held during 1995–96, and I was approved to take over a division as a two-star general. As I had not served in Western Command for almost twenty years, I wrote to the military secretary if he could consider posting me to command any formation in the western theatre, so that I could gain the required experience. My request was acceded to and my appointment as the GOC of 9 Infantry Division was announced in June 1996.

9 Infantry Division was a part of Indian 3 Corps during the Second World War. It took part in operations against the Japanese in Malaya. Finally, it was merged with 2 Indian Division and fought in the battle of Singapore Island. This division was re-raised in August 1964 by Major General P.S. Bhagat, VC, at Saugor, as a result of the expansion of the Indian Army after the 1962 war. It was converted into a mountain division and was moved to Ranchi. Major General Prem Bhagat, the only Indian officer to be awarded the Victoria Cross for outstanding bravery during the Second World War, was a dynamic leader. He forged the division into a highly motivated team with well-set operational drills and procedures. The division has a symbol of a pine tree in its formation badge, and hence is also referred to as the pine division. During the Indo-Pak war of 1971, the division fought extremely well under the leadership of Major General Dalbir Singh, and won the battle honour of Jessore. Several of its brave officers and men were decorated with gallantry awards. Later, the division moved to Meerut, near Delhi. So, I did not have far to go, and took over the formation from Major General K.G. Pitre in July 1996.

My foremost aim was also to forge a war-winning team, and enhance esprit de corps. I got my formation commanders and staff together and shared my aim and priorities with them. We adopted 'Fight to Win' as our motto. Since training for our operational missions was our most important challenge, I wanted to ensure that my brigades and units were well-led and trained, and in a good state of operational preparedness. Since most combat units in my division had come to peace stations after a three-year stay in operational or high-altitude areas, they also needed to have time for rest and recuperation. I had given orders that as far as possible, units should not be away from their peace locations for more than two months each year.

The moment my posting orders were issued in mid-1996, I started preparing for this assignment. An important war game had been planned by the Western Command HQ for 11 Corps, and Pine Division was a part of it. Therefore, I requested my boss at the Army HQ, Major General M.P.S. Kandal, for permission to go on area familiarization visits to 11 Corps zone. It was critical for me to do so, as my knowledge of the western theatre was inadequate. I could not take any chances with an army commander like Lieutenant General A.K. Gautam, who was reputed to tear into anyone who did not measure up professionally. After the formal welcomes, some of them lukewarm, as most people in Meerut believed that 9 Infantry Division was on its way out, I proceeded on the reconnaissance of my area of operational responsibility (AOR). There was a month to go for the war game. I got hold of my brigade commanders and we discussed various contingency plans. I may not have known each and every place by name, but I became very clear on the rationale, fundamentals and concepts of our war plans. Though we had a defensive role, yet offensive-defence was our byword. Once the war commenced, we could reach out and strike the aggressor even before he crossed the border. The sanctity of the border becomes meaningless when hostilities commence. That's exactly how we played the game.

We had set up our operations rooms within the precincts of the Corps HQ in Jalandhar. The tubular frame of the canvas structures was quite flimsy, yet we hung our maps and charts praying that the structure did not collapse on our heads! The war was initiated by Redland (exercise enemy) as it usually happens in our war games. During the first 24 hours, not much happened in our sector. The army commander went around all the Division HQs and other important Brigade HQs and was briefed by the commanders. He asked me a few questions and I responded as best as I could, but with confidence. After the briefing finished, quite a few people came over and congratulated me as nothing had gone awry. As I was quite new to my job and not so familiar with the area, it was some achievement.

The next day all hell was let loose in my division sector. It became clear that our defensive plans were going to be tested. The umpires kept on building the picture by giving us the progress of war. They also gave us the rulings on success or failure of our actions. At a critical juncture, the information given to us demanded immediate action on our part. I tried to get in touch with my corps commander, Lieutenant General H.B. Kala. He was moving around with the army commander and was thus unreachable. In the event, I ordered two companies to move from a flank that appeared less threatened, to beef up the defences of the area that was under heavy attack. This step caught the Redland off guard and their attacks got stalled. When the army commander asked me as to why I readjusted my defences on the first day itself, I replied that I acted before the enemy could create a critical situation for me. 'AKG', as he was known, then bowled a googly at me and said, 'What if the enemy does something on the side from where you have thinned out?' I did not lose my cool and replied, 'Sir, based on the information provided to us this was the best course of action in my reckoning. We will handle the situation in the other sector too by readjustments as rehearsed. Further, the enemy can't be everywhere.' AKG then asked, 'So you are not going to recall those companies?' I stood my ground and said 'No, Sir.' I believe I passed the test, as most of the other GOCs did not rise up the ladder subsequently. I was highly appreciative of General Kala, who held my hand because he was convinced that I had taken the correct decision. He was a thorough gentleman and a professional all his life. This was the first time I was serving under him.

Another major challenge I faced was to save the division from being pushed out from Meerut to Tibri, a small military station near Gurdaspur. For various reasons, both operational and administrative, it made little sense to cause so much of turbulence and expenditure. I earnestly appealed to everyone who mattered and was eventually successful in getting the decision put on hold and subsequently, reversed. There were some amongst the military brass who did not give a damn if there wasn't enough accommodation for married officers and men or schooling facilities in Tibri. The affect on the morale of soldiers was given short shrift. The relocation would have been perfectly understandable if there was a war in the offing. In hindsight, with the revised operational role which was also initiated by me, it was a prudent decision to abort the move.

The next year, we were asked to conduct a seminar on 'heavy breakthrough', a Russian concept. Since this involved large-scale employment of armour, mechanized forces and artillery, it should have been ideally conducted by the Strike Corps. For inexplicable reasons, the responsibility was given to our formation. Anyway, as is my wont, I took it up as a challenge. To begin with, we analysed the term 'heavy breakthrough', and tried to understand the fundamental issues involved in such an operation. We got eminent speakers to air their views and interact with the audience. Various scenarios on how to execute a heavy breathrough in our context were discussed. In my mind it was clear that this concept involved the delivering of a sledgehammer blow with mechanized forces at a given point to achieve a breakthrough. Having done that, we would need to continue the momentum by penetrating into the bowels of the enemy's defenses and turn the flanks. It became evident that the three stages of the battle, 'the break-in, dogfight and break-out', ought to be merged into a seamless operation and taken to its logical conclusion. The chief of army staff, General Shankar Roychowdhury, the army commander, Lieutenant General H.B. Kala, the corps commander and division commanders and high-ranking staff officers attended this training event. The essence of the seminar was that no linear fortification line, however formidable, could withstand a determined assault in overwhelming strength on a chosen point of attack.

Meerut is a very old cantonment and it has good facilities for sports and social activities. I laid great emphasis on shooting. We also improved the golf course and have fond memories of many a round of golf played there. At the same time, I encouraged many youngsters to play the game. Two of them, Jyoti Randhawa and Digvijay Singh, are leading professional golfers playing in the national, Asian and European circuits today. The Pine House, which is the official residence of the GOC, is a lovely colonial bungalow, and proved to be very lucky for us. We solemnized the wedding of our daughter, Urvashi, with Gagan Dugal in this house in November 1997. Gagan is the son of Major General M.S. Dugal, Vir Chakra, with whom I had gone to the Staff College. Interestingly, the marriage of Tajinder Gill and Nina, daughter of Major

General Prem Vadehra, also took place in this well-appointed house. One of my predecessors, Major General K.S. Brar, was himself married while he was the GOC and was living in the Pine House!

By mid-1996, Rohini had established her own office at Delhi, where she started creating new designs for Indian handicrafts and gift items. Therefore, she had to divide her time between her responsibilities at Pine Division and her entrepreneurial venture. Overall this tenure was a very satisfying period for both of us.

15

Masterminding Operations

While I was still commanding 9 Infantry Division, I was selected for a prestigious two-star-ranked appointment at the Army HQ, in the military operations directorate. For a hands-on soldier like me, it was like a dream come true when I took over as the additional director general of military operations (ADGMO) in early 1998. I had to report to the director general military operations (DGMO) and the army chief. The job carried great responsibility and entailed planning and execution of operations being undertaken by the million-plus Indian Army in the country or abroad, as also any aid to civilian authorities during serious law and order problems, or in disaster relief. During peace time, my primary task was the handling of the proxy war, counter-insurgency and counter-terrorism campaigns in J&K or the northeast, as well as guarding the sensitive northern border with China.

But I must admit that even with a service span of thirty-two years, I was a bit lost in the beginning, as I had served for only two-and-a-half-years earlier in the Army HQ. I was not very conversant with the ways of life in Delhi and its work culture or procedures. However, I made up for it with the exposure I had had in difficult border areas and the knowledge gained because of that, and could therefore make a meaningful contribution. I was certainly not a fair-weather soldier, and had a flair for fighting in the mountains and a vast experience in counter terrorism.

My eventful tenure of almost three years, from 1998–2000, has been the longest ever for that post. In the event, I served with four DGMOs and two army chiefs. The defence minister during this period was George Fernandes. The major events that occurred during this period included India's nuclear tests in Pokhran followed closely by those of Pakistan, the Kargil war, natural disasters like the supercyclone in Orissa, the earthquake in Bhuj and an outstanding military action, Operation Khukri, undertaken by the Indian Army and Air Force as part of UN operations in Sierra Leone. In this action, we were able to secure the safe rescue and relief of two companies (233 peacekeepers) of our battalion, which had been encircled by rebels at Kailahun. In addition, we were able to free seventeen UN observers who had been made hostage by these rebels. What made this operation stand out was that all peacekeeping contingents except ours laid down their weapons in front of the rebels. I recall that the UK government made a request that Major Andy Harrison, one of the UN observers from the British Army, be rescued on priority. We replied that the lives of all peacekeepers were equally precious and that efforts would be made to ensure their safe evacuation. Therefore we gave the go-ahead for Operation Khukri. I accompanied the defence minister to Sierra Leone to congratulate the Indian forces for their resounding success.

I met Brigadier Rajpal Punia in 2011, and he told me the story of their siege for about three months without any lifeline and with limited rations. He was a major at that time and was a part of the isolated position in Kailahun. A breakout with the support of attack helicopters was executed by the beleaguered sub units and link up established with the rescuing force. Thereafter, we flew out all the observers, including Major Harrison. This operation is spoken of as a 'great success' in case studies of UN peacekeeping, according to Brigadier Punia.

As part of our ongoing negotiations on the boundary dispute with China, I visited Beijing in the latter half of 1998 as a member of our joint working group comprising the representatives of the ministries of defence, external, home affairs, and the army. Our deliberations lasted for a day-and-a-half. Expectedly, nothing much came out of our discussions with the Chinese. We reiterated our position that we should exchange maps giving our respective alignment of the line of actual control (LAC), and commence the reconciliation from the area where we have the least variation. That is, from the central sector, which includes the Shipki La and Bara Hoti plateau in the UP-Tibet border area. We should be prepared for a long haul as far as these negotiations are concerned, as I did not think the Chinese appeared to be in a hurry to resolve the problem. This being my first visit to China, it was a great experience to see the Forbidden City, the Great Wall and the shopping malls of Beijing. To top it all, the hosts took us out for traditional Chinese cuisine, including the Peking duck.

During 1998, I also participated in the inconclusive Indo-Pak dialogue on issues like Siachen, Sir Creek, sharing of river waters – all this when the infamous Operation 'Badr' in Kargil was perhaps being planned by Pakistan. We maintained our stand that the first step to resolve the Siachen problem should be the authentication of the existing positions of both sides. Besides, we brought out that the issue in question should thereafter be the pull-back from the Saltoro range by the two armies. To call it the 'Siachen issue' is a misnomer as the Siachen glacier is well to the east of the Saltoro range, along which lies the actual ground position line (AGPL).

16

Stand-off in Siachen

Siachen figured prominently in the last decade of my military career, more so when I was the ADGMO at the Army HQ and thereafter. As many people are not well acquainted with the genesis of the Siachen problem between India and Pakistan, I have endeavoured here to cover its essentials.

Dividing the northernmost crown of India and originating from the mighty Karakoram range is the Siachen, the second-longest glacier in the world. As one flies northwards from the base camp along the 76.4-kilometre-long glacier, one is dazed by the awesome beauty of the sea of ice and snow with moraines on both sides right up to the horizon. It is a surreal sight as the panoramic view of Sia Kangri, Indira Col and the other craggy and rocky peaks and pinnacles on both sides of the glacier slowly emerge from the white haze (Panorama 16.1). There is a famous saying attributed to the people of the region: 'The land is so barren and the passes so high that only the best of friends and the fiercest of enemies come by.' On the west of the Siachen is the rugged Saltoro range, which forms the watershed between Baltistan and Nubra valley of Ladakh region. Siachen in the Balti language means 'the place which has abundance of roses'. It is the source of the Nubra river that goes on to join the Shyok river, which has its origin in the area of the Karakoram Pass. The Shyok drains into the Indus near Skardu.

At the end of hostilities in the Indo-Pak war of 1947–48, a ceasefire line in J&K was agreed to by both countries and was authenticated on the maps. This delineation was specific up to a point – NJ 9842 – and

Panorama 16.1: The Siachen glacier and Karakoram range (Courtesy: Shanta Serbjeet Singh).

beyond that the agreement went on to say, '*and thence north to the glaciers*'. This position was maintained even after the Shimla agreement in 1972, although the ceasefire line (CFL) was renamed as the line of control (LoC). As no human presence on a permanent basis existed in these icy wastes, no thought was given to extending this line right up to the boundary of the princely state of J&K with China.

During the nineteenth and twentieth centuries, the historical 'Great Game' was played out by the British Empire and Czarist Russian Empire on the roof of the world. This was the famous region of the Pamir, Hindukush and the Karakoram ranges where the natural divide of Central and South Asia occurs. This game in a different avatar is being enacted by Pakistan and China against India since 1963, when they colluded and entered into an agreement wherein the Shaksgam valley, a part of India, was 'ceded' by Pakistan to China. This valley covers an area of about 5180 square kilometres and is on the north of the Karakoram range. When seen in the context of the sinister and illegal extension of the LoC from NJ 9842 eastwards to the Karakoram Pass by Pakistan, and the publication in some maps of this interpretation, the rationale of this 'Sino-Pak game' becomes crystal clear. The Shaksgam valley was part of the Dogra kingdom of Jammu and Kashmir, and since the state acceded to India in 1947, it lawfully became a part of our nation. (See Map 11.1 and Panorama 16.1.)

For China it would be more convenient to have the entire Karakoram range in Pakistan's possession right upto the Karakoram Pass, as the ceding of the Shaksgam valley would get sanctified with a higher level of certitude, than if the eastern Karakoram range from Sia La to the famous Karakoram Pass was part of India, and under Indian control. In actual fact, after the decisive victory in the 1971 Indo-Pak war, India had every reason to insist on a settlement of the alignment of the LoC in a northward direction towards the glaciers from NJ 9842 as per the original Karachi agreement of 1949. However, we lost out on that opportunity during the 1972 Shimla talks. According to an engrossing account given by renowned adventurer Harish Kapadia, 'A desperate Bhutto had pleaded with the Indian Prime Minister Indira Gandhi that he be trusted to do so (to agree to delineate the borders along the Saltoro range, but later), as he did not want to antagonize his generals at that point in time. *Aap mujhpe bharosa kijiye* (Trust me), he is reported to have said.'[1]

The Siachen issue gained prominence when cartographic aggression or errors were made in internationally published maps and atlases, which unilaterally decided to mark the extension of the LoC from NJ 9842 to the Karakoram Pass (see Map 11.1). Neither does this alignment go northwards nor are there any glaciers emanating from the Karakoram Pass. The issue was flagged with the US government by the ministry of external affairs at the behest of the army. However, there was no response from the Americans for quite some time. Eventually, after a lot of prodding, they replied that the 'papers' stating the reasons for this decision could not be traced! This was conveyed to me by Lieutenant General Hridya Kaul, who was the director general of military operations in the early 1980s. The foreign secretary during this period was Ram Sathe.

The situation was further exacerbated when our army learnt that the Pakistani authorities surreptitiously began to give permission to foreign mountaineering expeditions to climb or trek in the Siachen glacier area, taking full advantage of that cartographic misrepresentation. The Pakistan Army conveniently began to assume that the triangle formed by NJ 9842–Karakoram Pass–Sia Kangri was Pakistani territory, knowing well that it was a falsehood. It is a historical fact that the Saltoro range has been a traditional boundary between the Balti people, who are predominantly Shia Muslims, and the Ladakhis.

We came to know of Pakistan's intentions of setting up its military and civil presence in the Siachen area in 1982–83, even if that was partly for mountaineering or adventure activities. Therefore, the Indian Army sought the government's approval and, in a pre-emptive action, occupied most of the important passes and dominating heights on the Saltoro range during April 1984. This ridge line follows a northward direction from NJ 9842, east of which is de jure Indian territory. The operation was named 'Meghdoot' (divine cloud messenger), and it commenced on 13 April 1984. In this joint heliborne operation, the

---

[1] Harish Kapadia, *Into the Untravelled Himalaya*, Indus Publishing Company, New Delhi, p. 234.

Indian Army was ably supported by the Air Force. 'Bilafond La and Sia La were the first to be occupied by infantrymen; two soldiers heli-lifted at a time in the Alouettes or their Indian versions, the Cheetahs, the only helicopters which could operate at altitudes above 18,000 feet. This was a stupendous feat that required about fifty sorties, just for the initial build-up of one platoon at each of these passes!'[2] Thus India effectively pre-empted the Pakistani plans, and not only reclaimed its rightful territory but also restored the alignment of the LoC in a northward direction. Indian troops are deployed on all tactically important places on the Saltoro range. Pakistan responded by deploying its army on the lower heights and slopes on the western side, but they were not able to come close to the Siachen glacier. This is now referred to as the AGPL.

By firmly holding the Saltoro range, we physically denied them even a peep into the Siachen glacier. Pakistan has been falsely projecting to its people and to foreigners that its soldiers are fighting on the Siachen glacier. The reality is that the contest is for the control of the Saltoro range, which as of now is firmly in Indian hands.

In the 1980s and 1990s, the Pakistan Army undertook many unsuccessful ventures to try and capture some of these important passes or heights. The first such attack by the Pakistani forces, comprising Northern Light Infantry and commandos from the Special Services Group (SSG) took place on 25 April 1984 but was repulsed and they suffered many casualties. On the other hand, 8 J&K LI, in a gallant action, captured the highest Pakistani observation post called Qaid in April 1987. For this mission Subedar Bana Singh won the Param Vir Chakra. In retaliation, Pakistan launched a major attack in September 1987 called Operation Qiadat,[3] with one infantry battalion and two SSG companies with TOW missiles alongwith artillery and mortars in support. Because of the altitude and glaciated terrain, a large-sized operation is impossible. Therefore, a series of attacks were

---

[2] V.R. Raghavan, *Siachen – Conflict Without End*, Penguin Books India, New Delhi, p. 54.

[3] Description of the battle as seen from the Indian side.

launched to capture some positions on the Bilafond La Pass from 23–25 September 1987. It is believed that Pakistani President General Zia-ul-Haq had entrusted this task to the then brigadier, Pervez Musharraf, who is said to have planned the attacks from the SSG base at Khapalu in Pakistan-occupied Kashmir (PoK). Reportedly, close to a hundred Pakistani officers and men died in this operation and more than that number were wounded. A chilling account of these foolhardy and ill-conceived operations, but with outstanding junior leadership and youthful bravado, is given in the book *Fangs of Ice – Story of Siachen* by Lieutenant Colonel Ishfaq Ali of the Pakistan Army.

Since then the Pakistan Army has been desperately trying to get a foothold on the Saltoro range, but we have managed to frustrate every design of theirs. Having taken a number of casualties each time, Pakistan finally gave up making any more serious attempts to attack our positions in the Siachen area. However, artillery duels continued with great intensity, till the ceasefire in 2003. Both sides suffered a number of casualties, more on account of the high altitude, avalanches, accidents and medical causes. Just to maintain the troops in those positions has been at a price. But the fact remains that Siachen is Indian territory and even if we withdraw from the positions on the Saltoro range, we would have to keep adequate number of soldiers fully acclimatized and ready to defend our territory in this region. These troops will perforce have to be kept in the base camp area, and we would have to bear that expense anyway. Therefore, the cost factor loses its relevance considerably. Further, the human cost in terms of casualties due to altitude and extreme cold conditions has also been brought down to fairly acceptable levels.

Apart from exercising our right to safeguard our territorial integrity, there are some important gains achieved by our deployment in Siachen. By holding the Saltoro range we are in a position to deny direct access to the Karakoram Pass to Pakistan, and also retain a capability to exert some influence on the Indian territory in the Shaksgam valley, which Pakistan has illegally ceded to China. However, in the agreement with Pakistan, the Chinese have taken abundant precaution of qualifying that the agreement would be subject to renegotiation with the side that has sovereignty over the area, once the issue of Kashmir is resolved.

Over the years, there have been a series of talks and meetings to find a way to resolve the Siachen issue. I participated in the seventh round of talks in 1998 in New Delhi as the ADGMO. During these talks, we made our position clear that we were prepared to disengage or withdraw from the freezing heights on the Saltoro range, provided the Pakistanis agreed to authenticate the existing ground positions on the maps. This was primarily due to the trust deficit between the two countries, which has been exacerbated by the Pakistani misadventure in Kargil in 1999. The Pakistani side did not agree to authenticate the present positions, and hence the talks ended on the first day itself. During my tenure as ADGMO, I also accompanied the then defence minister, George Fernandes, to Siachen in 1998. He was one of the few ministers who made a number of visits to these forbidding heights, and with his support, we were able to do a lot to improve the living conditions of soldiers serving there, specially the medical facilities.

Subsequently, on 23 November 2003, both sides agreed to extend the ceasefire along the AGPL in the Siachen area too. This truce has held since then.

As the army chief, I accompanied Prime Minister Manmohan Singh on his visit to the glacier on 12 June 2005. He was the first prime minister to visit the glacier. He called for a peaceful resolution of the problem and made an appeal to make it a 'mountain of peace'. We discussed various dimensions of this issue during this visit. When asked for my views, I had no hesitation in stating that the army was ready for disengagement of forces to fall-back positions, in a phased manner. However, I strongly recommended that this step should only be taken once the Pakistanis agreed to authenticate the present positions. Without doing so, there was every possibility that they might renege from the agreement, grab some of our vacated positions, and then claim that they had always been there!

Further, it is my considered opinion that whenever an agreement is reached and a disengagement and redeployment of forces has to take place, it should be in phases and to positions from where neither side would have an unfair advantage of being able to occupy the area previously held by the other side. Any violation of the agreement by either side should allow the other side to take measures as considered necessary to have the status quo ante restored. In 1989, a proposed agreement for the two militaries to pull back forces and create a zone of disengagement never saw the light of the day. The main reason for this was that the Pakistani side did not want to disclose its actual positions on the ground. But in case it had done so and the agreement had gone through, it would have left the Indian forces in a rather disadvantageous position with respect to the scenario discussed above. In this regard, I find that some strategists and journalists have failed to comprehend the operational nuances of war-fighting in the Siachen glacier, and also the political compulsions that would have an overarching bearing while looking at options for conflict termination. As rightly brought out by Lieutenant General V.R. Raghavan, '... Indians and Pakistanis have attributed motives and pressures to the political and military leaders of the two countries. What was the reality? Certainly, from the Indian side no Prime Minister can accept a solution which would be seen as unequal by the public and the Parliament.'[4]

Fundamentally, there really is no logic to support the alignment claimed by Pakistan, a dotted line direct from NJ 9842 to the Karakoram Pass as erroneously shown in some maps, covering a distance of approximately 80 kilometres as the crow flies. Neither is this alignment going northwards nor is there any glacier emanating from the Karakoram Pass, thus making a mockery of the agreement between the two countries, which unambiguously states that from NJ 9842 ... 'thence north to the glaciers'. Therefore, India has been compelled to secure its territory and keep a permanent military presence on the Saltoro Range.

---

[4] V.R. Raghavan, *Siachen – Conflict Without End*, Penguin Books India (P) Ltd, New Delhi, p. 145.

17

Kargil
The Pakistani Misadventure

Jehad cannot be conducted with lies.
— *Jasarat*, the mouthpiece of Jamaat-e-Islami Pakistan.[1]

The Pakistan Army's misadventure in Kargil resulted in the Kargil war during May-June-July in 1999. In my tenure as the ADGMO in the military operations directorate at the Army HQ, this war was the most important challenge the nation faced. The initial surprise gained by the enemy was countered by a fierce response by the Indian Army. India's commendable achievement of giving the adversary a bloody nose, and throwing most of the Pakistani intruders [principally comprising battalions of the Northern Light Infantry (NLI) and elements of the regular Pakistan Army such as the Special Service Group (SSG)] back across the LoC, has been remarkable. A large number of their soldiers perished due to the harsh conditions in this rash and miscalculated venture. Eventually, an unambiguous victory was achieved by the Indian armed forces, as the Pakistani leadership agreed to withdraw the remnants of their force to their side of the LoC. So much has been written about this quaint and queer localized war, in a region that comprises barren glacial and high-altitude wastes of the tallest mountain ranges in the world.

The response of the Indian nation, and principally its army and the air force, despite the initial confusion and shock, was a fine example of the

[1] *The Times of India*, 24 June 1999, 'Tell the World the Truth, Jamaat Tells Pakistan PM'.

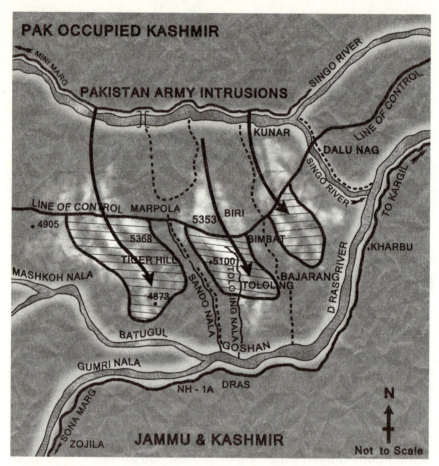

Sketch 17.1: The Pakistan Army's intrusions into Kargil (Mashkoh-Dras).

resolute will of the people and our armed forces, who were determined to avenge Pakistani aggression, and achieve victory at all costs. This was indeed beyond the comprehension of Pakistan, and therefore became the cause of much discomfort and embarrassment to General Pervez Musharraf and a few of his chosen field commanders and staff officers responsible for this costly and unmitigated military disaster. It was a hopeless and badly planned operation, not well thought through or professionally deliberated collectively, by the Pakistani military, ISI and civil leadership.

It was a war imposed on us by the Pakistan Army. Regular units of NLI, SSG and other elements of the Pakistan Army disguised as mujahideen intruded across the LoC in the Kargil sector upto a depth of six to eight kilometres, and occupied dominating heights in that rocky, barren and glaciated area. Some of them were wearing black Pathan suits as a measure to deceive the Indians, and came in through the unheld gaps. Historically, both sides considered such areas unviable for any worthwhile military operations, and consequently did not deploy troops to guard them. However, there were some posts that were occupied in summer and vacated in winter. It is worth mentioning that the average altitude of peaks in this area was in the region of 18,000 feet above sea level (see Sketches 17.1 and 17.2).

A first-hand account given by a Pakistani soldier who spent seventy-seven days in Indian territory in the Kargil area is recounted here:

> In the early days we mowed down many of them. Those Indians came like ants.... We also suffered a lot of casualties, many more than what officials in Pakistan are claiming.... The men who are fighting on those ridges know that they are in a hole from which they cannot come out alive.[2]

By attempting the unexpected, the Pakistani planners hoped to use surprise as a ploy and decided to launch this operation, named Badr, with the following objectives:

- Do a 'Siachen' on India, and thereby alter the status of the LoC for obvious gains. (Pakistan has not been able to live with India's pre-emptive securing of the Siachen area and thus planned to capture areas dominating National Highway 1A in an effort to interdict the road, and put pressure on India to vacate Siachen.)
- Internationalize the Kashmir issue.
- Give a boost to the flagging proxy war and terrorist activities in J&K.
- Isolate Turtok and Siachen by outflanking the Indian positions from the south.
- Open new routes of infiltration into the Kashmir valley from the Kargil and Turtok areas.

---

[2] *How I Started a War*, *Time* magazine, 12 July 1999.

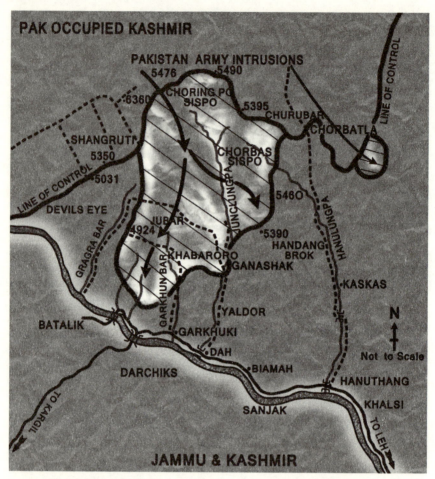

Sketch 17.2: The Pakistan Army's intrusions into Kargil (Batalik).

It has been revealed by researchers, including some from Pakistan, that as far back as 1987, a similar plan had been conceived. However, it was probably shelved as it was either considered foolhardy and impractical, or did not receive political clearance. On being appointed the army chief in 1998, General Musharraf, who is believed to be amongst the chief architects of Operation Badr, is likely to have taken out the earlier plan, brushed it up and fine-tuned it with his close confidants. 'There are indications that the plan (employing jehadis) was approved as early as October 1998 by Prime Minister Nawaz Sharif, when it was proposed to him by General Musharraf'.[3] It is believed that

[3] *Kargil Review Committee Report*, p. 95.

this core group, headed by Musharraf, included Lieutenant Generals Mohammad Aziz Khan, the chief of general staff, and Mahmud Ahmed, general officer commanding (GOC) 10 Corps, and Major General Javed Hasan, the force commander northern areas (FCNA). The plan was kept secret from both the air force and naval chiefs and also all other corps commanders. Key elements of the ISI would have been in the need-to-know loop. My understanding of this episode is that a generalized scenario employing *mujahideen* or so-called 'freedom fighters' might have been articulated to get the nod of the prime minister, without going into details or specifying that the Pakistan Army soldiers and officers would be undertaking this operation across the LoC.

Therefore, in my perception, to cloak this suicidal venture in a shroud of secrecy, a great fraud was committed by General Musharraf and his inner coterie on not only the people of Pakistan but also on the Pakistan Army. This is particularly so in the case of the gallant soldiers of the NLI and the simple people of Gilgit, Hunza, Skardu and others from the Northern Area. The truth began to emerge within a few weeks, when the battle was joined by the Indians. Despite denials by Pakistan, it did not take long for the world to become aware as to who was right, and who had committed the aggression.

The Indian military response was slow and measured, massive and ruthless, notwithstanding the hiccups in the beginning. While ensuring that we didn't create a strategic imbalance elsewhere along the western border, the Indian Army retaliated with everything that was necessary and could be put into the battle to recapture the heights of Kargil. Additional forces, including infantry formations, artillery, air defence, army aviation and other combat support and logistics units, were pumped into this theatre. The government approved the use of the air force on 25 May 1999, albeit on our side of the LoC only. For us in the military operations directorate, it was like a war, whether declared or not. We began working 24×7 since we got the first situation report from the Corps HQ at Srinagar on 8–9 May 1999. Frequently, we had to stay up all night and follow the progress of the battle. After all we were dealing with blatant aggression and a rogue action by the adversary to capture our territory. We accepted the challenge and adopted a mission mode. It was our firm determination to get the intruders out and restore the sanctity of the LoC. If it called for a hard kick on their butts, so be it.

Initially, in the second and third weeks of May 1999, we suffered quite a few setbacks. It must be admitted that our forward troops and commanders were caught off guard and their early assessments of the situation were totally off the mark. Firstly, the enemy situation was not at all clear, and secondly, pressure was being put from all directions for early action to throw the intruders out, as a result of which hasty and uncoordinated attacks without adequate artillery support were launched by our units and formations. The fog of war, coupled with total denial of any involvement by the Pakistan Army, resulted in inaccurate assessments of the aim, strength and dispositions of the intruders in the initial stage. It took us almost a week or two to get the overall picture right. Having got our act together, the strategy evolved was to obtain the details of the intrusions, contain them and systematically clear them. We laid down priorities and planned to capture the enemy positions accordingly. Features dominating Dras, like Tololing and Tiger Hill, were accorded the highest priority. However, we had to keep in mind the caveat by the government that the LoC should not be crossed. This imposed certain constraints on our operational plans as we could not isolate and cut off the enemy positions from the rear in all cases.

Waves of well-planned and coordinated infantry assaults, mostly from the flanks or rear, with overwhelming artillery support, including multi-barrel rocket launchers, and debilitating air attacks using precision-guided munitions, presented the Pakistani soldiers on our side of the LoC with a hopeless scenario, and a clear verdict – surrender, die or withdraw. There was just no other option, despite the tall claims made by General Musharraf and some others.

The first position of tactical importance to be captured was the Tololing peak on 13 June 1999. This feature was about five kilometres from the highway and the village of Dras, and was dominating both effectively. It fell after repeated attacks as the Pakistanis gave stiff resistance. The next prominent objective to be captured was the Tiger Hill. This battle was also well contested and the pinnacle-shaped peak was eventually captured on 4 July. There were celebrations in the Indian Army and the nation looked on with pride and awe at our achievements. It was celebration time with champagne and chocolate cake. The TV channels had galvanized the people and taken the war into every home. At a press briefing as the army spokesperson during mid-June '99, I was asked by one reporter as to when the war was likely to finish. I replied that it was the Pakistanis who initiated this conflict, but it is we who shall end it, and on our terms.

On the same day that Nawaz Sharif was in Washington, Tiger Hill was recaptured by us. Seeing the writing on the wall, he had sought an urgent meeting with President Clinton. Before Nawaz Sharif left Pakistan for the meeting, he was told by the Americans in no uncertain terms that restoration of the sanctity of the LoC as decided during the Shimla Agreement and ceasefire was 'non-negotiable and Pakistani forces would have to fall back'.[4] As events unfolded, 'the Americans bluntly told him of the seriousness of the situation, including the nuclear dimension, and he signed the joint statement'.[5] The purpose of this statement, however, was to give a veneer of face-saving to the Pakistan Army. The average citizen of Pakistan and even their armed forces, not knowing the truth, have unjustly placed the entire blame on the political leadership of their country for the withdrawal of their troops from the remaining positions in Kargil.

During the period up to 7 July, several other peaks were recaptured by our troops, such as Pt 4875 and a few more features to its north in the Mashko sector; Pts 5140, 4700 and 5100 to the north of Tololing in the Dras sector; Pt 5203 and the Jubar area in the Batalik Sector. Towards the end it became an unequal fight, with the situation getting more and more precarious and hopeless for the Pakistani troops with each passing day.

The real villains of this sad chapter of Pakistan's history will only be exposed if an official review of the events leading to the Kargil war and

[4] Bill Clinton, *My Life*, Knopf, 2004, p. 865.
[5] Bruce Reidel, *American Diplomacy and the 1999 Kargil Summit at Blair House*, Center for the Advanced Study of India, 2002, pp. 11 to 13.

the operational handling of the conflict is undertaken in Pakistan. The whole edifice of lies and subterfuge will be shattered, but so will the national honour. Hence, the cloak of secrecy is unlikely to be lifted officially in the forseeable future. But can the people of the Northern Areas and other Pakistanis whose kith and kin were used as cannon fodder, and what is worse, were left abandoned in the battlefield without proper burial, ever forget it? This has happened earlier too – one has only to look at the misadventures of Pakistan in 1947 and 1965. It was reassuring to read that 'the PPP-led Government has decided to close the gates for any Kargil-like misadventure in future through legislation that will require the Cabinet's approval for declaration of war'.[6]

The ill-conceived and Machiavellian Pakistani plan was based on wrong assumptions and a foundation of deniability. As I saw it in my assignment as the ADGMO in the Army HQ, where we had to grapple with the challenge in Kargil, and in higher appointments later on, the following points stood out:

- Operation Badr was based on secrecy, deception and the belief that once Pakistani soldiers had secured the peaks, their positions would be unassailable. Their ingression would present a fait accompli, and their contention that the LoC was vague might even get accepted by the world.
- The planners underestimated the resolve and determination of the Indian Army to throw them out, and the guts to take the casualties that were inevitable. They thought that the Indians would acquiesce.
- Pakistan felt that once skirmishes took place, they would raise the ante and ask for intervention and ceasefire by the UN or the West. The nuclear sabre could always be rattled.
- The provision of deniability was inbuilt in the plan as till the very end, the Pakistan Army officially maintained the façade that the intruders were mujahideen and that their army was not involved. This was a ridiculous stand to take in the face of irrefutable evidence emerging every day as the conflict raged on. Pakistani soldiers taken as POWs, a large number of identity cards of Pakistan Army, and

[6] Shafqat Ali, *The Asian Age*, 10 September 2009.

some of the heavy weapons and equipment captured by our troops made the Pakistani position totally untenable. As a result, they blatantly disowned a large number of their dead soldiers, which is highly shameful – a stamp of disgrace that no army in the world could possibly live with. Some of their fallen soldiers, whose bodies were retrieved by the Pakistanis, were handed over to their families in Gilgit or Skardu areas at night with the instructions that the bodies should be buried before daybreak, all in the name of secrecy. The sordid facets of Operation Badr have been highlighted by both Pakistani and Indian authors:

'Gafoor Khan, a resident of village Hamaidas, told Ilyas that, "on June 8, 1999 they got the body of his brother, Sepoy Shakur Jan of 12 NLI. His wife, three daughters and others were shocked at the furtive way in which these bodies were brought by soldiers in civil clothes in the dead of the night – as if they were bodies of criminals." There were no honours, no last post and no civic receptions.'[7]

'Because of the lack of factual information given to the population, rumours and negative stories were bound to spread, which continue to hold sway even today.'[8]

- As a measure of surprise and deception they had used wireless operators fluent in Balti, Pushto or other Northern area dialects. Most of the transmissions were in these languages. So besides being difficult to interpret, this was another ruse to create the false impression that they were mujahideen.
- Another false justification trotted out by General Musharraf, who has stated in his memoirs[9] that the Indians were preparing to attack in the Shaqma area in PoK, was never mentioned on any occasion either before or after the conflict. As the Pakistan Army prepared for the intrusion from October 1998 to May 1999, the Indian Army was in winter configuration.
- To accuse Prime Minister Nawaz Sharif of a sellout in Washington on 4 July, instead of taking the blame himself, was another example

[7] Anil Bhat in the *Sentinel*, 13 September 2009.
[8] Shireen M. Mazari, *The Kargil Conflict 1999*, Institute of Strategic Studies, Islamabad, p. 76.
[9] Pervez Musharraf, *In the Line of Fire*, Free Press, New York, 2006, p. 88.

of passing the buck by General Musharraf. In the Pakistani system, as brought out by Bruce Reidel, in his paper on American diplomacy referred to earlier, even the preparations for possible deployment of nuclear missiles by the Pakistan Army were not known to Nawaz Sharif, and he was shown the relevant satellite photos by the Americans. Similarly, it is unlikely that he was given the full picture of what Operation Badr was all about and what it involved.

Another major adverse fallout of the jehadi cover for Operation Badr was that Pakistani media did not know how to project the actions of the Pakistan Army. In fact, they were also fed false information and accordingly kept eulogizing the initial success of the mujahideen, when they should have been praising the actions of the Pakistan Army. This was in stark contrast with the role played by the Indian media and the handling of the media by the Indian side. The electronic and the print media became force multipliers, and as described earlier, television took the war to people's living rooms. Though there was some critical reporting, by and large the media was very positive and raised the morale of the soldiers, and made every Indian feel that they were a part of the war. This was the first time such a thing had happened. We allowed the media everywhere, as we had nothing to hide. I was involved in deciding the media policy as the 'operations guy', and was the military's spokesperson or interface with the media on important occasions during the Kargil War, along with Air Commodore Bhojwani and Raminder Jassal from the ministry of external affairs. The media moulded the minds of the people worldwide, bringing out the righteousness of the cause for which the Indian soldiers were fighting. This was not the case in respect of the Pakistan Army, as has been very aptly put across by Shireen Mazari in her book, *The Kargil Conflict*:

> The information war was lost from the start because of the decision not to inform the public at home and an equally half-hearted approach regarding what to give out to the international community.[10]

[10] Shireen M. Mazari, *The Kargil Conflict 1999*, Institute of Strategic Studies, Islamabad, p. 76.

General Musharraf's lies have been exposed by the honours and awards announced by Pakistan after the war concluded. There were two Nishan-e-Haider (equivalent of our Param Vir Chakra), twenty-five Sitara-e-Jurrat, thirty-two Tamgha-e-Jurrat and many other awards given to Pakistan Army officers and soldiers. Captain Karnal Sher Khan was killed while leading a counter-attack to recapture Tiger Hill, which was about 5–6 kilometres inside our territory. He was awarded the highest gallantry award by Pakistan. Was his action in support of the mujahideen or as a Pakistani soldier masquerading as a freedom fighter?

In his book *In the Line of Fire*, Musharraf avoids talking of the number of casualties taken by the Pakistan Army. According to one estimate, the Pakistan Army suffered 772 fatalities. These included sixty-nine officers and seventy-six soldiers from the SSG. Over a thousand were wounded, while eight were captured alive by our troops.[11] Bodies of over 200 of their soldiers were left behind in Indian territory, lying in the open or partly covered by stones. These were then buried as per Islamic rites by Indian troops, as the Pakistanis did not make concerted efforts to take them back! They specifically asked for the return of the bodies of three officers only, including Captain Karnal Sher Khan and Captain Taimur Malik, which was done by us. This will be recorded as an extremely shameful episode in their military history. (In 2010, the Pakistan Army released names of 453 officers and men who died in the Kargil war. This figure is believed to be on the lower side.)

One more lie trotted out by the Pakistanis was that the LoC was vague in the Kargil sector. Even a Pakistani map captured during this conflict clearly showed the LoC printed on it joining one prominent peak with the other. When this was shown to the Pakistanis, along with other documents such as identity cards and diaries during the meeting of the directors general of military operations at Attari near the Wagah border outpost on 11 July 1999, their faces turned red.

As far as our side was concerned, the Kargil Review Committee did a great service to the nation by bringing out their report in record

---

[11] Amarinder Singh, *A Ridge Too Far*, 2001, p. 102.

time. They have comprehensively brought out the lessons that emerged during this war and I have no desire to go into those details. We in the MO directorate assisted this committee in preparing this report by making available all relevant records of Operation Vijay, the name we coined once the hostilities commenced in May 1999. All the same, I wish to share my personal observations of how we fought the war:

- We were indeed taken unawares and overwhelmed by the unexpected developments in Kargil. Though we had been getting some driblets of information in 1988–89 about Pakistani activities in the Kargil area, our focus remained on counterterrorism operations in J&K. It was a collective failure at all levels for us not to be able to make a cohesive analysis and see the big picture. I distinctly recollect reports of underslung loads being carried by helicopters in the valleys laterally along the LoC. There were some other reports of heightened activities across the LoC in Kargil sector. As the forward troops and the brigade, division and the corps HQ did not find anything unusual or amiss in that activity, we also let it pass. But what beats my comprehension is that the Pakistan Army was able to penetrate six to seven kilometers and occupy positions overlooking Dras and the highway, without being detected. There was not much snow on some of these very high and rugged features and therefore, our surveillance plans, which included ground patrols and aerial surveillance, left much to be desired. These intruders should have been discovered much earlier.
- As for the evolution of the strategy and the higher direction of war during Operation Vijay, the MO operations' room was the hub of activities and we worked as a well-knit team. Lieutenant General N.C. Vij was the DGMO. Although we had the guidance and directions of the vice chief, the presence of the chief, General V.P. Malik, during the initial stage of this conflict would have made a difference. We made a number of presentations to the Cabinet Committee for Security (CCS), headed by Prime Minister A.B. Vajpayee, Deputy Prime Minister and Home Minister L.K. Advani, Defence and External Affairs Minister Jaswant Singh, Finance Minister Yashwant Sinha, National Security Adviser Brajesh

Mishra, the service chiefs, heads of IB and R&AW and the cabinet secretary, starting 18 May.

At that time, based on the reports of the forward troops and formations as well as the IB and R&AW, our assessment of the intrusions was hazy. We accepted the analysis of HQ 15 Corps and Northern Command that the intruders were mujahideen who were being supported by the ISI and the Pakistan Army, and that they would be evicted in two or three weeks. Yet there was something that was not gelling. We had discussions in the MO directorate and started planning for various eventualities. Orders were given for certain forces to be sidestepped within the divisional sector, the corps zone and the command theatre and gathering of intelligence. Orders for relocation of some Army HQ reserves and other formations from the Eastern Command were also issued. The strategy that was emerging was to contain and limit the intrusions, punitive engagement with artillery, mortars, rockets and long-range direct firing weapons, isolation of the intruders, and their eviction in a systematic manner. In this period, certain hastily planned local actions taken at brigade and division levels met with failure and led to avoidable casualties. In the meanwhile, the Pakistani establishment continued to make ridiculous statements, such as the one by their foreign minister Sartaj Aziz, 'that the infiltrators could be fighters from Afghanistan who may have crossed the LoC in support of the local mujahideen forces, and that the LoC was vague and undefined.'[12]

- The presentations, particularly the review of the operational situation and the progress of our operations in the MO operations room, were my responsibility as the ADGMO. I was present during all discussions on the progress of operations. We were told that we should take care not to cross the LoC, and keep the conflict localized; further, diplomatic and other pressure would be put on Pakistan to vacate. The employment of the air force was approved by the CCS on 25 May 1999, albeit on our side of the LoC only. During the course of the war there were four or five occasions when this high-powered body met

---

[12] Jaswant Singh, *A Call to Honour*, Rupa & Co, New Delhi, p. 208 and *The Asian Age*, Wednesday, 11 June 2008.

to review the progress of operations. In one meeting towards the end of June, when the tide had definitely turned in our favour, a question was posed, 'What if the Pakistanis agree to withdraw?' Since no one responded, I got up and suggested that we should continue our operations till we finish the assigned task. When asked as to how long that would take, I responded that it could take a few weeks more. Then there was some discussion on the number of casualties that might occur and so on. Such interactions ensured that well-considered decisions were taken by our political and military hierarchy after a deliberate analysis. This did not seem to be the case as far as Pakistan was concerned, in view of the hush-hush manner in which the Kargil war was prosecuted. Shireen Mazari hit the nail on the head when she articulated that, 'Essentially, the advantage Pakistan gained at the tactical level was lost at the strategic level – especially the initiative, primarily for lack of an institutionalized national response.'[13]

- At first the Indian Army did not make much headway as it tried to mount assaults along the spurs. These approaches were well defended. It was my suggestion to move trained mountaineers from the high-altitude warfare school in Gulmarg to each infantry battalion along with soldiers from Ladakh Scouts. This gave our troops the capability of attacking the formidable 'sangar' (a defensive position made by heaping stones and rocks) from the steep flanks or the rear by using mountaineering skills and rock-climbing techniques. The attack on Tiger Hill in this manner overwhelmed the enemy with surprise, and our soldiers achieved a glorious victory. Such attacks tilted the scale irrevocably in our favour, and heralded the beginning of the end of Operation Vijay.

- By 10 July 1999, through a series of pincer movements, most of the Pakistani-held positions were in the process of being isolated and their logistics chain severely disrupted. The ration stocks at most of the captured localities were at precarious levels. There was little or no medical cover at most locations. It must be appreciated that to evacuate one casualty in such altitudes two teams of four soldiers

---

[13] Shireen M. Mazari, *The Kargil Conflict 1999*, Institute of Strategic Studies, Islamabad, p. 77.

each would be required. Where would the manpower come from? Either the post would have to be abandoned or else the wounded soldier left to die. In some positions there was an acute shortage of drinking water too. The Indian Army was closing in on all positions. The Mashko valley was addressed in the later phases as it was on a flank, but it was just a matter of a few more weeks. The remainder of the positions held by the demotivated and demoralized Pakistani NLI and other regular army soldiers were falling like nine pins. In the MO operations room it was a welcome sign to see the red pins (indicating positions held by Pakistani troops) being replaced by blue at a faster pace every day. The claims made by General Musharraf that the remaining Pakistani positions could have held out, were utopian, wishful and unrealistic.

- The effective use of artillery and the air force gave us an unbeatable edge over the Pakistanis. Most of the attacks were launched with overwhelming fire support of over one hundred guns, mortars and multi-barrel rocket launchers. Thousands of shells, bombs and rockets carrying many tons of TNT breaking into warped shrapnels of metal, wreaked havoc on the enemy. We were aware that hitting the targets in such a difficult and rocky terrain with knife-edged ridges was very difficult, yet the boom of the guns and sound of the blasts reverberating in the mountains played on the minds of the soldiers of both sides – positive and morale-boosting in our case, and demoralizing for the Pakistani soldiers. It is estimated that a large percentage of Pakistani casualties occurred due to the artillery shelling. At Muntho Dhalo, which was an important logistic base in the Batalik sector, the air force and artillery caused heavy casualties – the Pakistan Army lost five officers and many troops in one of these bombardments. The gunners innovated and perfected their skills of direct shooting and the performance of the 155mm Bofors gun was indeed praiseworthy.
- The invaluable contribution of the Indian Air Force during the Kargil war in offensive air strikes against enemy strong points and administrative bases, aerial imagery and logistics support by its fighter and transport aircraft, including helicopters, proved to be a war-winning factor. Air operations were named Operation Safed

Sagar, in which our air force demonstrated to the world how air power could be applied at such high altitudes even with constraints like non-violation of the air space beyond the LoC. The operations branches at the Army and Air HQ worked in close coordination during this war. As ADGMO, I conducted the briefing of ground operations for the air chief and senior commanders at the Air HQ during the crucial phase of this conflict.

- The crucial role played by the Indian Navy is a lesser-known fact of this war. The navy was put on a full alert from 20 May 1999, in order to meet any challenge at sea and for surveillance. To put pressure on Pakistan, strike elements from the Eastern Fleet were moved to the North Arabian Sea. This use of naval power opposite the Makaran coast forced Pakistan Navy to move its fleet from Karachi and get into a defensive mode. We also moved some amphibious force elements from Andaman and Nicobar islands to the western coast. This naval operation was named 'Talwar' and proved to be an effective deterrent to escalation of hostilities beyond Kargil and also to safeguard our maritime interests.
- The Indian Army suffered a total of 522 fatal casualties, which included twenty-six officers and twenty-three junior commissioned officers, and over a thousand were wounded as conveyed by the defence minister in Parliament. For their conspicuous gallantry and sacrifices, four Param Vir Chakras, nine Mahavir Chakras, fifty-three Vir Chakras and many other gallantry and distinguished services medals were awarded to our officers and men.
- The Air Force lost three officers and two airmen. Flight Lieutenant Nachiketa became a POW as his aircraft crashed after being hit by a stinger missile, and he bailed out and landed on the Pakistani side of the LoC. The air warriors were decorated with two Vir Chakras and twenty-three Vayu Sena Medals besides other distinguished service awards.

When the conflict ended, the DGMO asked me to prepare a historical record of the Kargil war. I formed a team from the MO directorate and made out a broad framework for the task. We asked for the detailed account of operations carried out by all the formations in 15 Corps during Operation Vijay. Once we got these reports, we worked in a time-bound manner and within a few months produced the history of this war. It was printed in-house in the MO directorate and disseminated down to division level. This is perhaps the only war where a history has been written by the MO directorate. It is a voluminous record and has an executive summary and four or five volumes covering all dimensions of the war. Hopefully, someday it would be declassified and available in the public domain. Many officers were decorated amongst our team at the MO directorate. I was awarded an Ati Vishisht Seva Medal and was decorated by the president in 2000.

During my tenure, we were able to get a special allowance sanctioned by the government, named as the highly active field area (HAFA) allowance. There has always been a clamour for an 'infantry allowance' to compensate the infantry rank and file for the high percentage of casualties, hardships of service and the separation from their families that they have to endure. Though justifiable, I was sure that this idea would not be acceptable to the officialdom within the army and also in the ministry of defence. On the other hand, it occurred to me that everyone who serves within selected zones classified as 'highly active' along our long and unsettled border, should get an allowance that would be higher than that of a field area or counter-insurgency area allowance. In this case we called the joint secretaries from the ministry of defence, defence (finance), and finance to the MO operations room and after showing them these zones on the map, gave them the rationale, logic and the financial implications related to the proposal. In just one meeting, it was agreed to in principle by everyone. We moved the file after that, and got the government's approval in a month or two. Over 90 per cent of the beneficiaries of this allowance, which is in force even today, happen to be from the infantry.

On 29 October 1999, a massive and unforgettable natural disaster struck in the coastal districts of Orissa near Cuttack. The supercyclone, called Paradip, a deadly mix of a hurricane and a gigantic tidal surge, left about 10,000 dead, and over a million homeless. The massive surge travelled upto 10–15 kilometres inland, destroying everything in its wake. It was one of the biggest cyclones to have hit India. The state government sought help from the ministry of defence and the armed forces were requisitioned. All communications with the region had been cut off. Army columns were rushed in by road from Ranchi to the disaster-hit areas. Air force and army helicopters as well as naval ships were pressed into rescue and relief operations. The defence minister, George Fernandes, asked me to accompany him to Orissa as he wished to oversee the aid being rendered by the armed forces. We could not land in the state capital as the air traffic facilities and communications at Bhubaneswar airport had been disabled, and therefore had to land at Ranchi, and then proceed ahead by helicopter.

We were horrified to see the devastation caused by this twister. Like a giant vacuum cleaner it had wiped out many villages without any trace. The only shreds of evidence that remained were small clean patches where people's homes were once! The army columns moving by vehicles faced a herculean task of clearing hundreds of trees and other obstructions from the roads, and a journey of eight hours took them two to three days. The administrative set-up and the law and order machinery was in a traumatized mess. Not surprisingly, everyone had gotten busy trying to reorganize their own personal lives. The sad reality was that their official duties and functions had taken a back seat.

My stay in the Army HQ as the ADGMO was one of the longest ever in that post. It happened because the government announced a two-year extension of service across the board for all. In fact, our promotion board from major general to lieutenant general had to be held two times.

It was during this tenure that my son, Vivek, got married to his French girlfriend, Anna. We went to attend their wedding in Normandy during the summer of 1998. It was a simple but elegantly arranged function, with a registered marriage followed by a reception and a lovely dinner which carried on till the wee hours. In the merrymaking we danced and most of us had more than our share of champagne, cheese and wine. Later in the year they came to Delhi for celebrating the wedding in true Punjabi traditions in the gurdwara. They have two wonderful daughters, Anne-Tara and Marie-Sana, and live in a country home near St Lo, in Normandy. Vivek runs a business in designing and developing handicrafts, household accessories and gift items and sources them from India, while Anna works for a social organization. My daughter, Urvashi Kaur (Sonia as we call her), is an acclaimed fashion designer, and her husband, Gagan Dugal, runs a successful global company that provides services for cellular communications. They have three wonderful children – Seerat, Suveer and Sumair – and live in Delhi.

18

Command of Strike Corps and Exercise Poorna Vijay

Towards the end of 2000, while I was still serving as ADGMO, I was told that I would soon be taking over the 'Strike Corps' located at Mathura. It was a matter of great pride for me to get the command of 1 Corps, which had a glorious history and the distinction of winning Param Vir Chakras in both the 1965 and 1971 Indo-Pak wars.

As was the norm, every major formation was put through an exercise with troops once every three to four years. 1 Corps had not been exercised for quite a few years. It was suggested that the exercise should be conducted in the summer of 2001. For a newly promoted corps commander like me it was a great challenge. During peace, exercises like these are the closest that we can get to actual war. Importantly, they help the officers and men of the entire formation to get to know each other, rehearse their respective missions or roles, and become more conversant with their weapon systems and equipment. Moreover, the real state of our operational readiness comes to the fore.

Taking over the corps in January 2001, I settled down as fast as possible, as within a few months we were to leave for Rajasthan for the exercise. It had been named Exercise Mayhem, but no one could tell me why!

What is so important about the name of an exercise or manoeuvre? I believe that the name of an important corps-level exercise should connote the conceptual essence of the mission, or else convey a telling message not only to the troops participating in it, but to the army and the nation at large as well. It would amount to professional sacrilege if the name of a major exercise was decided nonchalantly, without relevance to the aforementioned aspects, and more so on the whims and fancies of the commander concerned, howsoever humorous his intentions might have been. In my reckoning, 'Mayhem' did not gel as a name for an exercise with troops at a corps level. What motivation or inspiration would the officers and soldiers draw out of it? Though these manoeuvres were to be held in the month of May, and there is always an element of confusion in every exercise, yet it did not justify being called Exercise Mayhem or Summer Madness.

Once the initial formalities and visits were over, I sought a meeting with the army commander, Lieutenant General Pankaj Joshi, to discuss issues relating to operational tasks, training and administration and the forthcoming exercise. A seasoned soldier, the GOC-in-C welcomed me and we had a pleasant conversation. I also discussed the exercise with him and he approved the overall strategic theme, aim, scope and the lessons to be brought out. Finally, I told him I would like to change the name of the exercise to Poorna Vijay. He agreed.

While flying in the Cheetah helicopter (an indigenous version of the French Alouette) from Mathura to Lucknow for this meeting, I had a brush with death. Brigadier Jasbir Lidder, an outstanding professional, was my brigadier general staff. The lanky officer wanted to explain something on the map. In the process of opening the mapsheet, he spread his legs and stamped his boot on the collective lever of the chopper. There was a cracking sound and the chopper went down with a jerk. The pilot, who had momentarily taken his hand off the collective when this happened, quickly grabbed the lever and arrested the fall. For a moment I thought we were gone!

In my long military career, I was often witness to unprofessional higher commanders trashing an exercise while it was being conducted, and that too in the presence of junior officers and men. This could only happen if the big boss hadn't bothered to give clear directions regarding what the exercise ought to achieve, and importantly, how, when and where it was to be conducted. This definitely reflected poorly on such higher commanders. Besides, such actions lowered the confidence of the junior leaders and tended to confuse the rank and file too. We must remember it is these junior leaders who would actually conduct the manoeuvres, and also lead their men in battle.

On getting back I held a conference of my team. It was my first encounter with my staff and advisers posted at the corps headquarters.

'When was the corps exercised last, and are there any documents or after-action reports available?' I demanded. Since no one had any answer, I realized that we would have to start from scratch. Hence, I directed everyone present, as well as all others concerned, to get on with the preparations for Exercise Poorna Vijay on a war footing.

Having prepared my subordinates mentally, the next challenge was to field the tanks, armoured fighting vehicles, guns and other combat weapons platforms for the exercise. The equipment-intensive Strike Corps is like an Anaconda and the slumber from which it had to be woken up also meant making up the deficiencies and bringing the obsolete or off-road equipment back in shape. Considering the time constraints, this was no mean task. But thanks to the Kargil conflict, the Army HQ was more receptive to our requests and we were able to receive most of the equipment, though some of this happened because of my previous posting as ADGMO. My staff worked out the approximate cost of our inventory of tanks, guns, missiles, transport and equipment, and it came to a whopping 25,000 crore rupees!

Exercises in the desert of Rajasthan were generally conducted during the winter period to avoid the hot summer, when the temperatures could shoot up to 50 degrees Celsius. This time we wanted to test man and machine in the scorching heat.

For any professional military leader, there is no greater joy or satisfaction than to take his command out for a manoeuvre and rehearse his assigned tasks or mission. For me it would be a great learning experience to conduct an exercise of the Strike Corps, with over 50,000 troops taking part in it; an infantry and an armoured division, a couple of artillery brigades, an air defence brigade, a para battalion, an engineer brigade, signal regiments, electronic warfare elements, a special forces unit, army aviation units and the air force projecting its firepower and its transport and heavy drop capabilities, and the entire gamut of logistics units, including a nuclear, biological and chemical decontamination unit being fielded for the first time. In this exercise the air force was co-opted from the inception and planning stage, right through to the conflict termination phase. This exercise was a rare occasion when the parachute battalion was dropped at night with the chief of army staff and other top brass witnessing it. This was one of the largest exercises since 'Brass Tacks' held during the late 1980s. The GoC-in-C, Lieutenant General P. Joshi, was present for the major part of the exercise. The media was allowed unprecedented access to actions taking place. It was a 'media blitz' aimed at sending a message to Pakistan, as noted by analyst Vikram Vyas.

The plethora of equipment we possessed was put to test not only in the offensive manoeuvres, but had to withstand the harsh conditions of immense heat and sand storms. Modern warfare has brought in heavy reliance on technology. I wondered how the IT experts got the computers and the network connectivity going in such high temperatures and sandstorms where the fine dust permeated into every space. I was constantly worried about the missile storage and resupply, which needs a sanitized, dustproof and cool environment. Each modern gadget or gizmo that contributes to efficiency needs power supply, and we had to face the challenge of making it work in a highly mobile environment. The total wattage produced by all the generators required to keep the Strike Corps energized, could easily meet the needs of a small town in India. The corps of EME (electronic and mechanical engineers) smilingly provided what was almost an electricity department to handle the task. The communications were through a 'rolling grid' based on the concept of the commercial mobile phone network that we use extensively today. In our case, it was purely an exclusive military network providing multiple and secure connectivity. I was always through to my HQ even when I was airborne in the helicopter.

We left our peace stations in March and moved by road and rail to the exercise area in Rajasthan. The role of the corps is such that we have to acquire the capability of moving across the breadth of the country rapidly and by different means of transportation. In our case some units and formations had to cover about 1400 kilometres to gather for the exercise. We were able to rustle up 80–90 per cent of the posted strength so that this war-like experience was of benefit to maximum officers and men. It was also a good opportunity to assess the knowledge, capabilities and leadership qualities of the higher commanders as well as of the junior leaders. During such manoeuvres, one could identify the professionally sound or unfit individuals, sub units and units; an experienced eye could easily gauge the state of morale and motivation of men and the units as a whole.

In this joint army-air offensive exercise, we had planned to try out new concepts, strategy and tactics. These included use of high technology, employment of UAVs and sensors, exploitation of enhanced night fighting capabilities, IT, information warfare, joint operations and fighting through a nuclear environment. Air power and army aviation assets were effectively enmeshed as war-winning factors and their capabilities optimally showcased. For the first time, we tried out the concept of a mobile forward surgical centre – an 'operation theatre on wheels'. This was achieved by joining four air-conditioned vehicles and connecting them with an airtight passage to make this facility dust-proof and air-conditioned. This was located next to the field hospital. We also fielded a nuclear, biological and chemical (NBC) warfare shelter and a decontamination unit.

Being an important exercise, and also because of the hype created by the media, we had many visitors and observers during various phases of this event. In fact, the presence of the defence minister, Jaswant Singh, the army chief, General S. Padmanabhan, Air Chief Marshal A.Y. Tipnis and other army, air force and naval higher commanders was morale boosting. The presence of defence attachés of friendly countries, and a host of mediapersons, including those from the BBC and CNN, heightened the profile of the manoeuvres even further. Often, these visitors were the cause of avoidable disruption and distraction. Some of the senior officers even went to the extent of interfering in the conduct of the exercise. Hence, they had to be politely but firmly put in their place. It was conveyed to participating units and formations that all outsiders were to be treated as visitors irrespective of their rank or status. However, it boosted our morale to have the defence minister and the army chief amongst us in May, sharing the heat and dust storms of Rajasthan. The defence minister decided to live with us in the Corps Tactical HQs tucked away in the sand dunes, as did General Padmanabhan, rather than in the circuit house nearby. He was quite at home living for two nights in my caravan based on a 3-ton Shaktiman truck, which I had christened Chetak. He was also happy to move around in my custom-built jeep that was my operations room on wheels. Air Chief Marshal A.Y. Tipnis not only attended the exercise, but also flew a MIG 21 sortie in support of Blueland.

The defence minister was very keen to see the tanks in action, as he had himself served in the cavalry before joining politics. Therefore, it was planned to fly him in a MI 17 helicopter over the exercise area, and make him witness a modern tank battle. Unlike many such high-profile events that are stage-managed and rehearsed, this one was not. I wanted the defence minister and my chief to see the exercise as it was unfolding, the real stuff, warts and all. Before taking off, I briefed the pilots on the map about the axis on which the armoured columns were advancing, and the few prominent landmarks to follow, so that we could fly over the area and see the activities from the air.

Unfortunately, the pilots were new to this area, having flown all the way from Delhi only a day back. The helicopters for the minister and the army chief belonged to the elite VIP Squadron. We seemed to have run out of luck as despite their best efforts, we could not spot any movement of tanks or even the odd blaze of dust in that vast featureless desert that we could see up to the horizon! The pilots kept trying for almost an hour, and eventually gave up. They sought my directions to turn back to base. I went into the cockpit and asked the crew to give it one more go. Sitting in the cockpit on the bench meant for the navigator, I put on the headphones and got into the navigation act, but to no avail. Just when we thought that it was pointless to go on, I suddenly sighted a few small dust clouds on the horizon.

I asked the pilot to fly in the direction of those specks, and lo and behold! we came across the most wonderful sight; that of a whole regiment of armour blazing rapidly across the desert. Each tank was furiously churning the sand and leaving a trail of dust and tracks behind, as it wove its way through the sand dunes. It was hard to contain my joy; I returned to my seat and pointed towards the manoeuvres. The pilots, who seemed to enjoy the view as much as us, sharply banked the helicopter, and continued to circle around the area till we had a fill of that extraordinary battlefield scenario.

Thereafter the pilots were asked to return as we were getting low on fuel. Interestingly, on our way back, we flew along the axis on which the tanks had advanced the previous night, and where the 'follow-on' forces had consolidated the crossing over the canal. Here, we saw a bridge being launched. This unexpected event was a bonus. We hovered for a while at this spot, and finally headed for the Corps HQ. The minister and the army chief were quite pleased and satisfied to see these operational actions being undertaken by the troops in the scorching heat. Besides, with their vast experience, they must have also realized that there was nothing put on for show.

Unfortunately, we had a fatal Mig 21 crash during a ground attack sortie during the early phase of the exercise. We could only salute the gallant air warrior for making the supreme sacrifice. I was later told that the young pilot got so engrossed and mesmerized while engaging the 'enemy' column of tanks, that he lost a few milliseconds in pulling up, and unfortunately crashed in the sand dunes. We did not have any other fatal casualty in the entire exercise. Also, very few cases of heat stroke were reported.

It was 9 May 2001 and it happened to be my thirtieth wedding anniversary. When we left for the exercise, I knew that that year, Rohini and I would not be able to celebrate this special day. Notwithstanding this, I had asked the ADC to carry some champagne for the occasion, which I could share with my personal staff. At that time, none of us had any inkling that we would have very high-ranking visitors in our midst on that day.

As it happened, I invited the defence minister and my chief and the other senior officers to join me for a drink in my caravan in the evening. As I opened the champagne bottle, I ardently hoped that the cork would pop out with the typical, conversation-stopping sound of good champagne, and it did! It was a Moet et Chandon, which had been chilled in the mini-refrigerator in my caravan. I can say without any hesitation that I would have done the same even if we were in the midst of a war, if the situation permitted. In the event, everyone joined in raising a toast to Rohini and me. One amongst this elite, who professed to be a no-alcohol type, made an exception that evening. Was it for felicitating me or double standards, I wondered. It turned out to be a perfect evening, and a wonderful way to end a hot and hectic day. I missed Rohini very much and told her so when I spoke to her later in the night.

As soon as I saw off the minister and the chief and the other brass the next morning, I asked for a briefing on the progress of the exercise. I was happy to learn from the director that everything was on course, barring a few minor hiccups. Except for the unfortunate air crash, there had been no other mishap. I then told them that I would like to fly to the area where the parachute battalion was air-dropped at night, and meet the troops.

We took off in the light Cheetah helicopter and after about half an hour we were over the area where the para battalion should have attacked. We couldn't see any activity. When we eventually landed in the midst of the defences of the para battalion, I was shocked to see the men crouching in shallow trenches. It was a comical sight, as the burly paratroopers tried to fold themselves into the small dugouts. It was unbelievable that during the last 12 hours they had dug for themselves only knee-deep pits! The fact was that they didn't expect anyone to visit them, least of all the corps commander. It was but natural that I blew my top, and gave the commanding officer the dressing down of his lifetime. If it had happened during an actual war, I would not have hesitated to sack the CO on the spot. Since the aim of such exercises is to train and to learn from mistakes, I did not harm his career. Instead, I gave them another 12 hours in which to prepare and occupy a well-sited and dug-up battalion-defended area capable of withstanding an armoured assault accompanied with heavy shelling. The next morning, their defences would be inspected by my brigadier general staff, who would then report to me.

Similarly, I went to observe the tank and infantry manoeuvres, and gave orders to increase the tempo of the exercise even higher. In such major exercises, it had become the accepted norm that once the main offensive force had captured and secured the areas up to the first phase line, and the air drop of the para battalion with the 'heavy drop' had been accomplished successfully, the exercise was terminated. So at first, my decision to continue the manoeuvres caused some consternation in the fighting formations as well as the logistics units. But soon thereafter, it felt great to see the adversaries going for each other, and trying to win their battles. We had put in place an effective umpire organization.

It was tasked to announce the result of each engagement as fast as possible, if not almost instantaneously. These decisions were not based on gut feelings of the control organization, but on the basis of scientific value-based software evolved by us, keeping in mind both the tangible and intangible factors.

This important training event came to a successful conclusion once we had achieved the aim set out by us. The final act was the summing up, in which we highlighted the lessons learnt and our strengths and weaknesses. It was an important occasion for me to share my views with my leaders – the battalion and regimental commanders, the brigade and divisional commanders and the staff officers. I literally flew into the site of the summing up, and landed right in front of a huge dome made of camouflage nets under which my gallant team of warriors had been assembled. There were about 400 officers, including quite a few women officers, who had participated in the exercise. In my address, I reminded them of our philosophy of a 'warrior and a winner', and my motto for our corps, 'Fight to Win'.

A few days after the exercise, I received a letter of appreciation from the defence minister saying how happy he was with the whole experience. A copy of the letter is reproduced on the next page.

On the culmination of the exercise, no one could have guessed that within a few months, the corps would be headed for the real thing – an actual bout with Pakistan. Terrorism had begun to rear its ugly head all over the world. First came 9/11, which gave a rude shock to America along with the rest of the world, followed by a constitutional crisis in Nepal. Then came the attack on the Indian Parliament by a group of Pakistani terrorists, taking us to the brink of a war. There were other incidents of terrorism – at Akshardham in Gujarat; at the Raghunath temple in Jammu; at the Kalu Chak military station in J&K. Since we had honed our war-fighting skills, we were fully prepared to carry out our assigned mission, and were just awaiting the green signal. Alas, it never came or we could have created history (see also Chapter 20).

We moved into a new sprawling office complex of the Corps HQ at Mathura on returning from the exercise. The corps commander's office was located on the first floor and had a beautiful view. I was the first GOC to occupy that office. We planned and constructed a small war

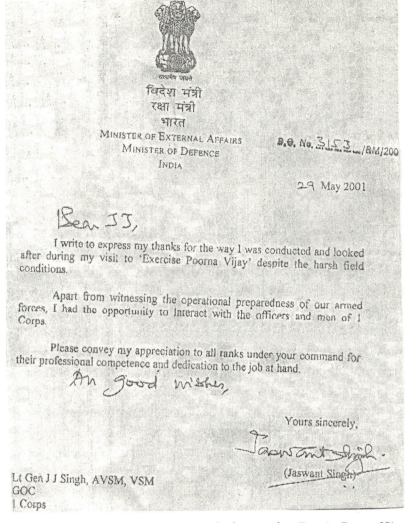

A letter from Defence Minister Jaswant Singh after attending Exercise Poorna Vijay.

memorial adjacent to the Corps HQ. In the battle of Basantar in the 1971 Indo-Pak war, Second Lieutenant Arun Khetarpal of 17 Horse was decorated with a Param Vir Chakra and his tank – a Vijayanta – had the pride of place in the memorial. It was one of the best office buildings in those days, and we worked very hard to do up the interiors. During a visit to Mathura in February 2011, I was amazed to see the improvements made over the past decade in the Corps HQ and the cantonment by my distinguished successors.

19

Colonel of the Regiment

During the summer of 2001, besides Exercise Poorna Vijay, there was another important development taking place. And that was the election of the colonel of the Maratha LI, one of the oldest and most renowned infantry regiments of the Indian Army, with a glorious history going back to 1768. The election was necessitated due to the retirement of Lieutenant General V. Oberoi, the vice chief of army staff. Every regiment or corps in our army has traditionally elected a colonel to be their father figure, and to look after their interests. This is the only position in the army where elections take place and as far as the infantry and cavalry are concerned, it is not necessary that the seniormost becomes the colonel. However, the measure of an officer's standing in the regiment is reflected when the ballots are counted. There is a predetermined electorate – all battalion commanders, serving colonels, brigadiers and generals of the regiment have a vote. The commanding officers' vote reflects the mandate of the soldiers. Since our regiment was doing exceptionally well, we had four generals in the fray besides me. This was certainly a record of sorts. It became a matter of life and death for all of us as our regimental reputations were at stake.

Eventually, I was chosen with an overwhelming majority, and I consider this to be a great honour. This was reflective of the high level of trust that all ranks of the regiment reposed in me. I felt humbled, vindicated and redeemed at the same time. My regimental service and extended tenures in command of troops paid off. In a hierarchical and seniority-ridden organization, like armies all over the world, it can become terribly embarrassing for the senior if a junior gets elected. But

I wasn't the seniormost! We were all friends and had grown up in the same regiment. I had a successful tenure as the colonel of the regiment for six years till I retired in September 2007.

During this period, I focused on policy decisions for the good of the regiment and improvements of infrastructure and accommodation in the Regimental Centre at Belgaum and in regimental assets at other locations. Based on research and deliberations and importantly, with the consensus of the entire regiment, we reverted to the custom of wearing our green lanyard not around the neck but on the left shoulder, except the 5th Battalion, which proudly wore the royal blue lanyard on the right shoulder as before. Besides that, we introduced the black pouch belt to be worn on ceremonial occasions.

Five significant events occurred during my tenure as the colonel of the regiment. The first was the bicentenary celebrations of 5 (Royal) Maratha LI at Kota in December 2001, which was raised during the Raj period on 21 December 1800. As covered earlier, I had the privilege to command this very fine battalion from 1985–87 at Hyderabad.

The 5th Royals bicentenary was conducted in a grand manner from 11 to 14 October 2001. It was a gala reunion, with a ceremonial parade reviewed by me as the colonel of the regiment, the Maratha pageant, followed by a 'bara khana' (a combined dinner for all ranks), and the bicentenary dinner in the officers' mess. The Bicentenary Cup was unveiled that evening for which all officers had contributed. Made of sterling silver, it was a matching trophy to the Centenary Cup presented by all officers on 21 December 1900 (they were all British), and is proudly displayed in the ante-room of the mess. Former colonels of the regiment, Generals E. D'Souza, Bachhitar Singh, Vijay Oberoi, along with Generals K.S. Brar, D.B. Shekhatkar, S. Satpute and C.K. Karumbaya, were present at these functions.

On 30 January 2003, we had an impressive affiliation ceremony on board INS Mumbai, one of our navy's latest warships – a state-of-the-art guided missile destroyer, with the motto 'I am invincible.' I reviewed the joint Guard of Honour and told the gathering that the affiliation of INS Mumbai with the Maratha Light Infantry was a historic occasion. The ceremony was an apt reminder of the prowess of the naval exploits of Chhatrapati Shivaji Maharaj and Admiral Kanhoji Angre. The domination of the west coast from Mumbai to Vengurla by the Maratha warriors laid the foundation of a rich tradition of valour enshrined in countless sacrifices of sailors in wars, was the essence of my address on the occasion.

On 30 November 2006, we got affiliated with the 20 Squadron of the Indian Air Force, nicknamed the 'Lightnings', located at Pune. The squadron's crest depicts three bars of lightning in conjunction with the Himalayan Eagle. It is one of the most highly decorated squadrons of our air force. This time the ceremony was conducted at our regimental centre in Belgaum, which included a joint Guard of Honour, exchange of trophies and an address by me and Air Marshal T.S. Randhawa, the commodore commandant of the 20 Squadron. One of our elite fighter squadrons, it is currently equipped with the state-of-the-art Sukhoi 30s. The highlight of the ceremony was the flypast by three Sukhoi 30 aircraft of the squadron.

Our regiment thus achieved the distinction of being affiliated with both the Indian Navy and the Indian Air Force. Both INS Mumbai and the 20 Squadron of the air force acquired the status of battalions of our regiment. I have often been asked the logic behind inter-services affiliation. My response is that unlike mergers and acquisitions witnessed in the boardrooms of the corporate world, our bonding is etched in the battlefields, where these very affiliations make the difference between life and death, victory and defeat. Our deep bonds are an example of close integration with our sister services, which will stand us in good stead in the years to come.

The fourth event was the 150th Raising Day celebrations of the 22 Maratha LI (Hyderabadis) at Hyderabad in November 2003. Colonel Pannu of the Hyderabadis, who happened to be my colonel military secretary when I was GOC I Corps, and later my deputy military assistant, made sure that we attended this event. This battalion has about 50 per cent soldiers who are Marathas, and the rest are Muslims. They frequently share the same barracks for their temple and the mosque.

The fifth event was the regimental reunion held in April 2007. It was the first reunion held with the army chief as the colonel of the regiment, and evoked great bonhomie and regimental spirit.

Finally, I would like to place on record the magnificent contribution of the House of Kolhapur, a royal family which has descended from the great warrior king Chhatrapati Shivaji Maharaj. The present maharaja, Shahu Chhatrapati, has rendered yeoman service to the Maratha Light Infantry, following the footsteps of his illustrious father, Major General Shahaji Chhatrapati. During the Second World War, his grandfather, Rajaram Chhatrapati Maharaj, made available his palace guard battalion (which was known as Rajaram Rifles and later 19 Maratha LI) to help in the war effort. During my tenure as the army chief, in a touching honour ceremony held at Kolhapur on 29 May 2006, the Maharaja Saheb presented me with a traditional silver sword, which now has the pride of place in the Regimental Centre Officers' Mess. Shahu Chhatrapati has made it a point to visit the Maratha battalions even in remote field areas to boost the morale of our soldiers, and remains in personal contact with the officer corps of the regiment.

In 2009 he visited Arunachal Pradesh and joined me in unveiling an imposing equestrian statue of Shivaji Maharaj installed at Tawang on the road going to Bumla on the China border, named as Shivaji Marg. He was accompanied by Colonel Sambhaji Patil of the Hyderabadis, who was the CO when the road was initially constructed under the overall responsibility of 22 Maratha LI. The officers and men worked day and night alongwith engineers and completed a 30-kilometre road in seven months in high altitude and rocky terrain.

During my tenure as the colonel of the regiment and army chief, Colonel Vasanth V., CO of 9 Maratha LI, laid down his life as a brave warrior. Fighting against the terrorists along the line of control in the Uri sector of Kashmir, he became a martyr in the finest traditions of the Indian Army on 31 July 2007. He was decorated with the highest peace-time gallantry award of Ashoka Chakra. Another 'bravest of the brave' of our regiment, Lieutenant Navdeep Singh of 15 Maratha LI, was also decorated with an Ashoka Chakra in 2011 for displaying conspicuous gallantry while facing terrorists in J&K. We salute them both.

On my superannuation, the government appointed me as the honorary colonel of the Maratha LI for life. In the meanwhile, I had already handed over the baton to the newly elected colonel of the regiment, Lieutenant General Narendra Singh.

20

Attack on Parliament and Operation Parakram

On 13 December 2001, we were aghast as the Indian Parliament came under a terrorist attack. Five terrorists on a suicidal mission (later learnt to be from Lashkar-e-Toiba and Jaish-e-Mohammad) had managed to enter the precincts of the Parliament House. The Parliament was in session though it had been adjourned some time before the attack. The terrorists were heavily armed and tried to rush into the main building while firing indiscriminately. However, due to effective action taken by the paramilitary forces on guard duty and some fortuitous circumstances, none of the terrorists could gain entry into the main hall, where many political leaders and parliamentarians were deliberating on the proceedings of the day. The exchange of fire took place for a few hours, by which time the site of the encounter was sealed and the army was placed on standby. Eventually, all the five terrorists were killed, though in the shootout seven paramilitary personnel also lost their lives. No member of Parliament or minister was hurt. All nations of the world condemned this brazen act of terrorism, including Pakistan (*sic*). On the other hand, the statement of the Pakistani military spokesman, Major General Rashid Qureshi, that, 'this attack was a drama staged by Indian intelligence agencies to defame the freedom struggle in occupied Kashmir,' was ridiculous and horribly repugnant.

In a matter of a few days, we received orders to mobilize for war and move to our designated areas for Operation Parakram. By early January, my corps was ready. Pakistan responded similarly, but took more time as it had to move back troops from its borders on the west. Having just completed Exercise Poorna Vijay, where we had ample opportunity to streamline our procedures, we were able to mobilize faster than other offensive formations. Having reached our locations, we commenced recces of our respective areas and held operational discussions to fine-tune various plans and contingencies. Fortunately, we had made up a lot of our equipment deficiencies and put maximum number of tanks, guns and other equipment on road prior to our exercise. As most of my troops were under canvas, my caravan Chetak was my home for the next ten months.

We kept waiting for orders and the green signal but none came. However, we took our responsibility very seriously and carried out preparations for our mission as per the national strategy. Pakistan was taken aback by our alacrity and, in the early stages, was quite unprepared for a military showdown. On 12 January 2002, President Musharraf gave a speech in which he categorically stated that Pakistan would not allow its soil to be used for propagation of terrorism and attempted to defuse tension on the border. What that country actually did was something else. According to me, he used it as a clever ploy to buy time by saying the right things at a juncture when India could have gone in for some level of retaliatory military action. Musharraf did that once again by making a statement on 27 May 2002, which reiterated an assurance to end cross-border terrorism. This was soon after a cowardly attack by terrorists in a small military station near Jammu in which thirty-four people, most of them wives and children of army personnel, were killed. We were almost ready to go in once again by the first week of June, though by that time Pakistan was much better prepared compared to the opportunity we had in January 2002. A retributive military response has, in my view, a fleeting window of opportunity. Further, the international ramifications of an armed action have to be factored in before undertaking such a step. When provoked by a serious act of aggression or state-sponsored terrorism, the strike back has to be precise, short and swift.

However, the situation was defused this time too, perhaps due to international intervention, mainly by the US. Pakistan also resorted to some carefully-calibrated nuclear sabre-rattling during this period. Musharraf said on 5 June that he would not renounce Pakistan's right to use nuclear weapons first, in response to our external affairs minister saying that India would not be the first to use nuclear weapons. We military leaders or other decision-makers sometimes overlook the fact that whatever happens in a volatile region such as ours would have a great impact on the rest of the world. This is more so because of the nuclear dimension. That it is not just going to be an India-Pakistan affair, as was the case in 1965 or 1971, is something we must always bear in mind. How successful the military build-up against Pakistan proved to be is debatable, but eventually a military conflict did not take place. The thrust of the government's strategy was on 'coercive diplomacy.' Pakistan was put under tremendous pressure during this stand-off. But after a certain stage, I was not sure whether the operation was serving any purpose, or had became an exercise in futility. Waiting endlessly for months out in the open sapped the energy of even the fittest and most motivated troops. Was this the best way to achieve our aims? My response is, perhaps not. Did we have an exit strategy? To the best of my knowledge, the answer is no. Perhaps this reflects a lack of clarity or fuzziness about our overall national strategy at that time.

On the other hand, there were many plus points of this operation too. There was some clamping down of terrorist infrastructure in Pakistan and reduction in terrorist activities in Kashmir, the results of which we got to see in 2004 and thereafter. We got to know our operational areas thoroughly and refined our plans, the relationship between the leader and the led got cemented, and we made up our equipment deficiencies to a large extent. A peace dialogue between India and Pakistan was initiated, and a ceasefire along the LoC was agreed to in 2003 by both sides, which is still holding. Finally, Operation Parakaram was called off in October 2002 and we returned to Mathura.

The sad part of the previous two years was that most of us in 1 Corps spent about a year and a quarter living like gypsies under canvas or in caravans. I did not even get to see the face of Mathura properly. Soon after our return from Operation Parakram, I learnt that by January 2003, I would be taking over as the GOC-in-C of Army Training Command (ARTRAC), located in Shimla.

21

Army Commander
The Penultimate Rung

En route to Shimla, I called on the army chief, General N.C. Vij. He congratulated me on my new assignment, and during our interaction, he asked me to write the doctrine for the army as the GOC-in-C of ARTRAC. There had to be two parts to it – one for the public domain, and the other classified, covering operational aspects. I started working on this from day one. The salubrious climate of Shimla was extremely conducive for creativity and conceptual work. My office was in a historical building, constructed in the nineteenth century to house the General HQ of the British Imperial Army. Though the top two floors of the seven- or eight-storeyed building had got burnt down, it was still a very imposing building. The fact that the office had been occupied by the likes of General Lord Roberts of Kandhar (1885–93), General Viscount Kitchener of Khartoum (1902–09), General Sir Philip W. Chetwode (1930–35), whose words are enshrined in the Chetwode Hall of the Indian Military Academy, General Sir Claude J.E. Auchinleck and General Sir Archibald P. Wavell (the second last governor general of India), to name a few, who were all commanders-in-chief of the Indian Army, was an unbelievable high. What must have happened in the exalted wood-panelled and teak-floored chambers and corridors of this famous building is impossible to imagine or describe. The Command House, where we lived for a year, was named the Retreat. It was one of the best houses that I have ever stayed in, and was constructed in 1904 during the glorious period of the Raj.

I formed a team to do research for writing the army doctrine. It was evolved keeping in mind the lessons learnt in previous wars, including Kargil and the recently concluded Operation Parakram. We had frequent review meetings and discussed various issues that arose. My experience of Exercise Poorna Vijay, Operation Parakram, and the seminar on heavy breakthrough helped me in formulating the doctrine for offensive operations in the plains and desert. It also addressed our concerns in the mountains. This doctrine was a visionary document in which the futuristic challenges were analysed and we talked of fighting the future war. By the end of the year, we had the draft of the document ready. After considerable deliberations, it was approved and released the next year by the army chief.

All important training institutions of the army came under the Army Training Command. Therefore, I had a lot of travelling to do. We reviewed and published a book on leadership and another on training in the Indian Army, called *Quest for Excellence*. During the annual training conference in 2003, I laid great emphasis on information technology, geographical information systems, aerial and satellite imagery, communications and night fighting capabilities. We developed indigenous war gaming models based on computers and began training officers at unit level in a facility in Delhi Cantonment. I also encouraged the development of simulators for gunnery, driving, aviation and in other applications. Where necessary, we made our bids for import of such equipment. We raised a simulator division in the Electronic and Mechanical Engineering College at Secunderabad. Computerized war gaming and simulators reduced the need for exercises in the field and enhanced the life of equipment due to less wear and tear, thereby generating a lot of savings. Citing the example of Operation Desert Storm, the US campaign in Iraq during 1991–92, I exhorted officers to study the use of high technology, especially surveillance, acquisition and destruction of targets, with precision-guided munitions, so as to be able to obtain a decisive result in the shortest possible time frame, and with the minimum casualties.

During December 2003, it was announced that I would be the next GOC-in-C of Western Command. It is one of our most prestigious commands with its HQ at Chandimandir, a military station near

Chandigarh. We felt very sad at the thought of leaving the pristine environment of the Shimla hills.

Towards the end of January, Shimla and its surroundings again witnessed very heavy snowfall. It was snowing in the morning as we left for Chandimandir and the road was covered with two feet of snow. It was sheer coincidence, but it had also snowed the day I took over the reins of the Army Training Command at Shimla, and it proved to be a good omen. Our Ambassador cars got stuck so we had to abandon them and get into 4x4 jongas fitted with non-skid chains to drive down.

Western Command is an operational command unlike the ARTRAC, which had no operational role. It was responsible for the defence of the western border from J&K upto Rajasthan during the 1965 and 1971 wars. Later, Northern Command was carved out from it to assume operational responsibility for J&K. Presently, it looks after the defence of the most politically sensitive and precious heartland of Punjab.

Therefore my first priority was to visit and familiarize myself with the latest situation in our area of operational responsibility (AOR). Though I had commanded 9 Infantry Division, which formed a part of Western Command, things had changed after Operation Parakram. We had realigned the theatre boundaries on the entire western border with Pakistan. At the end of my tenure as GOC 1 Corps, I had been entrusted by the army chief to do a study to bring out the lessons from Operation Parakram. Based on the recommendations of this study, the inter-command boundaries were changed and a new South Western Command was raised at Jaipur, as well as a new Corps HQ at Yol, about 70 kilometres east of Pathankot. This readjustment of boundaries came about after a lot of discussions and the overruling of many objections raised by HQ Northern Command – the objections smelt of petty turf issues. My first concern was to integrate the additional AoR in the Jammu sector into the Western Command plans. This arrangement would inherently create greater synergy for the defence of our AoR. Besides, we were also able to create more reserves and enhance the inherent offensive defence capabilities in the theatre.

In order to validate the new doctrine, the Strike Corps was asked to conduct an offensive exercise, named Sange Shakti, in the obstacle-ridden plains of the Punjab. Besides launching appropriately grouped task forces within a short time from their peace locations, the exercise also highlighted our capability in network-enabled functioning and the use of UAVs. A number of visits were undertaken by me to review operational readiness and to meet soldiers in border cantonments. I stressed upon thorough knowledge of the operational task and the terrain, and a high state of maintenance of weapon systems and equipment. All ranks should know the ground like the back of their hand. During this tenure, I was honoured by President A.P.J. Abdul Kalam with the Param Vishisht Seva Medal for distinguished services of the highest order at the Rashtrapati Bhawan.

Realizing the growing importance of the role of the media, we held a seminar on army-media relationship and were successful in conducting useful interactive sessions. Many important strategic analysts and media personalities participated in this event. There were unusually heavy monsoon rains in Himachal Pradesh and Punjab in 2004. The cloud burst that took place in the catchment areas of Himachal Pradesh resulted in the flooding of the entire Ambala-Patiala belt. Many people became homeless and there was a huge loss of property and livestock. We made a large number of army aviation sorties with relief material alongwith the air force, and saved lives of many marooned people.

Around September–October 2004, inspired and motivated articles began to appear in the media about the race for the next army chief, as General N.C. Vij was scheduled to retire on 31 January 2005. I was cautioned by some friends that there were a lot of 'dirty tricks' played by rivals in such succession battles not only in the armed forces, but in all domains of public service. There was nothing that one could do about it except to guard one's flanks through friends and well-wishers, and leave the rest to destiny. I was the natural successor to the then chief of army staff as I was not only going to be the seniormost at that time but also equally good, if not more meritorious, as compared to other competitors. Although it was never a consideration as far as I was concerned, some people were speculating whether or not the government would appoint a Sikh officer as the army chief. If it did so, it would be the first instance in the history of independent India of a Sikh leading a 1.3-million-strong Indian Army. Setting aside all speculation, the government decided to do precisely that. The greatest chapter of my life was about to begin.

Laying a wreath at Amar Jawan Jyoti,
India Gate, New Delhi, 1 February 2005.

Dad and Rohini pipping me as a 'four star' general, 31 January 2005.

Blessings of mom and dad on my becoming the chief of army staff, 31 January 2005.

Ceremonial Guard of Honour by 7 Maratha LI on my taking over as chief of army staff, Army HQ New Delhi, 31 January 2005. (Maj Rohit Choudhary commanded the parade.)

Reviewing the passing out parade at the Indian Military Academy, Dehradun, December 2006.

A content chief and first lady of the army, February 2005.

Tête-à-tête with General Guo Boxiong, vice chairman of central military commission, Great Hall of the People, Beijing, 21 May 2007. Nirupama Rao, then ambassador to China, is on extreme left.

Calling on His Majesty Jigme Singye Wangchuck, king of Bhutan, 2005.

Receiving the medals of Field Marshal S.H.F.J. Manekshaw for the Indian Army, Stavka, Nilgiris, 2006.

Ceremonial welcome on board PLA Navy frigate at Shanghai Naval Base on 25 May 2007.

Reviewing the traditional and ceremonial Guard of Honour at Whipple Field, Washington DC, 7 November 2006.

Honouring the widow of a martyr and her braveheart son in combat dress at the Maratha LI Centre, Belgaum, 2007.

'Fight to Win' – raising the morale of my warriors at Siachen, 2005.

With 'glacier warriors', Siachen, 2005.

Affiliation of the Maratha LI with the air force and navy.

The first visit by a prime minister to Siachen: with Dr Manmohan Singh, M.K. Narayanan, T.K.A. Nair and Brig Om Prakash, 2005.

Calling on President Pratibha Devisingh Patil, 2007.

Visiting earthquake-devastated Uri in Kashmir, October 2005, with Sonia Gandhi, Defence Minister Pranab Mukherjee, Chief Minister Ghulam Nabi Azad and Ambika Soni.

Receiving the 'traditional' sword of honour from Shahu Chhatrapati Maharaj, whose lineage goes back to Chhatrapati Shivaji Maharaj, Kolhapur, 2006.

'Aman Setu' cake at Army Day reception, New Delhi, January 2006.

Crossing the newly constructed 'Aman Setu' (bridge of peace) on the Line of Control in Uri Sector, Kashmir, 2006 (with Defence Minister A.K. Antony, GOC-in-C Northern Command Lt Gen A.S. Panag, GOC 19 Inf Div Maj Gen R. Halgalli and Deputy MA Col P.J.S. Pannu).

On board aircraft carrier INS Virat, with Admiral S. Mehta, the naval chief, and MA Brig V.S.S. Goudar, 2007.

Presiding over an army commanders' conference, October 2006.

With Russian Defence Minister Sergei Ivanov at the joint Indo-Russian exercise 'INDRA 2005' in Rajasthan.

Saluting the Colours of 61st Cavalry during review of the ceremonial mounted parade in Jaipur, 2007.

Defence Minister A.K. Antony bidding me farewell in the presence of the minister of state for defence, M.M. Pallam Raju, and senior armed forces officers, September 2007.

Rohini and I at the Pangong Tso lake near the Line of Actual Control with China in Ladakh, 2005.

Presenting the humane face of the army, Srinagar, 2006.

Receiving the Brahmos missile system from President A.P.J. Abdul Kalam and Dr Sivathanu Pillai, CEO Brahmos, 2006.

With Sonia Gandhi at Army Day reception, New Delhi, January 2007.

Meeting US President George Bush, with President A.P.J. Abdul Kalam and Laura Bush, Rashtrapati Bhavan, New Delhi, March 2006.

Part IV
THE PINNACLE

'I consider myself first and last to be an Indian.'

22

'Jangi Laat'
Becoming the Army Chief

Chandigarh, 28 November 2004

When the government announced my name as the next chief of army staff on 27 November 2004, it made headline news. It was the first time in the history of the Indian Army that a Sikh officer was going to head it. It was indeed a great honour and a unique privilege. The Command House at Chandi Mandir Cantonment was brimming over with the media, who were keen to pick my mind on various issues. The first was, 'How does it feel to be the first Sikh chief of the Indian Army?'

'I consider myself first and last to be an Indian,' was my immediate response. I added that I was proud to be a Sikh, and equally a Maratha, as I had spent over forty years with the Marathas. I carefully fended off many other queries by saying that the people must wait (I was still the army commander of Western Command), and give me time to reflect on my new position and responsibilities.

While narrating one of my poignant experiences in Kashmir, my eyes were moist, thinking of the intense pain and anguish of the innocent people in strife-torn areas. 'These young Kashmiri boys did not deserve to die like this,' I said, describing operations in Kashmir during which many AK-47-toting young men had lost their lives. I also recounted the story of the newly married misguided youth whom we let go after confiscating his AK-47. We gave him a chance to reform and start life afresh. There has to be a human touch while conducting counterinsurgency operations. Though I have a hard-as-nails exterior, I have a soft core too. This incident made good copy and the media went to town; it even got editorial comments, and led to a debate.

Another reason for the tears in my eyes that morning was the sinking in of my achievement and the recognition accorded by the nation. I had finally emerged victorious in the race for the top slot against three contenders who peeled out one by one, but not before playing out their parts as best as they could. I don't blame them for it, but I was the one whom destiny favoured. It was a subterranean fight. Finally one of the contestants had the grace to say to me, 'Congratulations, JJ.' I gratefully acknowledged his felicitations. Then he said, 'The King is Dead, Long Live the King!' As far as I am concerned, the final lap was the toughest.

'Are the emotive moments orchestrated? Is JJ just trying to repair the army's image, dented as it is with reports of fake kills and human rights violations?' wrote the *Tehelka* of 26 February 2005. These were some of the issues being raised by segments of our media. Continuing, the report in *Tehelka* went on to say, 'It is difficult to find an officer who has a problem with the first Sikh chief's style or manner. Ask former army chief General S. Padmanabhan what he made of a teary JJ and he says, "He has always been a man straight from the heart. It is not a sign of weakness to show emotion."' It further quoted General V.P. Malik, another former chief, as saying, '"JJ has a humane and yet a tough approach. He ensured that Kashmiris were neither alienated nor exposed to any hardship."'[1] [This remark was related to operations in J&K when I was a brigade commander and he (General Malik) happened to be my GOC.] The reaction of the people to this 'humane face' of a military leader was heart-warming. A minister from J&K, Muzaffar Hussain Baig, wrote a letter which, along with some media reports of that period, are reproduced as Appendices 2 and 3 respectively.

Being appointed the chief of army staff of the Indian Army, the second-largest standing army in the world, has definitely been, and

---

[1] Harinder Baweja, *Tehelka*, 26 February 2005.

'Jangi Laat' – Becoming the Army Chief

most probably shall remain, the most significant event in my life. It was a proud and yet a very humbling occasion when I was adorned with the rank badges of a four-star general by my parents and my wife, Rohini, on Monday, 31 January 2005. I happened to be the twenty-fourth chief of army staff since independence.

Our great army has been carefully nurtured by many illustrious predecessors and placed on a solid foundation of nationalism and the three pillars of being *apolitical, secular and professional*. Our ethos and traditions flow from these fundamentals. What would be my mission and key objectives during my tenure of two years and eight months as the army chief or the 'Jangi Laat,'[2] a term used by some elder veterans while addressing the chief? This thought was uppermost in my mind as I set about shouldering the responsibilities of my office. In fact, this process started as soon as I was nominated in November 2004 itself.

> An Army is to a Chief what a sword is to a soldier.
> – Marshal Foch: Precepts, 1919

I defined my aim in simple and precise terms – to lead the second-largest army in the world, a highly professional force that should be optimally trained, equipped and structured. The army should have the capability to operate successfully in a joint services environment in the entire spectrum of conflict in a network-centric battlefield. And, if and when challenged, our motto shall be – 'Fight to Win.'

Calling on President A.P.J. Abdul Kalam, Prime Minister Manmohan Singh and Defence Minister Pranab Mukherjee were my first few important engagements. I accepted their congratulations and the discussions that followed were brief, formal and cordial. I assured them that I would do my best in the service of the nation, and give the Indian Army the leadership that the officers and the men expected of their chief. The next on my agenda was to visit J&K, the northeast and the sensitive border areas, and observe things first hand. Travelling in the comfort of the Boeing executive jet of the IAF's VIP Squadron gave me time to think about and refine my ideas.

Having discussed various issues with the national leaders, field

---

[2] The Warrior Lord, as the C-in-C of the army was referred to during the Raj period.

commanders and my advisers at the Army HQ, I held my first conference in February 2005. This was to spell out the road map of the next three years to my principal staff officers, the heads of arms and services, and other senior officers of the Army HQ, and enunciate my aim, concepts, principles and key result areas (KRAs). A few months later, I reiterated these core policies and key objectives during the army commanders' conference in April 2005, where we discussed ways to improve the state of the army and achieve our aim. Excerpts of my concepts disseminated to the media and in the public domain are reproduced below:

> *Readiness to carry out our operational mission shall be one of our primary KRAs. To quote Chanakya, 'If a society seeks to live in peace, it should be prepared for war, and a unilateral desire for peace cannot ensure peace.' We are well aware of the live challenge of a proxy war that we are facing in Jammu and Kashmir and insurgency or terrorism that occupies our attention in the northeast. Besides, we have unresolved boundary issues with Pakistan and China. Consequently, there is a requirement to deploy the army and paramilitary forces to guard these frontiers. The strife and tension that has engulfed most countries in our region needs to be kept in mind. We must constantly review and refine our doctrine, operational and logistics plans and ensure the desired level of equipment fitness.*
>
> *We should ensure that we win the war against terror – the proxy war unleashed by Pakistan in Jammu and Kashmir, the insurgency in Nagaland and the actions of outfits like ULFA in Assam and Manipur. Our aim should be to carry out successful operations in J&K and the northeast and bring down the level of violence so that the civil administration, paramilitary forces and the police are able to function in an appropriate manner and provide good governance.*
>
> *There can be no substitute for realistic and operational-oriented training. We must train for the modern hi-tech battlefield and the future war, not the last one. The side which is adept at netcentric and information warfare and has the required night-fighting capability shall carry the day in any future conflict. The war doctrine should be incorporated in our exercises and practised at the tactical, operational and strategic levels.*
>
> *We must provide top class leadership to our soldiers, who are amongst*

the finest in the world. To quote Field Marshal Slim, 'The real test of leadership is not if your men will follow you in success, but if they will stick by you in defeat and hardship.'[3] Therefore, we need the best officers to lead the units and formations and give the kind of leadership our warriors deserve. They must be thorough professionals with adequate experience, particularly in command of troops.

We must inculcate an offensive spirit and a proactive approach in our subordinates. As no plan survives the first engagement, we must train ourselves and our commands to be dynamic and flexible and practise the directive style of leadership. Remember to be two steps ahead of the adversary. We must seize fleeting opportunities and take bold actions and calculated risks, but no gambles – lives are at stake! Surprise, deception and an element of cunningness should be ingrained into our thought process and plans. Our men are naive by nature and the average officer is too conventional. We must change the predictability in our approach and begin to do the unexpected. In fact, an unconventional plan could be the battle-winning factor. You will probably get your objective faster and certainly with lesser number of bodybags. Always be original and innovative and don't do the 'bhed chaal' (the way the sheep follow each other). In war as in peace, try to be the top dog – always in command of the situation. I have always been a practitioner of 'Chanakyaniti' (the principles of Chanakya).

This brings me to the most crucial element in any war, past, present or future – the fighting man. The man behind the machine should be well-trained, physically and mentally robust, highly motivated and imbued with great esprit de corps. I have often stated that our men should have their 'batteries' fully charged and be raring to go into action. Therefore it is imperative that we as leaders should see to it that our men have time for rest and recreation. A tired army shall never deliver. We must never forget that the soldier is the ultimate determinant of victory in the battlefield. The well-being of the soldier's family and dependents is a dimension that is also extremely important. Our welfare schemes ought to assure the soldier that his family would be looked after should anything happen to him.

---

[3] Field Marshal Bill Slim, *Defeat into Victory*, Cassell and Company Ltd, 1956, also republished by Cooper Square Press in 2000.

To evolve into an army of the twenty-first century, it is axiomatic that our 'mantra' should be modernization. I highlighted the need for acquisition of arms and equipment to replace some of our obsolete inventory, which had reached unacceptable levels. Therefore, I would like to see the results of the impetus given by the government for the modernization of the army and the induction of high-end technology and improvement of our night-fighting capabilities. This, along with information technology, information warfare and netcentric warfare, would be the essence of modernization during my tenure. India is known for its progress in the field of information technology all over the world and we are going to make sure that our armed forces exploit this strength optimally. I have thought of nominating the South Western Command, which is under raising, to be the test bed for IT and information warfare systems. Fighting in a synergized and joint manner calls for a joint doctrine and joint training, and greater level of inter-services cooperation. We in the defence forces today are in a state of transition from single-service entities to a synergized approach of jointmanship. The beginning was made by the creation of the Integrated Defence Staff with its headquarters at New Delhi, and the Strategic Forces Command and the Andaman and Nicobar Command, which are all joint structures. They have achieved a lot in their short span of existence. We still have a long way to go on the road to further integration in order to synergize our collective potential. Some of the areas which can be addressed without prejudice to respective domains include a common defence communications network, joint missile programme, exploitation of space by the three services, precision-guided munitions, combat potential evaluation model and, as far as possible, a common logistics infrastructure and human resources management strategy and training facilities.

The revolution in military affairs caused by battlefield transparency with the help of satellites, UAVs, radars and sensors, employment of hi-tech weapon systems and other force multipliers, is having an impact on our doctrine, concepts and structure for war fighting. In a modern battlefield success depends on tempo, lethality and survivability. The buzz word is manoeuvre and not attrition. Maximum firepower must be applied. All this calls for having a closer look at our doctrine, force structures, span of command and control and existing boundaries of our formations.

The other focus areas for us are assured and responsive logistics plans to support the operational plans, which are based on the principle, 'just enough and just when required'. Welfare measures to ensure the desired quality of life for all ranks at our military cantonments and stations remains one of our primary concerns. Importantly, we must give the highest priority to our schemes for healthcare and the welfare of our veterans, such as the Ex-Servicemen Contributory Health Scheme (ECHS). And finally, we need to ensure that physical fitness of all ranks and the importance of sports as a facilitator of building team spirit and camaraderie, continue to be given the highest importance.

For me, truthful reporting, loyalty and integrity are sacrosanct. I admire and appreciate frank and forthright subordinates, and do not want 'yes men'. The thrust of an argument or a dissenting note should be on the logic or rationale and pragmatism, rather than theory.

I am and have always been a team man. Therefore, my first step was to create a close-knit, loyal and dependable team of personal staff. This team was to act as my eyes and ears, and I encouraged them to give me honest feedback, frank views and pragmatic advice. Even till this day, my team continues to display an amazing spirit and camaraderie. They have never failed me.

23

The Security Perspective

The military operations room is the sanctum sanctorum of the Army HQ. It has a state-of-the-art projection system and video-conferencing facility. Crammed with maps and charts which go up and down or slide into and out of the walls, it is manned round the clock. As additional DGMO, I had the privilege of being the leader of the team that managed all discussions and presentations held in this room. Later, as the chief, I presided over the deliberations here and gave directions on issues of operational significance. Presentations, intelligence briefings and review of operational plans were keenly looked forward to by me. We had to be clear about the challenges that our armed forces faced and be prepared for them. A series of briefings were conducted to update me as the chief designate, starting from December 2004. Based on these interactions and my own study and experience, the security scenario as I perceive it has been covered in the following paragraphs.

During the last two decades, the global security environment has witnessed a paradigm shift. With more than one power centre beginning to emerge in the new world order, strategic partnerships and dialogue encompassing the security, socioeconomic and political fields have replaced the stratagem of coercion or containment. The impact of 9/11 has shaken the world. No nation, howsoever powerful, is secure from the scourge of terrorism, which today occupies centre stage in all security equations, thus transcending state boundaries. We are witnessing the birth of fourth-generation warfare, which goes beyond the canvas of conventional military operations. This has resulted in the global war on terror. Besides this, there are other drivers that are likely to shape the contemporary global and regional security environment in the future, such as economic or security blocs, spread of nuclear and other weapons of mass destruction, demographic shifts based on economic or ethnic considerations, and energy, water or other resource needs. Though the US will remain the unchallenged military and economic power for quite some time, the world is slowly moving towards a multipolar configuration. Asia has now assumed a dominant position with the rise of China and India along with the resurgence of Russia, and the presence of Japan. However, at the same time, the security situation in the region is very fragile and unpredictable. It is host to a historical baggage of problems relating to boundaries, religion, ethnicity and resources. The sudden spillover of an internal conflict beyond a country's border cannot be ruled out. This region also has the maximum number of countries possessing 'weapons of mass destruction', with the ever increasing risk of these being exploited by non-state actors. Most significantly, Asia has the epicentre of global terrorism located in the remote mountainous redoubts along the Af-Pak border and jehadi organizations entrenched in the heartland of Pakistan too.

The challenges facing India comprise the entire spectrum, from low-intensity conflict to a conventional war with a nuclear backdrop. On one hand we have internal security threats characterized by insurgency in some parts of the northeast due to geopolitical, tribal, ethnic or other causes, Naxal and left-wing extremism in the underdeveloped and forested areas in the heartland, and a proxy-war in J&K that is aided and abetted by Pakistan. At the other end of the spectrum, there are the conventional challenges that originate from issues such as unresolved borders and sharing of river waters with our neighbours. We are continuing our deliberations at the highest level to find a pragmatic and mutually acceptable solution of our border dispute with China. The border with it extends from the Karakoram, Ladakh, Himachal Pradesh, Uttarkhand to Sikkim and Arunachal Pradesh – a distance of 4056 kilometres. We also have many issues to settle with Pakistan, of which J&K is the foremost. At the same time, the sanctity of the LoC in J&K and the LAC along our Himalayan borders has to be ensured.

Since the 1980s, India's neighbourhood has turned into a volatile, unstable and strife-prone region. Therefore, we have to be capable of defending our sovereignty and national integrity from both external and internal challenges and safeguard our national interests by an effective presence in the Indian Ocean region. The modernization and enhancement of the capability of our armed forces is an imperative need and this has to be done on priority. To address these major security concerns, the first step I took was to review the overall state of readiness of the army to carry out its assigned tasks for the defence of the nation. Were my formations and units adequately trained and equipped, and were the men well led and motivated? I visited all the important insurgency, and terrorism-affected and sensitive border areas, and met the formation commanders, other officers and troops to get a first-hand feel of the actual situation on the ground. Although I was fairly satisfied with many aspects, there were some issues that I felt had been inadequately addressed, or not in the way I would have liked. I was cognizant of the fact that the mantle of leading the Indian Army rested on my shoulders now, and that the buck would stop with me. Thus, I gave directions for improvement or making changes wherever necessary.

It was my impression that over the previous two decades, commencing from the early 1990s, our focus had shifted to our western border and J&K. The Kargil war in 1999 had accentuated the situation further as more formations, troops, weapons and equipment were moved to the Northern Command at the expense of the eastern theatre. Now, as the situation kept improving in J&K, there was an imperative need to restore the strategic imbalance and fill up the voids existing in the east. Accordingly, I ordered the reversion of units and formations to their areas in Eastern Command and also built up other assets like armoured and mechanized units, artillery and missiles, UAVs and aviation units. This process commenced in 2006. We were able to successfully achieve force restructuring, once the raising and validation of the operational tasks of the South Western Command and 9 Corps was completed. We also initiated the plans for force accretions to enhance our defensive capability by raising a Corps HQ with two infantry divisions and supporting arms and services for the east, and improvement of infrastructure, roads, railway, airports and capability building in the northeast. The air force has similarly upgraded its capability by improving the airfields and has inducted state-of-the-art aircraft in this theatre. These transformational steps have provided the much desired strategic balance to our posture in both the western and eastern theatres. Our endeavour has been not to allow 1962 to be repeated under any circumstances.

The consolidation of the new South Western Command and 9 Corps, and their capability to effectively carry out their operational responsibilities, was an operational KRA for us. During my tenure as the chief, a number of operational discussions, war games as also exercises with troops were conducted to validate our new doctrine for war fighting. A lot has appeared in media reports about the so-called 'cold start strategy' of the Indians. In our doctrine and military lexicon, there is no such term or strategy. However, the slow and cumbersome mobilization demonstrated during Operation Parakram has been replaced with procedures that imply a swift response and fighting 'light and mean'. As a part of strategizing for various scenarios and contingencies, we have put into place, defined and practised specified courses of action which will be unravelled if and when we are challenged. I am confident that the Indian Army will successfully execute these plans.

24

Internal Security and Countering Terrorism

The Indian Army has a long experience in handling insurgency, terrorism and other forms of low-intensity conflict. This area has been my forte. I have had hands-on experience in counterinsurgency operations in Nagaland in the 1960s as a young officer, in Tirap district of Arunachal Pradesh in the 1980s while leading a battalion, and as a brigade commander in Kashmir in 1991–92. This experience helped me make a handsome contribution towards bringing down the level of violence and contain terrorism in J&K and the northeast. However, such challenges are comparatively new for many armies; and therefore, we see that the campaigns of the multinational forces in Afghanistan and Iraq have been extremely costly not only in terms of human lives but also financially. These wars have of late acquired serious political undertones along with a big price tag. Further, the end does not seem to be in sight.

In an asymmetric war, the preponderance of firepower does not give the same advantage as would be the case in conventional warfare. In such conflicts there is no front, and the adversary follows no rules. He can appear from anywhere, and may not even be recognizable. Very often he uses innocent citizens as human shields. When we look at urban insurgency that we are confronted with in parts of J&K or the northeast of India, or for that matter by the multinational forces in Afghanistan, the messy situations that the soldiers have to confront so often are unbelievable, and at times unimaginable! Those of us who have conducted such operations have been through some of these unpleasant experiences. Furthermore, there are no manuals to guide our junior leaders or troops in effectively handling various delicate and tricky situations that develop all of a sudden. As the stakes are very high, they have to take decisions quickly and correctly. Counterinsurgency operations are battles fought by junior leaders and bring out the best in them.

My conviction is that there is no purely military solution for such problems. If that was possible, then by now superior military power and strategy of the West would have prevailed in Afghanistan. The most fundamental step to be taken by us is to carry out a thorough analysis of the disturbed region. We must endeavour to study the people, their history and culture, the characteristics of the terrain, the development status of the area, and consequently, the political, social, economic, ethnic, religious and other causes that have led to the situation becoming critical. Once we have deliberated on these issues we should evolve a multidimensional and multipronged strategy at the national and state level to address the problem. Unfortunately, to the uninitiated, such situations appear as military problems that will require military solutions. Nothing can be further from the truth.

It has always been my belief that the principal reason for the emergence of an insurgent movement in any region is the lack of good governance. This compels segments of society to take recourse to agitations, which are initially peaceful. However, if these go unheeded, they end up resorting to violence. It has been our experience that at times external support is provided by inimical neighbours to people in a disturbed area to stoke the fire. An important means of getting to know the 'issues espoused by the insurgents' so as to gain the sympathy of the people and enlist their support, is to get hold of and study the propaganda material, such as booklets, brochures, leaflets, and video and audio cassettes which the insurgents disseminate to the public. Some of these causes may be genuine, some mere exaggerations of issues, while many are likely to be baseless and untrue. But when uncontested or not acted upon, these facilitate the rallying of people around the banner of revolt. Furthermore, these result in a kind of brainwashing of the ignorant masses, and help the insurgents get moral, financial and logistical support, and fresh recruits for their cause. Therefore, in order to counter their vicious propaganda and take the wind out of their sails, the 'crunch issues' raised by the insurgents need to be addressed with despatch by the central and state governments, security forces and administrators, beginning at the grass-roots level.

To tackle the challenge of insurgency and terrorism, it is imperative to create an apex core security group at the national and state levels. It is necessary that such evil must be 'nipped in the bud'. It is easier to do so in the initial stages. This core group should work towards evolving an overall security aim and a counterterrorism strategy.

I am convinced that conventional armies and paramilitary forces need reorientation training to handle terrorism or insurgency. We have accordingly established counterinsurgency institutions in J&K and the northeast. It is being ensured that prior to their induction in a disturbed area, every soldier or unit is put through a specially structured training programme of about eight weeks. Our armed forces have also been carrying out joint training on counterterrorism with foreign armies such as those of the US, Russia, the UK, China, Singapore and other friendly countries. This has been to the mutual benefit of the forces involved. Our police and paramilitary forces have often been outgunned and outmanoeuvred by the Maoists, and have suffered serious reverses in the forested areas of central India, Chattisgarh, West Bengal and Orissa. It is clear that they need to be equipped, trained and led better, and thereby given the capability to successfully wage the campaign against the Maoists and Naxals. It is reassuring to see that many states are modernizing their police force and have created counterterrorism schools for their training, so that they can meet this challenge more effectively.

The people in the conflict zone are the 'centre of gravity' and all operational strategies should be focused on winning their hearts and minds, and their support and cooperation. Actions that demean and alienate the population should be scrupulously avoided. After all, they are the helpless victims caught between two warring sides. Very often, the people would give vent to their feelings and say, 'we are caught in the crossfire between the jehadis and the army. *Jenab, ham badkismat, chakki mein pise jaa rahe hain* (We, the unfortunate ones, are like grain that is being ground in a mill).' Therefore, the security forces must reassure the people that, unlike the terrorists, they are responsible and accountable for all their actions. No counterinsurgency strategy can succeed without the active support of the people who, in our case, happen to be citizens of our nation. Special efforts should be made to identify the opinion makers and to convince them that our 'cause' and their 'aspirations' coincide. It should be unambiguously conveyed to the people that our actions are essentially focused upon achieving peace and prosperity and their well-being.

The Indian Army evolved and promulgated a doctrine of sub-conventional operations/low-intensity conflict during my tenure as the chief of army staff. This is based on lessons learnt from decades of counterinsurgency and counterterrorism operations. A basic tenet of this doctrine advocated by me is the concept of 'an iron fist and a velvet glove'. This was widely covered during 2005 by our national media based on my interactions with them. *The Times of India* called it my pet theme. The 'iron fist' denotes a ruthless and 'no-nonsense' approach while tackling the insurgents or terrorists, and the 'velvet glove' demonstrates the compassion and humane face of the security forces while dealing with innocent citizens. This concept hinges on the fundamental principle of employing armed forces to enhance the effectiveness of the government machinery, while painstakingly avoiding the alienation of the masses. While countering insurgency, the army's role is to provide security to the population and a secure environment for the administration to be able to provide good governance. Only then can the development of remote and inaccessible areas of such disturbed regions take place and the other grievances of the people addressed. This concept lays emphasis on 'people-friendly' operations, upholding of the laws of the land, and an abiding respect for human rights. It has to be understood that 'wanton killing of innocent civilians is terrorism, not a war against terrorism', as stated by Noam Chomsky. Every soldier operating in a counterinsurgency campaign or fighting terror carries the army chief's commandments in his breast pocket. Ten commandments of the chief were enunciated by General B.C. Joshi in 1993. Thereafter, during

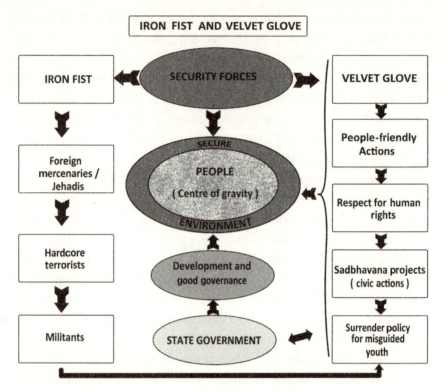

A representation of the concept 'iron fist and velvet glove'.

my tenure, ten more were added. These have been reproduced in Appendix 4. Successful and professionally conducted operations based on hard intelligence, causing minimum inconvenience to the local populace, and with little or no loss of innocent lives or other collateral damage, would greatly help in the elimination of the terrorists, and more importantly, in winning over the people as well.

It is of vital importance that the security forces avoid the use of excessive force, and conduct themselves in an impeccable manner at all times. In one of my first statements on becoming the chief of army staff, I laid great emphasis on projection of the 'humane' face of our army, and an even greater focus on respect for human rights. And further, I made it clear that there would be 'zero tolerance' for custodial deaths or other unlawful acts that sometime took place at the hands of the forces. I also directed that the term 'kill' would not be used while reporting about terrorists killed in actions or operations conducted by our troops.

These operations are not like the hunting expeditions during the Raj period, where, at the end of the day, asking the question, 'How many "kills" did you have?' was the norm.

WikiLeaks documents released in London and Delhi on 16 December 2010 make a mention of a secret briefing of US diplomats by the International Committee of the Red Cross (ICRC) in 2005. While describing some forms of ill-treatment and torture of detainees, the briefing said 'that the situation in Kashmir was "much better" as security forces no longer roused entire villages in the middle of the night and detained inhabitants indiscriminately, and there was "more openness" from medical doctors and the police.' In the same cable, American diplomats approvingly quoted media reports that 'India's army chief, Lieutenant (*sic*) General Joginder Jaswant Singh, had "put human rights issues at the centre of a (recent) conference of army commanders."'[1]

Use of force happens when the security forces are severely provoked and in an adverse situation, and consequently under great stress. If we drop a bomb on a village to kill two terrorists, and instead, destroy a house with twenty innocent civilians, including women and children, the result will be the creation of twenty families of sworn enemies! One has read of such mistakes having taken place in Afghanistan and Iraq.

Despite these steps, some mistakes are invariably committed by the troops on the ground. We couldn't afford to have any more cases that happened before I took charge – such as that of Manorama Devi, who was alleged to have been raped and killed by the security forces in 2004 in Manipur. These charges were denied and it was claimed that she was shot while trying to escape, but the army's version drew flak from some media and human rights activists. There was also the case of Major Rehman, who was accused of rape in Kashmir. Such incidents take the government and the security forces many steps back, besides consuming a lot of time and energy of those in higher echelons of the government, including the Parliament and the state assemblies. Directions were issued that any allegations of such violations were to be speedily investigated in a fair and transparent manner. Each infringement or mistake by our men in uniform would give the Pakistani propaganda

---

[1] Jason Burke, WikiLeaks cables, www.guardian.co.uk, 16 December 2010.

machinery the leverage to justify their calling us an 'occupation army'. The media loves to play up such stories, which furthers the cause of the insurgents and helps to raise their morale. I endeavoured to make this fundamental issue understood by every soldier. As a result, the local population became appreciative of the army's efforts and change in attitude and began to readily share information about terrorists, leading to successful operations. Growing signs of normalcy in the state are reflective of this change.

At the same time, action needs to be taken to provide solace, financial aid and other help to the aggrieved families by the government and the army. To win over the hearts and minds of the people, Operation Sadbhavana has been going on for a long time. This operation comprises a number of socioeconomic and civic action programmes undertaken by the army in the remote and underdeveloped areas to improve the lot of the people. These projects comprise the building of roads, bridges, model villages, goodwill schools, handicrafts development centres, and water and electricity supply schemes. These projects are executed by the army and have the formal support and funding of the ministries of defence and home affairs. They have been a huge success both in J&K and in the northeast. The armed forces have also been praised by the citizens for responding instantaneously whenever natural calamities like earthquakes, floods or heavy snowfall have struck these areas. Also, efforts were continuously made to encourage surrenders by the local misguided youth – they were given an opportunity to rejoin the national mainstream. This was a step in the right direction. Giving these surrendered terrorists some vocational training along with a viable financial package to help them rehabilitate themselves was definitely cheaper than a long-drawn-out counterterrorist campaign.

A majority of the population of such conflict-prone areas tends to be that of silent spectators or fence-sitters. They keenly observe the actions and the results of the encounters between the security forces and the insurgents, and invariably lean towards the winning side. Hence, the overall strategy and ground-level tactics must ensure that we succeed always. When we don't, we must analyse our actions and draw lessons from the mistakes that resulted in our failure. We have to outwit the terrorists and keep them on the run. We ought to think better and fight smarter, that is, plan to be two steps ahead of them, so that they are the ones who are reacting to our moves and strategy and we retain the initiative, and not the other way around.

Experience is a great teacher. We learnt the hard way and became wiser after many years of mountain- and jungle-bashing; and many unsuccessful attempts to carry out vague, pointless and impractical orders from higher HQs, mostly without accurate information, such as 'comb the forest', 'flush out the terrorists', 'carry out area domination', 'seek and destroy', and 'wipe out terrorism'! These are clichés quite commonly bandied about, which make one realize that unless the core philosophy and the fundamental principles of counterterrorism are focused upon and addressed, little can be achieved. Besides, one ought to have precise and actionable intelligence on the terrorists and their supporters, in order to get meaningful results. This is an imperative that is unexceptionable. But I have experienced that this is a major area of weakness while conducting operations. Accurate intelligence is generally hard to come by. Our intelligence agencies need to be strengthened and must be on the ball always, to meet this challenge.

The government's public information set-ups should expose the game plan of the terrorists, their false propaganda, and their utter contempt for human rights, so that the people do not fall prey to their machinations. We must highlight the incidents of rape, torture, killing of innocents, extortion and other atrocities carried out by the terrorists, so that we drive a wedge between the masses and them. We must also seek some accountability from the human rights watchdogs, as quite often they conveniently look the other way on transgressions by the terrorists. It is demoralizing for the security forces to see that only their heads roll when things go out of control or mistakes happen, while the terrorists walk away with impunity even after committing heinous crimes. At times, not a word is spoken by the traumatized people, the media and the human rights organizations against the atrocities of terrorists. For example, when the media or the intelligentsia call such criminals who live by the gun culture and spread 'dahshat '(terror) as militants instead of terrorists, it is indeed sad and ironic! Some do so in order to be able to buy their peace and a safe passage in the disturbed areas. What an enormous price we pay for such compromises! It has rightly been said by counterinsurgency expert Paul Wilkinson that 'fighting terrorism is like being a goalkeeper. You can make a hundred brilliant saves but the only shot that people remember is the one that gets past you.'[2]

Important factors discussed heretofore and which should be kept in mind while planning and executing a counterinsurgency/terrorism campaign are summarized in Appendix 5.

Countering Terror in J&K

In J&K, we were able to achieve satisfying results in counterterrorism operations and against the ongoing proxy war. 'Our attrition ratios increased from 1:4 to 1:7 in our favour during 2005–07, which was a quantum jump. This is a simple yardstick that conveys who is getting the better of whom in tactical-level encounters or engagements. Simultaneously, there has been a perceptible drop in the levels of violence in the state. Elections have been conducted peacefully despite the usual threats from the jehadis, and there is an overall yearning for peace. The tide has successfully turned in our favour, which is evident from the increased level of intelligence forthcoming from the locals, and the spurt in the number of surrenders.'[3]

But this was anathema to the terrorists and their mentors across the border. In the summer of 2010, large processions became the norm in Srinagar and some other places in the valley, where the youth resorted to provocative stone-throwing, violence, and slogan shouting. At places the paramilitary forces or the police had to open fire when the mobs got out of control, resulting in the death of ninety-eight civilians over the next few months.

In the rest of J&K, however, the situation is well under control. The ceasefire along the line of control is holding, barring the odd occasion when the Pakistan Army indulges in unprovoked firing, presumably to facilitate infiltration. The number of terrorists operating in J&K has also come down. They hesitate to engage the army and many have surrendered.

[2] *The Daily Telegraph*, London, 1 September 1992.
[3] Interview given by me to FORCE, September 2007.

Indo-Pak government talks at various levels and confidence-building measures remain the cornerstone for solving the long-standing issue between the two countries. As part of the confidence-building measures, it was decided to enhance people-to-people contact on both sides of the LoC. The most important step in this direction was the start of a bus service from Srinagar to Muzaffarabad. The terrorist organizations and jehadis were vehementally opposed to this idea. Perhaps they did not want the people of J&K to see the underdeveloped state of Pakistan-occupied Kashmir (PoK). I directed HQ Northern Command, and 15 Corps in particular, to meet the deadline to operationalize the historic Srinagar–Muzaffarabad bus link on 7 April 2005. We had to undertake demining operations of the border on our own side and improvement of the road for the final ten kilometers beyond Uri.

The last 300 metres, including a bridge with a span of about 50 metres, had to be made against time. Our military engineers did a marvellous job and we named the bridge as 'Aman Setu' (the Bridge of Peace). Many families were reunited after decades because of this road link. We anticipated that the terrorists might try to derail this process and target the buses. In the beginning we took the precaution of aerial as well as ground surveillance to sanitize the route and were prepared to take prompt action in case the terrorists struck the bus. Fortunately, no adverse incident happened, except once when the terrorists carried out some blasts to disrupt the bus service. However, this ill-advised action boomeranged and the people did not hide their anger. It exposed the real agenda and dichotomy of the jehadis. Soon we opened the Poonch-Rawalakot road and further enhanced the people-to-people contacts.

However, we have been unable to optimally utilize the capability of the media to brand Pakistan as the aggressor for all the wars fought over Kashmir. The people of Kashmir on both sides of the LoC have been misled by the Pakistani media and their propaganda machinery. It was quite surprising to note that people from PoK, travelling by bus from Muzaffarabad to Srinagar, asked if they could do the namaz when they crossed over to the Indian side. Such is the scale of disinformation that the people are being subjected to. They are quite astonished to see the development on the Indian side as compared to PoK. Perhaps it is for this reason that when the people of PoK wanted to cross the LoC en masse in the 1990s, it was the Pakistan Army that placed roadblocks on the road from Muzaffarabad to Baramulla.

There is no apparent change in Pakistan's intent to provide the terrorists moral, diplomatic and financial help. Occasional restrictions placed on terrorist groups remain calibrated, cosmetic and reversible. Pakistani senior officers often brag in typical Punjabi that the 'tooti' (tap) is in their hands. The infrastructure of the terrorist organizations remains intact in PoK and in Pakistan as well. General (Retd) Mirza Aslam Beg's improvident idea that with the nuclear deterrent, 'he could convert the Kashmir intafada into an armed insurgency,'[4] is revelatory. Besides that, Ayesha Siddiqa has recounted being told by General Pervez Musharraf, 'What makes you think that once Kashmir is over, there will be an end to the conflict with India. That's what drove his thinking and that's what drives the thinking of most of our generals.'[5] It would serve us well if our policy-planners keep these statements in mind. The threats to our security, I dare say, would continue in the years to come, and even beyond Kashmir! The recent terror attacks in Bombay and Delhi portend the challenges that lie ahead for us.

Having said that, the overall situation in J&K is improving gradually. The visit by Prime Minister Manmohan Singh on 7 June 2010, the formation of a body of interlocuters and various other initiatives for dialogue aimed at engendering peace are indeed laudable. Greater autonomy under the Constitution is also being talked about. These steps, along with relentless pressure of the security forces and waning local support, are leading to increasing frustration among the terrorists. As a result, they look for soft targets like minority community members, tourists or migrant labour to carry out acts of violence and terrorize innocents. The elected democratic government in the state is functioning with reasonable efficiency and a majority of the Kashmiris are tired of the strife and violence of the past two decades, and are yearning for peace.

As Sheikh Abdullah declared in a famous speech in June 1948, 'We the people of Jammu and Kashmir have thrown our lot with

---

[4] M.B. Naqvi, *The News* (Pakistan) 15 May, 2001.
[5] Murtaza Razvi, *Musharraf – The Years in Power*, HarperCollins, p. 207.

Indian people not in the heat of passion or a moment of despair, but by a deliberate choice. The union of our people has been fused by the community of ideals of common sufferings in the cause of freedom.'[6] Jammu and Kashmir is not only an integral part of our country, but it has reinforced our traditions of moderation, secularism and peaceful coexistence. It gave us the concept of Kashmiriyat, which, in essence, is the basis of our nationhood.

To achieve the goal of conflict resolution in J&K, I would like to re-emphasize the following aspects:

- Over 3000 years of history convincingly proves a shared civilization and culture between Kashmir and Hindustan. The accession of Jammu and Kashmir to India was ratified by the elected leadership of the state in 1954 during the rule of Bakshi Ghulam Mohammad, and later in 1975 under the Sheikh Abdullah accord.
- The political dialogue should now be taken forward with the participation of all segments of the people of Jammu and Kashmir. The views of people on both sides of the LoC, including the Gilgit, Skardu and Hunza areas, must also be sought. Further, the heterogeneous nature of J&K cannot be lost sight of. The composite dialogue between India and Pakistan to resolve various issues should take the views of the people of J&K into consideration.
- The military has performed its role perfectly by bringing down the levels of violence considerably, and shall continue to do so. Now it is for the elected representatives of the people to meaningfully address the problems of the common man. These are primarily related to their socioeconomic development. In this regard, the sincerity of purpose of the current government led by Omar Abdullah is beyond doubt and praiseworthy.
- There must be peace and the gun culture must end. The people must not provide support to organizations which use violence as a tool to achieve their vested interests. This requires the same level of courage and determination as was shown by the people of Punjab to root out extremism.

---

[6] Sheikh Abdullah, *Aatish-e-Chinar*.

- The psyche of the 'awaam' (people) has been seriously traumatized due to the violence of the past two decades. A healing touch is needed, and a humane approach needs to be adopted while dealing with the common man.
- It would be a step in the right direction to ensure that besides the army, the law enforcement agencies, such as the paramilitary forces and the police, should have a reduced signature and benign presence.
- Greater people-to-people contacts may be allowed along the LoC, along with an enhanced level of border trade, covering more areas.
- Economic activity should be accelerated so that more avenues are created for the employment of the youth. Tourism, industry, handicrafts and horticulture have great potential, which is yet to be exploited. But these would need a peaceful environment, above all else.

Militancy in the Northeast

Having served in the northeast for over twelve years, I have a fairly good understanding of the region. It has been plagued by a large number of secessionist or militant movements since independence, starting with Z.A. Phizo's call for independence for Nagaland in the 1950s. Initially, when the army was called to restore law and order, it adopted the 'scorched earth' policy and tried to suppress the insurgency with force. It was trained for conventional warfare and was new to counterinsurgency tactics. After making mistakes that antagonized a large part of the population and not achieving much success, it realized its folly. As a result, the Counter Insurgency and Jungle Warfare School was created in 1966–67 at Vairangte, to train the Indian Army units and junior leaders before their induction into insurgency-prone areas of the northeast. The Naga insurgency is the mother of all armed secessionist movements there. The high point of my experiences in the late 1960s was when we caught self-styled General Mowu Angami and a large number of rebels of his group who had just returned from China. It was the first major setback to the decade-old insurgency at that point and has been covered earlier in Part II. The pressure put on the underground by effective and professionally conducted counterinsurgency operations by the army resulted in containing the insurgents and winning the hearts and minds of the Nagas to some extent. The next major development was the change of heart of a group of about 1500 underground members of the 'Revolutionary Government of Nagaland' led by Scato Swu and the self-styled General Zuheto Sema. They had asked for a peaceful settlement within the Indian Union with some conditions. 16 August 1973 is the historical day when the ceremonial handing over of their arms to Governor B.K. Nehru took place at Zunheboto, the heartland of the Sema tribe. On that occasion, Scato Swu said, 'I would once again sincerely appeal to those who continue to mislead the people to totally give up the cult of violence and join us in our march forward to make Nagaland a modern and progressive state in our Great Country.'[7] Most of the surrendered cadres were rehabilitated in a battalion of Border Security Force under the command of Zuheto Sema and other police or paramilitary forces. Scato Swu was nominated by the Government of India to represent his people in the Rajya Sabha.

I would like to highlight a factor that has not received due recognition: the resounding and unsettling impact of India's decisive victory in the Indo-Pak war of 1971 on insurgencies in the northeast. During this campaign, we were pleasantly surprised to bag self-styled General Thinouselie and members of his gang undergoing training in erstwhile East Pakistan. Their surrender to our forces was an unexpected bounty, and it definitely had an adverse effect on the Naga rebellion. On 11 November 1975, the Shillong Peace Accord was signed between the Government of India and representatives of the Naga underground organizations, including the Naga Federal Government, which ended the two-decade-old insurgency. In this accord, they agreed of their own volition to unconditionally accept the Constitution of India, lay down arms and formulate other issues for the final settlement of the Naga problem. However, this agreement ran into heavy weather as the Isaac Swu- and T. Muivah-led gang, returning from China in 1975, 'denounced the Accord'.[8] They formed the National Socialist Council of Nagaland

---

[7] Murkot Ramunny, *The World of Nagas*, Northern Book Centre, New Delhi, 1988, p. 310.

[8] Ibid, p. 357.

(NSCN), which subsequently split up following a bloody clash in April 1988. This saw the emergence of another faction of the NSCN, led by S.S. Khaplang, a Burmese Naga. Besides the NSCN, there were some other dissidents of the Shillong accord too. Sadly, this accord could not usher in an era of peace. A phase of violence erupted, which was initiated by the NSCN. Eventually, after a decade of bitter fighting, a ceasefire agreement was signed between the NSCN (IM) and the Government of India in July 1997, which has been periodically extended.

At present, there is a ceasefire between the army and both of the Naga armed factions, namely the NSCN Isaac & Muivah (IM) group and the NSCN Khaplang (K) group. They have parcelled out territories in all Naga-inhabited areas of the region, including Myanmar, Manipur, Assam and Arunachal Pradesh, based on ethnic and tribal affinities. There are ongoing inter-factional clashes in which both sides have suffered a number of fatal casualties. To add to the prevailing confusion, recently a further split has taken place in the NSCN(K). One group under Khaplang is entrenched mainly in Myanmar and the breakaway faction under self-styled General Khole Konyak and Kitovi Zhimomi, predominantly comprising of Indian Nagas, is Nagaland-based. The latter group has expelled its founder-chairman, Khaplang, and the leadership has passed into the hands of Khole and Kitovi. This statement has been repudiated by the Khaplang faction. These groups have imposed on the people a 'parallel government' and levy taxes, fines, extortion demands and carry out other illegal acts. However, there is a public outcry against this mindless violence and taxation burden. The people have unequivocally rejected the idea of an armed struggle for independence and other demands of the NSCN groups. They want a peaceful resolution of the problem. A historic covenant for peace had been signed on 18 September 2010 by the leaders of various Naga groups, including NSCN-IM General Secretary Muivah, NSCN-K General Secretary Kitovi Zhimomi and their Federal Government of Nagaland/Nagaland Nationalist Council counterparts. A ceasefire monitoring group handles all complaints of violation of the ceasefire agreement. At the same time, there has been an ongoing dialogue between the Government of India and the leaders of the NSCN-IM to find a peaceful solution to the Naga problem. The Government of

India has committed that it is prepared to discuss any solution within the Constitution of India and I am hopeful that permanent peace will return to Nagaland. Recently I met with General Thinouselie, who is in his late seventies, in Dimapur, and he categorically told me that the anti-Shillong accord groups have misled the people all these years. The people are looking forward to the end of strife, and ushering in of an era of peace and prosperity.

The Naga insurrection was followed by Mizo and Manipuri rebel movements in the 1960s. The Mizo National Front (MNF), which launched a vicious armed rebellion on 1 March 1966, had its origin from the Mizo Famine Front, an organization that was created to alleviate the sufferings of the Mizo people as an aftermath of a widespread famine in 1959. The apathetic attitude of the administration and lack of governance provided the ballast to the rebel movement. After two decades of violence and strife in the region, we finally succeeded in resolving the problem in Mizo hills. Under the peace accord of 30 June 1986 between the MNF and the Government of India, the new state of Mizoram was carved out of Assam. The Mizos have been reaping the benefits of peace since then. On the other hand, the Manipur imbroglio continues. It has by far the maximum militant outfits in the entire northeast. There are ceasefire or cessation of operations agreements with many of them, but notwithstanding that, there is rampant extortion, illegal taxation, violence, inter-factional clashes and other terrorist activities. Tripura is a typical example of conflict of interest among the tribals and non-tribals. A demographic shift has taken place over the past few decades in favour of plainsmen and the tribal population is below 30 per cent. As of now, the law and order situation is well under control, and the state seems to have turned around. It is, in fact, one of the most peaceful states in the northeast.

In Assam, an agitation was started by the All Assam Students' Union in 1979 against illegal migration of Bangladeshis and outsiders, and the exploitation of oil, mineral resources and tea without adequate benefit accruing to the people of Assam. This peaceful agitation continued for six years and as a result, the Asom Gana Parishad, a political party, was created after the signing of the historic Assam accord on 15 August 1985. On the other hand, an armed movement sprouted on

7 April 1979 as an offshoot of the parent organization, and is known as the United Liberation Front of Assam (ULFA). Subsequently, some other militant groups, representing minorities like Karbis, Bodos and Dimasas, surfaced. There is a sense of deprivation among these ethnic minorities and hence, these people are seeking a greater say in their own development and some form of autonomous structure for their areas. However, today, most of these organizations are bereft of any ideology and have almost become criminal groups that are carrying out acts of terrorism, extortion, kidnapping for ransom and killing of innocents. Terrorism has, in fact, become a sort of industry in this region. The crackdown on northeast terrorist outfits by the Bangladesh government in the last two years has given a terrible blow to these groups, and now more and more of them are coming around for talks with the Government of India. Many of their leaders have been arrested by our security forces and the police. The authorities in Bangladesh have also handed over many of their cadres, including some prominent leaders, to our Border Security Force. The chairman of the banned ULFA, Arabinda Rajkhowa, was released on bail on 1 January 2011, and he has publicly stated that ULFA is committed to working for lasting peace in Assam. Many other leaders of this organization have also similarly been released so that meaningful peace talks could be commenced with the Government of India. This development augurs well for peace and prosperity in the region.

The ULFA signed a suspension of operations agreement with the Government of India on 4 September 2011. However, after the heat raised in Bangladesh, the self-styled commander-in-chief of ULFA, Paresh Barua, and others moved to Myanmar. These groups are opposed to any dialogue without the sovereignty issue being on the agenda. On 8 September 2011, the Myanmar army launched operations on the camps of ULFA, NSCN (K) and other terrorist groups holed up in Myanmar. The government is hopeful of arriving at a peaceful solution of the Assam problem as a result of the ongoing parleys with the ULFA leaders. At present there is a democratically elected Congress government led by Tarun Gogoi, which has won the elections for a second term.

Sikkim, Arunachal Pradesh and Meghalaya are amongst the most peaceful states in the NE. There are two districts of Arunachal Pradesh bordering Nagaland which have a spillover of Naga insurgency, where cases of illegal tax collection, extortion, coercion, kidnapping and forcible recruitment have been taking place. However, the situation has not been allowed to deteriorate or spread to other parts of the state. More than a hundred misguided youth from Tirap District surrendered during 2009–10 because of frustration and a desire to return to the national mainstream. Sikkim has shown a remarkable improvement in governance. It is forging ahead in the domain of tourism. The socioeconomic condition of the people has shown an upward trend. The 2011 earthquake in Sikkim caused massive destruction of the infrastructure, though loss of lives was less than what was feared. The reconstruction process is on, with the army, air force and other agencies lending a helping hand.

Insurgency, terrorism and militancy are getting out of fashion, and the world has got united against terror. The 30 million people of the northeast are fed up of the strife and violence of the past five to six decades. They aspire for peace and prosperity in their part of the world. They need good governance and the connectivity to be able to engage with the global economy, as they are landlocked at present. The fact that Southeast Asia begins from the northeast should be remembered by the national leadership and our policy planners.

The prime minister has stated that Naxal extremism is one of the most serious internal security threats faced by our country. Lack of governance and many deep-rooted socioeconomic problems have led to a major law and order problem in thirty-four districts of eight states in the heartland of our country. In all, a total of eighty-seven districts in nine states are affected by Naxals or Maoists in some form or the other.[9] This area is often referred to as the 'red corridor' or the 'Compact Revolutionary Zone'. Interestingly, the worst-effected areas are the most remote, thickly forested and underdeveloped. The natural resources, including minerals, in these areas are immense and mostly untapped. Various hues of left-wing extremists (LWE) have gotten together under one umbrella, and are espousing the causes that have

---

[9] Statistics from the Ministry of Home Affairs website.

the greatest appeal to the poor tribal people inhabiting these areas. Their stated aim is to 'overthrow the semi-colonial, semi-feudal system under neo-colonial form of indirect rule'.[10] The nerve centre of this zone is the Dandakaranya forest area, which lies at the junction of Madhya Pradesh, Chhattisgarh, Maharashtra, Orissa and Andhra Pradesh.

A rising power needs all the resources that are available in the country, and therefore, law and order and peace are essential in this resource-rich heartland of India. The government has adopted an integrated approach to tackle this threat. An empowered group of ministers under the home minister has been created to oversee a coordinated approach to counter the Naxalite violence. And a standing committee of chief ministers of the affected states, also working under the home minister, has been formed to address political, security and socioeconomic development issues. At the executive level, there are various organizations that have been set up to tackle the menace. Integrated action plans covering sixty of these districts are being launched, but the principle of 'effective governance before development' would be sacrosanct before these plans are put into action.

The army has been carefully monitoring the developments and playing an advisory role to the government. It is also providing training assistance to the police and the paramilitary forces in various states on their request. We helped to set up the first counterinsurgency school at Kanker in Chattisgarh. I have been clear from the beginning that the army should not get embroiled in this problem as that would play into the hands of inimical forces, and detract us from our primary task of defence of our nation. I maintained this stance as the chief as it was not in our national interest. I am happy to see the policy has remained unchanged since then.

As army chief, my views on the repealing of the Armed Forces Special Powers Act (AFSPA) 1958 created a lot of ripples. Some people have termed it as a 'draconian law' that gives unbridled powers to the armed

---

[10] Constitution of the CPI (Maoist), http://www.bannedthought.net/india/CPIMaoist-Docs/index.htm, last accessed on 12 December 2010.

forces while they conduct operations against insurgents or terrorists. I believe that the armed forces are the instrument of last resort for a nation. Therefore, they must be given the responsibility of restoring law and order in a specific area only when all other means have failed. When such a situation arises, it becomes mandatory for the state to ensure that the armed forces are provided the necessary moral, material and legal support and wherewithal to overcome the challenge. When asked by the media, my categoric reply was that I would not like my soldiers to fight with one hand tied behind their back, or to be dragged to the courts on flimsy charges. While we shall take all steps to prevent human rights violations and punish those guilty of an offence, we would not want to restrain them from carrying out effective and speedy operations against the unscrupulous and faceless terrorists who strike and disappear instantly. National cohesion and integrity will be seriously jeopardized if the armed forces fail in their mission. However, if there are any ambiguities in the AFSPA, they need to be sorted out; value additions to make it more humane would also be welcome.

25

Chief of Defence Staff
The Way Forward

Would the appointment of the chief of defence staff (CDS) be the pill to solve the ills that exist in our higher defence set-up, as some analysts seem to suggest? The CDS has been in the news off and on ever since the Kargil war, and on occasions even before that, in discussions on defence leadership and national security. In the deliberations of the Kargil review committee, which was appointed soon after the termination of this conflict, the subject of higher defence organization once again came up.

The military operations branch, particularly the group that was led by me as the additional DGMO, is responsible for the planning and conduct of operations during war and peace, the defence of our borders, particularly the LoC in J&K and the LAC along the Himalayas in the north, and the ongoing counterterrorism operations in Kashmir and the northeast. Therefore, my team and I interacted extensively with this committee.

Their report indeed recommended the creation of the post of a chief of defence staff. Subsequently, to the credit of the government of the day, a group of ministers (GoM) was promptly appointed to study the Kargil review committee report. Four task forces were then constituted to study and offer concrete recommendations in the domains of enhanced capabilities for gathering of intelligence, management of the borders, internal security and defence management. This having been done, the recommendations of these task forces were discussed by the

Cabinet Committee for Security and, after approval, passed down for appropriate action.

However, though many of the recommendations of the GoM have been implemented, the government has not taken a decision on the appointment of a CDS as yet; the ostensible reason being offered is lack of political consensus and unanimity amongst the services. Some of the important findings that have seen the light of day are the creation of the Integrated Defence Staff, the Strategic Forces Command, the tri-service Andaman and Nicobar Command, the defence intelligence agency and the defence procurement board, and enhancement of the delegated financial powers of the defence and finance ministries and the services for procurement of arms and equipment.

As an interim measure, an inter-service organization with a chief of Integrated Defence Staff (CISC), a three-star ranking officer (from one of the three services) heading it, has been created to assist the chairman of the chiefs of staff committee (COSC) in dealing with tri-service operational and administrative matters and other specific issues assigned by the COSC, besides streamlining the long-term integrated planning process, prioritization of acquisitions, and bringing about greater jointness in the armed forces. From my experience as the chairman, COSC, and as chief of army staff, the CISC set-up has been working satisfactorily. The effectiveness of the CISC and the exploitation of the full potential of the Integrated Defence Staff depends entirely upon the chairman and members of the COSC and the ministry of defence.

Notwithstanding this, the question that still needs to be addressed is whether there is a necessity for a chief of defence staff and if so, in what time frame? Further, will the higher direction of war in India be handicapped without one? These issues have engaged the attention of the political elite, the defence ministry, the national security set-up, strategic thinkers and scholars. Unfortunately, a lot of lip service is paid in this regard by some of them; these issues tend to get raised from time to time, more so at the time of retirement of some service chief or the other – a feeble attempt to get a four-star general's post created, in the hope that it might benefit the individual concerned! At the same time, I do believe that the parliamentary committees for defence, on more than one occasion, have urged the respective governments to go ahead with the creation of a CDS without further delay. I also accept that there are some genuinely convinced adherents of the view that the CDS must be appointed as early as possible.

There are some fundamental considerations that need to be kept in mind and examined by the government before a decision is taken. First, *integration* in the true sense must imply not only integration within the services, as is the case at present, but also within the ministry of defence and the service HQs, with a complement of experts at the appropriate level from ministries of external affairs, home, finance and so on. It should be normal to see officers of these ministries and the defence services working together as a 'team' in various offices, as is the practice in all democratic nations. This has to happen sooner than later, but is not in place yet.

Secondly, each country must evolve its own *defence structure at the apex level*. Conceptually, there cannot be one formula that would apply to all. Whatever structure is created, it must ensure the highest level of security of our nation. No turf-guarding exercises should be permitted to compromise or dilute the steps required to safeguard the country. The CDS has been pronounced as the single-point adviser on defence matters for the government, and so it should be. He should have unfettered access to the prime minister and defence minister at all times. His presence at the highest decision-making fora in the country during discussions on national security should be institutionalized.

The next issue that needs to be examined is about the *command and control* of the armed forces. In most of the countries that have adopted the CDS formula, the operational control of the armed forces has been vested in his hands. In our case, the GoM report has recommended 'status quo' as far as the command and control of the forces is concerned. That would render the CDS a toothless tiger, a 'super adviser' without a definable responsibility or accountability. One could call him a modern-day Birbal! A dangerous guy to have around, I would think. Further, it is debatable if in our hierarchical and seniority-driven system, a 'first among equals' concept would work, more so if he happens to be a junior. We shall take some time to be ready for that.

We must begin first with an *inclusive and substantive integration* of the ministry of defence with the service HQs at the policy formulation and planning level, and going down to the theatre commands. There must be cross postings that would ensure meaningful integration on a functional basis, so as to include officers of the three services, officials of the ministries of defence, home, external affairs and finance and others as required, on the same lines as is the practice in other major democracies. Without this being in place, we would be handicapped as far as an integrated response to national security challenges is concerned. It is about time that the 'we' and 'they' syndrome is unshackled.

At the same time, we must create *an effective integrated military hierarchy,* with officers at the higher levels who have been exposed to conditions in other services and various theatres of our country and abroad. For example, high-calibre officers of the three services must be exposed to things like life in a submarine, the freezing Himalayan border areas, the tropical forests of the northeast, the desert of Rajasthan and so on. Finally, and importantly, such officers must also have a clear vision of the big picture at the national level, with an exposure in the ministry of defence, or the service HQs. I have come across some brigadiers and major generals who haven't been out of the country even once. As the chief, I desired that selected brigadiers and above should be given an opportunity to travel abroad at least once, so that they could learn by seeing things first-hand. Then alone, in due course of time, can one hope to become a useful 'single-point adviser'. This process of capacity building can start without delay.

Therefore, in the next ten to fifteen years, we should create integrated theatre commands and specialized commands – such as training and doctrine, aerospace, network-centric warfare and joint logistics in addition to the existing Andaman and Nicobar and Strategic Forces Commands. Cross attachment and posting of middle- and senior-level leadership and tri-service training, war games and courses could commence from 2013. At the theatre or command level and HQ Integrated Defence Staff, the posting of officers representing the MOD, MEA, finance ministry and the Defence Research and Development Organization should also be implemented simultaneously. As an interim measure, the CISC could be upgraded to a vice chief of defence staff of four-star rank to oversee the transformation and restructuring of the armed forces. Alternatively, we could consider having a permanent chairman of COSC at four-star level with specific responsibilities as being advocated by Lieutenant General V.R. Raghavan, who is a member of the Naresh Chandra Committee that is looking at higher defence set-up and national security issues. However, neither of these iterim proposals, if adopted, should get enshrined as a permanent arrangement.

It would be fair to surmise that we could have a CDS by 2020, who should be vested with operational command of the three services and be of a five-star rank. He would then be an effective and meaningful 'single-point' adviser on defence matters.

26

The Nuclear Dimension

The baton of the chairman of the chiefs of staff committee was handed over to me by Air Chief Marshal S.P. Tyagi in February 2007, and I held this position till I superannuated at the end of September that year. This committee is chartered to discuss and evolve joint military strategy focusing on national security challenges and to advise the national leadership on all service matters. During this period, three important events or issues took centre stage: a tri-service delegation led by me to China, the formulation of the recommendations of the armed forces to the 6th Pay Commission, and the implementation of the A.V. Singh Committee Part II report dealing with cadre review of senior ranks. These issues have been dealt with separately.

This was also the first occasion when one took a very close look at the nuclear component of national security. Though we had carried out a peaceful nuclear explosion (Pokharan I) in 1974, we had not demonstrated our capability of nuclear weaponization till the testing of five nuclear devices on 11 and 13 May 1998 (Pokharan II or Operation Shakti). It was in the wake of these tests that on 14 May 1998, Prime Minister Vajpayee stated, 'India is now a nuclear weapons state. We have the capacity for a big bomb now. Ours will never be weapons of aggression.'[1]

The nuclear dimension of India's national security strategy is based on the doctrine of a credible minimum nuclear deterrence, and our

---

[1] http://nuclearweaponarchive.org/India/IndiaArsenal.html

stated policy that there will be no first use of nuclear weapons, and that these will not be used against non-nuclear states. Our policy clearly lays down 'a continuance of strict controls on export of nuclear- and missile-related materials and technologies, participation in the fissile material cut-off treaty negotiations, and continued moratorium on nuclear tests.'[2] Our national leadership has maintained for a long time that we would work to achieve the goal of a nuclear-weapon-free world through non-discriminatory nuclear disarmament. I firmly believe that such a capability is not for fighting war but for deterrence. But should deterrence fail, we should not be found wanting in mounting an adequate and effective retaliation.

On India's nuclear capability, an article, *India and Weapons of Mass Destruction*[3] states, 'India possesses nuclear weapons and maintains short and intermediate range ballistic missiles, nuclear-capable aircraft, surface ships, and submarines under development as possible delivery systems and platforms.' Speaking about the three-dimensional capability of the delivery systems, it mentions, 'Although it lacks an operational ballistic missile submarine, India has ambitions of possessing a nuclear triad in the near future when INS Arihant, the lead ship of India's Arihant class of nuclear-powered submarines, formally joins the Indian Navy in 2012 after undergoing extensive sea-trials.'[4]

As part of risk reduction and confidence building, an agreement on the prohibition of attack on each other's nuclear installations and facilities was signed between India and Pakistan on 31 December 1988. In accordance with this agreement, the updated lists of such installations and facilities were exchanged on 1 January 2010.

I must admit that the Indian government and the nuclear establishment continue to display the highest level of secrecy, control and maturity required of a responsible nuclear power. This has been acknowledged and appreciated worldwide. Even in the highest positions that I have held in the military, I was in the decision-making loop only where required. In 1998, when Pokharan II tests took place, I was the additional DGMO in the Army HQ. It was only when the

[2] http://www.indembassy.org.ua/english/news10.htm
[3] http://en.wikipedia.org/wiki/India_and_weapons_of_mass destruction
[4] Ibid.

prime minister made the announcement to the media that I came to know of them. The fact that till the very end, the prying eyes of the world were kept away from Operation *Shakti* and total surprise was achieved, speaks volumes of the sense of security maintained by all those concerned with the project.

As mentioned in his well-researched book, *Weapons of Peace*, Raj Chengappa once asked Dr A.P.J. Abdul Kalam, 'You, more than anyone else, had the unique choice of building vehicles of peace at the space department or making weapons of war in defence. Why did you choose the latter when you know that it is capable of so much destruction and bloodshed?' Kalam answered: 'I had no qualms. By building such arsenal I actually ensure peace for my country. Now no nation dare attack us. These are truly weapons of peace.'[5] The world sat up to notice the emergence of India as a nuclear-weapon state.

The reaction of Pakistan was as expected. India's nuclear tests were described as 'reckless and highly provocative'. Prime Minister Nawaz Sharif stated in his address to the people, 'We will take all necessary measures to safeguard our security, sovereignty, territorial integrity and national interests.'[6] Gohar Ayub Khan, the then foreign minister, said, 'Indian actions, which pose an immediate and grave threat to Pakistan's security, will not go unanswered.'[7] Despite vigorous efforts and inducements, as also veiled threats by the US, Pakistan went ahead with its retaliation to India's tests by exploding five nuclear devices in the Chagai Hills on 28 May 1998, and a sixth two days later. These tests took place barely fifteen days after ours.

Pakistan has made it known that it would not be averse to the 'first use' of nuclear weapons in case its territorial integrity is threatened. It has blatantly indulged in nuclear sabre-rattling and blackmail both during the Kargil war and during the showdown in 2002 after the terrorist attack on the Indian Parliament. The same veiled threats emanated from Pakistan in October 2011 to deter another unilateral US military action inside Pakistan, after the strike that took out Osama Bin Laden in Abbotabad.

[5] Raj Chengappa, *Weapons of Peace*, HarperCollins, 2000, p. xi.
[6] Jaswant Singh, *A Call to Honour*, Rupa & Co, 2006, p. 129.
[7] Ibid.

27

Snow Tsunami and Earthquake in Kashmir

One of the worst natural disasters in recent years struck Kashmir in February 2005, soon after I became the army chief. Two spells of unprecedented heavy snowfall and inclement weather, the first being around 6 February and the second ten days later, brought Jammu and Kashmir to a standstill for almost one month. Nature does not differentiate between man-made boundaries, and hence the Pakistani side of the LoC was equally badly affected. Large areas were cut off, rendering even assessment of the damage and destruction impossible. Heavy accumulation of snow on the hill slopes triggered a series of avalanches and landslides, which buried numerous villages, crippled electricity and water supplies and blocked most roads and airfields. The army, by virtue of its extensive grid deployment in far-flung areas, was able to respond quickly and spearhead the rescue and relief effort. I gave orders to provide assistance without waiting for formal or written requisition from the state government. Rescue columns of the army saved the lives of sixty-nine people. Food and medical assistance was provided to about 1800 people. Besides that, clothing, blankets and tents were made available to hundreds of marooned passengers and destitute villagers who would otherwise have frozen to death. We recovered 208 bodies buried under the snow. As a humanitarian gesture, I ordered the release of 70 per cent of our war reserves of petrol, diesel and rations to provide succour to the people.

The main artery connecting Jammu with Srinagar remained cut off till 1 March 2005, when the border roads and the army finally cleared it. During this period, I accompanied Defence Minister Pranab Mukherjee to the state for an aerial survey of the worst-hit areas. It was heart-rending to see entire villages covered by a carpet of snow. The silhouettes of some of the houses were visible under the snow. We tried to look for people but found no signs of life in most places. Unfortunately for the terrorists, many of them perished as their hideouts in the hills and forests got totally snowed in. The people of Kashmir were very grateful and for once, the usually acerbic local media also showered praise on the army and the air force. We suddenly became angels! The central government stepped in and poured a lot of aid. Army relief teams spread out to the remotest corners of the Pir Panjal range and its valleys, which were the worst hit. Kashmir limped back to normalcy.

Later that year, on the morning of 8 October 2005, a severe earthquake caused tremendous loss of life and devastation in PoK and in some adjoining areas on our side of the LoC. This was the second disaster that struck the Kashmir region in the year. It was of an intensity of 7.6 on the Richter scale, enough to flatten out most of the capital town of Muzaffarabad in PoK and practically all the villages around it. It was about the same intensity as the earthquakes in Quetta (1935) or in Gujarat (2001) and this tragedy resulted in over 70,000 deaths and injuries to over one lakh people in PoK. On the Indian side, the worst-hit areas were Uri and Tangdhar along the LoC. There was colossal loss of property in the area, though not so much loss of life. Terrorist training camps in PoK were also hit. 'When entire villages have been wiped out, it is most likely that these terrorist camps (in Muzaffarabad area) have also been affected,' was my response to questions by the media.

'...a majority of the training camps were located near the epicentre of the quake with Lashkar's office and hospital in Muzaffarabad being completely razed to the ground. Harkat-ul-Mujahideen's training centre at Balakot and Batrasi, Jaish-e-Mohammed's camp at Attock, Al Badr's at Oghi, Lashkar's at Mansera and Hizbul's recruitment camp at Jungle-

Mangal had been damaged to a great extent.'[1] Was it divine retribution in the case of these terrorists?

Once again, without waiting for a formal request for aid from the state government, we reached out to the calamity-struck people of Baramulla and Tangdhar districts of Kashmir. Rescue and relief measures were effected on a war footing under the name Operation Imdaad (Succour). Even though we also suffered casualties along the LoC, and some of our posts were badly hit, my directions were to send out search and rescue mission patrols to the remote areas and give a helping hand to the people in distress. The forward piquet in Tangdhar sector just disappeared from the face of the earth as the fractured edge of the mountain was sliced by nature and tumbled down a few thousand feet.

As a humanitarian gesture, composite relief points were set up by our army for the people of PoK too. These were established at Kaman, Tithwal, Chakan-da-bagh, Roshni and Silkot, so as to facilitate transfer of relief material across the LoC to the Pakistani authorities. 'Pakistan Foreign Minister Khurshid M. Kasuri on Tuesday (11 October 2005) spoke to External Affairs Minister K. Natwar Singh and expressed appreciation for India's assistance to the quake-hit. India's 25-tonne relief supplies, including tents, plastic sheets, blankets, mattresses, food items and medicines, will fly out from New Delhi around midnight Tuesday.'[2] The total count of relief provided was much more, as shown in the news snippet below. The Indian Air Force and army aviation also made a commendable contribution and effected an air bridge from the affected areas to the hospitals in Srinagar and saved many lives.

Further, the army adopted three villages that had been destroyed by the earthquake and were raised from the rubble as model villages. These were Churunda and Tithwal in the valley and another in Poonch area called Khari Karmara. Along with my wife Rohini, I inaugurated the Tithwal model village on 22 June 2006. This village is within earshot of the LoC, with only the turquoise-blue Kishanganga river flowing between PoK and India. I also inaugurated the Churunda model village on 6 October 2006. In these villages we created community development

---

[1] *The Asian Age*, 12 October 2005.
[2] *The Indian Express*, 12 October 2005.

centres, new buildings for primary health centres, roads, pathways, piped water supply, sports fields and schools. Later, the Indian Air Force also adopted a village called Urusa and helped to reconstruct it. The comparison of the spontaneity of the relief and rescue operations on two sides of the LoC was inevitable, and I am happy to say that our efforts won praise and acclaim on the other side as well, albeit grudgingly at places.

28

Defence Diplomacy and Neighbourhood

As the army chief, I endeavoured to enhance our level of military cooperation with other countries within the ambit of the foreign policy parameters enunciated by the government, and contribute towards achievement of our national objectives. This was one of my key result areas. I laid down guidelines for augmenting the level of army-to-army cooperation and directed the newly created defence cooperation cell, which was an extension of the foreign division in the Army HQ, to identify the areas of mutual interest and make out a road map for defence cooperation with friendly countries. I undertook a number of goodwill visits as the army chief, and as the chairman of the chiefs of staff committee in my last year in office. My priorities were our immediate neighbours and countries with which we have a strategic partnership, followed by those with which we have traditional ties and enduring military relationships.

The experience gained by me during my tenure of three years as the defence attaché of India in our embassy in Algeria gave me valuable insights into the world of diplomacy. It also brought out the importance of military diplomacy as a vital component of our foreign policy. As is the case with other developed nations that have enshrined international defence cooperation as an important mission to further their national diplomatic aims, we also need to give this dimension a similar place. The need for defence cooperation, including an array of other activities such as high-level strategic dialogue and goodwill exchanges, joint training, sharing of intelligence relating to terrorism or other mutual security concerns, professional military courses of instruction, and weapons and equipment transfers, is unexceptionable. Furthermore, participation in joint counterterrorism, peacekeeping and disaster management exercises between our armed forces and those of friendly countries in and around our neighbourhood and other important nations of the world has proved very beneficial. Well-orchestrated military diplomacy can help in the achievement of our foreign policy goals and in addressing the security concerns in our region.

This is particularly true in the case of countries where the military has an overarching role in policy-making or governance. I was able to make bridges for effective military-to-military cooperation between the armed forces of Algeria and India as a defence attaché. Colonel Chadli Bendjedid was the president of Algeria at that time. Due to India's moral and diplomatic support to the freedom struggle of Algeria, our standing in the Arab countries and my army background, I was able to get easy access to their military and political hierarchy.

I have been a great advocate of involving the armed forces during the evolution and formulation of our foreign policy with respect to our neighbouring countries. This will further our national interests, build mutual trust and confidence, and thereby engender peace and stability in the region. A strategic-level military-to-military dialogue helps in evolving a shared perception of emerging challenges as also the possible steps to overcome them. The process comprises high-level defence interaction with key global and regional players through exchanges at various levels. We have been pursuing these in a focused manner with our neighbours like China, Bhutan, Nepal, Afghanistan, Myanmar, Sri Lanka, and recently with Bangladesh, as also with the US, Russia, the UK, France, Japan, Australia, Singapore, Indonesia and a few other countries. With Pakistan, there have only been diplomatic parleys and a composite dialogue, which has been 'off and on' due to Pakistan's complicity in terrorist attacks against our country. We have conducted joint training exercises with many of these countries, as also with China. The agreement for this was signed between the foreign ministers of the two countries, but the modalities were concretized during my visit to China in mid-2007. Because we are regarded as a thoroughly professional and battle-experienced army, there is a great clamour among other countries for seeking vacancies for courses of instruction in our armed forces training institutions.

Joint exercises between two armed forces are designed to evolve common operating procedures that could be used during the conduct of counterterrorist or peacekeeping operations and disaster management. They could also be designed to counter emerging threats such as the use of weapons of mass destruction. Such exercises are mutually beneficial to both sides as they help to develop better understanding and improve interoperability. Military training exchanges, both bilateral and multilateral, are an important component of military diplomacy and a valuable instrument of building bridges between armed forces, with the purpose of promoting national interests. These activities comprise conduct of professional courses, making available of training advisers, and provision of training teams. It may be recalled that we raised the military academies in Ethiopia and Nigeria and our officers helped to run these training institutions for a number of years. Similarly we had air force training teams in Egypt and Iraq, which trained a whole generation of pilots from these Arab countries.

When I visited Nigeria as the chief of army staff, a brigadier at their Kaduna academy remarked that on seeing my olive green uniform his hair stood on end, as he was reminded of his Indian Army instructors. In a meeting during that visit, when I pointed out that their president, General Obasanjo, was an illustrious and distinguished alumnus of the Defence Services Staff College in India, the president remarked, 'Gentlemen, have you heard what the Indian army chief has just said.' Similarly, King Jigme Khesar Namgyel Wangchuk, the present king of Bhutan, and General Irshad, the former president of Bangladesh, are graduates of the National Defence College, New Delhi. There have been at least six chiefs of armed forces of countries like Sri Lanka, Nigeria, Malaysia and Afghanistan who have graduated from the National Defence College in India. It is but natural that such training programmes generate a lot of goodwill and bonhomie which, if nurtured, could prove to be a great asset while dealing with these countries.

The exchange of military hardware is another area that has an important bearing on building friendly relations between countries. Our strategic partnership with countries like the US, Russia and others has been enhanced by military weapons and equipment transfers. We need to have a strategy of helping our smaller neighbours achieve a reasonable capability of defence against the challenges they face. We must remember that in case we fail to seize the opportunity, someone else will fill the vacuum and meet their needs. I am also of the opinion that whatever we give to another country should be our best indigenous products that are currently in service with our defence forces, even if we are gifting the equipment or undertaking the transfers at nominal prices. This would help in strengthening our ties and keeping inimical forces at bay.

When I was in Algeria, many requests were made for us to help them overhaul their Soviet-origin weapon platforms and equipment. I conveyed those requests to our government, but our response was tardy. Our armed forces have acquired a high level of expertise in optimization of Russian tanks, guns, aircraft, ships, submarines and other equipment. We have innovated many techniques of employing this hardware, which has astounded even the Russians at times. This expertise is something many countries that have similar equipment are looking for. We must make best use of this advantage and build bonds and enduring relationships.

Another important dimension of military diplomacy is the active participation of Indian armed forces in UN peacekeeping operations. We have been the largest contributors to such operations, beginning with the first deployment in Korea in 1950. Our aspiration for a permanent seat in the UN Security Council has been reinforced by the sterling performance of our armed forces in forty-plus peacekeeping missions all over the world; our professionalism in these operations has won universal praise for us. We have provided brigade-group-sized forces in missions at Korea, Congo, Somalia and Sierra Leone, and a large number of battalion groups in many other conflict-prone areas in Africa and Asia. These deployments helped to bring about peace and stability in those areas. Significantly, at the request of the UN, we made available thirteen force commanders to lead missions in Europe, Africa and Asia. Many of our gallant soldiers laid down their lives; some of them have been decorated with the highest gallantry awards. We have created a training facility for UN peacekeepers at New Delhi, which again has been in great demand in our region. It trains leaders as well as observers for UN assignments. Besides that, all units assigned UN missions are put through a comprehensive training programme for four weeks, and some persons from the core group are also imparted language skills.

From the global point of view, as the dust began to settle after the cataclysmic break-up of the USSR in 1990, it appeared that a unipolar world had emerged, with the USA as the most powerful nation on earth.

However, during the past two decades, we have witnessed the diffusion of political, military and economic power, with the rise of China, the European Union, Japan, Russia, India, and Brazil. The US no longer believes that it can go it alone or that its best interests would be served by being in the lead role in every situation. Therefore, a 'defining strategic partnership' between the two largest democracies of the world, as emphatically stated by President Barak Obama during his November 2010 visit to India, assumes great importance. Indo-US relations are gaining a momentum of their own. This is a golden opportunity for us to forge a meaningful long-term relationship with America which, in the words of President Obama, 'will be indispensable in shaping the twenty-first century'. With shared democratic values and more convergence in views than differences, our mutually beneficial partnership portends well for peace and stability in the world.

These very heartwarming and welcome sentiments are in stark contrast to the perceptions in America about our country during the Cold War period. I recollect reading and rereading an international weekly magazine that had done a cover story on 'Democracy' in the late 1970s. India was not mentioned even once in that story, leaving all right-thinking Indians aghast. From 'not figuring' on the American radar screen to becoming a 'strategic partner' is remarkable. The wheel seems to have taken a full turn.

During my visit to the US in November 2006, we were very warmly received and taken around. During the discussions and meetings at the Pentagon, I had the privilege of meeting Defence Secretary Donald Rumsfeld. There was a detailed interaction with General Peter J. Schoomaker, their chief of staff of the army, and other officers. We visited the US military academy at West Point; the training and doctrine command at Fort Monroe; and Forts Benning in Georgia, Lewis in Seattle, and Irwin near Los Angeles. At Fort Irwin we were taken to the national training centre and were shown a training facility depicting an Arab village called 'Medina Jabal' in the desert. All troops going into deployment in Iraq were trained at this institution.

After the disintegration of the Soviet Union, there was a period of uncertainty and political upheaval in that region for a few years. Russia has been a time-tested friend of our country. India and Russia are in the process of enhancing their cooperation in various fields such as space research, defence, science and technology, trade and energy. The landmark visit of Prime Minister Manmohan Singh to Russia in December 2009 gave a further boost to our existing close ties. During this visit, 'six important agreements were signed apart from the adoption of a joint declaration on "further deepening the strategic partnership", thus reflecting the shared vision of the two countries on many global issues.'[1]

We have a vibrant relationship as far as defence cooperation is concerned, with a regular exchange of visits, joint training exercises, courses of instruction, transfers of weapon systems and equipment and transfer of technology. Certain joint projects have been initiated for the development of missiles and futuristic fifth-generation aircraft. The Brahmos supersonic cruise missile is an outstanding example of such collaboration. While we improve our relations with other countries, we must consolidate and further strengthen our ties with the Russian Federation.

We had carried out the first counterterrorist exercise called 'Indra' in Rajasthan in October 2005, with the Russian airborne forces and the paratroopers of the Indian Army. The defence minister of Russia,

---

[1] Ministry of External Affairs, Annual Report 2009–10.

Sergei Ivanov, was present along with the chief of their airborne forces. It gave me immense satisfaction to see our troops carrying out joint operations to destroy a terrorist camp along with the simultaneous capture of an advanced landing ground. In this exercise we showcased the capability of heavy drops in which a few latest Russian armoured personnel carriers (BMDs), weighing 8 tons each, were dropped, as also a few mortars and light vehicles, which came down in clusters of four parachutes each. It was an awesome sight. We were lucky to avert a serious mishap as one of the crates carrying a mortar landed a few metres behind us, making the Russian defence minister quip, 'Perfect air-dropping of cargo is next to impossible, even during war.'[2] This was followed by over 200 parachutists coming down in front of us. In a few minutes they got hold of their BMDs, mortars and jeeps and got into action to attack the terrorist stronghold.

I visited Russia on two occasions, first in August 2006 as the army chief and then in September 2007 as the chairman, chiefs of staff committee. The highlights of the first visit were meetings at the Kremlin with the chief of general staff of Russian armed forces, General Yuri Baluyevsky, and Colonel General Alexie Maslov Feodorovich, the C-in-C Russian land forces; the laying of the wreath at the Tomb of the Unknown Soldier; visits to the Mikhailov Artillery Academy at St Peterburg; 106 Airborne Division at Tula and a live firing demonstration organized by the 2nd Motorized Guards Rifle Division at Alabino. The main purpose of my second visit was to witness the Indo-Russian Joint Exercise, 'Indra 2007', which was conducted at Kislovo near Pskov. It was a very impressive paradrop and I was proud to see the performance of our paratroopers matching the Russians.

France is a major European power and our ties have always been cordial and close. With the signing of the strategic partnership in 1998, our cooperation has touched new heights in diverse fields such as space, nuclear energy, defence, education, economy and culture. It was the first country with whom India has an agreement on nuclear energy. We

---

[2] *Hindustan Times*, 17 October 2005.

need to study the independent approach and policies adopted by France on various global issues. There are many things we could emulate from such countries as we climb on to the higher rungs of the ladder as a world power. There is a dependability factor in our relationship with France. Weapon systems, equipment and technology transfers from France do not come with many conditions.

My visit to France in June 2007 as the chairman of the chiefs of staff committee was very useful. I met the chief of defence services, General Jean Louis Georgelin, and the chief of the army staff, visited the naval academy and the nuclear submarine base at Brest (they took us on board one of their nuclear submarines), and the headquarters of the special forces and the centre for planning and conduct of operations. It was a great honour to visit the First World War memorial at Neuve Chappelle. We also visited the beaches in Normandy and the Second World War memorial at Caen. France gave our nation and our armed forces the great privilege and rare honour to lead the Bastille Day parade on 14 July 2009, with a big military contingent. On this historical event, Prime Minister Manmohan Singh was the guest of honour and we had a 400-strong armed forces contingent marching impressively on the Champs Elysses in Paris. For me, as the honorary colonel of the Maratha Light Infantry, it was a proud day to see the gallant Marathas leading this parade.

India and the UK not only have historical ties but also an enduring strategic partnership and cooperation in diverse fields, including that of defence. My family ties with the British Indian Army are almost a century-old. Therefore, my official visit to the UK from 5–8 July 2005 had a special significance for me. Our army inherited the traditions, culture and customs from the British Indian Army and therefore we share many values. The visit started with the ceremonial guard of honour at Wellington Barracks in close vicinity of Buckingham Palace, where I took the salute and reviewed the parade in the presence of General Sir Mike Jackson, the chief of general staff of the British Army. My late grandfather and father would have felt equally honoured to witness this ceremony.

Reviewing the Guard of Honour at the Wellington Barracks near Buckingham Palace, accompanied by General Sir Mike Jackson.

Over the next four days there were meetings at the ministry of defence, the foreign office and visits to formations and institutions such as HQ Land Command at Wilton, the defence academy at Shrivenham and 2nd Division at Edinburgh. I was impressed to see the training facility created in the combined arms tactical trainer, where all arms manoeuvres could take place with live firing. The equipment display was very interesting as they had laid on a demonstration of their latest weapon systems and equipment. At the defence academy, I addressed the students on security issues and leadership. At the army banquet hosted by General Sir Mike Jackson, I was presented two medals of the Great War which my grandfather had earned but which had been lost at the time of Partition. It was a very touching gesture, and must have gladdened the spirit of the grand old man too. It was a matter of great pride for me. They have been mounted on a silver stand and find a pride of place in our home today.

Talking about our neighbourhood, our relations with China assume the greatest importance for peace, prosperity and stability of the region. We have a 'strategic and cooperative partnership' in place. There is enough space for sustained economic and social development and trade for both of us. The paths we have chosen are different but the aim is common – the well-being and prosperity of our people. Therefore, I believe that we may be competitors but we are not rivals. Our leaders have adopted a statesman-like approach and agreed to resolve our intractable boundary and other problems in a peaceful, mature and pragmatic manner.

The Government of India's response to the Chinese argument – that the boundary between the two countries had never been formally delimited – was: 'the Sino-Indian boundary, based on custom and tradition, follows natural features, and for the major part this customary and traditional boundary is also confined by treaty and agreement (between British India and Tibet, though the Chinese shied away from most of these treaties on some pretext or the other). This boundary has been fixed and well known for centuries. According to international usage and practice, a customary boundary which follows well known and unchanging natural features like the main watershed, stands defined and does not require further and formal definition.'[3]

A comprehensive review of the boundary dispute between India and China brings out that our northern border is sanctified by tradition and history over the centuries; that certain sectors of the boundary crystallized during the nineteenth and early twentieth centuries due to the British empire's security concerns and that the internationally accepted principle of the watershed or the highest crest line along the northern mountain chain became the basis of determining the boundary.

> 'The idea of a demarcated frontier is itself an essentially modern conception, and finds little or no place in the ancient world,' Lord Curzon observed at the beginning of the 20th century. Further, he pointed out that until then, 'it would be true to say that demarcation has never taken place in Asiatic countries except under European pressure...'[4]

[3] White Paper issued by the Government of India, No. III, p. 85.
[4] Lord Curzon, 'Frontiers', Romanes Lecture of 1907.

The Sino–Indian border issue needs to be addressed at a faster pace, of that there is no doubt. For years both sides have been adopting fixed positions. The visit of the Indian prime minister, Rajiv Gandhi, to China in 1988 was a landmark event. It laid the foundation for a more vibrant relationship between the two Asian giants. It resulted in the signing of the agreement on maintaining peace and tranquillity along the border in 1993, during the visit of Prime Minister Narasimha Rao.

During Prime Minister A.B. Vajpayee's visit to China in 2003, both countries agreed to appoint a special representative to explore the framework of a boundary settlement. Any mutually acceptable solution will have to be an exercise carried out objectively based on the agreement on 'political parameters and guiding principles' signed in 2005. This approach will benefit both countries.

During my tenure as the chief we had an important visit by a Chinese army delegation led by General Liang Guanglie, the chief of general staff, during which we had meaningful discussions at the Army HQ and visits to field formations.

Subsequently, as the chairman, chiefs of staff committee, I led a tri-service delegation to China, during the last week of May 2007. I was privileged to have called on Vice President Zeng Quinghong and Foreign Minister Yang Jiechie in the Great Hall of the People, besides meeting the hierarchy of the People's Liberation Army, namely, General Liang Guanglie, the chief of general staff of People's Liberation Army (presently the defence minister) at the HQ of the Central Military Commission (CMC), and General Guo Boxiong, vice chairman of the CMC, and other defence officials. While shaking hands with the vice president and conveying the good wishes of our people, I summoned the courage to say, 'Excellency, when our two nations shake hands, the world sits up to watch.' He smiled. We agreed to hold the first-ever defence dialogue in New Delhi in a few months' time and also agreed upon the modalities of joint training between the two armies to be held once a year. For army officers of our generation and our predecessors who had been through the 1962 showdown, this was something incredible. The same may have been the case on the Chinese side.

On my farewell visit to HQ Eastern Command during September 2007, an interesting incident concerning China happened quite innocuously.

In my customary interaction with the media, I was asked a number of questions relating to my visit to China and the infrastructure being built in Tibet. My response covered the extremely positive developments in our bilateral relations, the confidence-building measures in place and so on. The media was not satisfied and continued harping on the point that we were not doing enough to meet the future challenges. I assumed that the media was projecting the feelings of the people. Therefore, to give them the desired level of reassurance, I highlighted with great emphasis that we were doing everything that was required to improve our capabilities and the infrastructure so that we could effectively respond to any challenge, and that 1962 would not be repeated.

The next day we were amazed to learn from ambassador Nirupama Rao that the Chinese foreign office had queried her if the Indian army chief had issued a warning to China! We were quite surprised as no such thing had happened. When we checked up on this, it turned out that one of the media reports had titled the story of my interaction in Kolkata – 'Indian Army Chief warns China against misadventure.' The heading given by the editor had no relationship with the text of the article. Nirupama Rao deftly explained to the Chinese that this was an example of irresponsible and sensational reporting by an element of our free media. Fortunately the issue was not allowed to be blown out of proportion by this timely intervention.

Pakistan has been inherently and consistently antagonistic towards India over a host of issues. Prime amongst them is that Pakistan has not been able to reconcile itself to the fact that the predominantly Muslim state of Jammu and Kashmir acceded to India in October 1947. We have had four wars over Kashmir; a war by proxy is still continuing; and our bilateral relations have become hostage to this issue. There was frequent cross-border shelling, sniping and skirmishes at the LoC till 2003, when both countries decided to have a ceasefire that is still holding. Pakistan has hopefully realized that it cannot take Kashmir by force. However, after 9/11, things changed drastically for Pakistan. It had to decide whether to go with the Taliban or join the US in the global war on terror. Pakistan chose the latter option but did a partial U-turn in its relations with the Taliban and jehadi organizations that had proliferated in the tribal border areas. They did not take any action against certain terrorist networks whom they classify as strategic assets, like the Haqqani faction. The spillover of the messy situation in Afghanistan has also been adversely affecting the stability and progress of Pakistan.

While dealing with internal turmoil and taking action against the Al Qaida and other terrorist organizations on its border with Afghanistan in areas like Swat and South Waziristan, Pakistan has simultaneously continued to upgrade its conventional and strategic capability. It is building its nuclear arsenal, honing the delivery systems and testing its long-range nuclear-capable missiles. It seeks to achieve conventional parity with us and accordingly has enhanced its defence spending to unaffordable levels. This is definitely at the cost of development.

Who is in control in Pakistan? Going as per media reports and books written by some well-known authors, including some from Pakistan, their army is all-powerful. Some have gone to the extent of saying that while other states have an army, in Pakistan the army has a state. Though on the face of it there is a democratically elected government in place, it is an unstated fact that the army calls the shots. This is particularly so when it comes to dialogue with India over Kashmir or other substantive and sensitive matters. Besides that, there are certain fundamentalist organizations like the Lashkar-e-Taiba, the Tehrike Taliban Pakistan, the Haqqani network or Jaish-e-Mohammad, which are treated as holy cows and are not touched, even though they are banned. They are said to enjoy huge public support because of which they have acquired immunity. Even General Musharraf, who was the army chief and the president of Pakistan, pleaded helplessness when it came to taking action against some of the jehadi leaders, afraid of the fallout. The French philosopher, Bernard-Henry Levy, towards the end of his book, *Who killed Daniel Pearl*, reaches this terrifying conclusion: 'I assert that Pakistan is the biggest rogue of all the rogue states today…what is taking form there, between Islamabad and Karachi, is a black hole compared to which Saddam Hussein's Baghdad was an obsolete dump.'[5]

[5] *India Today*, 22 December 2008, p. 34.

Since 2003, with the introduction of confidence-building measures such as the opening of the road from Srinagar to Muzaffarabad, the train connectivity between Delhi and Lahore, and increase in trade, India has been endeavouring to normalize relations with Pakistan. However, while Pakistan professes to welcome peaceful relations with India, it encourages the use of its soil and PoK for infiltrating trained and armed terrorists to carry out acts of violence in India. Primarily because of this dichotomy, there is a trust deficit. Therefore, despite India's best efforts, the 'composite diologue' between our countries stands frozen after the terrorist attacks on Mumbai. Pakistan is in a bind; it is treading on a dangerous path where it has to compromise and resort to double-dealing with key terrorist leaders and also draw a distinction between 'good' and 'bad' Taliban.

As far as proliferation of nuclear technology is concerned, Pakistan has had a dubious record. Is it conceivable that the Pakistani president and army chief, Pervez Musharraf, was unaware of the dealings A.Q. Khan had with Libya or North Korea or what was going on in their nuclear installations? How could Khan be using Pakistani Air Force planes to cart his shadowy cargo on his own? Now that he has been exposed, he has been conveniently dumped and put into cold storage. 'The enterprising father of the Pakistani nuclear bomb A.Q. Khan hawked his wares for years before my group at the CIA caught him red-handed and put him out of business for selling a nuclear bomb to Libya in late 2003.'[6]

There has practically been no bilateral military-to-military interaction between India and Pakistan except for the posting of defence attachés, weekly DGMO-level talks, and flag meetings by the formation commanders for resolving local issues. There is some interaction between the representatives of the armed forces during the composite dialogue process, which too is now on a 'pause mode'. It may be a good idea if, as part of our overall diplomatic strategy, our defence forces are given the opportunity to break the ice and meet their contemporaries formally or informally to thrash out some of our military-related irritants. This out-of-the-box idea to engage with their army is certainly worth trying. A moderate, peaceful and prosperous

---

[6] Valerie Palme Wilson, *Newsweek*, 9 August 2010, pp. 26–27.

Pakistan would be good for all of us, and be able to contribute to the stability of our region.

Our policy of helping in the reconstruction of Afghanistan and a development-oriented partnership has been hugely appreciated by the people of that country. We would like to see a stable and peaceful Afghanistan that would be able to establish its control and prevent the spread of terrorism by organizations like Al Qaida from its soil. An interesting conversation regarding Afghanistan took place between Dr Henry Kissinger and me at a private dinner in November 2008, when the gracious host, K.P. Singh, requested me to give company to the distinguished Nobel laureate.

Dr Kissinger began with the question, 'General, what are your views on the Afghan situation and what we should do?'

'Briefly Sir, Afghanistan has historically never been subjugated by any external power. The tribal chieftains or warlords are very powerful and their writ runs unchallenged. Nothing can be achieved without their support. You have to have them on your side. Having beaten the Russians, the Taliban and Al Qaida have their tails up,' I replied, and Dr Kissinger nodded.

'And as far as the second part of your question is concerned, with due respect I feel that the whole issue should have been discussed with us too before the operation in Afghanistan was mounted. But Sir, now that you are in the thick of it – don't quit, as in that case, the Taliban and Al Qaida would start believing that they have defeated the Americans too, and that they have the world on its knees,' I said.

'Why don't you join us?' Dr Kissinger asked. I replied that this question might be addressed to the right quarters in the government, as I was not the appropriate person to respond to it. I suppose he could comprehend the intricacies of our democratic set-up as is the case in the US too. During his visit to India in October 2011, the Afghanistan president, Hamid Karzai, signed a strategic partnership agreement, the first such agreement with any country. This confirmed to the world that they (Afghanistan) regarded India as a close and reliable friend of long standing. The agreement concretized bilateral relations between

Afghanistan and India and envisaged military-to-military ties that would include training and supply of arms and equipment, besides the building of strategic infrastructure and facilities like hospitals.

Nepal and India share age-old historical, cultural, social, religious and economic ties. We have an open border with Nepal that facilitates people-to-people ties, trade and job opportunities. One of the pillars of strength in our relationship is the presence of about 50,000 Nepalese soldiers in the Indian army, serving in various Gorkha regiments, and around 1.25 lakh Indian army pensioners in Nepal. The sacrifices, gallantry and dedicated services rendered by Nepalese soldiers in the Indian Army are legendary. These bonds forged during peace and war can take our relationship to great heights. Besides this, many of their army officers, including the highest ranks, have been trained in Indian training institutions. These issues need to be factored into our foreign policy formulation.

Unfortunately, due to certain misunderstandings caused by political, economic or ethnic issues in the past, both our nations have not been able to derive optimum benefits of these bonds. The political turbulence owes its origin to the king dismissing the government, and declaring a state of emergency on 1 February 2005. This event took place when I had just taken over as the army chief, and relations between the two neighbours nosedived. India's view was that the action taken by the king was violative of the constitution of Nepal. As a result, regrettably, I could not visit that country to receive the honorary rank of general in the Nepal army. In fact, in the wake of this action, there was a lot of bloodshed and violence perpetrated by the Maoists. The Nepalese army came down heavily on the Maoists, but suffered a fair number of casualties too. Finally, when the elections were held, King Gyanendra Shah was forced to step down and the monarchy was abolished. During this extremely turbulent period, the Nepalese army chief, General Ruk Mangad Katuwal, spoke to me on a few occasions and sought my advice. I recall advising him to follow our example of being an apolitical, secular and professional force doing the assigned charter of duties as per the Constitution, and taking orders from the democratically elected government.

Gorkha ex-servicemen of the Indian Army are disbursed their pensions running into several million rupees every month, through the Indian army-administered pension offices in various parts of Nepal, including mobile pension offices. For these veterans and their families, we have also been providing medical cover by sending teams into various parts of Nepal. These links make relations between our two countries special. But there is considerable scope to make them stronger by leveraging the bonds and ties of sacrifices made by our soldiers together for more than a century. The relationship is yet to achieve the solidity that should be there. There have been needless misunderstandings in the past, as some influential sections of their society have perceived us to be interfering in their internal affairs. Today, our positive approach towards the transition of Nepal to a democratic and progressive entity and help in its development under the aegis of Indo-Nepal economic programme is being welcomed by the people.

Bhutan is our closest neighbour and we have vital stakes in its stability and progress. Therefore, my first goodwill visit as COAS was to Bhutan. The traditional and warm welcome by the then King Jigme Singye Wangchuk and his government, followed by meaningful discussions, made the visit memorable. In 2005, Crown Prince Jigme Khesar Namgyel Wangchuk chose not to go for higher studies to Harvard or any other university abroad and instead preferred to do the year-long course at the National Defence College (NDC) at New Delhi, when I was the army chief. I found him to be one of the most wise, mature, clear-headed and articulate young men that I had met in years. I invited him to the Army House on a number of occasions, as both of us developed a close rapport and a shared vision of military cooperation and future challenges to our security. During his visit to the NDC in October 2010, he fondly remembered his time doing the course and stated, 'I feel it was destiny that gave me the most wonderful opportunity to spend my final year before becoming the king, in India.' Today, Bhutan is on the path of consolidating its democratic institutions and developing its infrastructure and other fields such as roads, hydro-power, IT, industry and agriculture, with some help from India. Camps established by

Indian insurgent groups like the ULFA and the National Democratic Front of Bodoland of Assam were destroyed in 2003 in operations conducted by the Royal Bhutan Army in coordination with the Indian Army, and even now they are being denied safe havens there.

The year 2009 witnessed a major change in the bilateral relations between Bangladesh and India, consequent to the establishment of the multi-party democratic government led by Prime Minister Sheikh Hasina. Landmark agreements were signed in January 2010 between the two countries for mutual benefit. India has committed US $1 billion for infrastructural development in Bangladesh. Enhanced cooperation on security issues, particularly action against terrorist groups who have established their bases in Bangladesh, has had a great impact on downsizing of terrorist organizations like the ULFA. Connectivity over surface routes was given a quantum jump by transit facility from Bangladesh to Nepal and Bhutan, and India was given access to the ports of Chittagong and Mongla. All these measures will contribute to the economic upliftment of the people of this region. A few years ago, this kind of cooperation, though highly desirable, was unimaginable. I had written in *The Telegraph* over four years ago of the benefits that would accrue to Bangladesh and the northeastern states of India by exploiting the Brahmaputra as a waterway from Kolkata to Dibrugarh with ports of call enroute in Bangladesh and Assam. Today, it is very satisfying to see some of these pathbreaking initiatives being progressed, and both nations should maintain this momentum in their national interest. However, keeping the extremists at bay would be fundamental for these initiatives to succeed.

The relationship between Sri Lanka and India had become very complex because of the historical, cultural and traditional affinity of the Tamil people of both countries. In the same breath, the close bonds and kinship between our people because of Buddhism and Tamil ethnicity make for an extremely vibrant relationship. For over two decades, Sri Lanka had been ravaged by the insurgency spawned by the Liberation Tigers of Tamil Eelam (LTTE). Unfortunately, because of the Tamil sensitivities and the LTTE, our government's foreign policy had to be crafted treading on a fine line. This posed an enormous challenge to our mandarins in the south block. To their credit they were able to avoid the pitfalls and managed to conduct the relationship adroitly. With the end of hostilities in Sri Lanka, we have begun to play an extremely useful and positive role in the reconstruction of the war-ravaged northern and eastern regions of Sri Lanka, which bore the brunt during the conflict. We must leave no doubt that we stand for a united, peaceful and progressive Sri Lanka. Things appear to be looking up already with India being the largest trade partner of Sri Lanka and the second largest investor.

An appreciable initiative has been the Government of India's 'offer of assistance of Rupees 500 crores for the relief, rehabilitation and resettlement of internally displaced persons belonging to the Tamil minority, and long-term reconstruction of the war-ravaged regions of the country.'[7] The military-to-military cooperation between our two countries has had to be nuanced and often done without publicity, keeping in mind the sensitivities involved. But below the surface, the defence relationship and military diplomacy have played an important role in building bridges between the two countries. A large number of officers and junior leaders of Sri Lanka's armed forces have been trained in India; now the military-to-military relationship can also be upgraded without the inhibitions of the past.

We share with Myanmar a land border of 1640 kilometres over thickly forested and rugged terrain where unfortunately a host of rebel organizations hold sway today. The areas to the west of the Chindwin river are extremely underdeveloped and can be more easily accessed from the Indian side. Taking advantage of the free trade regime upto 20 kilometres on both sides of the border, the Myanmarese Naga and other tribes depend heavily upon India and source everything from rations, medicines, kerosene, hardware and other necessities for day-to-day use from traders on our side of the border. It would be in the interest of both countries to open more trade routes and formalize the ongoing informal trade. The domain of defence cooperation has picked

---

[7] Ministry of External Affairs, Annual Report 2009–10, p. i.

up considerably during the past six years or so. We need to work closely with the Myanmar army to eliminate the camps and safe havens created by the Indian terrorist organizations in the vicinity of the border. The need to launch coordinated operations on both sides of the border simultaneously to eliminate these camps is an imperative.

The ongoing defence cooperation between our nations is multifaceted and includes exchanges of visits, training, supply of military equipment, construction of goodwill roads in the border areas, and sharing of information and operations against Indian insurgent groups. During my official visit as the army chief to Myanmar at the end of October 2005, we requested them to take action to deny such havens to Indian terrorist organizations. Though they promised to do so, in actual fact, it is believed that the Myanmar army is not in a position to take effective steps against insurgents in some of the remote border areas. Our government agreed to give a comprehensive military assistance package to Myanmar and I was happy to convey this to them. Besides that, I also promised to establish an IT facility for training their cadets on computers and other aspects related to IT. It was set up by our team of officers and men from the Corps of Signals within a year. General and Mrs Maung Aye hosted a dinner in honour of our delegation. We will never forget the beautiful golf courses that we saw and the pleasure of a round with General Maung Aye on one of them too.

We have a dynamic army-to-army cooperation with the Singapore army. We have been regularly doing joint training with them at sub unit level at Babina, near Jhansi, and Nasik. During my official visit to Singapore, we were given a warm welcome, and I had very meaningful interactions with their army chief, General Desmond Kuek, who is now their chief of defence staff. The island state has made phenomenal progress in all fields, including defence-related industry.

The reciprocal goodwill visit to Japan in April 2007 helped me to enhance the level of military cooperation and the rapport established with their military leadership, particularly with General Tsutomu Mori. He had visited India during my tenure as chief, and hosted a dinner for us when we were transiting through Tokyo in November 2006. By 2007, General Ryoichi Oriki had taken over and I had useful interaction with him and also called on the minister of defence, Kyuma Furnis. My programme included visits to 1st Airborne Brigade and the Middle Army HQ at Osaka. I was very impressed with the Japanese efficiency and warmth I witnessed during the visit.

I also made goodwill visits to Israel, Nigeria, Egypt, Chile, Brazil, Indonesia and Australia, which were helpful in building stronger military-to-military ties and for projecting the image of the Indian armed forces as a professional organization.

Our 'Look East Policy' has given a renewed focus on our relations with countries in East Asia and Japan. The visit by the Japanese prime minister at the end of 2009 provided impetus to India's comprehensive engagement with Japan, and imparted more depth to our strategic and global partnership. India's increasing engagement with multilateral global and regional groupings like BRIC (Brazil, Russia, India and China), SCO (Shangai Cooperation Organization), ASEAN (Association for South East Asian Nations), BIMSTEC (Bay of Bengal Initiative for Multi-sectoral Technical and Economic Cooperation), SAARC (South Asian Association for Regional Cooperation) and so on, is in keeping with the growing stature of our country. These multilateral relationships, though primarily designed to enhance cooperation in trade, commerce, social and cultural dimensions, are going to have security connotations as well. The creation of an environment of peace and stability would be a precondition for progress and prosperity in any region. Therefore, it is in our national interest that we take the lead in our region, and at times even offer asymmetric and non-reciprocal commitments to other smaller countries in the regional groupings to help them overcome their domestic problems.

29

Preparing for the Future

The Indian Army's plans for modernization are based on a fifteen-year perspective plan. The need to maintain a balance between development and defence expenditure constrains us to have a proportionate mix of equipment: the state-of-the-art as well as the nearly obsolete. As far as the mechanized forces are concerned, we are focusing on night-fighting capability of the vintage equipment as well as inducting T90 and Arjun tanks.

As I visualize it, the T90 shall be our main battle tank for the next few decades. The T72 tanks are being refurbished with improved fire control, night vision and communication systems. For the artillery, we could not induct new towed 155 mm guns because the systems under trials did not meet the desired parameters. The whole exercise is being repeated on priority as the artillery badly requires new equipment. Besides that, I was convinced that we needed to acquire a capability of 155-mm light howitzers with a longer reach, which could be underslung and lifted by helicopters, specially for the mountains, and out-of-area and amphibious operations. There were some amongst us who were content with the towed guns under trial, but had no answer for areas in the mountains where there were no roads or even if there were, the guns would not have been able to reach the desired areas easily. I believe such light howitzers are now being evaluated and tried out. To meet this operational requirement, the air force is also in the process of procuring heavy lift helicopters to carry these guns and undertake other missions as well. This capability will definitely take us into the big league.

The same applies to the air defence artillery, where the equipment is almost obsolete and the shortages need to be made up. In the domain of missiles we have had an impressive indigenous research and development (R&D) record. Whereas we had started the process of induction of the Prithvi and Agni missile systems in the last few years, it was my privilege as the chief to symbolically receive two mobile 'autonomous launchers' and a mobile command post of the Brahmos supersonic cruise missile system for the army from none other than President A.P.J. Abdul Kalam on the 21 June 2007. This missile project is a fine example of joint R&D by India and Russia, and was led by Dr Shivathanu Pillai, a dynamic scientist. For me personally, it has been a feeling of deep satisfaction to see this system developed. I had witnessed the launch of this missile on two occasions in the Pokharan ranges and observed at first-hand its devastating effect. As stated by Dr Pillai, the naval version of the Brahmos missile is also being inducted in Indian warships and the development of air-launched Brahmos is in progress.

Modernization of the infantry was one of my foremost KRAs. In the type of challenges that we are presently confronted with and are most likely to face in the future, the infantry will continue to be the battle-winning factor. The infantry soldier is thus being progressively transformed by the F-INSAS (Futuristic Infantry Soldier as a System) programme.

'The future infantry soldier must be equipped with tools for better situational awareness, light all-purpose weapons, day-night vision capability, single piece uniform containing climate control and monitoring system... Today's infantry soldier is certainly more operationally capable than his predecessor was a few years ago. He is equipped with a lighter weapon, i.e. INSAS 5.56...night vision devices and night sights on his weapon system...lighter infantry combat kit than he was carrying earlier...better surveillance and communications system... In a few years from now, we are going to actually see the infantryman holding a hand-held device on which he can at all times know his own position and that of his colleagues and also transmit a message by SMS or by data to his company commander and from there on to his battalion commander. So, we are going to see an army of the future, where a satellite image is received by frontline soldiers and they transmit messages and data through this system upwards to the headquarters. RMA is going to be manifest in a very effective manner at the cutting edge, that is, the infantryman.'[1]

The infantry urgently requires a state-of-the-art close-quarter-battle (CQB) carbine to replace the existing obsolete weapon. As the Defence Research and Development Organization (DRDO) made a bid to make an indigenous carbine, we had to give them a chance. Finally, their product failed to meet our requirements and we had to carry out trials of imported models. To keep the costs low and to give our ordnance factory an opportunity, I proposed that we should have two types of carbines in our army, one for the infantry for a specialized CQB role, which must match the best in the world, and the second for the rest of the army, which should be the best indigenous product. I am happy this proposal stands accepted by the government and the acquisition process is on. When I visited Oman as the chief in 2005, they scheduled a visit to the army's museum. I was shocked to see a 9-mm carbine of the type we are currently using, and which we had also supplied to the Omanese army in the 1960s, displayed as a museum piece!

The ageing fleet of army aviation helicopters is being upgraded. Since 2004, modern helicopters are being tried out so that we could replace the Cheetahs and Chetaks of 1960s vintage. In addition, our indigenous 'Dhruv' advanced light helicopters (ALH) are also being inducted. I distinctly remember that during the ALH desert trials, the prototype came to Rajasthan during Operation Parakaram (2002) and we had flown in it. I found it to be a very powerful and robust machine, though at that time there were some glitches noticed too. The biggest advantage that accrues with this aircraft is the carrying capacity. The entire 'R' (recce) group of the Corps HQ could move in one helicopter. As far as the engineers are concerned, modern equipment for mine laying and breaching is in the pipeline, as are bridges.

We are now ushering in the era of the digitized battle field. Commanders, their staff, the fighting units, weapon systems,

---

[1] Gurmeet Kanwal, *Army Vision 2020*, p. 200. Excerpts of an interview given by me to SP's Guide Publications, *The Chiefs Spoke*, SP's ShowNews (Defence Expo daily), 31 January 2006.

battlefield sensors and other entities will be interconnected by robust and fully secure digital information and communication technology infrastructure. The applications running on it will help us achieve information superiority. These will also provide us capabilities such as situational awareness, collaborative planning and sensor-to-shooter linkages as envisaged in our doctrine. Thus these network-centric systems and information warfare capabilities would act as war-winning force multipliers and give us the desired edge over the adversary.

India is renowned for its prowess in the information technology (IT) field but it was realized that we had not been able to exploit this IT dominance in the military domain. Therefore, I took the initiative to set up the Army Information and Technology Advisory Council. This council comprised prominent IT industry leaders, management experts, academicians and senior army officers. I was very happy to see the response of major IT companies like Microsoft, Wipro, NIIT, Hewlett Packard and Rolta, who nominated senior executives to be part of this council. This group was mandated to render advice in the formulation of an IT perspective plan for the Indian Army. The council holds a meeting twice a year to monitor the progress of various projects to make us into a network-enabled army. The first meeting of this council was held in April 2006 and was presided over by me.

To achieve the objective of network-centricity and IT dominance, projects like the battlefield surveillance system, the command information decision support system, and the artillery command and control and communications system received renewed focus. I am more than satisfied to see these projects being gradually deployed on ground. The information and communication technology projects that saw the light of day during my tenure are listed in Appendix 6.

As far as the logistics are concerned, two of my KRAs as the chief were modernization as well as improvement of the teeth-to-tail ratio. Therefore, my focus was on upgradation of the existing logistics infrastructure, pruning the strength of logistic units and offloading as many areas of administrative support of the army as possible to the public sector undertakings and trade. Holding of reserves of fuel, oils and lubricants, maintenance and repair of vehicles, and stocking of reserves of rations by the Food Corporation of India are some of the areas where the civilian sector has stepped in. Besides this, my thrust was on automation and computerized inventory control. As a first step, we were able to implement a pilot project of automation in the ordnance depot at Delhi. This is being followed up in other logistics installations in a phased manner. I firmly believe in the concept of 'just enough and just in time' in the domain of logistics. We have to grow out of the habit of overinsurance and overstocking by maintenance of reserves at all levels as if we are operating in an overseas theatre. As our indigenous production capability is going up, it must result in reduced holdings except items being imported, and thereby bring in savings.

The EME was given greater capability to carry out repairs in field conditions, and as far forward as conditions permitted. Major restructuring and modernization of the base workshops was commenced in a phased manner. This was to facilitate overhauls and base repairs of the tanks, guns and other equipment. Repairs of vehicles and other equipment was offloaded to the original equipment manufacturers and trade to the extent possible, so that EME manpower and facilities could concentrate on imported and sensitive equipment. Having grown up in a technical environment, it was but natural for me to have an attraction for mechanical things. My focus as far as repair and recovery was concerned was to have better capabilities to keep weapon systems and equipment in good working order. Because we had to keep a fairly large inventory of older equipment going, we had to fabricate spares and make innovations. I awarded the maximum possible chief's commendations 'on the spot' for good work done and for the most innovative ideas to encourage out-of-the-box thinking and creativity. The screening of the deserving individuals was done by their superior officers in advance.

As far as the medical infrastructure is concerned, my focus was on upgradation and creation of facilities to make the command hospitals and military hospitals, such as the one in Guwahati, on par with the Research and Referral Hospital at Delhi. The cases were taken up with the ministry of defence and hopefully, we shall see them materialize in due course. At the field level, the endeavour was to induct the latest life-saving equipment so that the 'golden hour' principle could be meaningfully implemented. As a result, the fatalities during evacuation have been brought down considerably.

Overall, we were able to carry out a fair amount of modernization and enhancement of our capability in terms of night-fighting equipment, sensors, battlefield surveillance radars and equipment for net-centric and information warfare as also in the domain of logistics. If some more of our proposals had fructified in a shorter time frame, I would have been even more satisfied. It was sad to see some of our major acquisition projects running into heavy weather in the last stages, for reasons which are best known to the government.

30

Leadership and Command Experience

'Good leaders command respect and not demand it; respect has to be earned,' my grandfather told me once, as he rambled on about British officers of his time. 'All of them were not the same,' he said. And I understood what he meant. As I went along in my military career, the import of what he said became crystal clear to me; to be held in high regard by one's subordinates is achievable only by dint of an officer's hard work, sincerity, professional acumen and a caring attitude. And the soldiers are the best judges of their leaders.

One can find a number of books and manuals dedicated to leadership in the armed forces. Therefore, I have no intention of traversing that broad canvas here. What I wish to do is to share my perceptions of what I saw, learnt and most importantly, practised, in my life. Fundamentally, military leadership is akin to leadership in the civil domain, be it government service or the corporate sector, except for three major differences. First, there is the question of national honour – the military has to remember that there is no silver medal in war, or to use the caption of my interview in *The Economic Times, Corporate Dossier* of 16 September 2005, 'You're No. 1 or You're Dead' (see Appendix 7). Second, human lives are at stake when a military command is given. And third, a small action can lead to catastrophic damage or embarrassment for the nation.

The raison d'etre for an army is to defend the nation and when challenged, to fight and win the war. Therefore, we have no option but to achieve victory every time the clarion call beckons us. So, for me the credo has been that of a 'warrior and a winner' – a warrior whose cause is just, and whose path is righteous. But for this to happen each and every time, thorough preparation and training along with the highest quality of leadership is called for.

Is one a born leader or are leaders made? This question has engaged military researchers since ages. In my view, barring an odd historical example, leaders are made. But in the same breath, I would like to add that a good leader must also have certain attributes that are inherited or come with the genes. A mule will remain a mule no matter how much training or hard work is put in. To be an effective leader one has to have an above-average intellect and be physically and mentally robust. Despite the revolution in military affairs, a good leader has to lead by example and from the front. Things haven't changed much from the days of Alexander or Hannibal in so far as setting a personal example and sharing the hardships and risks are concerned. 'Many have often seen Hannibal lying on the ground wrapped only in a military cloak amid the sentries and outposts of his soldiers,' wrote the Roman historian Livy. The relationship between the leader and the led will always remain an important factor, and a well-trained, -equipped and -led soldier will be the final determinant of success in war.

Ours is a command-oriented army. We have seen five wars in our six decades of history as an independent nation. The Indian Army is, therefore, a battle-hardened and combat-tested army. 'The million-man army actually fights, unlike the post-modern militaries of many of our European allies,' as stated by US Ambassador Robert Blackwill in the summer of 2005. India's hardwon victory in Kargil and successful prosecution of the campaign against jehadis in Kashmir would have been in his mind when he made those remarks. However, the last major war we fought was forty years ago. Unfortunately, today in our army there are very few veterans around with such war experience. There are not many officers and men who might have seen a bullet being fired in anger, other than those who have served in Jammu and Kashmir or the northeast, or a localized war such as the one we fought in the Kargil region during the summer of 1999. However, keeping in view our unresolved border issues with China and Pakistan and other national security challenges, we have to be 'ready and relevant' to defend our country. Therefore, it is of utmost importance that we select, train and groom the best officers and men or women to lead Indian armed forces of the future.

As the army chief, I tried my best to see that promotions, postings and appointments were based on performance, merit and qualifications, without extraneous influences playing any part. Yet there might have been some aberrations. For example, there were some very fine officers of my regiment and others who had served with me earlier, who got left out purely because of relative merit. Yet nothing gave me greater joy and satisfaction than giving a fair deal and a redress to any officer who was unjustly 'fixed' or bypassed for reasons other than professional. By and large, I can say with confidence, most of us have gotten a fair deal. Further, there is no perfect organization in the world. A few 'parasites' would anyhow worm their way into the best of them! And that brings me to my conviction that anyone with a perfect or near-perfect dossier needs to be looked at with suspicion or caution; some of these individuals could be frauds in disguise. Amongst them one is likely to find some very clever 'careerists', who are either great manipulators or individuals who have been fooling the system by taking the help of benign seniors, having served in personal appointments with those high-ranking officers in their early years, or are related to them. The system should be able to pick up such individuals, and sideline them before they reach senior ranks and damage the organization. Based on my personal experience and that of many others, it is my conviction that our armed forces do not write off a 'good guy' in a hurry. At the same time, I do admit that there have been a few genuinely deserving officers who got left out, despite the checks and balances in the system – they were victims of circumstances, I suppose.

There is no alternative to regimental service and command of troops for an officer of the combat arms in particular and all other officers in general. Handling of men, weapon systems and other equipment in different operational situations, terrain configurations, peacetime soldiering and training for war, is in itself a great learning experience. The essentials of leadership that are imbibed while serving in the regiment or the battalion; living, playing and eating with the men, cannot be learnt at any academy or by reading manuals. Today, I am given to understand that command tenures of one star and above are so short that they can hardly do justice to their assignment. In fact, most commanders want to conduct a war game or a sand-model discussion or some other major training event during their brief tenures – at times to score brownie points and prove that they are better than the others. Each of them is in a tearing hurry, often without caring about the adverse impact on their officers and men. Consequently, the commanding officers of units are away quite often, attending war games or other events, and the second-in-command are running the show. In some formations and units the term 'quick' result areas has replaced 'key' result areas!

In our system one has to command a unit or formation successfully to be eligible for the next higher rank. Hence everyone has to be given a chance to command, even if the tenures are ridiculously short. During my two years in command of 1 Corps, I saw three generals changing hands in my armoured division. The protocol welcomes and farewells were quite a strain on time. It required some genius for them to contribute anything substantial or to achieve their key objectives. I doubt if they were able to meaningfully visit all their formations and major units in that short period. Even if they managed to do so, how much time was left for looking at the big picture, with all the running around. It was neither fair to them nor to the organization. Till two years ago, the brigade commanders were getting about a year-and-a-half and the general officers-in-command of divisions were lucky to get over a year in command. We must find a long-term solution to the problem.

Our present system of selection has placed some officers in high positions, even after they had reached their limit. In higher ranks, we need leaders with greater vision, high professional competence, rich and varied experience and importantly, large-heartedness and conduct as a general. Besides, one would definitely prefer those who have served more with troops rather than the ones who have had long tenures in staff. The latter may have all the qualifications but many of them are clever and calculative opportunists or careerists, unbeatable on paper!

Leadership and Command Experience

They are ticket punchers. They are the ones who even count the months while they are in command. To such commanders, I had a standard refrain, 'are you pregnant?' whenever they spoke of the number of 'months' they had been in command of troops. Before one is selected to command a battalion or a regiment in the combat arms, one has to have a minimum of two performance appraisal reports as a company, battery or a squadron commander. This implies that an officer should have served with troops for at least one-and-a-half to two years. There are some officers who buck the system by doing just the bare minimum time in command assignments, and like a submarine, take a deep dive and resurface only when the next rank is due. During this interregnum they take up a safe staff job or study leave. Further, some of them try to manipulate their posting under someone they have already worked with and, if possible, in an area where they have served earlier. And there are some who are the smooth talkers and by flaunting terms and clichés used in foreign armies, they try to impress others. They might carry the day in a sand-model discussion, but when it comes to the 'real' thing on the ground, they begin to shiver under stress and give the impression that their knees are about to buckle under! Such fair weather high-fliers are potentially dangerous. Though some of them may reach high ranks in peace time, they make poor leaders and are more than likely to be disasters in war. Such cases are found in most armies and we are not an exception.

When the results of the first selection grade promotion of my batch (25th NDA Course) from major to lieutenant colonel were announced in 1980, I had put in about sixteen years of service. By then, I had earned four or five reports as a company commander, whereas there were a few of our course mates who got deferred for promotion, because they did not have even two mandatory reports! Where had they been serving all those years? It would be reasonable to assume that most of us would be reluctant to take a chance with a greenhorn cardiac surgeon, and would prefer to be operated upon by a more experienced one. Therefore, what makes us feel that our soldiers would be happy to be led by inexperienced or 'just-adequately exercised' leaders, who might be something akin to an untested missile! If we consider our lives as precious, so do the officers and men whom we have the privilege to lead in peace and war.

The soldiers are the best judges of their leaders and we have the world's finest soldiers. Therefore, we as their commanders are honour bound to give them the leadership that they expect and that cannot happen without a rock-solid foundation based on command experience.

I commanded two battalions for a total period of over four-and-a-half years, the first tenure as a lieutenant colonel and the second in the rank of a colonel. Not that I was given a choice, but in retrospect, I believe it did give me sound command experience. Further, this is not to suggest that everything was always 'hunky dory'; things did go wrong, but it was my constant endeavour to do the assigned tasks sincerely, honestly and with a sense of commitment, and I did not shirk responsibility for things that went awry.

In order to win a war, we require the best leaders, or at least better leaders than our adversaries. When speaking on the wireless, the code word for a commander is 'tiger'. It implies that he has to lead his men like a tiger. More importantly, he shouldn't acquiesce before his superiors and become a 'yes man', or what is worse, a doormat; that would qualify him to be called a 'mouse'! There are some leaders who are the 'half-tiger–half-mouse' type. These are the guys who pose as tigers in front of their men, and behave as mice with their bosses. But sooner or later they get found out. I recall that when I was commanding the battalion at Tezu, the brigade commander inspected the unit and commented on a few issues regarding administration, documentation and other procedures in a five-page demi-official letter. Unfazed, I examined all the issues and while accepting full responsibility for the lapses, I replied that corrective measures would be taken expeditiously and ended the letter by stating unequivocally that, *'This is to assure you, Sir, that there can be no one more concerned about the operational and administrative efficiency of this battalion than me.'* By writing so bluntly my head was on the chopping block. But I sincerely meant every word that was written. I survived, but only because we worked very hard and performed, and the results did the speaking.

Unlike movies or fiction where the underdog is romanticized, one should always endeavour to be the top dog in combat or for that matter while facing any challenge in life. In the business of war stakes are very high so there is no question of taking any chances. Having been a 'team man' all my life, I have always believed in delegating responsibility, as it is humanly impossible to do everything oneself. Having spelt out the aim clearly, most of the routine tasks are delegated by me to subordinates (about 80 per cent of the total), whereas a close watch and tight control is kept on few selected activities which would have a major impact on the success of the mission. Thus, the substantive issues remain under my watch. I have never believed in the 'zero error' syndrome, as mistakes are bound to happen and I didn't lose my sleep on some issues that went wrong. In this manner, a tension-free atmosphere was created where the subordinates were given the latitude to use initiative. I believe in the directive style of command and the performance of my team has mostly been beyond my expectations. As one goes higher in rank one has to be a visionary, a lion-hearted and compassionate leader – an 'asli jarnail', a true general officer. On the other hand, there are senior commanders who carry out umpteen rehearsals for any major event, and they personally ensure that even dinner menus are microscopically examined and rehearsed. They also tell the juniors how to do the assigned tasks. How on earth would these leaders have any time or enthusiasm left for looking at the macro-issues or for thinking ahead? In the same breath, what would their subordinates do in a war? There are some commanders who terrorise their subordinates. Such units do not have to hunt for terrorists as 'one' is commanding them! Haven't we seen such leaders?

No military leader can achieve greatness without being original, innovative and unpredictable. To follow the beaten path is pedestrian. Unless we take the adversary off guard, we cannot expect outstanding results. In fact, this approach will get us our objective fastest and with the least casualties. It would be a cardinal mistake to select an obvious option even if it's the best, as the adversary would be prepared for it. In fact, an objective analysis of the Second World War will reveal that the Allies suffered very heavy casualties while trying to land on the best beaches in Normandy. This was because the Germans were also expecting that and logically defending them in strength. I have laid great emphasis on encouragement of all ranks to *think and be original,* as I realized many officers and soldiers only did what they were told. They seldom used their mind. I would pull their legs and say, 'Are you guys preserving your brains for the next life!' In my career I took many innovative steps to inculcate this habit amongst all ranks of the army and used to give great incentives for original and creative ideas, innovations and inventions. As the chief, I also started a 'dreamers club' wherein anyone could email his or her idea to my office, which would then be passed on to the appropriate branch or directorate of the Army HQ. This initiative was hugely welcomed and a lot of ideas came in. Those which merited action were progressed. For example, we implemented one such idea of providing air-conditioned buses for conveyance from the residential areas to the Army HQ. This may not be of much significance to the advanced countries, where air-conditioned transport would be the norm, but in the Indian armed forces, air-conditioned buses were unheard of till 2005! So this step was greatly appreciated by the army. However, the dreamers club was a concept ahead of its time and did add on to the workload of the military bureaucracy. It wasn't followed up as enthusiastically as I expected. I hope it would get a new life in due course – when its time comes.

It is my belief that many military leaders don't really understand the essence of the phrase 'esprit de corps', or if they do, they do not practise the building up of such a spirit in their units or formations. For me it has been a magical phrase and I found its motivational and inspirational effect as a real force multiplier during my life. It helped me produce better results than others and run a happier team – the latter being very important to me. That is how I consistently overperformed even when I had been dealt a bad hand. When I commanded 9 Maratha LI we had two superseded officers, including my second-in-command. Despite this we did very well as we worked as a team and everyone put in his best. As a brigade commander in Kashmir, I was given the responsibility of guarding the LoC and preventing infiltration, without having the powers to write the confidential reports of officers of the units placed under my operational control. And yet, our operational performance was exceptionally good, and we were counted amongst the top achievers in the entire Northern Command. We learnt the cliché – pay, play and pray with the men – early on in regimental soldiering. Providing an environment in the unit or formation in which esprit de corps is omnipresent is the acme of true military leadership.

Only if the soldiers feel that you genuinely care for them, can one aspire to be remembered as a good military leader. Bonding with my subordinates and the soldiers has been one of my strengths. Wherever possible, I reached out to them and shook hands and spoke with as many of them as possible. During early August 2007, one of our patrols discovered by chance the debris of an old aircrash in the Lahaul region of the Himalayas. An AN 12 had crashed on the way to Leh in 1968, and despite our best efforts, the site of the wreckage had not been located till then. We were able to retrieve and hand over the bodies of four soldiers to their families with due military honours.

Another leadership trait that I have found very effective is perseverance and doggedness in pursuit of an objective. History has made us aware of the razor-thin difference between victory and defeat in many a battle. The side that refused to throw in the towel or persevered longer carried the day. Once a decision has been taken it must be relentlessly pursued to its logical culmination.

Regardless of how grandiose our war plans are, we cannot succeed without the 'fighting spirit' of our soldiers. To emerge victorious in any war we need a force that is well-attuned to operational tasks and is adequately rested. We must make sure the army is mentally and physically charged and is raring to go, if we wish to win the race from the start to finish. As commented earlier, some self-centred commanders want to make a name for themselves in peace time by conducting as many training and social events in their units or formations during their brief tenures of two years or less. This has resulted in combat units spending about 50 per cent of their time in peace stations out of their barracks. A feeling has crept in amongst the soldiers that they are better off in the field areas than in peace stations. This is definitely not good for morale. Hence, as the chief, I gave instructions that routine training and sports activities should be spread out over a time span of two years and, as far as possible, no unit should be out of their cantonments for more than two months in a year in peace stations.

The role of women in the armed forces has been a subject of discussion for quite some time. I have no doubt that the women would admirably complement the men and act as force multipliers in certain areas. However, at present, they are being inducted as officers in many arms and services other than combat arms like mechanized forces, infantry or artillery. Further, wherever they are able to do the mandatory command and staff assignments and qualify in career courses, there should be no bar to their elevation to higher ranks and tenure in service, akin to the men. During my tenure as the COAS, a furore took place when the vice chief made a remark that, 'the army could do without women'. His comments were blown out of proportion by some women's organizations and the media. Yet in order to defuse the situation, I advised him to clear the air and render a polite apology. This he did, the gentleman that he was, and the issue was resolved. However, the debate still continues.

The National Cadet Corps and the Sainik Schools are the feeder organizations which in recent years have provided a large proportion of the leadership in the armed forces and also in the civilian domain. A few million disciplined and patriotic young men and women have passed through the portals of these institutions over the past six decades. The NCC is a tri-service organization and has produced outstanding leaders in the fields of science, politics, public and private sector, sports, arts and culture, besides the military. It is a delight to see the radiant faces of these motivated young men and women during the Republic Day parades in Delhi and in the states.

Ethics, morality and propriety are issues that are gaining relevance more and more, particularly with regard to conduct of officers in higher ranks. Similarly, corruption has become endemic in our country and it has raised its ugly head in the armed forces too. It has been a perception that it was always there to some degree in the domain of contracts in works, supplies, clothing, stores and procurements. But by and large, the fabric of morality and probity in the armed forces was unblemished. The armed forces have been known to take action promptly against defaulters. Unfortunately, today, this disease has not left even the highest ranks unscathed. In the recent past, a few incidents have been played up by sections of the media, in some cases quite unfairly. The challenge has to be met squarely and collectively. We must ensure that the moral and ethical compass of all ranks of the armed forces does not deviate and lose direction. Therefore, we need to take urgent remedial measures, and the senior ranks have to show the way by displaying unimpeachable higher values and conduct for which the armed forces are renowned and revered by our countrymen.

We need to educate and forewarn the armed forces against adverse and corroding influences of some segments of society. It was reassuring to know of a 'public reverence survey' conducted by MODE on the occasion of the golden jubilee of our independence, in which the military scored over 80 per cent for honesty, bravery, efficiency and contribution to the nation and did better than civil servants, lawyers, doctors and businessmen. In another survey, carried out by *India Today* on India's fifty-fifth anniversary as a nation, it was heartening to see that the armed forces were rated as the first among fifty-five organizations or issues that Indians were proud of. Notwithstanding this, we must understand that in our context, 'value-based leadership' has today assumed greater relevance than before.

The top of the pyramid gives one an adrenaline-boosted euphoria, but also a feeling of loneliness, and at times, looking down gives a scary feeling. The responsibilities increase in geometric progression along with awesome accountability. Hence, the crown is always laced with thorns. In the highest ranks, qualities and traits such as vision, foresight, compassion, being lion-hearted with moral courage to stand up for organizational interest, and loyalty to superiors, peers and juniors assume greatest significance. Keeping one's cool under extremely stressful situations becomes imperative. It is equally important to pick the best team of advisers, who are competent, sincere and loyal.

The military leadership should advise the government in a frank, forthright and professional manner. However, when a directive is received, it should be carried out to the best of our abilities. An individual's personal views do not have a place at that stage. One cannot apportion or arrogate to himself the authority to question, or worse, defy the command of the lawfully elected government of the day. The tradition of 'not to question why but to do and die' was what we grew up with. In our history we have had one unfortunate case where a service chief challenged the orders of the government and was reported to have stated that they were 'un-implementable'. The government had no option except to remove him from the service. But his action caused irreparable damage to the institution. He could have honourably resigned if he had strong reservations. That step would have earned him the respect of the rank and file. Similarly, it may be recalled that during the Korean war, a highly distinguished hero of the Second World War, General D. MacArthur, was removed from command for not being able to 'support the policies of the Administration', and recently, another US general in Afghanistan was given the marching orders for his adverse comments against government policy. Admiral Arun Prakash, a former naval chief, had said this in 1999 about officers going to court: 'it is inevitable that he (the officer) will have to show either the Service or his brother officers, or both in a poor light. The officer will also feel the need to enlist the support of bureaucrats, politicians and the press to bolster his case: in the process, demeaning himself and his Service further'.

In this vein, the recent unfortunate controversy about the age of the previous army chief, General V.K. Singh, has saddened many of us. Since my name has been mentioned in this regard in some motivated articles and talk shows on the TV, I would like to clear the air on this issue. The fact that every soldier's honour is equally important needs no reiteration. Thus, I consider it appropriate to express my views now, lest my silence be misconstrued.

The 'age row' has its genesis with the contradictory dates of birth (DoB) entered in the threshold documents submitted by the general officer himself in the mid-1960s. The problem surfaced almost forty years later, when this discrepancy was pointed out by the ministry of defence in April 2006, while processing the papers of this officer's batch for promotion from major general to lieutenant general. Accordingly, the Army HQ (MS Branch) wrote to then Major General V.K. Singh in May 2006, seeking his clarification on the discrepancy observed. In his reply, the officer claimed that 1951 should be treated as his year of birth and attached certain documents to support his contention. However, after a detailed examination in the Army HQ in August 2006, it was conveyed to him that 'after due consideration of his reply and in view of the existing rules, the request cannot be processed at this belated stage', and therefore 1950 would remain as his recorded year of birth. Thereafter, I was informed of this fact by the military secretary, and was told that the issue had been closed. There was neither an exchange of correspondence directly between the officer concerned and me, nor did he represent or complain against the decision of the Army HQ at that time. In case the officer had any reservations against the decision, he was free to take up the matter with the Army HQ or the ministry of defence by means of a non-statutory or statutory complaint and have the matter resolved one way or the other. Rationally speaking, he should have done so but for reasons best known to him, he chose not to raise the issue then.

Comments made against me recently that this issue was raked up by me in 2006 with a 'succession plan' (*sic*) and parochial agenda in mind are preposterous, malicious and incorrect, to say the least. More seriously, these are loaded with dangerous portents that can play havoc with the secular and apolitical fabric of the great institution that we have given the best part of our lives to, and also cause incalculable harm to the nation as well. In fact, during my tenure as the COAS from 1 February 2005 to 30 September 2007, there was no controversy on this matter at all. In 2006, as the army chief, I recommended V.K. Singh (then major general) to be GOC 2 Corps, one of our strike corps, which is considered a prize assignment, so as to give him the requisite experience of handling large mechanised formations. Besides, in 2005, I had taken him with me on my first official visit abroad to Oman and the UK. Thus such insinuations at this stage by some of the army chief's advisers or 'well-wishers' have deeply appalled and angered me. Furthermore, in a recent interview with a magazine, he himself has implied motives regarding the decision of the Army HQ on his age issue.

I had so far maintained a stoic silence on the unfortunate controversy as the matter was sub-judice. However, the deliberations and the sagacious judgement of the Supreme Court on the army chief's petition, said it all. There are many who feel that in a personal matter such as this, the case should have been handled with the utmost discretion, sans the unsavoury media hype. What is certain is that the organization that we cherish so much has lost a lot of its sheen. A challenge every chief faces is his responsibility towards the future of his service; this was my main concern and I did not allow anything to come in the way during my tenure as COAS or later.

Unfortunately, the matter was once again raised with a vicious spin by filing a motivated and an utterly malicious public interest litigation (PIL) before the Supreme Court, raising the 'communal angle' and some allegations against the army chief-designate. This irresponsible and mischievous plan was nipped in the bud on 23 April 2012 by the curt dismissal of the PIL by the apex court as the honourable bench saw through the nefarious design of the the complainants, thereby vindicating the stand of the government. This entire episode has left a sour taste and vitiated the environment of the army in particular, and the ripple effect has been felt by the navy and the air force too.

We have had two cases in the past where extremely competent, highly decorated and meritorious generals were superseded in the race for the chief's appointment – Lieutenant Generals P.S. Bhagat, the only Indian officer who was awarded the Victoria Cross during the Second World War, and S.K. Sinha, vice chief of the army. But both of them accepted the decision of the government with dignity and grace and decided to fade away. They are held in high esteem and remembered even today. Perhaps we ought to learn a few things also from our civil service colleagues.

On completion of my tenure as the CO of 5th (Royal) Maratha LI and of the 9th before that, my wish on being commissioned as a second lieutenant was fulfilled – what more could one ask for. 'Anything else that comes my way now shall be a bonus,' is what I said to myself as described in Part II. Many of us have got much more, but happiness? I'm not sure.

> Many are those who see others' faults;
> There are some who see their virtues as well,
> Of those who can see their own faults,
> Alas: their number is very small.

In our context, there can be no better example of an officer and a gentleman and a charismatic leader than Field Marshal Sam Manekshaw. At the highest levels of military leadership, one is required to have the moral courage to call a spade a spade and to render professional advice keeping national interest uppermost. Not only was General Manekshaw gifted with this important quality, but he was also endowed with the ability to put across his views tactfully and effectively. The manner in which he displayed these attributes in early 1971, when the occasion demanded, during the briefing and discussions regarding the Bangladesh war, is legendary. A lesser person would not have been able to do what Sam Bahadur did. Sam also lived life fully. He was disarming and friendly. Endowed with social charm and grace, he was an extremely popular general. He led a happy team and believed in the motto, 'Work hard and play hard.' He has many admirers and friends in Kolkata because of his stint as GOC-in-C of Eastern Command. I would fail in my responsibility if I do not mention Sam Bahadur's concern for his men, the gallant soldiers of his regiment, the 8th Gurkha Rifles, and the Indian Army. For most of us who had the privilege and good fortune to serve under his leadership, he was our role model. Equally important as icons of leadership are Field Marshal K.M. Cariappa and Marshal of the Air Force Arjan Singh. As a couple, Arjan Singh and his charming and gracious wife, Teji, shall forever remain as a role model for both Rohini and me and for the fraternity of the armed forces.

31

The Man behind the Machine

The Indian Army has for long been visionary in its approach to welfare of all ranks. I had made it an act of faith to improve the service conditions of all ranks of the army and lead a well-trained, happy, highly motivated and spirited team. With this in mind, I pushed for an assured career progression plan for officers and men. The scale and number of soldiers who would benefit from this initiative would certainly have far-reaching implications on the morale and satisfaction levels of our soldiers. The sepoys, non-commissioned officers and junior commissioned officers would be eligible for 'three steps assured' progression in their careers. For instance, a soldier would be assured of the pay scale of a naik (corporal), a havildar (sergeant) and a junior commissioned officer after putting in eight, sixteen and twenty-four years of service respectively. The government approved this proposal and it has been implemented from 1 January 2008. The officers too would get a time-scale promotion to the rank of colonel on completion of twenty-six years of service. While implementing the A.V. Singh Committee (Part II) recommendations, there was a lot of wrangling by the other services to try and corner more posts of two- or three-star ranks. I stood my ground and insisted that the distribution of these additional vacancies be on a pro-rata basis. The other two services already had an edge vis-à-vis the army and I didn't want the situation to be skewed further. The problem got accentuated in the tri-service institutions where the juniors in service belonging to the navy or air force would be commanding their seniors from the army, because of this differential. Eventually, logic prevailed and we got a fair deal.

One of the most important issues was the presentation of the armed forces case for the 6th Pay Commission. This happened when I was the chairman of the chiefs of staff committee and the army chief. The three services adopted a highly synergized strategy to get the best possible pay and perks package for all ranks. After preliminary deliberations, the broad principles to be followed by the pay commission cell were enunciated by me. These were:

- All three services pay cells should adopt a joint and unified approach. We should not work at cross purposes on any issue, but support each other's service-specific demands.
- The proposals should seek an equitable and just package to make the armed forces an attractive career. We must consciously pitch at a higher level, so that we get a substantial raise in the pay and allowances package.
- The 'X' factor should be quantified keeping in mind the unique and hazardous working environment. The service conditions and early retirement should be compensated adequately.
- 'One rank one pension' and disability or special pension should be strongly projected.

Certain key issues were spelt out by me for the army, and our pay commission cell was set up with effect from May 2006 under the supervision of Major General K.R. Rao, the additional director general (personnel and services). Under the guidance of General Rao, the pay cell did a magnificent job. After achieving unanimity amongst the three services, we made a forceful presentation to the 6th Pay Commission during March 2007. Thereafter, a memorandum was submitted to the Pay Commission containing the proposals of the armed forces on 15 April 2007. The commission announced its report in March 2008. All along we insisted that the award of this Pay Commission should be made effective from 1 January 2006. We were happy that the government finally agreed to do so. The major achievements of the armed forces on this issue were:

- Common pay scales for the soldiers, sailors and airmen with the same entry-level qualification.
- A separate military service pay was introduced which would be treated as pay for all purposes, including calculation of basic pension.
- Pension of all ranks at 50 per cent of last pay drawn, irrespective of the length of service.
- Pay band-4 to be applicable to lieutenant colonels, colonels and brigadiers.
- Near 'one rank one pension' for those who retired prior to 1 January 2006.
- Higher Administrative Grade (HAG) plus pay scale for one-third of the lieutenant generals.
- All officers from lieutenant upwards to be entitled to travel by air while on temporary duty or when availing leave travel concession.
- An allowance of Rs 1000 per child for education – for two children.
- Pay for acting rank would be admissible without any conditions of continuous service for a fixed number of days.

We also recommended a separate pay commission for the armed forces in the future, as is the practice in many other democratic countries. We were fairly satisfied with the final outcome, though there were a few areas where our recommendations were not given the desired weightage. All ranks and the veterans are getting a handsomer pay and pension package today.

An area which caused me great concern was the poor financial state of our soldiers, particularly after they retired. Veterans who have sacrificed so much for the country and served the army with dedication during their youth, most certainly deserve a better deal as far as pensions are concerned. During the deliberations of the Pay Commission we insisted that the pensions be enhanced to make it possible for these veterans to live with dignity and honour, and emphasized 'one rank one pension' with all the force at our command. When we meet these old warriors at reunions, they appear to have aged prematurely, although their spirit remains undiminished. We as leaders need to help them achieve financial security while in service. It is a matter of pride that we have been able to create viable and self-sustaining institutions serving the cause of serving and retired personnel and their dependents, as also for war widows.

I have strong views on the system of giving honours and awards. First and foremost, recognition must be given for acts of gallantry in a fair and unbiased manner and as close to the date of the action as possible. To arrest the trend of an unhealthy race for awards by showing more 'kills', I banned the use of that word on becoming the chief. I declared that commanders and units would be judged by their overall performance and not just by the number of terrorists killed. We could not afford any more cases such as the one of fake killings videofilmed in Siachen. Besides, it is my view that 'yudh seva' (distinguished service for war) medals should be given only in exceptional cases in peace time. Even during the Kargil war, I could not reconcile myself to the fact that some senior officers were given the 'yudh seva' series of awards when most of the others in the same headquarters were awarded distinguished peace service awards. Indiscretion and double standards of this kind lower the sanctity of the awards. No system can be foolproof, yet it should be our endeavour to see that deserving cases get honoured appropriately and at the right time. Furthermore, I strongly recommend introducing a system where a 'sena', 'nau sena' or 'vayu sena' medal (equivalent of a military cross) could be pinned on the spot in the field by the chiefs. There can be nothing more inspiring or motivating for the officers and men. The government needs to look into this important factor and, if required, guidelines could be spelt out for this step.

'The army marches on its stomach' is a famous saying. Therefore, the quality of rations supplied to our officers and men was an important issue for me. I was encouraged by the caring attitude and interest shown by Defence Minister A.K. Antony, who often enquired about the standard of rations. Practically during every conference, I would make it a point to convey to my army commanders and principal staff officers that they must ensure that all ranks get their authorized rations and of the specified quality. I believed that the specifications needed to be upscaled if we wanted to see a genuine improvement. In fact, we began sending the feedback received from the lower formations for the information of the defence minister. One day, I asked for a meeting with the minister wherein a presentation would be made about the need to enhance the qualitative specifications of rations. I ensured the presence of the secretaries of defence and finance so that we could get an approval in principle on the spot, and move the file thereafter. I am grateful to the minister that he approved our proposals, and today the armed forces are getting a much better quality of basic rations (rice, wheat, lentils, tea, salt and sugar). We received a complaint from the ministry of defence against the head of supplies relating to some irregularities in procurement of rations. This matter was investigated and as a result, some of the individuals found blameworthy are now facing a court martial or other disciplinary action.

As mentioned earlier, one of my foremost key result areas was the health care of our serving and retired soldiers. It was projected to the ministry of defence that we needed the latest equipment and diagnostic facilities – as are available at the Research and Referral Hospital in Delhi – at all our command hospitals, namely at Udhampur, Chandigarh, Pune, Calcutta, Lucknow and Guwahati. This process started in 2006–07. I won't be amiss in stating that the armed forces medical, dental, nursing officers and paramedics are amongst the best in the country; some of them are indeed world class. All they need is state-of-the-art facilities and equipment. And this received my undivided attention. It was also my desire that the Ex-Servicemen Contributory Health Scheme (ECHS) emerges as the best health care project for our veterans. Even though the Army HQ launched this scheme a bit prematurely in 2004–05, as the army commander, Western Command, I ordered the deployment of doctors and paramedic staff along with equipment of our combat medical units on an ad-hoc basis, to make sure that our veterans were looked after in the best possible manner. It took a year or so to procure equipment like X-ray machines and other diagnostic apparatus for the ECHS clinics spread all over the country. I held a meeting in Delhi with the managing directors and chief executive officers of empanelled private hospitals, dental and diagnostic centres to discuss the aim and scope of the ECHS. The meeting was attended by eminent doctors such as Dr Naresh Trehan and Dr S. Khanna. Measures to streamline the timely clearance of bills of the hospitals were discussed and I also appealed to the medical fraternity not to exploit the veterans and the ECHS. In the long run it would definitely prove to be a win-win for all the stakeholders.

Orders were issued by my adjutant general, Lieutenant General A.S. Jamwal, that it would be the responsibility of the nearest army station HQ to take care of all the funeral arrangements and related expenses whenever any veteran passed away. This was to facilitate dignified and befitting funerals and last rites of veterans. I was happy to see that this measure was very well received by the rank and file and particularly by the families, for whom it became a matter of pride and a source of comfort.

From the point of view of morale and motivation, judicious, equitable and timely grant of leave is a very important function of command. Some leaders are stingy about leave and some go to the extent of clamping down on it before an important event to make sure that everyone is present. Consequently there are bound to be some demotivated soldiers around, and things that could go wrong often did. As a leader, leave was never an issue with me. If an individual had a genuine personal problem he was given leave. The only thing that I have always insisted upon is that whoever goes on leave must hand over his charge properly to the next in command and not leave behind an orphan organization. Besides, I felt that there was a huge need for enhancing the leave travel concessions for all ranks, particularly for those serving in operational areas and along the borders. I was very happy that we were able to get the MOD's approval for the grant of a second free railway warrant annually to travel to one's hometown. We did away with the ridiculous distance stipulation for concessional travel by train; this began in the British days, but made no sense today. In addition, as a landmark achievement, we were able to get the government's approval for chartered civilian flights from Leh and Partapur to Delhi and from Imphal to Kolkata. The weekly air force courier flights from Guwahati to Delhi continue to operate as well. These leave travel concessions benefited all ranks immensely and helped to raise their morale and motivation level. As far as the military special trains were concerned, we were able to induct new air-conditioned first- and second-class bogies as also proper kitchen cars. This was a great milestone and resulted in a quantum jump in the quality of train journeys as compared to military special trains of the past era, as described in Part II.

Many of us joined the army for the lure of action, adventure, appeal of serving the country and the love of uniform. Very few armies are engaged in fighting insurgency and terrorism or are deployed in guarding their borders in such large numbers as ours. Therefore, those of us who are in an operational area, which is approximately 30 per cent of the army, adorn the combat dress most of the time. In our nation, despite the law forbidding use of army uniform or accoutrements by people not entitled to wear it, there has been a proliferation of similar-looking uniforms and what is worse, by personnel from civilian security companies. The combat dress was introduced in the 1980s, and sad to say, also proliferated to a ridiculous extent. Different patterns and colours of camouflage dresses began to appear every day. Presuming that the fabric used for the army uniforms was very robust, its misuse as suitcase covers or on seats in buses or holdalls became commonplace! Since the officers have to buy their uniforms they purchase the cloth available from the local markets and get their uniforms or camouflage dresses tailored. So, no two officers were dressed alike or wore the same disruptive pattern dress and accoutrements. To say that we could be mistaken as army officers from different countries wouldn't be an exaggeration! Though the soldiers were issued with government-supplied combat dresses, the quality was poor and the colour faded very fast.

To me the combat dress symbolizes the dress of warriors. I believe that it ought to be given the same importance as the ceremonial dress. Therefore, I felt that the standardization of army uniforms, specially the battle fatigues, was an imperative need. We decided on a different cloth and camouflage pattern, based on the advice of professionals in the field of fabrics, and to prevent unauthorized usage, put the logo of the Indian Army on the fabric itself. We also standardized the belts and combat shoes and the manner of wearing the trousers – they had to be tucked into the boots. During my service in combat situations, I sometimes felt that we were two armies – one fighting terrorists or guarding the borders, facing bullets and braving hazards, and the other in higher HQs or in peaceful cantonments. They wore different uniforms. Its a fact of life that the higher the HQ, the more remote it is from the hardships being faced by those fighting it out, whether against the terrorists or in harsh living conditions.

Once, while I was commanding the brigade in Kashmir, we had a serious casualty in a counterinfiltration operation. This wounded soldier's life was at stake and we needed to evacuate him to the hospital at Srinagar even though it had become dark and the road protection was not in place. However, at the Corps HQ no responsible staff officer was available who could authorize us to move the convoy at night. This was because there was a party going on in the Corps HQ – some dining out or the other. But surely there must have been a duty officer. Whose war were we fighting anyway? I said to myself. Finally, after getting no response, only when I asked to be put through to the corps commander, did someone come on the line and we got the OK. A life was saved.

Therefore, I made it a point as the army chief to wear the combat dress with much pride and elan whenever I visited field formations or forward areas. Besides, in a display of camaraderie and to empathize with approximately 300,000 men in arms serving in the operational areas, it was decided by me that the rest of the army would wear the combat dress every Friday. To be honest, it did create quite an impact not only amongst the services but also in the ministry of defence. The people definitely welcomed this initiative. At least on Fridays no shop assistant in the market was likely to ask us as to which security company we were working for! Soon the air force and the navy followed suit. Once a week, we felt like warriors even if we were far removed from the battlefield. This was one way of showing solidarity and conveying that we shared their challenges and hardships in spirit. I was very clear about wearing of medals and regimental badges of rank on the epaulettes: in peace it was okay, except in a combat zone or during training exercises, when we would need no orders to strip everything off from the combat dress.

A very significant development took place when we, the three service chiefs, happened to attend the presidential fleet review at Visakhapatnam on 13 February 2006. Most of us from the army or the air force had never participated in such an event before. For the navy, it is a very important professional event where they showcase their *'shipshapeness'*, or the state of operational readiness, standard

The supreme commander, President A.P.J. Abdul Kalam, with the army, navy and air force chiefs and their better halves – Visakhapatnam, February 2006.

of training and battleworthiness of ships. The president was taken on board a submarine by the naval chief for a brief diving manoeuvre. The rest of us had a briefing session followed by tea. There were a host of mediapersons present at the event. As usual, they were looking out for some interesting story. And as happens so often, the breaking news is not related to the event of the day. This time around too, it happened something like this – sensing an opportune moment, a group of journalists swooped down on me. Before I knew what was happening, a few mikes were jabbed towards my face. Then, one of them asked me if it was true that the Indian Army had refused to cooperate with the Sachar Committee. It was a seven-member committee, led by Justice Rajinder Sachar, which was carrying out a Muslim-specific survey as part of the government's efforts to promote 'minority welfare' by studying their social, economic and education status.

'In which manner have we not cooperated?' I queried, composing myself and trying to fathom their response. 'General, we have learnt that the army was strongly opposed to any quota for any religious minority in the army, and is yet to provide the required data to the committee. Whereas in the case of the navy and the air force they have already done so,' asked one of the mediapersons.

Without commenting on what the air force or navy had done, I said, 'the system for entry into the armed forces and for enrolment is based on merit and qualifications; on the ability of an individual to perform the task assigned. We never look at things like where you come from, the language you speak, or the religion you believe in. That has always been our ethos and policy. We are an apolitical, secular and a professional force. Therefore, we consider it important that all Indians get a fair chance of joining the armed forces.' This innocuous statement was aired live by the electronic media as 'breaking news' with the title 'Army Chief rejects the Sachar Committee', or words to that effect, which created quite a stir. It was also carried prominently by most newspapers the next day. As a matter of fact, in an editorial in a leading newspaper the next day it was said, 'The Prime Minister's Office has distanced itself from the move as the committee has exceeded its terms of reference, and by raising these questions is actually belittling the secular character of the Indian military. Army Chief General J.J. Singh is absolutely correct in expressing a certain reluctance to tabulate religion based data, with the armed forces taking great pride in their ability to keep their heads far above communal waters. He could not be more precise and Justice Sachar must draw a lesson from the spirit of the Army Chief's remarks.'[1] Similar views were expressed by many other national dailies too. The government accepted our viewpoint, and the matter was not raised thereafter.

Having a roof over the head is the cherished dream of all officers, JCOs and men. The fact that most of the beneficiaries of the Army Welfare Housing Organization (AWHO) projects have been officers and JCOs, made me wonder if that was our objective in starting AWHO in December 1978. What about the 'jawans' or soldiers? They could apply for a home only if it was affordable. The homes we were making were simply out of reach of the other ranks. Hence I conceived of a low-cost housing scheme dedicated to serving and retired soldiers. We tried out this concept at the Maratha Light Infantry Regimental Centre, where a sample dwelling unit was constructed using locally available material. I was amazed to see that a one bedroom, sitting room and kitchen unit

---

[1] *The Asian Age*, 15 February 2006.

with all fittings for lights, fans and Indian-style toilet, cost about one-and-a-half-lakh rupees to construct. This did not include the cost of the land. This is how the 'Jai Jawan Awas Yojana' scheme came about and has become very popular. During my tenure as the chief, the first project located in the city of Jaipur was finished in less than two years, on a fast-track basis. Flats were allotted by a computerized draw, and handed over in August 2007 to soldiers at around Rs 6 lakhs; the going market price of such flats was three to four times more. Besides, they were given loans at concessional interest rates, which were lower than bank rates, from the Army Group Insurance Fund. Encouraged by the response, I asked the managing director of AWHO to carry out a survey of other locations where the soldiers would like to own homes. The men were advised to choose places where there was an army cantonment nearby so that they could avail of their entitled medical and canteen facilities, and where they would have schools for the children. Today, it gives me satisfaction to see that many more such projects have been completed or are under construction in Belgaum, Pune, Allahabad, Secunderabad, Dehradun, Bhatinda and Lucknow, besides another one in Jaipur.

The Army Group Insurance Fund (AGIF), which was registered as a society in January 1976, has grown in an impressive manner, thanks to the dedicated and selfless services of officers who managed it, in particular the late Lieutenant General (Honorary) K. Chandrasekharan. Today, it provides an insurance cover to the officers and other ranks of an amount of Rs 30 lakhs and Rs 15 lakhs respectively. Post-retirement, an extended insurance scheme of Rs 4 lakhs for officers, and Rs 2 lakhs for other ranks has also been introduced. During my tenure as COAS, we took a principled stand to protect the nature and identity of this institution when the government wanted to bring it under its regulatory control. AGIF has been providing outstanding services and schemes. It remains professionally managed and is operated with considerable financial prudence.

Army Welfare Education Society (AWES) was instituted by COAS General K.V. Krishna Rao during the early 1980s to meet the educational needs of the children of army personnel. Due to the expansion of the army in 1962, the existing Kendriya Vidyalayas (Central Schools) could not meet the demand and there were no schools in some of the army stations. The AWES, which started with a modest beginning of twenty-eight schools, runs 127 army schools today. The year 1994 was yet another milestone when General B.C. Joshi, the then COAS, took a bold decision to set up our first professional college, the Army Institute of Technology (AIT), in Pune. This indeed was an inspiring concept. The AWES added almost one professional institute every year and now has thirteen colleges or institutions. The AWES has thus filled a major void by providing avenues to our wards to join professional colleges for higher education. We had overlooked the need for such institutions in the northeast. Hence, I directed that an Army Institute of Nursing be set up at Guwahati to meet the aspirations of children of our soldiers from this region, and was happy to inaugurate this college on 7 August 2006.

Rohini, in her position as president, Army Wives Welfare Association, instituted some pathbreaking measures to ameliorate the condition of widows of soldiers, and help them gain respect and financial security. She believed that the suffering of one widow was no less than that of the other, whether her husband was a battle casualty, or had died in circumstances attributable to military service, or died post-retirement. The empathy or approach required for reducing their suffering and providing the best opportunities for their children, was the same. This enabled her to address them as 'veer naris' and put across the need for their socioeconomic empowerment. She conceived the programme 'ability beyond disability', which aimed at removing the barriers that have relegated the disabled from the mainstream of life and aimed at reintegrating them by provision of assisting devices, rehabilitation training and opportunities for their economic empowerment. The project was successfully conducted with appliances worth Rs 2.3 crore distributed in twenty-one camps. Those camps were conducted with the support of ministry of social justice and empowerment.

Both Rohini and I have imbibed the values of helping the underprivileged from our parents, who suffered so much during Partition. Hence, we thought of bringing up and educating orphans or needy children. The first child whom we took under our wing was

Kuljit, in 1997. He was all of seven years and came from a poor family in terrorist-infested Doda and Kishtwar area in Kashmir. An insecure lad, traumatized by the terrorism in his region, he took some time to settle down in Delhi. In his native village, he was taught in Urdu and didn't know a word of English. We put him in different schools depending on where I happened to be posted. He finished high school with credit, from the Army Public School, Delhi, and joined the army as a soldier as he was overage for the NDA. He is today an aspiring army officer, for he worked extremely hard and made it to the Army Cadet College, Dehradun. He plays volleyball for the college and is doing well in academics. He was perhaps the first student from the Army Public School to have joined the army as a soldier. God willing, he shall be commissioned from the Indian Military Academy as an officer in December 2013. It would be a proud day for Rohini and me. Soon after I became the chief, a media report about Kuljit went like this, 'Seven years ago a young, trembling boy travelled all the way from Doda in Jammu and Kashmir to Delhi where he was being given a new home. Kuljit, the seven year old who used to sleep under the bed for fear of militants today hopes to become an officer in the Indian Army. He's just written out his story and a line of it says, "I met someone like God seven years ago…." The "God", he was referring to, is General Joginder Jaswant Singh, the new Chief of Army Staff'.[2]

The second child is James, who was in a children's home in Kohima, the capital of strife-torn Nagaland. We took on the responsibility of his upbringing in 2006, when he was about ten years old. He was also educated in the Army Public School, Delhi, during my tenure as army chief. Thereafter, I got him admitted to the Sainik School, near Kohima, Nagaland. He has recently completed his tenth board examination and is doing very well. He is a prefect in the school and the captain of the football team. He will shortly be taking the NDA exam to be an army officer. A Christmas and New Year card that gives us unending joy every year is a handpainted one that has the signatures of over a hundred boys and girls from Father D'Souza's home at Kohima, the children's home from where James came (see Appendix 8).

---

[2] Harinder Baweja and Nitin A. Gokhale, *General Action*, *Tehelka*, 26 February 2005.

Two decades ago, when I was a brigadier, I had taken my ailing mother to the hospital. There I met an officer whose wife had been diagnosed with a malignancy. I met the lady and told her to imagine that she was confronted by a tiger in a jungle. She could either close her eyes and let the tiger finish her or she could pick up a stick and fight it. She might survive or die fighting the beast, I told her. We never met again. When I became the chief, I was quite amazed to receive a letter of congratulations from the same officer, who went on to say that his wife never forgot my story, and survived fighting the 'tiger'. It gave me much joy to read about something good that was done many years ago and forgotten.

32

Sports and Adventure Activities

The Indian Army has traditionally been the fostering ground for many luminaries in sports and adventure activities. In fact, these activities are the bedrock of regimental soldiering. In order to create the esprit de corps, camaraderie, leadership qualities, self-confidence and perseverance to achieve the assigned mission despite the challenges, the army has encouraged sport and outdoor activities.

After independence, army sportsmen dominated in athletics and field games. Dhyan Chand and Shankar Lakshman (hockey), Milkha Singh and Sriram Singh (athletics), Narinder Kumar and M.S. Kohli (mountaineering) and Rajyavardhan Singh Rathore, Olympic silver medallist, are a few of our legendary sportsmen from the armed forces. In the early 1950s, my father discovered the athlete in Milkha Singh, when he joined the EME Centre in Secunderabad as a recruit. Dad was his company commander and he nurtured young Milkha like a son. As kids we simply loved to see him running, and practically winning all the sprints at the station sports meets. In two years he rose to be our national champion in 400 metres, and thereafter made history at the Rome Olympics – and became known as 'the flying Sikh'. Unfortunately, the army's priority and focus of attention got totally reoriented to the operational side after the wars in 1962, 1965 and 1971. Besides, we needed a lot of funds for the creation of modern sports facilities, equipment, coaching and foreign exposure to produce international-level sportsmen. This was not forthcoming from any quarters. Consequently, the standard of sports deteriorated.

Realizing the need for government funding, during General Padmanabhan's tenure as the chief, a case was taken up. 'Mission Olympics' was the name given to the long-term project to rejuvenate sports in the armed forces. Funds were released to create the infrastructure, procure equipment and coaches and give international exposure to our sportsmen. The results began showing from the Commonwealth Games held in Melbourne in 2006. Our performance further improved at the CWG at Delhi, and the at the Guangzhou Asiad. I inaugurated the Army Sports Institute at Pune and gave renewed impetus to Mission Olympics. Disciplines like shooting, boxing, wrestling and rowing received greater attention, as I believed we had better chances in them. I presented the COAS trophies for shooting and golf and had the inaugural tournaments for these games at Mhow and Delhi. It gives me great satisfaction to see these competitions being keenly contested each year.

The 'Catch them young' scheme was introduced by me, wherein the children of armymen were given an opportunity to compete in a few selected disciplines. The children who had the best potential were then given a sports scholarship and trained in Delhi. Their educational needs were also taken care of. A few of them have made a mark at the national level in just three or four years. Unfortunately, this scheme went into cold storage after my tenure, much to the disappointment of all ranks of the army. Soldiers who could not afford the cost of equipment and training of their children with potential in a sport, had some hope because of the 'Catch them young' scheme. In fact, I once went to one of these selection competitions. Young kids with their parents had come from army stations from as far away as Guwahati, Thiruvananthapuram or Jammu and Kashmir. There was so much excitement in the air and a competitive spirit was palpable. In case funds were a problem, I am sure some way could have been found through government or corporate support. If we want to produce world champions, they have to be picked up at the age of ten or twelve years.

Mountaineering has always attracted me. It is true that very few senior officers have trained as mountaineers, and perhaps those who became mountaineers did not rise to high ranks. What greater fortune can one have than to learn the rudiments of climbing in the Himalayas

The army women's successful Everest expedition flagged in by Defence Minister Pranab Mukherjee and me in June 2005.

from Tenzing Norgay. This legendary mountaineer, who had the unique honour of being the first man to climb the mighty Everest, along with Sir Edmund Hillary, was the director of field training when I did my basic and advanced mountaineering courses at the Himalayan Mountaineering Institute, Darjeeling in the 1960s. This experience and knowledge came in very handy for me later in life, while dealing with the challenges on our high-altitude border with China – along the LAC in Ladakh, Joshimath Sector and the northeast, and the AGPL or LoC in Siachen, Kargil and Kashmir regions. In our case, for reasons that are obvious, it is of vital importance to understand, particularly at the senior levels, the challenges posed by mountainous and high-altitude terrain in warfare. We learnt this lesson to our bitter cost during the Chinese aggression in 1962.

It was a great pleasure for me to flag off the 'first' women's Everest expedition launched by the army on 18 March 2005. This expedition made history as for the first time, the Indian Army successfully put on the summit four courageous women – Captains Sipra Mazumdar and

Major D.J. Singh of the Maratha Light Infantry and his team on the summit of Everest.

Ashwini Pawar, Cadet Tshering Ladol and trainee Dechen Lhamo – and five more members of the support team on 2 June 2005. This included Major (now Colonel) S.S. Shekhawat. This expedition used the northern route to climb the peak known as 'Sagarmatha', the Nepalese name of the Everest, or 'Chomolungma', the Goddess Mother of the World in Tibetan, and had to approach the peak from Lhasa in Tibet because of the disturbed conditions in Nepal.

It was also my desire that an expedition comprising officers and men from the Maratha Light Infantry should scale the Everest during my tenure as the chief. Accordingly, the selection and training of the best mountaineers of the regiment commenced nearly one year ahead. They trained hard in the Siachen glacier and attempted other peaks like 'Bhagirathi' (6,510 m) and 'Mana' (7,273 m). To ensure a balanced composition of the team some outstanding mountaineers from other units of the army were also included in the team. Lieutenant Colonel I.S. Thapa from 4 Maratha Light Infantry was the leader of this expedition, which had a total of twenty members. The team was flagged off on 28 March 2007 and their plan was to climb the Everest from the tougher north face, like the earlier women's expedition of 2005. They put on the roof-top of the world a total of twelve army mountaineers and an equal number of sherpas on 15–16 May 2007. In the first successful summit attempt, Captain D.J. Singh, Subedar M. Khandagle, Havildars Tshering Angchok, Balwant Singh Negi, Amardev Bhatt and Sepoy Sachin Patil scaled the peak on the 15 May. The next day, another six climbers reached the summit. These were Havildars Nandkumar Jagtap, Dayanand Dhali, Ram Bahadur Mall, Mingmar Gurung, Tejpal Singh Negi and Khem Chand. Defence Minister A.K. Antony was there with me to flag in the expedition on 10 July 2007. I was happy that both these Everest expeditions had returned safely without any mishaps.

33

Adieu

To wrap up my innings I addressed a letter to all commanding officers of battalions, regiments or units and higher command and staff officers of the army on 28 September 2007:

Dear member of the great Indian army team,

I am honoured to have commanded one of the finest armies in the world. As I pass the baton, I wish to place on record my sincere appreciation to all my commanders, commanding officers, staff and the gallant soldiers who helped me uphold the honour, dignity and the professional ethos of our great army. I also pay my solemn tribute to all officers, junior commissioned officers and men who made the supreme sacrifice in the service of our motherland.

I had set out a number of priorities on assuming command in February 2005. These were addressed in right earnest, enabling us to achieve a high level of satisfaction in most areas. I take this opportunity to reminisce with you some of these priority areas, which, with your dedication and unstinted support, have been completed or are in various stages of fructification… (elaborated in earlier chapters).

I am hanging my spurs after forty-three years of responding to the call of the nation through war and peace. You can be sure of my continued association with our glorious organization and with all of you. My commitment to the army will be a lifelong call.

As I hand over the reins of this 'Great Army', I wish you all great success in your future endeavours.

Thank you. God speed and God bless you all.

General J.J. Singh

4 Rajaji Marg was our home for more than two-and-a-half years. The official residence of the chief of army staff was a well-appointed bungalow. Moving into this house was a special event. Rohini had done up the interiors very elegantly and that gave the house warmth and good vibes. We had the privilege of hosting many important visitors, intellectuals and foreign dignitaries, including army chiefs of many countries. The Army Day reception and the garden party for ladies of the station were well-attended annual events.

Our last morning in the house was truly memorable. The home looked empty as the baggage had already been moved to our new abode in the cantonment. After our morning tea had been served, it occurred to me that we would have nothing to do after midday, once the formalities of handing over the command of the Indian Army to my successor had been completed. Having led such a hectic life for over four decades in uniform, here was something that I was certainly not used to! However, for a change, we decided to relax and spend a quiet day together. Nostalgia flooded our emotions and we wished to savour the warmth and memories of what had been our beautiful home for the past two years and eight months, reliving the happy memories of our stay. On this, our last day amidst these lovely surroundings, we wanted to soak in as much as possible of the gracious colonial bungalow so reminiscent of the 'Raj', with its colonnaded portico and verandahs, its impeccably manicured lawns and garden, complete with a waterfall and lush verdant surroundings. We walked around the house at peace with ourselves, which was a most tranquil and soothing experience. We spoke to our children and the rest of the family, recounting the events and activities of the past few extremely busy days. They were proud of our achievements and appeared content that we would now have more time for them. Life had been full of surprises and 30 September 2009 was no exception. Around midday I went through the formal ritual of handing over charge to my successor. That done, it was a very satisfied 'chief' accompanied by the 'first lady' of the army, together with the military assistant and other personal staff, who walked briskly along the corridor and then downstairs to the main gate of the ministry of defence in South Block. We were also accompanied by many senior officers from the Army HQ.

After the customary high tea, we bade our farewell to all those present, among whom were some of my principal staff officers, other senior colleagues, civilian staff from my secretariat and members of my team. I was then escorted to a flower-bedecked open jeep that was drawn by officers, junior commissioned officers and soldiers – a ceremonial send-off with the accompanying 'Jais' (victory or glory). This was a very moving moment for me since it represented my 'Farewell to Arms', and was a fitting finale for three generations of my family who had served the army. Adorning the ceremonial dress of a general of the Indian Army, my chest swelled more than usual with pride and my eyes were moist, as I realized that it was the last time I would be doing so! It had been the magnetic aura and attraction of the army uniform some forty-seven years earlier that had drawn me, a stripling of some fifteen years of age, to the portals of the National Defence Academy. What an epic journey it had been; carrying me from a 'one pipper' to the rank of a four-star general. Our cavalcade then drove past 4 Rajaji Marg, that had us glancing fondly at the 'White Gates', our recent home, and on to 20 Mandir Marg in the Delhi Cantonment, which was to be our temporary residence for the next year or so.

We dressed casually for the evening's 'dinner for two'. Suddenly, we had company. My team of the chief's secretariat, led by 'Bunny' Chetinder Singh and Venkat Gouder, descended upon us. They proceeded to invite us to an exclusive dinner that they had organized at the infantry officers' mess. They had quietly invited our entire family, including our parents and children. It was touching beyond compare to find my entire former personal staff and their wives present in the mess to welcome us, together with the bags and pipes band so beloved of the true infantryman. There was a carnival air in the mess and a joyful time was had by all with merrymaking, music, singing and dancing. The party seemed unending and carried on till the wee hours of the morning. It could be labelled as the *Balle Balle* evening, what with all of us singing and dancing, *Mauja hi Mauja* and *Saadhe Naal Rahoge te Aish Karoge*. The British left us some wonderful precepts, one being to 'work hard and play hard'.

Later in the evening, we experienced another wonder being unravelled in our midst. All of a sudden there was silence and everyone was asked to gather in the ante-room of the mess. A specially designed stand to hold my much-valued military baton was brought into the room, along with my baton, and presented to me. My deputy military assistant, Colonel P.J.S. Pannu from 22nd Maratha Light Infantry (Hyderabadis), had observed the care and pride with which I always carried my baton since it bore the crests of all the units and formations that I had commanded in my over four decades of service. He felt that this baton should rest on a special stand painstakingly designed by him and which, on its base, bore the names of all the officers of my secretariat. It was a superlative gesture, notwithstanding my once casual personal expression to Colonel Pannu that my baton and medals, along with many other trophies, should appropriately be housed in the Maratha Light Infantry Centre Museum. The baton finds a pride of place in my home today.

As we emerged from the officers' mess, another surprise package greeted us! Our car was nowhere to be seen. A 'two in hand' ceremonial horse carriage or buggy was waiting in the porch instead. The carriage was accompanied by a mounted escort of five cavalry troopers in full ceremonial attire from the Indian Army's only horse-mounted regiment, the 61st Cavalry, of which I had had the privilege of being the colonel commandant in my capacity as the chief of the army staff. In all, there were seven horses – an auspicious symbolism! We were escorted to the carriage by my aides-de-camp and instead of the usual farewells, everyone, including the graceful ladies present, broke into a choral rendition of 'For he's a jolly good fellow'. Our pleas to end this affectionate display fell upon deaf ears till we reached our destination, 20 Mandir Marg, a distance of almost one-and-a-quarter kilometres.

Now it was my opportunity to turn the tables on my team. I declared that this was not to be the end of the evening and that I would not let them depart without a 'thank you' drink. This provided the ideal opportunity to uncork some fine champagne in honour of the first guests to our new home.

That was the day, as they say, on which I hung up my spurs. I no longer was the 'Jangi Laat'. Except for the two of us, it would be life as usual the next day for everyone present that evening – just another working day. *C'est la vie*!

I have tried to project in this story the soldier that I was and my performance in the assignments that were given to me, and I stepped out of uniform with grace, dignity and with my chin up. The rest is for the people to judge.

> And when you have reached the mountain top, then you shall begin to climb.
>
> – Kahlil Gibran

All the 'chiefs' at the Conclave–2006 at Army House: (From left to right) Generals S. Padmanabhan, S. Roychowdhury, V.N. Sharma, O.P. Malhotra, the author, K.V. Krishna Rao, S.F. Rodrigues, V.P. Malik and N.C. Vij.

34

Musharraf and I

General Pervez Musharraf and I are peers in a curious way, though we have never met. There have been many interesting and some coincidental events in our lives. We were both born in India in the 1940s against the backdrop of the Second World War, when we were still a colony of the British Empire. We came from middle-class families that were on the wrong side of the border when the country was partitioned in 1947. The Musharraf family migrated from Delhi to Karachi, and my ancestors moved in the opposite direction, from Rawalpindi to Patiala. Both families faced untold hardships as refugees or mohajirs as they were called in Pakistan, and still are! The experience of growing up in nascent nations that had fought a war over Kashmir in 1947–48, was shaping our young minds. We joined our respective military academies in 1961, and also got commissioned in the same year – 1964. Adventurous and fond of the outdoors, we have both been fairly skilled marksmen. As youngsters, we fancied Bengali damsels, but unlike Musharraf, mine was a briefer friendship as recounted in Part II.

From what I have read, Musharraf got married in 1968 to Sehba Farid, a pretty and talented young lady. It was an arranged marriage. They have two children, a girl and a boy.

I was also a captain when I was married, albeit in a different fashion. I met and fell in love with an attractive young girl of nineteen at the 'New Year's Eve' dance at the Army Club in Poona. Two months later, we were engaged, and got married in May 1971. We also have two children, a boy and a girl.

THE RAISON D'ETRE OF A SOLDIER

Medals earned by my grandfather, Sep Atma Singh, 1/67 Punjab Regt – World War I, Mesopotamian Campaign, 1914-1918.

Medals earned by my father, Lt Col J.S. Marwah (EME) – Second World War and the Indo-Pak wars, 1943-1973.

My decorations and medals, 1964-2007.

My baton with crested silver bands of all command assignments – the widest band representing the command of 9 Maratha LI.

With the ladies of Adi and Memba tribes of Upper Siang district during a tour to interior areas at Tuting in Arunachal Pradesh, 19 February 2009.

Prime Minister waving to the crowd with (from left to right) Union ministers Prithviraj Chavan and Mani Shankar Aiyar, Chief Minister Dorjee Khandu and I at the Indira Gandhi Park, Itanagar, 31 January 2008.

Inaugurating the Singa micro hydel project near the China border, February 2009. Rohini and I in Memba dress flanked by ADC Ravi Gonte, Aloke Dutt, former chief minister Gegong Apang, Prashant Lokhande and others.

With Vice President Hamid Ansari and Minister Kalikho Pul at Kibithoo, Anjaw district, on 27 November 2008.

Reviewing the progress of State Secretariat Complex along with Chief Minister Dorjee Khandu, Itanagar, 4 January 2011.

Addressing the state legislative assembly on 3 March 2011. In the chair is Speaker Wanglin Lowangdong and seated in front row (right to left) are Chief Minister Dorjee Khandu (in white shirt), and ministers Jarbom Gamlin, Nabam Tuki and Tako Dabi.

Releasing a book on the Arunachal Education Act 2010 by Minister Bosiram Siram, February 2011.

Near the border at Taliha, flanked by ministers Chowna Mein and Tanga Byaling

Home Minister P. Chidambaram inaugarating a bamboo processing centre at Poma, near Itanagar, on 2 April 2010.

Swearing in of Arunachal Chief Minister Nabam Tuki on 1 November 2011.

After the swearing in of Chief Minister Nabam Tuki (second from left). With Dr (Col) D.R. Shandil, Mrs Tuki, Rohini and Union minister S.K. Shinde, Itanagar, November 2011.

Rohini and I along with family and friends after rafting in the Suru in Ladakh, 2009.

Rohini and I with Kuljit and James, our foster children, at Army House, New Delhi, 2007.

With Marshal of the Air Force Arjan Singh, DFC on 16 July 2011.

With Tiger Woods, Dubai Desert Classic, 2009.

Taj Mahal, Agra, 2001.
Sitting: Sonia, Rohini, I,
Anna , with Seerat and
Anne-Tara. Standing:
Gagan and Vivek.

Team Arunachal, Itanagar, 2012:
Sitting: Rohini and I;
Standing (left to right): Ankur
Garg, Swati Sharma, Tage Napi,
Tage Habung, Dr T. Kampu,
Monika Punia, Sqn Ldr Rajesh
Punia, Dr Tripti Dabral, Maj
Kuldeep Dabral, Atum Potom.

The Jangi Laat's (army chief's) team, Army House, 2007.

Family reunion on my father's 90th birthday, July 2011.

After doing the staff college we both held the prestigious post of brigade major and subsequently, commanded our battalion/regiment. Both of us served in our respective Army HQs in the military operations directorate, in senior capacities. Later, as lieutenant generals, both Musharraf and I commanded the elite 1 Corps of Pakistani and Indian armies respectively. We are survivors, too: I was shot and seriously wounded by terrorists in Kashmir, and his car was blown up by a terrorist's bomb, and both of us have had a few more close brushes with death.

Finally, we became the army chiefs of our respective countries, and held this coveted appointment during the period 2005–07, though Musharraf had also appointed himself as the president after a coup in 1999. I retired on 30 September 2007, and was appointed by my government as the governor of Arunachal Pradesh in January 2008. In the case of Musharraf, though he reluctantly doffed his uniform in 2007, he continued wearing his other hat – that of the self-appointed president of Pakistan. Sadly for him, from that dizzy height, he had to step down unceremoniously on 18 August 2008, as he had been served an ultimatum by the political coalition that was then ruling Pakistan to resign by 19 August or face impeachment. What an inglorious end to his innings as the head of state! He lives in London these days, and according to media reports, he is contemplating a return to Pakistan to be in active politics and run for elections. I hope it is not another case of gross miscalculation on his part of his support base in Pakistan or in the hierarchy of its army. Anyway, it will be a test case and I wish him good luck. As of June 2011, besides the notices served to him to appear in the court at Rawalpindi as a 'proclaimed offender' and his failure to respond, Pakistani prosecutors are likely to proceed with impounding his assets, as per media reports. Time seems to be running out for him as the Pakistan government has issued an Interpol alert for his arrest.

As an army chief, purely from the professional point of view, I always considered myself as having an edge over my counterpart in Pakistan. There was nothing to distract me, and I could apply myself in a single-minded and focused manner to the task of leading the Indian Army. On the other hand, circumstantially, Musharraf had taken upon himself the responsibility of running the country as well. This was at the cost of motivating and inspiring his troops and the army, who would have liked to see more of their chief! A case in point: while I could make a number of visits to the border areas of Jammu and Kashmir and the northeast and do my best to pep up my officers and men, the same could not be said of my peer. Contrary to his actions after the coup d'etat, Musharraf in his book has himself stated that 'whenever the army gets involved with martial law, it gets distracted from its vital military duties. Military training and operational readiness suffer.' But the dichotomy in his words and actions stands out.

It is interesting to see two soldiers of the same era, with more or less the same background, growing up and professionally advancing right to the top rank of their armies, in two neighbouring countries that have fought four wars since their independence in 1947. Both of us experienced the vicissitudes of military life, but grew up in two highly contrasting systems. Mine was an apolitical, secular and professional army functioning as per the Constitution, an army of a democratic nation. In the case of Pakistan, it was an entirely different ball game. In between bouts of democracy, the country has mostly been ruled by the army, in one form or the other. Even when the elected civilian governments have been in place, the army has continued to wield power from behind the curtain.

Musharraf has been labelled as brash and arrogant and one who lied on Kargil. Perhaps the last word on him was pronounced by Murtaza Razvi, who wrote, 'The tragedy is not that he (Musharraf) ran a banana republic in his heyday, but that by the time he left his doomed republic it had run out of bananas.'[1]

As for me, I have been described as as an 'odd ball', a maverick, 'the architect of the Indian Army's doctrine', 'a general with a difference who shoots both from the hip and the lip', 'has a heart that's soft to the core', and so on.

How I would have felt on meeting Pervez Musharraf I cannot say. Though I was invited to the *India Today* conclave at New Delhi in 2008 and we could have met face to face, I didn't have the inclination to meet the mistrustful architect of the Kargil war, someone with double standards and one who does not hesitate to tell lies!

[1] Murtaza Razvi, *Indian Express,* 9 October 2010.

Part V
GOVERNOR OF ARUNACHAL PRADESH

Being sworn-in as governor of Arunachal Pradesh on 27 January 2008.

35

The Second Innings

After I hung up my spurs as the army chief on 30 September 2007, Rohini and I just relaxed for a few days and took stock of our personal matters. These had taken a back seat during my service career – things like personal correspondence, bank accounts, passports, housing, car loans and the like. During this period Rudrangshu Mukherjee from *The Telegraph* approached me to write for their op-ed page. I agreed to write one article every month. During my tenure as the army chief, I was requested by some organizations to receive their awards in appreciation of my services for the nation. I had politely declined their requests at that time citing exigencies of service. Having retired, I had no hesitation to say yes to such honours provided the organizations were non-political and reputed. Therefore, in October that year, I received the 'Sikh of the Year 2007' Award from the 'Sikh Forum International', at the famous Lincoln's Inn in London. Thereafter, we spent a few days with Vivek and his wife Anna, and their two lovely daughters, Anne-Tara and Marie-Sana, at their cosy home in the countryside in Normandy, France. We enjoyed this holiday like free birds soaking in the wonderful ambience of the French countryside.

The word retirement has never appealed to me. I look at life ahead as a batsman who is taking the crease for the second innings. For both Rohini and me there is no question of sitting on past laurels; we always try and find something constructive and meaningful to do. We came back to Delhi and got immersed in reorganizing our lives in the new milieu and environment. Golf came to our rescue and we tried to play as frequently as possible. It kept us sane and fit. One day around mid-November 2007, I received a call from the office of the national security adviser (NSA) asking me to meet him. The next day we met in the NSA's office. After the usual pleasantries, he mentioned that the government was considering me for a gubernatorial position, and asked for my views. Frankly, I was not expecting such a question and after a pause, replied that it would be a great honour to serve my country. Then he threw another bombshell and said that he had learnt that I would prefer to be an ambassador. I had no hesitation in telling him that he had been misinformed. I had tea and while leaving his office, I turned back and expressed my desire that if something was going to come my way, it would make me happier if there was a challenge in it. I came back and shared the gist of the conversation with Rohini. Then we forgot all about it. In the meanwhile, a close friend of mine offered me a vice-presidentship and an equal status to him in his multinational company, with unbelievably attractive terms and conditions. I requested him to give me six months' time. If nothing came up from the government, I would gladly join him after the 'cooling off' period.

On 24 January 2008 I received a message from the office of the home minister that he wished to have a meeting with me. It was a very brief and pointed meeting. The minister, Shivraj Patil, asked me if I was willing to accept a governorship in the northeast. I replied in the affirmative, saying that it would be a great honour. He said, 'I am moving the file now to the prime minister with the recommendation that you should be appointed as the governor of Arunachal Pradesh.' I thanked him and left his office. Till that day I had no inkling that the ministry of home affairs was the nodal ministry for the appointment of governors. Things moved with lightning speed thereafter. By mid-day on 25 January, I was rung up by the secretary to the president of India, Christy Fernandez, congratulating me on being appointed as the governor. I thanked him and asked him if the warrant of appointment could be sent to me. He confirmed that it was on the way. I asked him if any date had been specified. He said it was left to me, and that my appointment would take effect from the day I was sworn in. I got the first congratulatory call from Arunachal Pradesh from Prashant Lokhande, the secretary to the governor. An extremely sincere and efficient officer, Prashant gave me

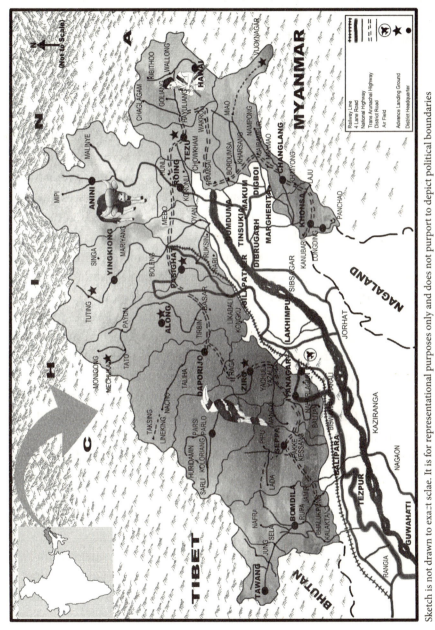

Sketch 35.1: Arunachal Pradesh

a brief description of the capital, Itanagar, and also apprised me of the forthcoming visit to the state by the prime minister on the 31st of the month. That left Rohini and me with no other option but to pack our bags and leave the next day.

When the country was celebrating its 61st Republic Day, both of us flew into the enchanting state of the rising sun, Arunachal Pradesh. I was to take over as the governor on 27 January. We took off from Delhi in the morning and two hours later reached Guwahati, where we were received by a minister from Arunachal and our state's resident commissioner, besides some other officials from the state of Assam. From Guwahati, it was a six-hour journey by road or else a helicopter flight for an hour. We preferred to travel by the chopper to save time.

As we flew over the Brahmaputra valley, memories of my travels and stay in various places of the northeastern region flashed across my mind. During my army career, I had done three tenures and had served in three out of the seven northeastern states, namely Nagaland, Sikkim and Arunachal Pradesh. It needs to be stated that when the sun rises over India, its rays fall over the northeast at least an hour before they do on Delhi. I have always felt that there was a necessity of having an eastern standard time in India. Further, if one looks at the map and focuses on Guwahati or Shillong and draws an arc with a radius of 1000 kilometres, the circle would encompass eight countries. And it would include cities and towns like Kolkata, Dhaka, Kathmandu, Varanasi, Thimpu, Lhasa, Kunming, Mandalay, Chittagong and the border areas of Vietnam, Laos, and Thailand. Therefore this area assumes geo-strategic importance and is, in fact, the land link between India and Southeast Asia.

Historically, the Brahmaputra valley, surrounded by densely forested hills which rise northward to the Great Himalayas, is a land inhabited by an ancient civilization of plainsmen and tribals. It has a vibrant culture and was once a flourishing centre of trade. Assam tea has been exported to the UK since 1838. Oil was discovered in this area and a refinery was set up at Digboi in 1890. Even at the time of our independence in 1947, the northeastern region was amongst the most prosperous of the country. Abundant in oil, minerals, coal, forests and water, a large area is yet to be explored. It produces a huge quantity of tea and fruits like pineapples, oranges, leechies, apples and kiwis. Bamboo, cane, ginger, and other herbal and medicinal plants are aplenty. There is tremendous scope for these natural products to be exploited commercially. This region has some of the world's untouched rain forests, thus earning for itself the status of a biodiversity hotspot. Handicrafts of the area are a novelty. The people are handsome, sincere, content, hardworking and proud of their culture and martial arts. They are fun-loving and have music in their blood. Yet today, the northeast is generally lagging behind the rest of the country as far as development is concerned.

I reminisced of the many crossings of the 'pagla' (mad) Digaru river on elephant back to reach Tezu, the district HQ, in the early 1980s; the freak accident when the jeep overturned and we nearly fell hundreds of feet into the Lohit river; trekking over a thousand kilometers; and my battalion's participation in operations on the Indo-Myanmar border. We were accorded a warm reception, with a ceremonial guard of honour, at the Raj Bhawan helipad at Itanagar, where Chief Minister Dorjee Khandu and his entire cabinet and the who's who of the state had gathered to welcome us.

Arunachal Pradesh, earlier known as NEFA (North-East Frontier Agency) has always been considered a geo-strategically important part of our country, with a common boundary with Bhutan, China and Myanmar. Therefore, successive leaderships at the centre have always given it a very special and unique status while formulating the development priorities for the country. It is well known that our first prime minister, Jawaharlal Nehru, had tremendous love and respect for the tribes of Arunachal and their culture and traditions. He had a firm belief in the policy of letting the people here develop at a pace and in a way that was determined by them rather than imposing any development model on them (Nehru-Elwin Policy). Much before the Indo–China war of 1962, he had visited this frontier state in the 1950s. The strong bonds continued during the tenures of Indira Gandhi, who accorded Arunachal the status of a Union Territory, and Rajiv Gandhi, who bestowed on it full statehood in 1987. The people of the state have, in turn, reposed their faith in the policies of the central government. In fact, the famous incident of one of the 'gaon-burhas' (a title for a respected villager elder) of Apatani plateau proposing to marry Indira and offering a large number of 'mithuns' (a prized animal of the oxen family) as bride price, is still fondly remembered by many Arunachalis!

It is a sensitive state as the Chinese continue to wrongly show a major part of it in their maps as their territory. Therefore, the state cannot be allowed to be destabilized either politically or from the law-and-order point of view, and development has to be given the highest priority. The feeling that I couldn't have got a more challenging assignment gave me immense satisfaction.

On my swearing-in on 27 January 2008, I silently prayed for courage, strength and wisdom to live up to the expectations of the people and do justice to the oath that I was taking. Almost twenty-seven years ago, I was the commanding officer of 9 Maratha Light Infantry, which was one of the units tasked to defend our borders in Tezu district. Little did I realize then that one day I shall be back in Arunachal Pradesh as its first citizen. However, when I look back to the two-and-a-half years spent by me in the state in the early 1980s, it is disheartening to see that not much development appears to have taken place in all these years. Although there was some development of infrastructure, more could have been achieved. Very little was done as far as tourism was concerned. Further, there was no industry worth the name. So, there was indeed a challenge for all of us in Arunachal to give greater momentum to development in all spheres.

36

A Proactive Approach

Within a week of my assuming charge as governor, Prime Minister Manmohan Singh arrived in Itanagar, the capital of Arunachal Pradesh. It was a landmark event and the whole state was eagerly looking forward to it. On this occasion, Dr Singh announced a huge infrastructural development package of over Rs 20,000 crores, including an airport, a rail link to Itanagar, a four-lane highway from Guwahati, a trans-Arunachal highway of over 1500 kms connecting most of the district HQs, and many hydel power projects. This much-needed initiative has launched the state into a new trajectory of growth and development. (A list of these projects is given in Appendix 9.)

This was the first occasion since independence that such a massive development programme was initiated in the state. The prime minister then had a meeting with me and the chief minister and his team of ministers at the Raj Bhawan. He was given a comprehensive briefing about the security situation and the development needs of our state. He stayed with us for the night and the next day, accompanied by the chief minister and me, he flew to Tezu. There, Dr Singh addressed a gathering of army officers and soldiers of a mountain brigade, which is also known as the hathi (elephant) brigade, and had a cup of tea with them. It was a coincidence that I had served as a battalion commander in the same location during 1981–83. The brigade then had an Assam Rifles battalion, which was authorized an elephant as there were numerous rivers and channels which were not bridged and the elephant helped us cross all these obstacles. Prior to the prime minister's visit, I met

Chief Minister Dorjee Khandu and his cabinet to discuss issues that needed to be raised with Dr Singh. We are now witnessing a historical phase of development of infrastructure. With its estimated hydro-power potential of about 55000 MW, Arunachal is gradually emerging as a potential powerhouse of the country, with around one-third of the country's energy needs being met from what we shall produce here. I perceive that in a decade from now, the Arunachalee people will be amongst the highest per capita income earners in our country.

Besides these major projects, I visualize tremendous potential for tourism, organic farming, floriculture, horticulture, tea, bamboo, handicrafts and cane products and small-scale industry for fruit processing. These activities will result in generation of more jobs for the people. A number of initiatives have been taken by the state government and the Raj Bhawan to encourage people to create self-help groups or become small entrepreneurs, and exploit the potential of the 'gold mine' they are sitting on. As the constitutional head of the state, I see my role as that of a guide, mentor and catalyst and the head 'gaon bura' too. By the end of my tenure, if I am able to earn and justify the sobriquet of being a 'people's governor', my ambition in my second innings would be realized.

Therefore, I got my 'swearing-in oath' framed and put on my desk, so as to be constantly reminded of it. There are two fundamental issues included in our oath, as our constitution framers had conceived it. The first is to uphold the constitution of India and the rule of law, and the second, which I consider to be of equal importance, is to work for the well-being of the people. Besides these, the governor's office has been given a special responsibility for the maintenance of law and order under Article 371 H of the constitution. Thus, I have a somewhat greater span of responsibilities as compared to most other governors.

As soon as we had settled down, I planned a visit to the district of Tirap, which is affected by the spillover of decades of insurgency from the neighbouring state of Nagaland. On 2 February 2008, I flew to Khonsa, the district HQ. I was accompanied by Ankur Garg, an enthusiastic young IAS officer who was to take over as the deputy commissioner of Tirap on the same day (he later joined as my secretary in November 2009). I was pleasantly surprised when an elderly 'gaon bura' approached me and said, 'Sir, I worked with you during your battalion's operation in this area in 1981.' At Tirap I gave a clear message to the security forces, the civil administration and the citizens that law and order will be given the highest priority, and insurgency would not be tolerated. A strong message went across that the governor had accorded prime importance to this issue, and had made sure that his first visit was to this disturbed area. In accordance with the aforementioned special responsibility, I analysed the overall security situation and recommended measures for enhancing the effectiveness of the law and order machinery. At that time, Tirap and Changlang districts were witnessing violence and strife and a vicious struggle for dominance by the two NSCN groups. Forced recruitment, illegal taxation, extortion and coercion were the order of the day. The state police and other security forces were unable to take effective action against these terrorist outfits because of inadequate strength, lack of modern weapons and training. Thus, the modernization, expansion and training of the police and beefing up of force levels in these districts became a priority for us.

The need for a cohesive strategy and coordinated actions of various agencies responsible for combating terrorism in the two affected districts and other areas bordering Assam, where the Bodo or the ULFA terrorists often seek refuge, also emerged clearly. Therefore, I recommended the creation of an apex body – a state-level core group on security with the chief minister as the chairperson with high-ranking representatives of the army, police, paramilitary forces alongwith the chief secretary and other civilian officials as members. As usual, initially we faced resistance from the bureaucracy in Delhi, but eventually, we were able to convince them of our rationale, and this set-up was created. In one of their meetings, important guidelines were conveyed by me to this group. 'First and foremost an overall security aim should be evolved which would ensure law and order prevails throughout the state and that no terrorist group is allowed to establish its roots or dominance in any part of Arunachal Pradesh. To achieve this aim, a strategy must be worked out by the core group that should accord priority to the tenets of counterterrorism elaborated in Part IV earlier. As a result, there has been greater effectiveness in the law enforcement, and the overall situation is better, though not yet as peaceful as is desirable.

Keeping in mind the security challenges faced by the state, I was convinced that there was a need for raising 'Arunachal Scouts', a force on the lines of Ladakh Scouts, to act as a force multiplier for the army for the defence of Arunachal Pradesh. Accordingly, a proposal was forwarded to the government in 2008. Chief Minister Dorjee Khandu and I lost no opportunity to impress upon the decision-makers in Delhi the need to sanction this proposal at an early date. On 22 January 2009, I wrote to Defence Minister A.K. Antony:

> It is beyond any doubt that the establishment of Arunachal Scouts is of the greatest importance for strategic and other reasons. Further, when we start recruiting the local youths we are ensuring productive employment to a large number of youngsters in Arunachal Pradesh who otherwise may be misled by anti-social elements. The youth selected for Arunachal Scouts would be force multipliers wherever we face a challenge to our security. They would get an opportunity to defend their homeland, act as guides and interpreters, would not require much acclimatization in the high altitudes and would know how to live off the land. It may be recalled that during the Kargil War, the Ladakh Scouts played a vital role in the eviction of the Pakistani intruders, and facilitated the operations of the army tremendously.

The idea of Arunachal Scouts had taken strong roots by then. After almost two years of pushing the project to make it a reality, it was a source of great satisfaction to see that the first battalion of this force has been raised at Shillong. Both the chief minister and I joined in the raising day ceremonies during November 2010. I congratulated the officers and men and complimented them for their high morale and esprit de corps. After my address to all ranks of 1st Arunachal Scouts, I presented a silver trophy to the battalion. Eventually, Arunachal Scouts is likely to comprise four battalions and a training centre. During a visit to Itanagar, the defence minister was happy to announce that the government had cleared the raising of the second battalion. This process could take upto five years.

Most of my illustrious predecessors, barring a few like K.A.A. Raja, Mata Prasad, A. Dave and S.K. Singh, had short tenures in office and some only held additional charge. As such, there appeared to be lack of continuity and an urgent need to streamline the functioning of the Raj Bhawan. Therefore, we set about doing so in right earnest and resultantly, we evolved many new standard operating procedures (SOPs) and streamlined others. We decided to throw open the Raj Bhawan to the public once a week on Sunday. There have been a couple of thousand visitors since then. Rohini and I also decided to make the Raj Bhawan a crucible for new ideas that could make a difference to the lives of the people. Therefore we set up an organic farm with vermin compost as the manure (and banned the use of pesticides or fertilizers), a country chicken farm, bee colonies for production of honey, a small fish farm making use of a rainwater harvesting tank and a green house for an orchid nursery. We also created a lawn and terrace garden which has covered up an ugly-looking rooftop of the Durbar Hall. Florida tifdwarf grass was obtained from Chandigarh. After making a nursery to propagate the grass, the same has been used extensively to beautify other parts of the Raj Bhawan too, as also to make a pretty nine-hole golf course with the expert advice of Colonel Gurdial Singh. We also added to the guest accommodation as Itanagar does not yet have decent hotels. Two bedroom suites were constructed as an extension of the existing guest house as also a unique wooden cottage of four small bedrooms that came in a prefabricated kit, and took only a few weeks to assemble. The interiors and furnishing of these rooms of the 'Hornbill' cottage, as it has been named, were done using local materials such as cane and bamboo, the designs for which were created by Rohini. These suites could serve as benchmarks for guest rooms all over the state. Besides this, we have recently added a modern gymnasium, a badminton court, an auditorium, a children's park and store houses in the Raj Bhawan.

Being a team person always in life, it was but natural for me to make an appeal for 'Team Arunachal' and design an appropriate badge for it. We finally chose to make a badge and lapel pin with the hornbill motif on it. I have been liberally presenting the Team Arunachal badge to all citizens who do outstanding work. I have a cherished desire to see the majestic yellow-beaked Indian hornbill in full flight in Arunachal.

The natural beauty and the diversity of flora and fauna have placed Arunachal Pradesh amongst the very few remaining biodiversity hot spots of the world. The state has different climate zones, ranging from the glaciated and alpine climate along the Himalayas to the tropical rain forests in the foothills, with the cool and temperate region with coniferous forests in between. It is a part of the world with places where perhaps no human has ever set foot. There is over 82 per cent area under forest cover, which is amongst the highest in the country. It is also the most sparsely populated region of India with about 17 persons per square kilometre as against the national average of over 382 people. During the past three years alone, four new or extremely rare species of fauna have been found: a multicoloured small bird called Bugun Liocichia, a catfish with grey head and brown body (*Erethistoides senkhiensis*), a butterfly known as Bhutan Glory (*Bhutanis lidderdalii*) and recently, a rare mammal, Black Pika (*Ochotona nigrita*), sighted for the first time in India.

However, it was astonishing to see that despite the enormous potential for tourism, this sector had not seen commensurate development of infrastructure. [According to *Lonely Planet* (2012 edition), Arunachal Pradesh has been rated 'fourth' among the top-ten regions to be visited in the world.] Tourism had thus become one of my foremost thrust areas and I had to somehow get things moving on this front. Besides that, in my meetings with the concerned ministers in the central government, I stressed the need for making more areas accessible or opened up for tourists. Importantly, we also took up the case for issuance of the inner-line permit 'online' and for streamlining the procedures to make them tourist-friendly. In view of the absence of road communications, many scenic places are out of reach of the people and thus I advocated the concept of heliports. We were very pleased when the tourism ministry agreed to develop Mechuka, one of the most beautiful valleys in Arunachal, as the first tourist heliport in the state. Arunachal Pradesh is an inalienable part of our country and we must provide easy access and facilities to as many Indian and foreign visitors as possible so that they can see the natural beauty of the state.

37
Development of Northeast and 'Look East' Policy

Keeping in mind the strategic importance of the northeastern region and its unique and vitally important developmental needs, the Government of India set up a separate ministry for the development of northeast region (DoNER) in September 2001. Prior to that, in October 1996, the central government had put into effect a policy of earmarking at least 10 per cent of planned budgets of various central ministries or departments for the development of northeastern states. Another important step taken by the planning commission is that it allocates special plan assistance funds every year to eleven special category states, which include all the northeastern states.

Even prior to the creation of the DoNER ministry, a northeastern council (NEC) was constituted in 1971 by an act of Parliament. This high-powered apex body, comprising the governors and chief ministers of all the northeastern states, marked the beginning of a new chapter of focused and rapid development of the region. The mandate of the NEC is to take action in the fields of economic and social planning, transport and communications, and matters relating to power and flood control concerning the region as a whole. The council also has a role to review the security situation in the member states and recommend action as required. However, because of numerous reasons, most important of which is the lack of infrastructure and connectivity, the desired pace of development has not taken place. Therefore, with the active participation of all states, a comprehensive study was carried out under the aegis of the NEC to spell out the goals, identify the challenges and suggest implementation strategies. This resulted in the evolution of a document titled, 'Peace, Progress and Prosperity in the Northeastern Region: Vision 2020'. At an NEC plenary session at Agartala on 13 May 2008, all the governors and chief ministers became signatories to this important document, and it was formally released by the prime minister on 2 July 2008 in New Delhi.

> India's Look East Policy is not only an external economic policy, it is also a strategic shift in India's vision in the world and India's place in the evolving global economy. Most of all it is about reaching out to our civilizational neighbours in Southeast Asia and East Asia.
> – Prime Minister Manmohan Singh.[1]

Although the results of this policy have not yet manifested themselves in the northeastern states, there is huge potential of boosting the economy of this region by linking it to Southeast Asia through surface trade routes. Thus, the answer lies in encouraging Indian investment in infrastructure in neighbouring countries, and resolving outstanding issues of investment, trade and transit. Prime Minister Manmohan Singh's government deserves to be complimented for giving a boost to our Look East policy. His visit in October 2010 to Malaysia, Vietnam and Japan is a pointer to India's increasing engagement with Southeast and East Asia. Analysts who see this as encirclement of China are looking at it in an unreal and sensational manner. India needs to open up with its eastern neighbours for the economic benefits that would accrue to people in our northeast. No doubt this initiative also has its ramifications on the political and security domains. An encouraging development is the expression of intent by the ASEAN to jointly fight terrorism and transnational crime.

With a highway connecting Kolkata-Dhaka-Guwahati-Myitkyina-Mandalay-Kunming-Hanoi or going to Laos, Thailand and Singapore, the whole economic profile of the region would get transformed. Having seen the benefits of the 160-kilometre Tamu-Kaleywa (India-Myanmar)

---

[1] http://www.southasiaanalysis.org/%5Cpapers37%5Cpaper3662.html

friendship highway to Mandalay, we need to focus on the opening of the historic Stilwell Road that linked Assam, Myanmar and Kunming in Yunnan province of China during the Second World War. Only a small portion of about 150 kilometres needs to be made motorable from Pangsau Pass (which is connected on our side by a national highway) to Shingbwiyang. This road would connect Ledo, an important logistics base of Second World War fame in Assam, with Myitkina through the Pangsau Pass on the Arunachal Pradesh-Myanmar border, and on to the frontier area of Yunnan province of China, a distance of about 600 kilometres. (The original distance from Ledo to Kunming was 1760 kilometres.) This recommencement of formal border trade will truly give a boost to the economy of the northeastern states, particularly Arunachal Pradesh, Assam, Nagaland and Meghalaya. As timber will be one of the major items of import, it would help in the revival of wood- and timber-based industries in the northeast. These had to be closed down following the Supreme Court's restrictions on timber operations in 1996. I have been making this point ever since I took charge as the governor. Since this subject concerns many ministries and agencies, the decision-making has been delayed. But I understand that it is still under consideration of the NSA. If media reports are to be believed, the Chinese have beaten us to it and might probably go ahead and complete this road upto Pangsau Pass from the Myanmar side.

38

Upliftment of Rural Areas and Tourism

The prime minister's visit was followed by the visits of an unprecedented number of important dignitaries. We had the unique privilege of hosting President Pratibha Devisingh Patil, Vice President Hamid Ansari, Deputy Chairman of Planning Commission Montek Singh Ahluwalia, Speaker of Parliament Meira Kumar, Chief Election Commissioner Navin Chawla, His Holiness the Dalai Lama and some ambassadors, including the British ambassador, Sir Richard Stagg, during my tenure. The president presided over the convocation in the North-East Regional Institute of Science and Technology at Itanagar and visited the border areas of Tawang and Kibithu. She was driven around the Raj Bhawan by me in a small battery-operated car, and was visibly impressed to see the various experiments and initiatives being taken by us, including the essentials of the bamboo project that has now come up in Poma village.

So many high-profile visits had never happened in such a short period in the state's history. These sent out the right message: that the Government of India was doing its best to bring Arunachal at par with the other leading states of our country. Therefore, huge investments were being made in basic infrastructure projects of roads, railways and airports.

Accompanied by Rohini, I have travelled across the length and breadth of this vast state. The aim of these visits was to meet the people of different tribes and get to know their problems, to interact with government officials and observe the state of development and to meet with army, paramilitary and police force officials and get briefed on the security and law and order situation. I consider these visits as an important part of my duties. There were two occasions when we flew to remote villages, Singha and Gelling, close to the border with China, where I inaugurated mini-hydel projects of 30–50 KW. The roads have not yet reached some of these areas. The generators were stripped into head loads and carried by porters to these remote destinations. There they were assembled and the projects completed. In many places I was told that the people were seeing a governor for the first time. All over Arunachal Pradesh there are 651 border villages covered through micro- and mini-hydel projects, and 523 villages have been provided with solar home lighting systems. These developments are part of the prime minister's package announced in 2008, and the remaining 1000-odd villages in the border belt would be provided electricity by the end of 2012.

We had been hearing of an important bridge over the Siang river being constructed by the Border Roads Organization in collaboration with Gammon India since the 1980s. This mighty river flows into India from Tibet, where it is called Tsang Po, and becomes the Brahmaputra as it joins the other major rivers like Lohit and Dibang.

It enters Arunachal Pradesh near Gelling village and flows into the Brahmaputra basin about 160 kilometres downstream. It is one of the most challenging rivers in the world for white-water rafting. The bridge over the Siang river (as it is called in Arunachal Pradesh) at Pasighat has great importance as it facilitates east to west movement in the foothills of Arunachal. This project had already taken more than two decades and was far from completion in February 2008 when I first toured the area. I flew over it a number of times and visited the site for a briefing. Considering the fact that it was a vital surface link and that none other than Prime Minister Rajiv Gandhi had laid the foundation stone in the 1980s, the inordinate delay in its completion was incomprehensible. It was after three visits to the site and a warning that I would strongly recommend that some heads roll, that this languishing project was finally completed in August 2009 and opened to the public. Similarly, another significant road connecting the southern side of the Brahmputra basin to the Lohit district in the north, including a 2.1 kilometre-long bridge at Alubari Ghat, has been successfully pushed by us and would be a reality in five to seven years. This would reduce the journey from Tinsukia in Assam to Tezu in Arunachal from four hours (a whole day during the monsoon period) to an hour or two.

I have made it a habit to drive into the rural areas of the state to meet people and see the developments taking place in the interior areas. Travelling by helicopter does not offer the same opportunities. On weekends, we sometimes also go on excursions in the vicinity of Itanagar. On one such exploratory visit, we came across a beautiful valley with paddy fields on both sides of a small river. We started trekking along the river and walked uphill, leaving the road and a sleepy little village behind. The water flowing in the river was spring-fed as a large number of perennial streams originating from natural springs flowed into it. There were rain forests on both sides of the river. After walking for an hour along a forest trail, we spotted a nice place where the river formed a big pool. The water was emerald green and its attraction was difficult to resist. We decided to relax and enjoy nature's bounty. This was pure mineral water as there was no habitation uphill that could have polluted it. We enjoyed our picnic lunch and swam in the river. On our way back we stopped at the same small village. As was our practice, we distributed sweets among the children and spoke to the villagers. Besides agriculture they had no other source of income or means of livelihood. It was subsistence living. Except for electricity and an unmetalled road, not much had changed in their lives for decades. This village of around 300 inhabitants, about an hour's drive from Itanagar, is called Poma, and the river has derived its name from it.

In the absence of any industry or with tourism yet to see the light of day, some avenue had to be found to enable income generation. I had read of the Cane and Bamboo Technology Centre (CBTC) at Guwahati. On my next trip there, I decided to visit the CBTC and meet Kamesh Salam, its director. It was a revelation as I found an answer to the issue of sustainable income generation by the villagers of Arunachal Pradesh.

All that was required was to add value to the raw bamboo and cane that is found in abundance in Arunachal. A pilot project was

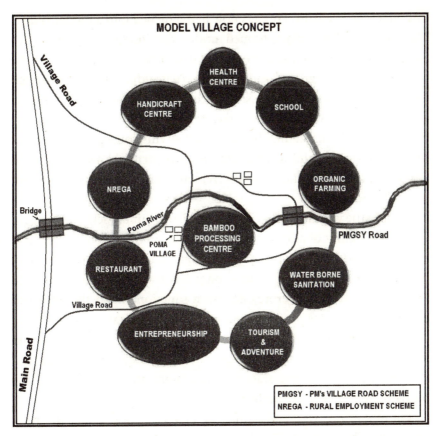

Poma village in Arunachal was developed as a model village.

conceptualized by me in Poma village, where we created a workshop and put in a few low-technology machines that would enable the youth and women to process the bamboo and make simple products. This project was facilitated by the departments of planning and environment and forests, and implemented by the Forest Corporation Limited of Arunachal Pradesh. A few young men and women were sent to Guwahati to undergo a short training capsule, and the Poma project was off to a start. It has been handed over to the village development society management. Today, it is a source of great joy and satisfaction to see the village humming with activity with about forty families actively involved in producing thin bamboo sticks for the incense sticks and other handicrafts to meet the unending orders. More importantly, entrepreneurial instincts and skills have been generated in the people of this once sleepy village. Poma is now being turned into a model village. The road has been black-topped under the Pradhan Mantri Gram Sarak Yojana (PMGSY) and the special plan assistance programme, the school has been upgraded and the primary health centre has also been renovated. Now we are witnessing a growing demand from other rural areas of Arunachal Pradesh for starting similar projects. Taking a step further towards facilitating the expansion of this concept as demanded by the people, a training programme for a fortnight was conducted at Poma, and was attended by villagers and small entrepreneurs from other districts.

During the visit of the minister of tourism, Kumari Selja, we brought up the possibility of a tourist resort along the Poma river in the same area. We made an effective presentation and she promised to have the project examined and cleared on a fast track basis. To her credit, a project worth Rs 3.9 crores has been sanctioned and the work has already started. This project is one of the exceptional cases where the central government has released the funds to create a green tourism resort using wood, bamboo and grass for thatched roofs. The project is being executed by the state tourism department and involves the participation of villagers of the area.

On one of our weekend jaunts, we chanced upon a very beautiful and scenic lake about 15 kilometres from Itanagar. It was a sorry spectacle to see the lake, known as 'Geykar Sinyi' or Ganga lake, and its surroundings in such an unkempt state. Even the inaugural plaque, carrying the name of a former governor, had creepers and undergrowth all around. Instead of a place to cherish nature's bounty, the area had something sinister about it. Hence, I decided to request the Indian Navy to send a team of divers so that we could do a hydrographic survey of the lake. Having done that, the navy was kind enough to mark the dangerous areas with colourful buoys. The next step was to procure some paddle boats. The state's tourism secretary was requested to get funds released so that they could place the order for boats. It was then brought to my notice that there was no electricity or water supply at this site. To make it into a worthwhile destination for tourists, a new power line and water pipelines had to be laid. Besides these, there was a languishing swimming pool project at this site which needed to be funded so that it could be completed. All these have been put into place on a fast-track basis, with constant nudging of the Raj Bhawan. This tourist facility has been leased out as part of the tourism department's public-private partnership scheme, and is today humming with activity. This complete transformation has been achieved within a period of two years. The downside of it is that young boys and girls are bunking school to romance in the environs of this enchanting lake!

I am convinced that Arunachal Pradesh has huge potential in apiculture too. Pure Himalayan organic honey has a huge demand and sells at a high premium. Therefore, we have taken the lead by setting up a few bee colonies in the Raj Bhawan itself. A lesser-known fact is that Punjab is the largest producer of honey in our country even though it has very little forest cover or flowers and no support of Himalayan flora. In Arunachal, we have all three, yet we produce a negligible quantity of honey, an aspect that I keep emphasizing to our people. There have been some encouraging developments in this field, and I hope to see my vision being realized one day. Further, seeing the potential for the production of tea, I talked to the tea board officials and recommended that they should open a chapter in Arunachal Pradesh as they had no presence till then. It didn't surprise me when I learnt that even the Darjeeling variety of tea could be produced in Arunachal Pradesh. Consequently, we have made good progress in this field. Moreover, I have been telling the state's farmers to grow the organic variety of tea because of the high returns it would give.

Arunachal has the longest stretch of Himalayan mountain chain (about 1000 kilometers) in the country. In fact, other than Sikkim and Arunachal Pradesh, no other state in the northeast has the Himalayas. Therefore, all-out efforts to create a mountaineering institute in Arunachal Pradesh were being made by the state government. For this we needed the sponsorship and financial backing of the ministry of defence and accordingly, I was constantly in touch with the minister. Eventually, on the state's twenty-fifth statehood day on 20 February 2012, the defence minister, A.K. Antony, announced the sanction of this project by the Government of India.

Three Everesters of Arunachal Pradesh being felicitated by the author: Tapi Mra (top), Tine Mena (left) and Anshu Jansempa (right).

The first and only Everester from our state till recently was Tapi Mra. His was a one-man expedition to Mount Everest. During his daring bid in the summer of 2009, I received a desperate call from him from the base camp for financial assistance of $1000 or his sherpa would desert him. I assured him of this help and as a result he was able to go ahead with his mission. He climbed the Everest taking only 53 hours from the base camp to the summit. This is the fifth-fastest time in the world. On 1 April 2011, I had the pleasure of flagging off the first women's expedition to Mount Everest by two Arunachalee women, Anshu Jansempa and Tine Mena, who had earlier climbed Mount Nepal Peak (7169 metres). It is a matter of great pride for all of us in Arunachal that both the women climbed the Everest and established a record for being the first women from the northeast to do so. Tine Mena created history on 9 May 2011 and Anshu Jansempa, a mother of two, summited three days later. Not content with that, Anshu, the determined and intrepid mountaineer that she is, made a second successful ascent of the Everest on 21 May and created a world record. Basking in the glory of these achievements, we now hope that the National Institute of Mountaineering and Adventure Sports at Dirang would become a reality in two or three years.

To increase the availability of better habitat for tourists, we proposed to the northeastern council to upgrade seventeen of our most beautifully located forest inspection bungalows. Some of them provide a view that is out of this world. Most of these structures are in a woeful and completely rundown condition. As funds are being released now, the renovation of these bungalows will be done in a phased manner. This project will be a landmark achievement in the field of Arunachal tourism. In a meeting in 2008 with the then tourism minister, Ambika Soni, I was able to get a commitment of Rs 12 crores for the creation of an institute of hotel management with a hostel for the students. It is satisfying to see the project coming up already in the area of Bandardewa. The first course shall commence in the academic session 2012–13.

Rohini has spearheaded various campaigns such as a breast cancer awareness programme, blood donation, and 'ability beyond disability' to help the challenged children and adults. So far, thirteen poor children have been provided free heart surgery in Delhi through the aegis of rotarians like Sushil Gupta and the National Heart Institute.

39

Captives of Geography

One of the easternmost points on the mainland of India is a quaint little settlement in Arunachal Pradesh known as Vijaynagar (see Sketch 35.1). It is situated in a narrow valley at the tri-junction of India, China and Myanmar. It lies in a salient about 100 kilometres deep, jutting into Myanmar like a dagger, and has high mountain ranges on both sides. My visit to this remote area was an unforgettable experience. It takes a trek of six days to reach Vijaynagar, which is the circle HQ. After concerted efforts for almost a year, an Assam Rifles outpost was established in November 1961 and christened Vijaynagar. Subsequently, after the Sino-India war of 1962, on the advice of the army, our government set up a colony of ex-servicemen from Assam Rifles in this sparsely populated but strategic area. Therefore, the population of this area comprises, besides the tribals (belonging mostly to the Yobin and Lisu tribes), Nepali-speaking families of Assam Rifles ex-servicemen. They subsist on farming and forest produce. At the eastern tip of this salient is the Chaukan Pass, which is almost equidistant from Guwahati in the west and Kunming in China, which is about 600 kilometres to its east. I do not think there is any other circle HQ in India that requires a trek of six days from the roadhead over such treacherous terrain.

In April 2010, I decided to visit Vijaynagar and see for myself the situation on the ground. We took off at 7 a.m. in an MI 17 helicopter. Although the weather was not ideal we landed an hour later at Dibrugarh to refuel. There we received frantic calls about the poor visibility and bad weather conditions at Vijaynagar, and in the narrow valley that we had to fly through. My advisers recommended that we should call off the trip. However, I didn't agree and asked the pilots to give it a try provided the weather permitted. Soon we were on our way. What greeted us fifteen minutes into the flight was a scene unlike any I had ever seen before. Vast green plains changed into a narrow river valley with densely forested hills. The helicopter threaded its way in the valley, flying along the Dihing river. The view was unbelievable – and surreal. We were overflying the famous Namdapha reserve forest, home for much of our wild life, particularly the great Indian hornbill and a few remaining tigers. Finally, we reached Vijaynagar, where a colourful reception awaited us. We landed on a disused runway, which used to have regular maintenance and communication sorties of AN 32 transport aircraft of the air force till recent times. Despite the isolation and difficult living conditions, the people were warm and welcoming. This was the first visit by a governor in recent times to this place, and a big crowd had gathered to meet me. After the welcome address by the circle officer and my response, the people's representative handed over to me a memorandum of their demands, which I admit were very genuine. I assured them that I would do my best to ameliorate their problems and distributed gifts to the village heads and 'gaon buras' and a cash grant to the circle officer for the welfare of the people. Then I went across to the Assam Rifles post and interacted with the soldiers. I was very pleased to see the state of morale of the gallant officers and men of 18 Assam Rifles.

On the way back, I pondered over the plight of these people. Their ancestors were settled here with promises and they trusted us blindly. So, I decided that if I was to pick one single development challenge facing the state, it would definitely be to provide road connectivity to these 6000 or so inhabitants of Vijaynagar area, and to do so with a sense of urgency. To begin with, I initiated the idea of a jeepable fair-weather road connecting Miao to Vijaynagar, a distance of approximately 175 kilometres. Thereafter, the state government released some funds and the work commenced. The chief engineer, Toli Basar, a dedicated official, had promised to complete this task by January 2011 subject to weather conditions. This road was being constructed more or less on the same alignment as that of an earlier road that had been abandoned many years ago. I sought the help of the defence minister, A.K. Antony, and then Air Chief Marshal Naik to expedite the repairs and lengthening of the runway of Vijaynagar airfield. Consequent to that, airlifting of heavy earthmoving machinery to Vijaynagar has already been accomplished by two or three MI 26 sorties so that work on the road could commence from that end as well. I had promised the people of Vijaynagar that I would lead the first convoy when this road project was completed. Though I couldn't keep my promise, I was delighted to learn that from early May 2011, jeeps and light trucks commenced moving on this road. At a later stage it could be converted to a single-lane black-top road except probably the stretch that goes through the famous forest reserve. As of April 2012, the road has been made motorable except during the monsoon period. Rohini and I flew in by helicopter on 18 November, preceded by Air Marshal S. Varthaman, C-in-C of Eastern Air Command; it was the first landing by an AN32 airforce transport aircraft in the newly repaired and upgraded airfield at Vijaynagar. The scenic beauty, wildlife, flora and fauna of the Namdapha national park makes it a tourist's paradise, and hopefully it would soon begin to figure in the tourism map of the world. This would totally transform the living conditions of the people and the economy of this neglected area.

40

A New Dawn

At the time of independence, there were less than 100 kilometres of roads, three schools with fifty students, one hospital and three dispensaries in Arunachal Pradesh! This in a state that is twice the size of Switzerland! There are twenty-six major tribes and over 100 sub-tribes in the state. Traditionally, they used to trade with people in the Assam plains. They very rarely had any dealings with the Tibetans across the Himalayas except the Monpa, Memba, Khamba, Mishmi and Sherdukpen tribes in the north. The people of Arunachal are fiercely patriotic and nationalistic and take umbrage at the Chinese laying claims over areas of their state. During my tenure I have witnessed a number of events where the people of Arunachal have expressed their anti-Chinese feelings. The youth organizations have held a 'dharna' at 'Jantar Mantar' in New Delhi, taken a motorcycle rally with anti-China placards upto Bumla on the border, banned Chinese goods in the local markets and burnt the effigies of Chinese prime minister as a protest against the issue of stapled visas being given to people from Arunachal Pradesh.

Arunachal Pradesh is the only state in the northeast where Hindi is universally spoken. In fact, it has become a link language amongst the people as most Arunachalees do not understand the language or dialect spoken by tribes other than their own. The state has come a long way now, with the focus on vitally important infrastructure development. A greenfield airport will come up at Itanagar, and across the state, eight subsidiary airfields are being upgraded and extended for short-take-off-

and-landing aircraft. As mentioned earlier, a trans-Arunachal highway is under construction, which will enhance connectivity manifold by joining the major valleys laterally and link up with most district HQs. During a recent visit, I was happy to see the progress being made in the construction of the state legislative assembly, the civil secretariat and the housing project for the members of the assembly. These projects, alongwith the drinking water supply scheme, would change the face of Itanagar upon their completion by 2012–13. The state is eagerly looking forward to December 2012, when the railway connectivity with the rest of the country is scheduled to be established (see Sketch 35.1).

During my Republic Day speech in 2010, I made an appeal for a clean, green and plastic-free Arunachal Pradesh. I have ensured that the Raj Bhawan's people-friendly initiatives do not tread on the toes of the executive and, in fact, act as force multipliers to their efforts. Yet some may consider these steps as being proactive. For me the oath taken at the time of my swearing-in is supreme, and I believe that I am only doing my duty.

Democracy has struck deep roots in Arunachal Pradesh. The people exercise their franchise enthusiastically. Despite the allurements which various candidates promise, they generally vote for the best candidate. The fact that some bigwigs failed to get elected to the current legislative assembly is an indicator that the will of the people prevails. The message is loud and clear: the votes will be cast for someone who will deliver. Elections were conducted peacefully with impressive turnouts for the panchayat (79.16 per cent), Parliament (68.16 per cent) and the state assembly (79.5 per cent). In a poll carried out by *India Today* (27 December 2010), an overwhelming majority of Arunachalees said they were proud to be Indians, and felt that China was not justified in showing their state as part of it. It is a matter of pride for us that on 24 February 2011, Arunachal Pradesh was conferred the CNN-IBN and IBN7 Diamond State Award as the best performing state amongst the smaller states of India.

Although there are only a few hundred retired servicemen in the state, I was astonished to see that the state ex-servicemen (ESM) board was almost defunct. Hardly any of the benefits announced by the government or the ministry of defence for the veterans were being passed down to them. This dormant organization was kick-started and a few meetings and rallies were held thereafter. There is now a functional but ad-hoc set up for the ESM to take care of their needs. As proposed by me, a state-level rally was held on 4 December 2010 where we were able to get to know the veteran's problems. On the occasion, the chief minister, Dorjee Khandu, assured the gathering that he would create a full-fledged state soldiers board and look into the issues raised by the veterans. We have held a number of recruitment rallies to encourage the youth to join the armed forces and contain the rising unemployment. Besides that I have been pushing to raise additional NCC units, including a naval wing. We are hopeful that under the leadership of Lieutenant General P.S. Bhalla, the desired expansion of the NCC in Arunachal Pradesh would become a reality.

On 30 April 2011, a shocking and unfortunate event took place. Chief Minister Dorjee Khandu's helicopter took off from Tawang at 9.56 a.m. and ran into bad weather around the Se La pass. The chopper lost contact with the base and went missing. The spell of exceptionally heavy weather with snow and rain hampered search and rescue operations for the next few days. The crash site and the bodies were located after an intense search of four days. Dorjee Khandu had come to symbolize the strength of our democratic traditions, having served in the army and rising from the social fabric of Arunachal to become the chief minister for a second term. His humanitarian values, humility and simplicity endeared him to all. He will be remembered as one of the finest chief ministers the state has seen.

The Congress legislative party met on 5 May 2011 to elect a new leader. After hectic parleys, Jarbom Gamlin was chosen as the next chief minister. He was very close to Dorjee Khandu and soon after his swearing in, announced that he would complete the projects and plans undertaken by his predecessor. The swearing in of his council of ministers was conducted on 20 May. Unfortunately, Jarbom Gamlin's tenure was cut short due to political turbulence caused by various factors. Dissent against his government kept increasing by the day. Finally, after a period of uncertainty coupled with law and order problems during five months of Gamlin's rule, the Congress decided to make a change of guard. After due consultations with the elected members of the assembly and other people's representatives, it nominated Nabam Tuki as the new chief minister. His swearing in was conducted at the Raj Bhawan by me on 1 November 2011. Tuki couldn't have got a luckier beginning as he was asked to receive an award in the 'most improved small states' category from Pranab Mukherjee, the finance minister of India, on 4 November 2011. These awards have been instituted by *India Today* magazine. We hope to maintain our position in 2012 also. A grassroots politician, Nabam Tuki is proving to be a worthy successor to Dorjee Khandu and is focusing on development projects and good governance. This augurs well for Arunachal Pradesh and its people. I have always maintained that the people of the state should be the biggest beneficiaries of the development process taking place. At the same time, the indigenous faith, culture and rich traditions must be preserved.

I started my military career from Nagaland in 1965 and later served in Sikkim and Arunachal Pradesh. I shall cap my services to the nation with this tenure as the governor in 2013. In 2010, I was invited to be the chief guest at the Indian Military Academy passing-out parade of the 112th Regular Course. It was a great honour to be back at my alma mater from whose haloed portals I had graduated forty-seven years ago. This occasion became all the more memorable as my ninety-year-old father, who had passed out from the same academy in 1943, was also present. Excerpts of my address to the cadets are given in Appendix 10.

Part VI
REFLECTIONS

'Today, it would be unwise for any country to start a war that it cannot win, and to use nuclear weapons would be the height of folly.'

स्वे स्वे कर्मण्यभिरत:संसिद्धिं लभते नर: ।
(भगवद्गीता, 18-45)

Every individual attains fulfilment of life and fame only on account of discharging the duties prescribed for him/her.
— Bhagvadgita 18–45

41

A View from the Verandah

From the large verandah of the Raj Bhawan at Itanagar, the view of virgin forested hills, the different shades of verdure, the pure spring water of the rivers, the pollution-free environment and the blue sky, makes me go back to my carefree childhood when one read children's classics describing the life of Robinson Crusoe on an isolated but beautiful island. The scenery is perhaps the same, but the scenario of global politics is far more complex now. India is a young and vibrant nation, looking for its rightful place in the comity of nations. So much has changed in these six-and-a-half decades since our independence.

I regard India as a civilizational concept. This was the cherished dream of our forefathers, we are following it, and our children will witness its realization. 'India is not a rising power, it is a world power,' said Barack Obama, the US president, during his visit to India in November 2010. The Indian elephant with its gleaming tusks is taking confident strides into the second decade of the twenty-first century. This has been acclaimed as the century of India and China. With a rising economy and a steady growth rate of around 8 to 9 per cent for the past six to seven years, India is poised to make its impact in the global arena. It has come as no surprise that we hosted visits by the heads of all the P5 countries during 2010. It is a reflection of our growing importance and stature. We are emerging as a deserving permanent member of the UN Security Council and this has been acknowledged by nearly all important nations today. An empowered India can no longer be transgressed or taken for granted.

A vibrant democracy, a strong economy and a powerful military machine are the symbols of our nation's strength. The manifestation of this strength would come about with the indomitable will of our people, and the insurmountable resolve of its soldiers.[1] No nation can achieve greatness without overcoming challenges, and India is no exception. An analysis of India's national security has to take cognizance of both external and internal challenges to its national unity and territorial integrity. Quite often, internal threats can erode the cohesiveness of a nation more critically than any external danger. Though the last major conflict we had was the 1971 Indo–Pak war, the past four decades have been an era of 'no peace no war'. We have had the Kargil conflict in 1999 and two major stand-offs: the first in 1987 as a result of Exercise Brass Tacks, and the second, known as Operation Parakram, from December 2001 to October 2002, consequent to the Pakistan-sponsored terrorist attack on our Parliament. All three could have triggered an all-out war between India and Pakistan. Accordingly, national power based on political stability, social cohesion, military strength and economic progress would remain central to the future of India's national security. Therefore, India seeks to improve its relations with its neighbours and have a peaceful security environment so that it can concentrate on economic and technological development and inclusive growth of its people.

Unfortunately, India is situated in a turbulent and unstable region with the presence of failing or unstable states, declining regional powers, and states that have facilitated nuclear proliferation. The region has emerged as the epicentre of global terrorism and has the maximum number of countries possessing weapons of mass destruction, with the increasing risk of non-state actors laying their hands on such deadly weapons. Over and above these, we have unresolved boundary issues with China and Pakistan. There are not many countries in the world that have to face the full spectrum of threats as India does, from low intensity to an all-out conventional war in diverse terrain while keeping in mind the nuclear overhang. To deal with them we would

---

[1] *India Empowered*, excerpts from my article that appeared in the *Indian Express*, 3 September 2005.

require an array of defensive and offensive capabilities, so as to deter or blunt the aggressive designs of any adversary and thus guarantee our territorial integrity. Modernization and upgradation of the weapons and equipment systems and intelligence and surveillance capabilities, and an effective command and control set-up is the mantra for our armed forces. As has been our experience, capability building takes time, whereas intentions can change rapidly. It would be axiomatic to point out that this calls for a well-led, -trained and -equipped military with an updated and compatible joint doctrine to face the challenges of the battlefield of tomorrow, which will be digitized and netcentric.

This joint doctrine was approved by the chiefs of staff committee in 2007 and is being implemented. As a mature and responsible emerging power we cannot afford to be below par as far as capabilities are concerned. However, we have learnt our lessons from history, both ancient and recent, and have realized that a 'unilateral desire for peace cannot by itself guarantee a secure environment'. We need an iron fist and a velvet glove. We have to be strong to deter aggression, and we cannot be an economic giant without the ability to defend ourselves and safeguard our core values as a nation.

I started my innings as the chief of army staff with a clear aim that comprised operational readiness, high state of training, modernizing the army to cover enhanced night-fighting capability, use of information technology in warfare, success in counterterrorism operations, joint warfare, force restructuring and welfare of soldiers. It gives me immense satisfaction to note that we have achieved reasonable progress in these areas. Today, the army is much better prepared for any contingency as compared to the past. The doctrine for the army has been introduced and validated successfully. This has been complemented by realistic and well-phased training schedules, which focused on keeping the army 'ready and relevant', and at the same time gave the much desired rest to troops in peace stations.

As the army chief, I assiduously built up rapport and a working relationship with the political leadership and the bureaucracy at the national level, based on mutual trust and healthy respect for each other.

Consequently, there was greater synergy. I never had a problem of accessibility to the highest level of the national leadership. Whenever my views were sought, they were given in a frank and forthright manner, keeping in mind the national interest. Even though we disagreed on occasions, there was no acrimony. We faced some tricky situations, which were overcome in a sagacious and mature manner.

Ongoing inductions in the Indian Army have substantially enhanced our night-fighting capability at the level of the individual soldier as well as for major equipment like tanks, guns and other weapon systems. We have also inducted cutting-edge technology in the field of netcentric warfare not only within our service but also in conjunction with other services in an environment of increasing reliance on interoperability. Still, the pace of modernization of the Indian Army needs to be hastened.

We have also achieved very satisfying results in counterterrorism operations and the ongoing proxy war. During my tenure as the chief, the attrition ratios in J&K regarding casualties incurred by our troops vis-à-vis the terrorists had improved considerably in our favour. Simultaneously, there has been a perceptible drop in violence levels in the state. Elections have been conducted peacefully and there is an overall yearning for peace. The tide has successfully turned for us in the proxy war, which is evident through the increased levels of intelligence that is available from the locals and the spurt in the number of surrenders.

There is also an overall improvement in the security scenario in the northeast. The people have rejected violence by secessionist groups as a means of achieving their political goals. Furthermore, militant organizations like the NSCN, the ULFA, and the PLA of Nagaland, Assam and Manipur respectively, have been pushed out from their sanctuaries in Bangladesh due to the rapid improvement in our relations. We have been successful in persuading Myanmar also to put pressure on these unlawful outfits, which have created safe havens across the Indo-Myanmar border. A dialogue process is on with the NSCN and ULFA, and it is hoped that peaceful solutions would emerge out of these deliberations. Many of these groups are bereft of any ideology and have turned into criminal gangs that are resorting to extortion, kidnapping and groups murders to survive. However, the situation has turned in our favour and the rule of law is being enforced. The elected governments are focusing on development and other people-friendly initiatives. It is my view that the northeast would stabilize and see peace and prosperity in the coming decades.

As far as the Naxal problem is concerned, it has been created partly due to lack of governance and wrong policies adopted over the years vis-a-vis the tribal population in the remote parts of India's heartland. These have now been analysed and are being addressed in a sincere and objective manner. I agree with the present strategy of our government. Having identified sixty worst-affected districts of the country, concentrated efforts for ensuring good governance and re-establishing the rule of law are being put in place, to be followed by integrated programmes for the socioeconomic development of the people. Further, legislation has been enacted to alleviate the problems of the people with regard to forest produce and also to safeguard their other interests. This approach would definitely bear fruit in the coming years and meet the aspirations of the affected tribal population.

Force Restructuring

We have achieved successful force restructuring after the raising and validation of the operational tasks of the South Western Command and 9 Corps. At the same time we have reverted some formations which had been moved to J&K to the eastern theatre, and also inducted units to fill the voids. Besides that, we initiated the process of raising a corps HQ and two infantry divisions and supporting arms and services for the east, in order to enhance our capabilities to meet future challenges. These steps have provided the much desired strategic balance to our posture in both the western and eastern theatres. Keeping in view India's geo-strategic location, size and stature, it is my firm conviction that the time has come for us to shed the inward-looking image, and play a bigger role with regard to peace and stability in the region. To accomplish these tasks we would need to build up capability, which could also be employed for protecting our trade routes and sea lanes of communication, safety of overseas Indians and prevention of spillover effects of conflicts in the neighbourhood, including the Indian Ocean region.

Looking at our region, I would first like to focus upon Sino-India relations. Today the two nations represent almost one-third of humanity. Barring the border war of 1962, the relations between the two Asian giants have been warm and friendly. At times there has been friction on the border issue, but the mature and statesmanlike leadership of both nations has been able to resolve the problem. A series of landmark agreements beginning with the 'maintenance of peace and tranquility along the border' agreement of 1993 and culminating in the 'strategic and cooperative partnership for peace and prosperity' agreement signed between the prime ministers of our countries in 2008, have paved the way for a peaceful resolution of the boundary and other issues. We need to resolve our problems so that both countries can focus singlehandedly on alleviating the socioeconmic conditions of our people and contribute to peace and stability of the region and the world. China has become our largest trading partner with trade worth US $ 61.7 billion taking place in 2010. There is tremendous scope for enhancing bilateral relations and reaching consensus on vital global issues like climate control, financial order and sustainable development. A new equation is emerging in the balance of power in the world, with the centre of gravity shifting towards Asia. The cooperation in the field of defence has also grown phenomenally consequent to the highly significant memorandum of understanding on defence cooperation signed during the defence minister, Pranab Mukherjee's visit to China in 2006. It was the first of its kind MoU between the two nations, and was given a concrete shape during my visit to China in May 2007 as the chairman of the chiefs of staff committee.

Many theorists have been predicting a war between China and India. First it was supposed to have happened after the Beijing Olympics, and then it was forecast to take place in 2012, and now there is some talk of 2020. Some of these analysts haven't been to the high Himalayan regions on either side, or have merely undertaken whistlestop tours in fair weather. To comprehend the true dimensions of fighting a war in this region, one has to see the conditions during the freezing winter season, when the snow and the blizzards make life impossible, or during the monsoons, when it rains for days on end and even small streams become raging torrents, washing away bridges and major parts of roads. We need to understand that no modern war can be fought unless it is thought through in its entirety, and more importantly, only if the initiator is convinced that it can be won. Further, to start a nuclear war would be the height of folly. However, I do not wish to give an impression that we can afford to be complacent or let our guard down. In fact, we should continue to modernize our armed forces and improve the infrastructure, strengthen the intelligence agencies and provide them state-of-the-art wherewithal for giving real-time intelligence, and thereby enhance our capability to face the challenges of the future.

Sometime in October 2007, soon after I had handed over the baton of the army chief, I got a call from Professor Stephen P. Cohen, senior fellow, The Brookings Institution, Washington, requesting a meeting at my home in Delhi. I had heard about him and read his book on the army of Pakistan, apart from some other writings. Our free and frank discussion lasted much more than the scheduled 40 minutes. With due respect to the distinguished scholar, at times I found Cohen's perceptions of events a bit unconvincing, and I did not hesitate to speak out my mind. Discussing the situation in Pakistan and its neighbourhood, I highlighted the disastrous consequences of inherent schisms and deep-rooted contradictions within Pakistan, the uncontrolled activities of terrorist organizations all over the country and in the Af-Pak border areas, which have turned Pakistan into the fountainhead of Islamic extremism and terror, and the institution of a national strategy of 'deniability' and 'lies'.

Take the example of Musharraf's ill-conceived venture in Kargil. A fabricated story of 'freedom fighters' was trotted out, and to maintain the cover-up, the bodies of Pakistani soldiers were left behind. Only recently, during November 2010, some figures of casualties in that war have been officially released. It is amazing how one man's miscalculation can put an entire nation into such a mess. The American writer, Bruce Riedel, has clearly brought out that the US helped to bail out the Pakistan Army and gave them a face-saving opportunity at that time.

The policy of running with the hares and hunting with the hounds has thoroughly discredited Pakistan not only in the eyes of the world but also of their beneficiaries – the Taliban – who claim that the Pakistanis 'feed them with one hand and kill them with the other'. When the sordid tale of nuclear proliferation was exposed, they made A.Q. Khan the fall guy. The most recent nail in the coffin of lies has been the shocking discovery of Osama Bin Laden in the garrison town of Abbotabad, a stone's throw from Pakistani military academy at Kakul. But for the audacious, secretive and highly professional Operation Geronimo, the Pakistani establishment would have continued to put wool over the eyes of the world, as has been asserted by US Congressmen Dana Rohrabacher and Ted Poe. As brilliantly summed up by Cyril Almeida, a well-known Pakistani writer, 'If we didn't know [bin Laden was in Abbotabad], we are a failed state; if we did know, we are a rogue state,' (in a lead article, *Time* Magazine, 13 May 2011). This was perhaps another legacy left behind by Pervez Musharraf's regime.

Taking a realistic and rational view of the factors discussed above, it is very likely that despite the wishes of the US, India, China or the rest of the world to see a stable and prosperous Pakistan, it might still implode. In fact, I went to the extent of telling Cohen that the button for self-destruction might have already been pressed. Only the people of Pakistan could save their country by snapping the already-lit fuse cord before it reached the detonator, and arrest the downward slide into chaos and destruction. The reactions of Cohen could not be deciphered by me clearly – these varied from 'yes, I believe so' to 'is that so' or 'incredible', and at times just a gesture of his hand on his heart. Maybe I got some of it wrong. Nonetheless, it shall be a memorable interaction for me and my admiration for him as a scholar remains undiminished. However, anyone can go wrong.

Pakistan has gone through turbulent times in its chequered history, but today it faces its biggest challenge, that of the extremist monster created in the 1970s and 80s. The people of Pakistan are standing at the crossroads. They have to decide whether they want to be a moderate and progressive Islamic nation living in peace with their neighbours or let their destiny be decided by the Taliban and Al Qaida and other obscurantist elements. They cannot have both options if they want to move ahead. As discussed earlier, there are many other schisms and contradictions in their polity and society and unless these are resolved in an early time frame, the situation may go beyond control. We hope that this state of affairs changes for the good of Pakistan, and a stable and prosperous nation emerges. On the positive side one can sense certain signs of change in Pakistan, but it is too early to predict.

I am of the firm belief that the time has come for us to reinforce Prime Minister Manmohan Singh's idea of making our borders 'irrelevant' and ushering in an era of peace in subcontinent. We can definitely look at the resolution of all issues in a peaceful manner and dialogue. Therefore, it is to be considered whether India could set the ball rolling for the creation of a subcontinental economic union on the lines of the European Union or ASEAN. I believe that the foundation provided by SAARC could facilitate the creation of such a union. The burgeoning Indian corporate sector could increase its investments in our neighbouring countries and help to create employment opportunities in those countries. That is likely to help in arresting the illegal migration of their citizens to India. We must not forget that even the US has not been able to stop the Mexicans from crossing the border. Consequently, India and Pakistan, as also all other countries in our region, could focus on alleviating the misery of the underprivileged in our respective countries. The region would then be able to witness a period of peace and prosperity. I say this with conviction as the present approach doesn't seem to be working out in the desired manner.

We need to have a careful look at the existing structure of our national security apparatus and defence management at the strategic level. The institutionalization of the military component of this apparatus in the 'decision-making loop' is unexceptional. This is to ensure that expert military advice is available to the national leadership and policy-makers, as is the case in major democratic nations. While formulating and conducting foreign policy, particularly in our fairly volatile neighbourhood and also in those countries where the military is all-powerful, military diplomacy and the views of the service chiefs can prove to be invaluable. Timely advice can help in the prevention of a security situation from snowballing out of control. In a few security-related situations in the past, the armed forces were not quite aware of the big picture or were caught unprepared or without having the desired readiness levels when asked to execute a mission. Such instances are not in the best interests of the nation and hence, should be scrupulously avoided as far as possible. An integrated team with officials from the services and the ministries of defence, external affairs, finance and home makes sense. More importantly, an integrated team within the army, navy and air force at the theatre commands and at the service HQs is required. As has been articulated in Part IV, once this model has matured over a few years, we could have in place a chief of defence staff with the operational responsibility of the armed forces and the accountability that goes with it.

A vital component of national defence is the indigenous capability to research, develop and produce critical high-technology defence systems such as combat aircraft, ships, submarines, tanks, missiles, rockets, unmanned aerial vehicles, electronic warfare systems, radars, sonars, armaments and strategic weapons. We should definitely look at joint development of some of these major weapon systems with other friendly countries as well, as no country can go it alone due to prohibitive research and developmental costs. It is a matter of pride to see the Defence Research and Development Organization, other defence-related public sector undertakings and the private sector reaching significant milestones in these fields. There is a case for opening maximum areas of defence production, except certain strategic and sensitive domains, to the private sector. Our vision should be an India having a self-reliant defence industrial base, which will place us in the league of leading military industrial powers in times to come.

Though India has one of the largest arms industries in the developing world, the volume of defence exports is negligible. At the same time, we are amongst the largest importers of arms. Therefore we need to look into this important domain. Besides being instruments of foreign policy, arms exports are also driven by domestic economic imperatives. The high profits involved in such sales are an important factor in spurring new ideas and innovations by the armament industry and the private sector in the West. Also, by exporting, the industry can recover at least a part of the cost of research and development as well as reduce the cost of the production through economies of scale. Having visited a number of defence exhibitions in Europe and India, I feel that this is a great opportunity that we haven't seized. China has gone far ahead of us in this field. We must take our cue from them and gain influence among the developing countries by meeting their defence needs. Most of these countries can neither afford the expensive state-of-the-art Western arms and equipment nor have the need for them, and would be satisfied with what we are producing, which is cheaper, effective and reasonably advanced. We could also share our expertise in improving, adapting and servicing of equipment of common origin. We need to create a 'defence export board' or corporation, which should be an autonomous body chartered to enhance our defence exports, keeping in mind our national interests.

Post independence, the role of the armed forces in nation-building has been phenomenal. As an organization, the Indian Army has been a role model. Our principles, based on the three pillars of professionalism, secularism and an apolitical approach, have resulted in our gaining the respect and trust of the people. The Indian Army has played a vital role in disaster management and often without waiting for orders. The army has a diversity that in many ways represents a microcosm of India. It is seen as an impartial organization which deals with a situation on its merits, without any extraneous considerations. The moment people in a strife-torn area see men in olive green, their confidence automatically gets restored.

The contribution of the armed forces in hastening the decision of the British to give India independence is an aspect on which adequate research has not been done. Certain unorchestrated actions by units, officers and men of the armed forces indicated solidarity with the civil disobedience and freedom movements. The 1857 revolt had never really been obliterated from the British psyche. 'Wavell had noted in his *Journal* that Churchill had "the impression that the Indian Army was liable to rise at any moment; and he accused me [Wavell] of creating a Frankenstein by putting modern weapons in the hands of sepoys,"[2]

---

[2] Ronald Lewin, *Slim*, Leo Cooper Ltd, 1990, p. 137.

alluding to 1857'. The rebellion of 1857 'began as the mutiny of the Bengal Army, and was the defining moment for Indian Nationalism and can rightly be said to be the event that gave birth to an Indian national identity'.[3]

While the role of the army in war is well understood, in peace time it trains for war, a fact that is not well understood. The very existence of a disciplined, well-trained and potent military force deters potential adversaries, thus contributing to peace and stability. What do the armed forces expect in return? Only the respect and gratitude of a nation that recognizes and acknowledges the army's sacrifices. Dignity and honour are our prized possessions. When the soldier goes on leave he expects to be given a modicum of respect, especially while interacting with various civil authorities, and not be made to run from pillar to post for even the most mundane issues. There should be judicial and administrative edicts to ensure that his home and hearth is protected, and his family is not harassed while he is away guarding the borders or fighting terrorists. Sadly, that is not generally the case. I am reminded of the inscription on the Second World War memorial at Kohima, 'When you go back tell them of us and say – for your tomorrow we gave our today.' This should remind the people to honour its brave, undemanding and unsung heroes. We do not have any national war memorial or museum honouring our soldiers, sailors and air warriors who attained martyrdom in the wars fought by a free India, post independence. I strongly advocate that a befitting memorial-cum-museum should come up, as the armed forces have been projecting for a long time, in the area of the India Gate and, if required, a part of the construction could even be below the lawns of the Raj Path, like the underground armed forces museum I visited in Australia. This should not pose any problem as we have the expertise and we have recently made underground metro stations. Like all world powers, we should give the pride of place for such a memorial to our brave soldiers and veterans, at a central location, where the citizens could pay homage in large numbers as is the case in London, Paris or Washington.

[3] Centre for Armed Forces Historical Research, 2007, *The Indian Army: An Illustrated Overview*, p. 248.

To me, spirituality connotes a personal, direct and a very intimate connection with my God – my beliefs and my faith. It is something that I draw my strength from. I most definitely believe that I am guided and protected by a superior force. That force has been kind to me and helped me in following my philosophy of 'a warrior and a winner'. I am convinced that there is no short cut to success. On assumption of a new appointment, I looked at the big picture, looked forward and never backward, focusing on the horizon with my feet firmly on the ground. In life, I worked very hard at whatever I did and believed that one makes one's own destiny. It was my endeavour to be innovative and original and do things differently, rather than do the expected. That helped me to be an achiever. Eventually, I think my work always spoke for me. I have very frequently ticked off those officers and men who failed to use their intellect, imagination or initiative while executing an assigned task or mission, and would ask them, in a light-hearted manner, whether they intended to conserve their brains for the next life.

My positive and optimistic approach and attitude had a lot to do with my spiritual beliefs. It was not about going to the temple or praying every morning, or performing some rituals, but trying to be a good human being, someone who is constantly in touch with his faith. Due to this, I could not be subjugated by doubt, despite the challenges and rough weather I went through. For a soldier, and an officer in particular, faith is a personal issue and hence should play no part in his or her official work.

At times, on seeing some very high-ranking officers looking morose and unhappy over small or mundane matters, I would remind them of the high office they were occupying, and all that the organization had given to them. And also advise them to recast their definition of happiness or redraw the 'lakshman rekhas' (limits) of their desires, and be content in life. It is much better to be a happy colonel rather than an unhappy general, I would reiterate to them! In my view, this only happens to those officers who become 'rats' in the rat race, instead of being 'tigers'. They live their entire careers trying to ensure the happiness of their bosses instead of their own, and then keep complaining. I have always maintained that success and happiness are products of many factors, and as in any mathematical equation, a zero multiplied with any number makes the total 'zero'. For example, if one's son becomes a drug addict, or the daughter elopes with someone undesirable, or the wife ends up as a nervous wreck, is the next rank worth it? Success at what cost! One comes across both categories of officers amongst the serving and veteran fraternity. Fortunately, there are more happy guys, but some amongst the senior lot are fairly disgruntled too.

'What do I treasure most from my life's experience?' was a question once posed to me. 'The affection, trust and devotion that I received from my officers and men in arms whom I had the proud privilege to command is something that is priceless and I was fortunate to get it and hence, value it the most,' was my answer. And now, in my new assignment, which I call the second innings, I am striving to achieve the sobriquet of a 'people's governor'. I consider that for Rohini and me, this is the time to pay back to society for all that we have got in life.

Three generations of my family climbed eighteen rungs of the military ladder, from that of a soldier to that of a four-star general. It has been a century of service to the nation and the army. Whenever I hear the sound of the bugle, grandpa's face flashes in my mind, and his words resonate. 'When one's path is righteous and the cause is just, one will always be crowned with success.' And, 'sepoy da beta karnail, ate karnail da beta jarnail banega' (the soldier's son shall be a colonel, and the colonel's son will be a general). We were blessed to have had loving and caring parents. Rohini has been a wonderful companion and has played an invaluable part in this success story, and Vivek and Sonia have been adorable children. Life together, with its ups and downs, has been exciting and pleasurable. A lot has changed in the period between 1914 and 2012, but the core values and the bravery, courage, discipline and steadfastness of the Indian army soldier have not changed. An everlasting salute to my jawans is my modest acknowledgement.

> In the end spirit always conquers the sword.
> – Napoleon

APPENDICES

Appendix 1

Dated: 22 Dec 04

My dear General,

1. Reference my introduction with you on dinner 10th Dec.04 at 2 Corps Officers Mess.

2. I happened to be in BARAMULLA on a private visit to a distant relation, the day fatal attack came on you in the summer of 1992, and you are bestowed with second life. The militants had planned and rehearsed the operation so well that they were saying, "Even Allah cannot save Brig SINGH today".

3. The militants had placed 30 benches all along the outer boundary wall of the Govt. High School Baramulla, where 2 men were to stand on each bench and third man was to stand behind each bench for providing them with filled magazines. In addition they had two logs of wood with 4 men on each log to be placed as roadblock. They had also kept a sleeper studded with nails to be placed on the road for puncturing the vehicles.

4. Their EW system was working well to know about your movements. That is why as soon as your convoy reached the killing zone, all the militants who had taken positions on the benches stood up at once and started indiscriminate firing on you with the single aim of killing Brig Singh.

5. As the militants were sure of your death they had placed a powerful stop in a U turn on Sri Nagar road 2 km ahead of Govt. Degree College, Baramulla to snatch your dead body reaching Sri Nagar.

6. The next day when my relation came to drop me at Sri Nagar showed me this site on the way and also showed me the school from where they had brought very heavy fire on you. The benches were still there when I saw the site.

7. I shiver even today when I recollect this incidence. But then one always wonders the strange ways of God and no one can know what fate holds in store for each one of us.

8. May God! Give you long life and good health to lead one of the largest armies in the world.

With regards and best wishes,

Yours sincerely,

Lt Gen J J Singh
    AVSM PVSM
GOC – in – C
Western Command
Chandimandir

(names deleted for reasons of confidentiality)

Appendix 2

MINISTER
FINANCE, PLANNING AND DEVELOPMENT,
LAW AND PARLIAMENTARY AFFAIRS
JAMMU AND KASHMIR

Muzaffar Hussain Baig

No: FM/PS/2004-
Dated: December 2, 2004

Dear General Singh Sahib,

Please accept my heartiest congratulations on your appointment as the next Chief of the Army Staff. From whatever little I have heard about you, you are the most eminently qualified person to hold this position of great eminence and critical importance for the nation.

I was deeply touched when I saw you on TV channels speaking to the media at Chandimandir on 28th November. Only a great human being has the courage to express his inner feelings in public, the way you did. A renowned Chinese philosopher once said, "a nail is straight and stiff but it is made of wrought iron and not gold".

I expect that under your watch the people of our State will experience, in full measure, the new doctrine of winning the hearts and minds of the people of the strife-torn State of Jammu and Kashmir. This would certainly help towards strengthening the movement of peace and amity gaining momentum in the region.

With warm regards,

Yours sincerely,

(Muzaffar Hussain Baig)

Lt. Gen. J.J. Singh,
Chief of Army Staff (Designate),
GOC-in-C, Western Command,
C/o 56 APO

Appendix 3
Headlines after my taking over as army chief

Appendix 4

Ten Commandments of COAS –1993

The COAS, General B.C. Joshi, directed that all ranks would carry a card with his commandments:

1. No rape.
2. No molestation.
3. No torture resulting in death or maiming.
4. No military disgrace.
5. No meddling in civil administration.
6. Competence in platoon/company-level tactics in counterinsurgency operations.
7. Willingly carry out civic action with innovations.
8. Develop media interaction.
9. Respect human rights.
10. Only fear God, uphold dharma and enjoy serving the country.

Supplementary Commandments (2005)

1. Remember that people you are dealing with are your own countrymen. Your conduct must be dictated by this one significant consideration.
2. Operations must be people-friendly, using minimum force and avoiding collateral damage – restraint must be the key.
3. Good intelligence is the key to success – the thrust of your operations must be intelligence-based and must include the militant leadership.
4. Be compassionate, help the people and win their hearts and minds. Employ all resources under your command to improve their living conditions.
5. No operations without police representative. No operation against women cadres under any circumstances without Mahila Police. Operation against women insurgents be preferably carried out by the police.

6. Be truthful, honest and maintain highest standards of integrity, honour, discipline, courage and sacrifice.
7. Sustain physical and moral strength, mental robustness and motivation.
8. Train hard, be vigilant and maintain highest standards of military professionalism.
9. Synergize your actions with the civil administration and other security forces.
10. Uphold dharma and take pride in your country and the army.

Appendix 5

Factors to be considered while planning and executing a counterinsurgency/terrorism campaign

- First, an overall multipronged strategy must be evolved. Clear-cut aims and objectives must be spelt out for all players. This strategy should be worked out at the national and state level to include all dimensions of the problem – the political, socioeconomic, military, ethnic or religious.
- There must be maximum synergy amongst all forces and the government.
- Intelligence sharing amongst all agencies should be the norm.
- Good governance should be ensured by committed and motivated administrators and police machinery down to the district level.
- Implementation of the strategy of an 'iron fist and a velvet glove'.
- The people play a vital role as determinants of success.
- The terrorists adopt an irregular form of warfare that follows no rules, and has scant respect for human rights.
- We must employ tactics and plans that are innovative and unpredictable, and have an inbuilt element of surprise.
- The conduct of the security forces should be impeccable.
- An attractive surrender policy should be enunciated.

Appendix 6

Information and communication technology projects actualized

- A satellite layer was added to the terrestrial voice and data communications (LVSAT-I) to enhance redundancy, in March 2005.
- The Army Wide Area Network (AWAN) was put into place, which has revolutionized our archaic messaging system. This project has been a runaway success and now its second phase is being introduced. The pilot project was dedicated to the nation by President A.P.J. Abdul Kalam on 24 February 2006.
- Phase III of Army Static Switched Communication Network (ASCON Ph III) was commissioned on 13 September 2006. This brought about a quantum jump in communications by the introduction of ATM technology. The use of optical fibre cable (OFC) has enabled broadband connectivity and resulted in greater capacity for data and voice communications. This cabling was speeded up and many strategic alliance projects with the Bharat Sanchar Nigam Limited (BSNL), such as the Srinagar-Leh sector, have been completed or are in progress.
- The mobile cellular communication system for the army was conceived and progressed during 2005–07, and was commissioned in June 2008 in the testbed corps zone. This has proved to be a great success and is being expanded to cover more areas.
- Other important systems like Network for Spectrum, Tactical Communication System and Defence Communication Network, which are going to be a reality in the near future, were provided the launch pad and impetus during 2005–07.

Appendix 7

Important leadership tenets as I see them

- The army believes in the doctrine of the "Warrior and a Winner". In the battlefield, the "Winner Takes it All" and there's no space for the second-best

- The army rewards failure. Only leaders who have the courage to swim against the tide make mistakes. No good officer is written off for making mistakes or taking initiative that goes awry as ingenuity and creativity are important to improve processes

- The army believes that no plan survives the first engagement, howsoever brilliant it is. Changes have to be incorporated after the enemy faces the first offensive and counters it. It's important to be dynamic and flexible in decision-making

- The army believes that money can't bind an individual to an organisation. The ethos, work culture and scope to achieve satisfaction are more important

- Army leaders follow the dictum, "Know the way, show the way and go the way"

- The army follows the "directive style of command" where junior leaders don't have to look over their shoulders at every stage of the battle. Flexibility and individual empowerment are important and bureaucracy doesn't work in the battlefield

- The army doesn't quantify productivity and the system of motivation is not based on monetary considerations. Esprit de corps, camaraderie, regimental pride, act as motivators

- The army recruits through trial by fire and at the boot camp where the best and fittest survive. Many officers leave the Army mid-way as they can't be promoted or are not the best

- In the battlefield, speed and boldness is more important than perfection. Indecisiveness can be a fatal flaw. An average decision taken on time can carry the day while a brilliant decision that came late can result in defeat. The key is to pre-empt the enemy

Appendix 8

A New Year card from the children's home – Kohima

Appendix 9

List of projects comprising the prime minister's package announced on 31 January 2008

1. Projects for which foundation stones were laid by the prime minister:

    a) New secretariat building at Itanagar.
    b) Railway line to Itanagar capital complex/Naharlagun.
    c) 110 MW Pare hydropower project.
    d) 3000 MW Dibang multi-purpose project.
    e) Itanagar drinking water supply project.

2. Projects which were announced by the prime minister:

    a) Two-lane trans-Arunachal highway through 11 District HQs.
    b) Two-lane connectivity to remaining six District HQs.
    c) Four–Lane highway to Itanagar.
    d) Greenfield airport at Itanagar.
    e) Illumination of 2121 border villages.
    f) Providing road connectivity to 513 villages in the border blocks.
    g) Daily helicopter connectivity between Guwahati and Tawang.
    h) Providing Rs 50 crores corpus fund to R.K. Mission Hospital.
    i) Providing drinking water facilities in border blocks of the state.
    j) Functional airports at Pasighat, Along, Daporijo, Ziro and Tezu.
    k) Upgradation of Tuting, Mechuka, Along, Ziro, Pasighat, Vijaynagar and Walong subsidiary airports (ALGs).
    l) Rs 400 crores for restoration of flood-damaged infrastructure.
    m) Rs 455 crores for completion of incomplete projects.

Appendix 10

Address to the cadets – IMA passing-out parade: 12 June 2010

Lt Gen R.S. Sujlana, commandant, Indian Military Academy, parents, distinguished guests and gentleman cadets on parade.

It is indeed a great honour to review the passing out parade of the 126th Regular, 15TES, 109TGC, 18UES and 24 SCO courses of IMA. Your parade has been of an exceptionally high order and I wish to compliment each one of you and the directing staff for a fine display of a parade conducted with clinical military precision. It reflects the high level of training and professionalism achieved at the academy, which I am sure is precursor to a rewarding military career for all of you...

For me, gentlemen, 'India' is a civilizational concept... India empowered is the essence of this dream. To bear arms in the defence of one's country is a rare honour. However, the task of a military leader is, by no means, an easy one. It demands physical and moral courage, professional competence, physical fitness and leadership qualities of the highest order.

An India empowered can no longer be transgressed and trespassed... Our strength is reflected by a growing economy and a powerful military machine which is professional and modern.

We are amidst discernable and distinct changes which are shaping every sphere of life in general and the profession of arms in particular. The armed forces are no longer insulated from the socioeconomic-technological-internal security and geostrategic changes taking place, and are increasingly being impacted by the manifestation of these changes as we carry out our role and responsibility.

The nature of threat encompasses the entire spectrum of war fighting and includes... the entire gamut of socioeconomic challenges, which have resulted in a greater threat of terrorism, WMD proliferation, drug trafficking, fundamentalism and Naxalism... Thus, today the stability of our region is as critical for our progress as is the peace and tranquillity within our geographical confines.

Even as the possibility of conventional warfare is gradually receding, the application of irregular warfare or a 'proxy war' by inimical forces in the form of both state and non-state actors remains a serious threat. Thus, the seeds of discord are being sown through war by other means, by using terrorism and insurgency as a weapon of proxy, to keep forces of disintegration and discord alive and simmering. Naxalism today has emerged as the single biggest internal security threat to the country. These emergent challenges have ushered in the need for a new genre of fighting men; soldiers who are sensitive to these new nuances... soldiers who are required to be aware of economic realities, social transformation, technological advances and are adept at keeping pace with the ever-changing panorama of high-technology and information warfare.

While facing the challenge of terrorism, insurgency or Naxalism, I have advocated the concept of an 'iron fist and velvet glove'. The iron fist is for the terrorists, the hardcore militants or Naxals and the velvet glove is for the people, the citizens of our country, and 99 per cent of them are innocent. We have to win their hearts and minds if we want to win this war.

The demands on soldiers include a deeper insight into conventional, sub-conventional and non-conventional aspects of warfare and not merely proficiency in the traditional form of war fighting as your predecessors had learnt and implemented. Also, today, no one is insulated from the lenses of media, which is real-time, so transparency and application of professional conduct becomes critical. The organizational 'naam and izzat' is our beholden duty.

I am very impressed by a quote of Field Marshal Slim, who led our forces in Burma turning defeat into victory and the man who made this statement: 'The real test of leadership is not if your men will follow you in success, but if they stick by you in defeat and hardship.'

Our counterinsurgency operations and the Kargil war remain the finest examples of heroic deeds by junior leadership, who defied adversity, terrain, altitude, snow-bound jagged peaks at 18000-20,000 feet and above; officers and men who displayed unbelievable leadership qualities and courage under fire... and whose spirit echoes even today in the hills of Tololing, Dras, Batalik and Tiger Hill – a haunting warrior's credo immortalized in the words: 'Yeh dil mange more.'

The officers of the Indian Army have always led by example and from the front, and this is a sacred trust that you have imbibed from the collective consciousness of the valour of the Indian Army. A trust that translates into a saga of our officers' casualty ratio vis-à-vis the soldiers being the highest ever recorded in past campaigns the world over. A trust which commits the men you command to walk through a hail of bullets, which may take the soldier's life but never his spirit and sacrifice, a spirit which will always unfurl the national flag atop the peaks of victory. This telling tale of the power of flag was evocatively voiced two centuries back by Sir Edward B. Hamley:

> *A moth-eaten rag on a worm-eaten pole*
> *it does not look likely to stir a man's soul,*
> *'Tis the deeds that were done 'neath the moth-eaten rag,*
> *When the pole was a staff and the rag was a flag.*

I would like to share with you that I believe in the creed of a 'warrior and winner'. Live life with the determination that we will win; for me it has always meant 'Fight to Win'. And in fighting to win, in boxing, wrestling or other sports and even in battle, you can either win by points or you win by knockout. I would prefer that we succeed against every challenge by a knockout. Remember, there is no prize for the runner-up in war; it is tragic but true in life that the winner takes it all. Further, in real life and in war, I am of the conviction that the underdog is not the right situation to be in. We should always be the top dog. And therefore, my motto has been 'Fight to Win', which means you enter a battlefield with the determination and firm belief that you will emerge victorious.

Gentlemen, I have always endeavoured to be different by not following the beaten track. Being unpredictable, unconventional and attempting to do the impossible, and achieving 'surprise' were essential parts of my strategy in all facets of my life as a soldier. This has been fundamental to my success story.

You, the future officers of the armed forces, will be the custodians of the faith that your countrymen repose in you. You will be called upon to pitch in, in all aspects of nation-building. Gentlemen, you shall do well to recall the pride of place assigned to a soldier in our society. A warrior is looked upon as the last bastion of hope. The armed forces have successfully achieved all their objectives through three pillars of soldiering. These are: secularism, an apolitical outlook and professionalism. These are the values you shall uphold. This is the ethos that must guide every action of yours. Your 'dharma' is to defend our country and its people. It is, therefore, imperative that you arm yourselves with knowledge and train yourselves to fulfil your responsibilities as a warrior.

A revolution in military affairs is sweeping the Indian Army. Fresh thinking, prompted by the swiftly changing world environment, is revolutionizing the way military affairs are conducted and managed. Technological growth and scientific developments have radically transformed the military thought process. Information warfare, network centred warfare, integrated command and control systems (C4ISR) – this is the operational paradigm that modern armies have to train and equip themselves in, so as to retain the winning edge. It will be your responsibility to spearhead this revolution through a judicious mix of knowledge and actual local ground realities.

And now I would like to share my thoughts with the gentlemen cadets from friendly foreign countries. India has a time-honoured tradition of helping our friends. We have training teams in many countries, participation in UN peacekeeping operations and the proud privilege of training cadets of friendly foreign countries. It pleases me that thirty-six foreign cadets will pass out today. Dear cadets, please remember that you came here as friends and you will be leaving shortly as brothers in arms. I am sanguine that you will value this training as the bedrock of a successful and challenging career in the armies of your respective countries.

I wholeheartedly felicitate parents and guardians on this momentous day and salute their courage, support and love for sending their sons to be soldiers…

It was on 2 August 1964 forty-six years ago when my father, then Major J.S. Marwah, was here to see his son pass out from the portals of this military academy. He is a sprightly ninety-year-old young man, who is present here to witness today's magnificent parade; just to remind you that he also graduated and got commissioned from this academy sixty-seven years ago, and he is here today to bless all of us. Finally, my dear brother officers, may you rise to every challenge and have a satisfying and a fulfilling way of life in the olive greens. I have the great privilege to welcome you to the folds of our glorious Indian Army. I wish you success, glory and God speed in all your endeavours.

JAI HIND

Index

1 Maratha LI (Jangi Paltan), 7, 62
1/67 Punjab Regiment, 3, 7, 21, 88
10 Corps, 159
106 Airborne Division, 246
15 Maratha LI, 187
15 Punjab, 133
162 Mountain Brigade, 48
17 J&K Rifles, 102, 103, 133
18 Assam Rifles, 335
19 Maratha LI, 187
1st Airborne Brigade, 260
1st Battalion, the Parachute Regiment, 3–5
2 Maratha LI (Kali Panchwin), 7, 71
2nd Motorized Guards Rifle Division, 246
2/11 Gorkha Rifles (GR), 102, 116, 119, 132, 133
22 Maratha LI, 186, 187
26 Infantry Division, 26, 87
31 Baluch, 62
36th Sikh, 15
5 Maratha LI, 7, 88
68 Mountain Brigade, 133
6th Poona Division, 7
7 Maratha LI, 67, 71
7 Sikh, 113–14
79 Mountain Brigade, 94, 97, 99, 105, 132
8 Assam Rifles, 48, 49
8 Gurkha Rifles, 281
8 J&K LI, 151
8 Mountain Division, 47, 51, 52
81 Mountain Brigade, 44
9 Corps, 206, 207, 347
9 Maratha LI, 32, 43, 48, 51, 52, 54, 63, 66, 71, 73, 74, 79, 80, 90, 187, 274, 316

Abdullah, Farooq, 99
Abdullah, Omar, 219
Abdullah, Sheikh, 218, 219
   accord, 219
Actual Ground Position Line (AGPL), 146, 151, 153, 298
Advani, L.K., 166
Afghanistan, 59, 91, 108–09, 119, 167, 213, 241, 242, 252, 254–55, 278
Agashe, Maj A.N., 82

Ahluwalia, Montek Singh, 326
Ahmad, Capt Shakeel, 131
Ahmed, Mahmud, 159
Airy, Brig Ved Prakash, 77–79, 83, 85
Ali, Lt Col Ishfaq, *Fangs of Ice-Story of Siachen*, 152
All Assam Students' Union, 223
Aman Setu, 217
Ambala, 18, 128, 194
Anantnag, 100, 102–03
Andaman and Nicobar, 170, 202, 229, 231
Angami, Gen Mowu, 47, 49, 51–54, 220
Angre, Admiral Kanhoji, 185
Anjaria, Capt S.S., 116, 118, 119
Ansari, Vice President Hamid, 326
anti-Chinese feelings, 337
Aram, Dr, 45
Armed Forces Special Powers Act (AFSPA), 226, 227
Army Group Insurance Fund (AGIF), 292
Army Information and Technology Advisory Council, 264
Army Welfare Education Society (AWES), 292–93
Army Wives Welfare Association, 293
Army, British Indian, 7, 14, 21, 46, 247
Army, Royal Bhutan, 257
Arunachal Scouts, 320
Ashoka Chakra, 187
Asom Gana Parishad, 223
Association of Southeast Asian Nations (ASEAN), 260, 324, 351

asymmetric war, 208
attrition in combat, 14, 202, 216, 346
Auchinleck, Gen Sir Claude JE, 191
Aurangzeb, 13
Aurora, Lt Gen J.S., 61
Australia, 54, 89, 241, 260, 354
Awami League, 59
Awasthi, Lt Col K.L., 43, 50, 54
Aziz, Sartaj, 167

Bahawalpur, 19
Baig Muzaffar Hussain, 198
Balakrishnan, Col N.K., 63
Baluyevsky, Gen Yuri, 246
Bangladesh, People's Republic of, 60–61, 111, 223–24, 241, 242, 257, 281, 346
Bara Hoti plateau, 146
Barua, Paresh, 224
Beg, Mirza Aslam, 218
Belgaum, 31, 40, 43, 185–86, 292
Bendjedid, Col Chadli, 241
Bhagat, Lt Gen P.S., 139, 280
Bhalla, Lt Gen P.S., 339
Bhandral, Maj P.S., 75, 77
Bhatia, Air Marshal Jimmy, 138
Bhatia, Capt, Ramesh, 57
Bhojwani, Air Cmde S., 164
Bhutan, 241, 242, 256–57, 315, 322
Bhutto, Zulfikar Ali, 60, 149
Bilafond La, 151–52
Bingley, Capt A.H., 15
Blackwill, Robert, 268
Border Security Force, 221, 224
Borphukan, Lachit, 17
Boxiong, Gen Guo, 250
Brar, Maj Gen K.S., 29, 62, 143, 185

Burma, 46–47, 51, 324, 370; *see also* Myanmar

Cabinet Committee for Security (CCS), 166–67, 229
Cane and Bamboo Technology Centre (CBTC), 328
career progression in army, 282–83
chairman of chiefs of staff committee (COSC), 229, 232, 233, 240, 246–47, 250, 283, 345, 348
Chaki, Lt Col Ashok, 86
Chanakyaniti, 201
Chand, Dhyan, 296
Chandimandir, 192, 193, 197
Chattisgarh, 210, 226
Chaudhri, Col U.R., 117
Chaugule, Naik Parshuram, 89
Chawla, Navin, 326
Chetak, 179, 189
Chetwode, Gen Sir Philip W., 191
chief of defence staff (CDS), 228–32, 247, 259, 352
chief of integrated defence staff (CISC), 229, 231
China, 47, 51, 52, 144–46, 149, 152, 187, 200, 205, 210, 220, 221, 233, 241–42, 244, 249–51, 260, 269, 298, 315, 324–25, 327, 334, 337–38, 343–44, 348, 350, 353
Chinese, 37, 47, 48, 52–53, 145–46, 152, 249–51, 298, 316, 325, 337
Chomsky, Noam, 211
Churchill, Winston, 353
Clinton, Bill, 161
Cohen, Prof Stephen P., 349–50
confidence-building measures, 217, 251, 253

conflict resolution in J&K, 219
conflict, low-intensity, 93, 135, 205, 208, 211, 344
Counter Insurgency and Jungle Warfare School, 220
counterinsurgency, 54, 71, 106, 144, 171, 198, 208–11, 216, 220, 226, 362, 370
institute, 210, 226
operations, 198, 208–09, 211, 216, 220
counterterrorism, 97, 100, 166, 210, 211, 214–16, 228, 241–42, 245, 319, 345–46
counterterrorist exercise 'Indra', 245–46

D'Souza, Maj Gen E., 8, 185
D'Souza, Maj Gen Kevin, 104
Dalai Lama, His Holiness the, 326
Daultala, 5
Dave, A., 320
Defence Services Staff College (Wellington), 62–64, 67, 242, 307
Dev, Guru Arjan, 12–13
Dhana, 61, 62
Dhillon, Lt Col J.S., 68, 70
Dhingra, Brigadier, K.C., 99
Dimapur, 43–45, 223
disaster management, army's role in, 145, 241–42, 353
Dogra kingdom, 149
Dras Sector, 156, 160–62, 166, 370
Dugal, Gagan, 142, 173
Dugal, Maj Gen M.S., 142

East Pakistan, 60, 221; *see also* Bangladesh

Empire, British, 9, 15, 149, 249, 306
Empire, Khalsa, 14
esprit de corps, 36, 70, 139, 201, 274, 296, 320
Everest expedition, 298–300, 332
   by women, 298–300, 332–33
Exercise
   Poorna Vijay, 174–84, 189, 192
      collateral damage in, 180
      decontamination unit in, 176, 178
      harsh conditions in, 155, 177
      in the desert of Rajasthan, 176, 231
      joint army-air offensive, 178
      nuclear, biological and chemical (NBC) warfare shelter in, 176, 178
   Sange Shakti, 193
   Trishakti, 88
ex-servicemen (ESM), state board of, 338–39
Ex-Servicemen Contributory Health Scheme (ECHS), 203, 286

Feodorovich, Col Gen Alexie Maslov, 246
Fernandes, Col A.F. (Tony), 71, 73
Fernandes, George, 145, 153, 172
France, 5, 9, 91, 92, 241, 246–47, 311
Futuristic Infantry Soldier (F-INSAS) programme, 262

Gamlin, Jarbom, 339
Gandhi, Mahatma, 94
Gandhi, Indira, 88, 149, 315
Gandhi, Rajiv, 250, 315, 327
Ganpats, 6, 88

Garg, Ankur, 318
Gautam, Lt Gen A.K., 140
Geneva conventions, 62
Georgelin, Gen Jean Louis, 247
Germany, 6, 36, 93, 273
Gilgit, 109, 159, 163, 219
Gombu, Nawang, 54
Gouder, Maj Gen Venkat, 303
governance, 200, 209, 211, 223, 225–26, 241, 340, 347
Great Game, 149
Gromyko, Andrei, 60
Group of Ministers (GoM), 228–30, 226
Guanglie, Gen Liang, 250
Gulmarg, 71, 168
Gupta, Sushil, 333

Harrison, Maj Andy, 145
Hasan, Maj Gen Javed, 159
High Altitude Warfare School, 168
Highly Active Field Area (HAFA) allowance, 171
Hillary, Sir Edmund, 298
Himalayan Mountaineering Institute (HMI), 54, 59, 298
Hindus, 11–13, 16, 19, 20, 60
Hizbul Mujahideen (HM), 112, 237
hostages, rescuing, 15, 100, 131, 145
human rights, 52, 100, 112, 198, 211–13, 215, 227
Hussain, President Zakir, 54

impact of 9/11, 182, 204, 251
Imphal, 45, 287
Independence, India's, 19, 220, 277, 296, 308, 314, 317, 337, 343, 353, 354

East Pakistan, 60
for Nagaland, 220, 222
India and multilateral global and regional groupings, 259, 260
India, challenges facing, 205–07
Indian Air Force, 29, 92, 169, 186, 238–39
Indian Army, 3, 14–15, 19, 39, 108, 144, 159–60, 170, 184, 194–99, 206, 207, 264, 268, 281, 294, 298, 301–04, 307–08, 353, 356, 370–72
   and 6th Pay Commission, 233, 283–85
   and career progression in, 282–83
   and IAF, 151
   and Pakistan, 99
   and Royal Bhutan Army, 257
   and Sachar Committee, 290–91
   and sports, adventure activities in, 296, 299
   achievements of, 160–61
   basha, innovation of, 26
   cold start strategy, 207
   combat dress in, 288
   emergency commissioning, 37, 38, 41
   expansion of the, 139
   handling terrorism and insurgency by, 208, 211, 220, 245
   helped set up military academies in Ethiopia and Nigeria, 242
   martyrs of, 187
   Nepalese soldiers in, 255–56
   night-fighting capability in, 178, 192, 200, 202, 261–62, 266, 345–46
   plans for modernization in, 261–64, 346
   role of bania in, 42–43
   Sierra Leone helped by, 145
   transport requirements in, 136–37
   victories of, 61–62, 99, 150–51, 155, 159, 161–63
   welfare of all ranks in, 282
   women's role in, 182, 269, 275–76
Indian Military Academy (IMA), 5, 18, 37–39, 191, 294, 340
Indian Navy, 170, 186, 234, 330
Indian Parliament, attack on, 182, 188, 235, 344
Indo-Myanmar border, 76, 315, 346
Indonesia, 241, 260
insurgency, 97, 99, 112, 133, 200, 205–06, 208, 210, 211, 218, 220, 221, 225, 258, 288, 318–19
Integrated Defence Staff, 202, 229, 231
intelligence agencies, 188, 215, 229, 349
Intelligence School (Pune), 46, 56–58, 63, 103
Iraq, 7–8, 29, 119, 192, 208, 213, 242, 245
ISI, 156, 159, 167
Ivanov, Sergei, 246

J&K, conflict resolution in, 219
Jackson, Gen Sir Mike, 247–48
Jaish-e-Mohammad (JEM), 112, 188, 252
Jamalpur, battle of, 62

Jamwal, Lt Gen A.S., 287
Jangi Laat, 197, 199, 304
Japan, 46, 139, 205, 241, 244, 260, 324
Jassal, Raminder, 164
jehadis, 97, 99, 107–08, 111–12, 158, 164, 205, 210, 216, 217, 252, 268
Jehangir, 12
Jiechie, Yang, 250
Joshi, Gen B.C., ten commandments of, 211, 293
Joshi, Lt Gen P., 175, 177
Joshimath sector, 298
Jubar area, 161

Kadyan, Brig Raj, 94
Kahlon, Lt Gen R.I.S., 136
Kailahun, 145
Kala, Lt Gen H.B., 141, 142
Kalam, A.P.J. Abdul, 194, 199, 235, 262, 290
Kalkat, Lt Col Har Ranjit, 71
Kandal, Maj Gen M.P.S., 140
Kapadia, Harish, 149
Karachi agreement (1949), 149
Karachi, 18, 111, 170, 252, 306
Karakoram Pass, 147, 149, 150, 152, 154
Karakoram Range, 110, 147, 149, 205
Kasuri, Khurshid M., 238
Kaul, Lt Gen Hridya, 150
kendriya vidyalayas, inadequacy of, 292
Kenya, 138
Khan, A.Q., 253, 350
Khan, Capt Karnal Sher, 165

Khan, Mohammad Aziz, 159
Khandu, Dorjee, 315, 318, 320, 339–40
air crash of, 339
Khanjangkuki, 45–46
Khapalu, 152
Khaplang, S.S., 222
Khetarpal, 2nd Lt Arun, 183
Kiphire, 48
Kismaayo, 138
Kissinger, Dr Henry, 254
Kitchener, Gen Viscount, 191
Kohima, 45–46, 294
Kohli, M.S., 296
Koiboto, 52
Kokernag, 100–01
Kumar, Capt Suresh, 122–23, 125, 127
Kumar, Lt Col Narinder, 54, 296
Kumar, Meira, 326
Kut-el-Amara, 5, 7, 88
Kargil war, 62, 145, 153, 155–73, 206, 228, 235, 285, 308, 320, 370
and chief of defence staff, 228–31, 259, 352
Gen J.J. Singh's personal observation on, 166–70
historical record prepared by Gen J.J. Singh, 170–71
Operation Vijay, 166, 168, 171
Pakistan's role, 62, 155, 157, 161, 168, 235
Pakistani Operation Badr, 146, 157–58, 162–64
role of Indian Air Force, 169–70
Operation 'Safed Sagar', 169–70
role of Indian Navy, 170

Tiger Hill, 160–61, 164–65, 168

Ladakh region, 109, 147, 150, 168, 205, 298, 320
Laden, Osama Bin, 235, 350
Lakshman, Shankar, 296
Lashkar-e-Toiba (LET) 112, 120, 188, 237, 252
left-wing extremists (LWE), 225
Lidder, Brigadier Jasbir, 175
line of actual control (LAC), 145, 205, 228, 298
Line of Control (LoC), 67–69, 97–99, 104, 112, 113, 115, 116, 131, 132, 149–51, 155, 157, 159–62, 165–67, 170, 187, 190, 205, 217–20, 228, 236–39, 251, 274, 298
Lokhande, Prashant, 312
Look East Policy, 260, 323–24
LTTE, 135, 257–58

MacArthur, Gen Douglas, 278
Maharaj, Chhatrapati Shahu, 7, 187
    Chhatrapati Shivaji, 6, 7, 17, 185, 187
    Rajaram Chhatrapati, 187
Mahrattas, 5, 7, 9
Malari, 63
Malhotra, Brig S.S., 51
Malhotra, Brig V.P., 82, 83
Malik, Capt Taimur, 165
Malik, Maj Gen V.P., 101, 103, 166, 198
Manekshaw, Gen S.H.F.J. (Sam), 26, 48, 53, 61, 280
Manipur, 200, 213, 222, 223, 346
Mann, Maj R.P.S. (Rajpal), 115

Mao Tse-tung, 51
Maratha LI Regimental Centre, 7, 40, 41, 43, 54, 185, 186, 187, 291
Maratha LI, 5, 6, 29, 41, 43, 48, 51, 52, 54, 62, 63, 66, 67, 71, 73, 74, 79, 80, 88, 90, 184–87, 247, 274, 280, 299, 300, 304, 316
Mardana, 11
Mashko Sector, 156, 161, 169
Mason, Philip, *A Matter of Honour*, 15
Mayadas, Maj Gen Misbah, 77, 79, 81
Mazari, Shireen, *The Kargil Conflict*, 164, 168
media, 197
    and Gen J.J. Singh, 197–98, 211, 213–14, 215, 217, 227, 235, 251, 276–78, 290–91, 294
    and terrorists, 125–26
    Indian, 164, 177, 178, 237, 279, 325
    Pakistan, 164, 217, 252, 307
    seminar on army-media relationship, 194
Meghalaya, 224, 325
Mehta, Capt S.S., 63
Member of the British Empire (MBE), 15
Menon, V.K. Krishna, 37
Mesopotamian campaign, 7, 9
Mikhailov Artillery Academy, 246
military diplomacy, 240–43, 258, 351
Ministry for the Development of Northeast Region (DoNER), 323

Misra, Brajesh, 166–67
missile systems, Prithvi and Agni, 262
Mission Olympics, 297
Mizo National Front, 223
Mizoram, 107, 223
mobile defence, 77–80, 84
Model village, Tithwal, 238
Mogadishu, 138
Mohammad, Bakshi Ghulam, 219
Mombasa, 138
Mountbatten Plan, 20
Mra, Tapi, 332
Muivah, T., 47, 49, 52, 221, 222
Mujahideen, 112, 157, 159, 162–65, 167, 237
Mujib-ur-Rehman, Sheikh, 59–60
Mukherjee, Pranab, 199, 237, 298, 340, 348
Mukti Bahini, 60–61
Muntho Dhalo, 169
Musharraf, Pervez, 152, 156, 158–60, 163–65, 169, 189–90, 218, 252–53, 306–08, 349–50
In the Line of Fire, 165
Muzaffarabad, 217–18, 237, 253
Myitkina, 325
Myanmar, 76, 222, 224, 241, 258–59, 315, 325, 334, 346; see also Burma

Nachiketa, Flt Lt, 170
Naga rebels, 45, 47, 221
Nagpal, Lt Col Brij Mohan, 118
Naik, Air Chief Marshal, 336
Nalwa, Hari Singh, 14, 17
Nambiar, Vijay, 91
Nanak, Guru, 10–12

Nath, Lt Gen Surinder, 114, 118
National Cadet Corps, 276, 339
National Defence Academy (NDA), 33–38, 41, 42, 271, 294, 303
National Democratic Front of Bodoland of Assam, 257
National Heart Institute, 333
National Socialist Council of Nagaland (NSCN), 221–22, 224, 319, 346
natural disasters, army's role in
  earthquake in Bhuj, 145
  cyclone in Orissa, 145, 171–72
  Kashmir, (snow tsunami, earthquake), 236–37
Naxals, 205, 210, 225–26, 347, 369–70
Nehru, B.K., 221
Nehru, Jawaharlal, 33, 37, 44, 315
Nepal, 182, 241, 255–57, 299, 332
neutralization of Naga rebels, 54
night-fighting capability, 178, 192, 200, 202, 261–62, 266, 345–46
NJ 9842, 147, 149–50, 154
Norgay, Tenzing, 54, 298
Northern Light Infantry (NLI), 151, 155
NSCN (IM), 222
NSCN (K), 222, 224
Nubra valley, 147
nuclear tests in Pokhran, 145

Obama, Barack, 244, 343
Obasanjo, Gen, 242
Oberoi, Lt Gen V., 138, 184, 185
Operation
  Badr (Pakistani operation), 146, 157–58, 162–64

Index

Gibralter (Pakistani operation), 99
Just Resolve, 102
Khukri, 145
Meghdoot, 150
Mousetrap, 115, 120
Parakram, 188–93, 207, 344
Sadbhavana, 214
Shakti, 233–35
Topac (Pakistani operation), 97, 99
   botched-up, 101
   cordon-and-search, 104–07, 128, 130–31,
Orissa, 145, 171, 172, 210, 226

Padmanabhan, Gen S., 178, 198, 297
Pakistan army, 60, 61, 111, 150, 151–52, 155–56, 159–67, 169, 216, 218, 349
Pakistan-occupied Kashmir (PoK), 98, 109, 152, 163, 217–18, 237–38, 253
Pandu, 44
Pannu, Col P.J.S., 186, 304
Partition of India, 10, 19–20, 88, 111, 248, 293, 306
passing out from the Academy, 37, 38, 39, 340
Patil, President Pratibha Devisingh, 326
Patil, Sachin, 300
Patil, Col Sambhaji, 187
Patil, Shivraj, 312
Patkai, 46, 49
pay commission cell, 283
People's Liberation Army, 250

Phek, 45, 46, 48
Phizo, Z.A., 220
Pitre, Maj Gen K.G., 139
Pradhan Mantri Gram Sarak Yojana (PMGSY), 330
Pradhan, Col N.K., 102
Prakash, Admiral Arun, 278
Prasad, Maj Gen Niranjan, 23
Prasad, Mata, 320
prisoners of war (POWs), 8, 61–62, 162, 170
Punia, Brig Rajpal, 145
Punjab, 3, 5, 7, 9, 10, 11, 13, 14, 16, 18, 19, 20, 21, 57, 71, 88, 107, 111, 133, 172, 193, 194, 218, 219, 331
Pune (also Poona), 7, 33, 36, 46, 56–59, 61–62, 71, 135, 186, 286, 292–93, 297, 306

Quest for Excellence, 192
quick reaction team (QRT), 115, 116, 119
Quinghong, Zeng, 250

Radcliffe Award, 20
Raghavan, Lt Gen V.R., 76, 154, 232
Raja, K.A.A., 320
Rajkhowa, Arabinda, 224
Ram, Maj Gen Samay, 135–36
Randhawa, Jyoti, 142
Randhawa, Air Mshl, T.S., 186
Rao, Gen Krishna, K.V., 292
Rao, Maj Gen K.R., 283
Rao, Narasimha, 250
Rao, Nirupama, 251
Rathore, Rajyavardhan Singh, 296
Ravindranathan, C.P., 93

Rawalpindi, 5, 10, 18, 111, 306, 307
Rawat, Maj Gen J.S. (Jimmy), 88
Rawlley, Maj Gen N.C., 48, 52
Red Cross, 9, 213
Reidel, Bruce, 164
Roychowdhury, Gen Shankar, 142
Rumsfeld, Donald, 245
Russia, 92, 142, 149, 205, 210, 241, 243–46, 254, 260, 262

SAARC, 260, 351
Sachar Committee, 290, 291
sainik sammelan, 43, 66, 70, 74
Sainik Schools, 276, 294
Saltoro range, 146–54
Samasata, 19
Sandhu, Satpal, 63
Sangha, Rana, 17
Saragarhi, 15
Sathe, Ram, 150
Sawant, Naik Balwant, 52
Schoomaker, Gen Peter J., 245
Se La, 37, 339
security group, apex, 210
security scenario, 204–07, 346
Selja, Kumari, 330
Sema, Zuheto, 47, 221
seminar on, army-media relationship, 194
'heavy breakthrough', 142, 192
Sena medals, 52, 77, 114, 118, 133, 170, 285
Shaksgam valley, 149, 152
Sharif, Nawaz, 158, 161, 163, 164, 235
Sheikh, Fatta, 131–32
Shekatkar, Maj D.B., 48
Shillong Peace Accord, 221–23

Shimla talks (1972), 149, 161
Shinde, Maj. Y.S. (Baban), 48, 51, 52
Sia La, 149, 151
Siachen, 146, 147, 150–54, 157, 285, 298, 299
Sikhism, 10, 11, 12, 14, 17, 110
Sikkim, 64, 86, 205, 224–25, 314, 331, 340
Singapore, 139, 210, 241, 259, 324
Singh, 'Bunny' Chetinder, 303
Singh, Brig Harwant, 73
Singh, Brig Hoshiar, 37
Singh, Capt V.K., 115, 116, 123
Singh, Digvijay, 142
Singh, Gen V.K., 278–80
Singh, Guru Gobind, 13, 17
Singh, Jaswant, 178
Singh, Gen J.J.,
    a talk with Kashmiri villagers, 106–11
    accompanied PM (visit to glacier), 153
    achievements, 'Sikh of the Year 2007' Award, 111
        Ati Vishisht Seva Medal, 171
        commendation of the chief of army staff, 133
        compliment by JCO, 136
        conducted operations, 132
        letter of appreciation from defence minister, 182–83
        Param Vishisht Seva Medal, 194
        Vishisht Seva Medal, 77, 86
    ambush, escaped, 121–28
    and Indo-Pak dialogue, 146, 153

and media, 197–98, 211, 213–14, 215, 217, 227, 235, 251, 276–78, 290–91, 294
and Musharraf, 306–08
and sports, 56, 59, 66, 142, 203, 275, 297, 333
as brigade commander at Baramulla, 104–06, 112–133
as young officer at Belgaum, 40–43, 54, 185, 186
as CO at Binaguri, 86
as visitor to infantry brigade in Somalia on UN mission, 138
as 'A' Company Commander with 9 Maratha LI at Jalandhar, 66
as ADGMO at Army HQ, Delhi, 144, 147, 153, 155, 162, 167, 170, 172, 174, 176
as adjutant at Hyderabad, 56
as army chief, 29, 57, 153, 158, 187, 197, 199, 213, 226, 236, 240, 246, 251, 256, 259, 269, 279, 283, 289, 302, 345
  key objectives, 199–203
as BM of 123 Mountain Brigade at New Mal, 64
as brigade commander of 79 Mountain Brigade at J&K, 94, 97–103
as DDGOL, Army HQ in Delhi, 135
as defence attaché at Algeria, 89, 240–41
as GOC of 9 Infantry Division at Meerut, 139–43
as GOC-in-C of ARTRAC, 190, 191, 193

as GOC-in-C of Western Command, 192
as governor of Arunachal Pradesh, 307, 312, 314, 317–19, 323–25, 327, 330, 335, 340, 356
  swearing-in oath, 318
authored the doctrine for the army, 191–94, 207
brother: S.J.S. Marwah, 29, 33, 55
childhood, 22–23
CO of 5th Royal at Hyderabad, 88
CO of 9 Maratha LI at Tezu, 71
command of 1 Corps at Mathura, 174-83
commissioning, 5, 37
course
  Defence Services Staff Course, 63–64
  General Intelligence Course, 56
  Higher Command Course, 86–87
  mountaineering, 54, 298
  National Defence College Course, 133–34, 242, 256
daughter: Sonia, 63, 66, 71, 91, 142, 173, 356
daughter-in-law: Anna, 172
drill, 'khopdi', 104–05
elected colonel of the Maratha LI, 184
encouraged high technology, 192
family roots and traditions, 3

father: Lt Col J.S. Marwah, 6,
  18–21, 24–26, 28–29, 33, 39,
  111, 247, 296, 340
foster children: Kuljit Kumar
  and James Klengto, 294
Gen S. Padmanabhan on, 198
Gen V.P. Malik on, 103, 198
granddaughters
  Anne-Tara, Marie-Sana, 172
  Seerat, 173
grandfather: Sep Atma Singh,
  3–6, 7, 9
grandsons
  Sumair, 173
  Suveer, 173
gunshot wound in J&K, 116–20
honorary colonel of the Maratha
  LI, 187, 247
important events as chairman of
  CoSC, 233
in HQ 26 Infantry Division at
  Jammu, 87
instructor at Intelligence School
  (Pune), 56, 61, 71
'iron-fist-and-velvet-glove', 97,
  106, 112, 211, 345
Jai Jawan Awas Yojana scheme,
  292
key result areas (KRAs), 74, 100,
  200, 240, 270, 286
letter to bid adieu, 301–02
most significant event, 199
mother: Jaspal Kaur, 18, 29
motto, 'Fight to Win,' 139, 182,
  199
official visits to foreign
  countries, 134–35, 145–46,
  240–60, 263, 279

prepared official record of Kargil
  war, 170–71
schooling, 22, 25–26,
siblings, 29
son: Vivek, 63, 66, 71, 91, 93,
  172, 356
spirituality of, 10–11, 17,
  354–55
study on transport requirements
  in Indian Army, 136–37
superannuation, 187, 233
sword from Maharaja
  (Kolhapur), 187
'warrior and a winner', 182, 268,
  354
with 7 Maratha LI at Tangdhar,
  67–71
with 9 Maratha LI at Malari, 63
with 9 Maratha LI at Nagaland,
  43–55
Singh, K. Natwar, 238
Singh, Khushwant
  History of Sikhs, 11
  Train to Pakistan, 20
Singh, Lt Col Harjit, 131
Singh, Lt Gen Narendra, 187
Singh, Lt Gen P.K., 66
Singh, Lt Navdeep, 187
Singh, Maharaja Ranjit, 14–15, 17
Singh, Maharaja Ranbir, 26–27
Singh, Maj Gen Bachittar, 71
Singh, Maj Gen Dalbir, 139
Singh, Milkha, 296
Singh, Patwant, 14
Singh, Manmohan, 153, 199, 218,
  245, 247, 317, 324, 351
Singh, Rohini (wife, also called
  Anupama), 20, 57–59, 64–72,

and media, 197–98, 211, 213–14, 215, 217, 227, 235, 251, 276–78, 290–91, 294
and Musharraf, 306–08
and sports, 56, 59, 66, 142, 203, 275, 297, 333
as brigade commander at Baramulla, 104–06, 112–133
as young officer at Belgaum, 40–43, 54, 185, 186
as CO at Binaguri, 86
as visitor to infantry brigade in Somalia on UN mission, 138
as 'A' Company Commander with 9 Maratha LI at Jalandhar, 66
as ADGMO at Army HQ, Delhi, 144, 147, 153, 155, 162, 167, 170, 172, 174, 176
as adjutant at Hyderabad, 56
as army chief, 29, 57, 153, 158, 187, 197, 199, 213, 226, 236, 240, 246, 251, 256, 259, 269, 279, 283, 289, 302, 345
  key objectives, 199–203
as BM of 123 Mountain Brigade at New Mal, 64
as brigade commander of 79 Mountain Brigade at J&K, 94, 97–103
as DDGOL, Army HQ in Delhi, 135
as defence attaché at Algeria, 89, 240–41
as GOC of 9 Infantry Division at Meerut, 139–43
as GOC-in-C of ARTRAC, 190, 191, 193
as GOC-in-C of Western Command, 192
as governor of Arunachal Pradesh, 307, 312, 314, 317–19, 323–25, 327, 330, 335, 340, 356
  swearing-in oath, 318
authored the doctrine for the army, 191–94, 207
brother: S.J.S. Marwah, 29, 33, 55
childhood, 22–23
CO of 5th Royal at Hyderabad, 88
CO of 9 Maratha LI at Tezu, 71
command of 1 Corps at Mathura, 174-83
commissioning, 5, 37
course
  Defence Services Staff Course, 63–64
  General Intelligence Course, 56
  Higher Command Course, 86–87
  mountaineering, 54, 298
  National Defence College Course, 133–34, 242, 256
daughter: Sonia, 63, 66, 71, 91, 142, 173, 356
daughter-in-law: Anna, 172
drill, 'khopdi', 104–05
elected colonel of the Maratha LI, 184
encouraged high technology, 192
family roots and traditions, 3

father: Lt Col J.S. Marwah, 6,
  18–21, 24–26, 28–29, 33, 39,
  111, 247, 296, 340
foster children: Kuljit Kumar
  and James Klengto, 294
Gen S. Padmanabhan on, 198
Gen V.P. Malik on, 103, 198
granddaughters
  Anne-Tara, Marie-Sana, 172
  Seerat, 173
grandfather: Sep Atma Singh,
  3–6, 7, 9
grandsons
  Sumair, 173
  Suveer, 173
gunshot wound in J&K, 116–20
honorary colonel of the Maratha
  LI, 187, 247
important events as chairman of
  CoSC, 233
in HQ 26 Infantry Division at
  Jammu, 87
instructor at Intelligence School
  (Pune), 56, 61, 71
'iron-fist-and-velvet-glove', 97,
  106, 112, 211, 345
Jai Jawan Awas Yojana scheme,
  292
key result areas (KRAs), 74, 100,
  200, 240, 270, 286
letter to bid adieu, 301–02
most significant event, 199
mother: Jaspal Kaur, 18, 29
motto, 'Fight to Win,' 139, 182,
  199
official visits to foreign
  countries, 134–35, 145–46,
  240–60, 263, 279

prepared official record of Kargil
  war, 170–71
schooling, 22, 25–26,
siblings, 29
son: Vivek, 63, 66, 71, 91, 93,
  172, 356
spirituality of, 10–11, 17,
  354–55
study on transport requirements
  in Indian Army, 136–37
superannuation, 187, 233
sword from Maharaja
  (Kolhapur), 187
'warrior and a winner', 182, 268,
  354
with 7 Maratha LI at Tangdhar,
  67–71
with 9 Maratha LI at Malari, 63
with 9 Maratha LI at Nagaland,
  43–55
Singh, K. Natwar, 238
Singh, Khushwant
  History of Sikhs, 11
  Train to Pakistan, 20
Singh, Lt Col Harjit, 131
Singh, Lt Gen Narendra, 187
Singh, Lt Gen P.K., 66
Singh, Lt Navdeep, 187
Singh, Maharaja Ranjit, 14–15, 17
Singh, Maharaja Ranbir, 26–27
Singh, Maj Gen Bachittar, 71
Singh, Maj Gen Dalbir, 139
Singh, Milkha, 296
Singh, Patwant, 14
Singh, Manmohan, 153, 199, 218,
  245, 247, 317, 324, 351
Singh, Rohini (wife, also called
  Anupama), 20, 57–59, 64–72,

78, 86, 91, 103, 119, 180–81, 199, 238, 281, 293, 294, 302, 311–12, 314, 321, 326, 336, 356
   artist and an entrepreneur, 93, 143, 321
   as president, Army Wives Welfare Association, 293, 333
   parents of, 57
Singh, S.K. 320
Singh, Sardar Swaran, 52
Singh, Sriram, 296
Singh, Subedar Bana, 151
Singh, Zorawar, 17
Sinha, Lt Gen S.K., 280
Sinha, Yashwant, 166
Sino-Indian relations, 249–50, 348
Skardu, 109, 147, 159, 163, 219
Slim, Gen W.J. (Bill), 46, 201
Somalia, 138, 243
Somra Tract, 46
South Western Command, 193, 202, 206, 207, 347
Special Plan Assistance programme, 323, 330
Special Services Group, 151, 155
Sri Lanka, 121, 135, 241, 242, 257–58
Srinagar, 27, 28, 67, 97, 99, 117–18, 159, 216, 237, 253
Stagg, Sir Richard, 326
Strategic Forces Command, 202, 229, 231
Sultan, Tipu, 17
Summanwar, Maj Deepak, 78, 85
Swu, Issac, 47, 49, 51–52, 221
Swu, Scato, 221

Talwar, Brig N.K., 65–66

Team Arunachal, 321
terror attacks in cities, 218
terrorism, 94, 107, 182, 188, 189, 200, 204–06, 208–27, 241, 254, 288, 294, 319, 324, 344
terrorist, letter found on a dead, 109
Thailand, 314, 324
Thampi, Maj M.N.S., 48, 66, 82
Thapar, Gen P.N., 37
Thinouselie, Gen, 221, 223
Thosar, Hav Vinayak, 75, 77
Tiger Hill, 160–61, 165, 168, 370
Tinmaung, 52
Tipnis, Air Chief Marshal A.Y., 178, 179
Tololing, 160, 161, 370
treaty of friendship, 60
tri-service, integrated organizations, 33, 63, 229, 231, 233, 250, 276, 282–83
   considerations for, 230–32
Tuensang, 47–48
Tuki, Nabam, 340

Uban, Lt Col G.S., 78
UK, 145, 210, 241, 247, 279, 314
United Nations (UN), 138, 145, 162, 243–44, 343
United Liberation Front of Assam (ULFA), 200, 224, 257, 319, 346
USA, 134, 244
USSR, 244

Vadehra, Maj Gen P.S. (Prem), 64, 143
Vaidya, Lt Gen A.S., 48, 77, 81
Vairangte, 220

Vajpayee, A.B., 166, 233, 250
Varma, Maj Gen Inder, 121, 130
Varthaman, Air Marshal S., 336
Vasanth, Col V., 187
Victoria Cross, 139, 280
Vij, Lt Gen N.C., 166, 191, 194
Vijaynagar, 334–36
Vision 2020, 324

Wadke, Lt Col M.B., 43, 45, 46
Wangchuk, King Jigme Khesar Namgyel, 242, 256
war game, 87, 140, 207, 231, 270
War
    Anglo-Sikh, 14
    asymmetric, 208
    First World, 6, 7, 9, 20, 23, 88, 117, 247
    Indo-Pak (1947–48), 87, 147
    Indo-Pak (1965), 99, 174
    Indo-Pak (1971), 29, 60, 87, 111, 139, 149, 174, 183, 221, 344
    Second World, 18, 38, 46, 57, 79, 139, 187, 247, 273, 278, 280, 306, 325, 354
    Sino-Indian, 37, 334
Wavell, Gen Sir Archibald P., 191, 353
West Bengal, 210
Western Command, 61, 66, 139, 140, 192, 193, 197, 286
WikiLeaks, 213
Wilkinson, Paul, 216

Yunan province, 47, 51

Zaki, Lt Gen M.A., 99, 101, 103, 111, 118
Zia-ul-Haq, President, 93, 152
Zunheboto, 52, 221